MARCO POLO
Venetian Adventurer

UNIVERSITY OF OKLAHOMA PRESS : NORMAN

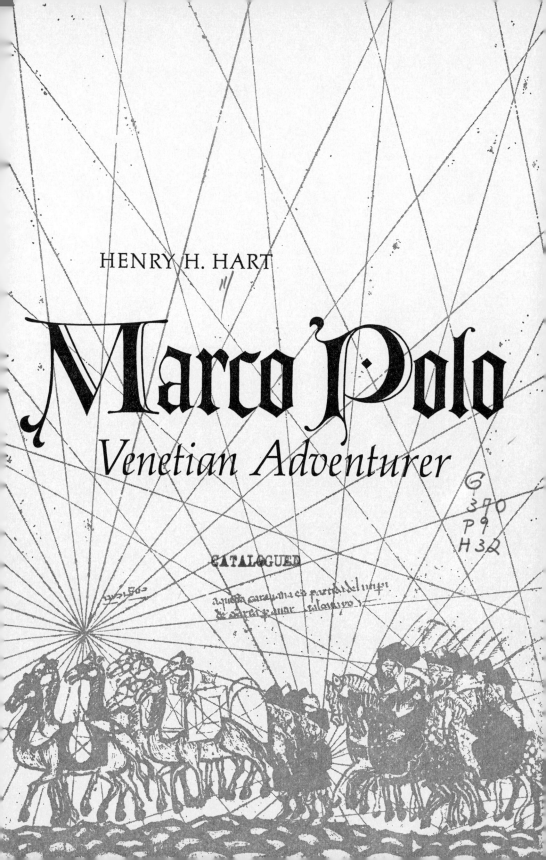

HENRY H. HART

Marco Polo

Venetian Adventurer

By Henry H. Hart

A Chinese Market
The Hundred Names
The West Chamber
Seven Hundred Chinese Proverbs
A Garden of Peonies
Venetian Adventurer
Sea Road to the Indies \ 1 5 0
Poems of the Hundred Names 1954
Luis de Camoëns and the Epic of the Lusiads 1962
Marco Polo: Venetian Adventurer

Library of Congress Catalog Card Number: 67–15585

Copyright 1967 by the University of Oklahoma Press, Publishing Division of the University. Composed and printed at Norman, Oklahoma, U.S.A., by the University of Oklahoma Press. First edition.

UXORI

Alice Stern Hart

QUAE HIC OMNIBUS VITAE MODIS MIHI FUIT COMES
ATQUE ILLIC EST SEMPERQUE ERIT DUX
HOC AMORIS SEMPITERNI
TESTAMENTUM FERO

Preface

THIS VOLUME is far more than a revision of *Venetian Adventurer* (Stanford University Press, 1942), which had the good fortune to pass through several editions in English as well as translations into Spanish, German, and Polish and a very large printing (Bantam Biographies) in paperback form.

In response to requests for a new edition I set out to bring the book down to date. However, in the interim the seventh centenary of Marco Polo's birth (1254) was the occasion for the publication of a number of new editions of his narrative in Italian, French, and English, together with a spate of volumes, symposia, and periodical articles on the man and his book. This interest has necessitated a recasting and considerable expansion of the former book and a new approach to the subject. Moreover, frequent returns to many of the sites, together with further studies in identification of persons, events, and materials, have clarified many ideas presented in the previous volume.

In spite of the new material that has been brought to light in recent years and novel theories that have been propounded, the tale of Messer Marco Polo is not yet complete, and there is always the possibility that further information and documents may come to light and even the original manuscript of his book may be unearthed at any time. Many questions remain to be answered, many problems that have puzzled and tantalized scholars ever since the first manuscripts were penned have yet to be solved.

In the light of recent discoveries and additions to our knowledge, I have, with the exception of certain basic paragraphs, rewritten the book in its entirety. I have also incorporated into the narrative many annotations on persons, places, and events in Messer Marco's account of the Polos' epic journeys to and from the realm of Kublai Khan, thus filling out numerous lacunae that existed in *Venetian Adventurer* because of limitation of space.

I quote from the preface to that volume:

"The author's concern has been to present the story of Messer Marco Polo as he has found it in the Venetian's own book, in contemporary chronicles, in later authoritative books and as the result of many visits and much personal research in Venice and elsewhere in Europe, America and Asia. More specifically he aims to release the man Marco from the mass of dusty documents and weighty scholarly tomes which have tended to obscure him. If he has here been brought to the reader as the vivid and sharply etched personality that he has become to the writer in the course of long association with him, the purpose of this book will have been accomplished.

"In but few instances has the author obtruded his own opinions, and then only when the facts as he has found them seem to warrant a departure from traditionally accepted conclusions. There has been no witting departure at any time from the strict truth as revealed in the documents and manuscripts, following careful investigation into the life of contemporary Venice, the Mediterranean and Eastern worlds.

"The meticulous scholar may perhaps be disappointed at not finding here controversial discussions of efforts which have been made to elucidate certain of the unsolved enigmas presented by Marco Polo's life and book—the making of mangonels for the army of Kublai Khan, the exact routes followed by the Polos, obscure place-identifications, and the like. These have been deliberately omitted because of the author's conviction that they possess little interest except to the specialist, and for fear that dissertations on them might weary the reader who is desirous of obtaining a picture of the man and his times but is in no way concerned with the minutiae of research.

"Every document used has been checked by me in the original language, and no reliance has been placed on quotations found in any work on the subject without verification, save in a few instances where it was impossible to consult the original. Except where acknowledgments are made, the author is responsible for all translations, including quotations from the various editions of the Polo manuscript and from other books and documents."

Excerpts from the narrative itself—and none of the six-score existing manuscripts is identical—are taken, with a few exceptions, from the masterly variorum edition (in English) prepared by the late Rev. A. C. Moule and Paul Pelliot, from Ramusio's[1] version or, in some instances, from the excellent edition in French and Latin, published by the *Société de Géographie* (Paris, 1824), adjudged by most scholars as the most authoritative text extant.

The bibliography does not pretend to list all the books covering life and travel in medieval Europe and Asia. It embraces only those actually used in the preparation of this volume, including such editions of the Polo text in various languages which contain introductions or annotations that may prove of value to the student. Quotations in the text from Chinese or other Asian languages are given in English translation, but as the original volumes themselves are for the greater part not easily available, they have not been included in the bibliography.[2]

It is with both pleasure and gratitude that I acknowledge my obligation to the officials of the British Museum, of the Bodleian Library at Oxford, and of the Bibliothèque Nationale of Paris for their co-operation in locating manuscripts and supplying photographs, and to the officials of the Marcian Library of Venice for permission to examine and have photographed the original testament of Marco Polo.

To the following persons I owe a debt of friendship and apprecia-

[1] See Appendix, page 265 below.
[2] Recent contributions to Polian studies, plus material that was not available to me in 1942, have added over four hundred items to the earlier bibliography.

tion: Cesare Olschki of Florence and Rome, for securing several very rare books on Venice and Marco Polo; the late Lionel Giles and Edward Lynam of the British Museum staff, for maps and photostats; R. A. Skelton, superintendent of the Museum's map room, for valuable advice; Jean Polak, wise and helpful antiquarian bookseller of Paris, for obtaining scarce printed material; Robert H. Haynes, former assistant librarian, and Foster M. Palmer, associate librarian of Harvard College Library, for their ever generous assistance in opening to me the rich resources of the Library collection; my late friends Leon J. Richardson of the University of California and Hon. Percy V. Long of San Francisco, for their constant advice and encouragement; and the late Douglas P. Anderson, F.R.P.S., for his patience and skill in photographing some of the material used in illustrating this volume.

Further, it is a pleasure to thank the following publishers for permission to quote or otherwise use the material indicated: Columbia University Press, for permission to quote from Edgar Holmes McNeal's *Conquest of Constantinople* (Robert de Clari); Harper and Brothers, for the privilege of quoting from Pero Tafur's *Travels and Adventures*, translated and edited by Malcolm Letts (Broadway Travellers Series); A. C. McClurg and Company, for the use of certain material from Pompeio Molmenti's *Venice*, translated by Horatio F. Brown; Messrs. Peaslee, Brigham, and Albrecht, New York City, for permission to quote from F. Marion Crawford's *Salve Venetia*; Charles Scribner's Sons, for the privilege of quoting and otherwise using material from Yule's *The Book of Ser Marco Polo* and Cordier's *Ser Marco Polo*; The Hakluyt Society of London, for permission to use material from several of its publications; Longmans, Green and Company, Limited, London, for the privilege of quoting from Howorth's *History of the Mongols*; John Murray, London, for permission to quote from Alethea Wiel's *The Navy of Venice*; and George Routledge and Sons, Ltd., London, for the privilege of quoting material from Moule and Pelliot's *Marco Polo*. The version of Marco Polo from which these quotations are made is a version of the French text (F) with additions, marked by the use of italic type from other texts inserted. In making the quotations, this use of italic type has naturally been dropped.

There are others, too many to list by name, who have contributed by knowledge and criticism to any value that this present study may have. To them I express my gratitude. Special thanks are due Miss Anita Merritt for her infinite care and patience in preparing the manuscript for publication.

To conclude, in the words of Thomas Coryat to his readers in his quaint and charming *Crudities*:

"Other faults there are also in the booke, at least halfe a hundred (I believe) unmentioned in this place, which I intreate thee to winke at and to expect a truer Edition, which I will promise thee shall make recompence for the errors now past."

Henry H. Hart

San Francisco, California
March 18, 1967

Introduction

IN THE MIDDLE YEARS of the thirteenth century, Venice, "the Bride of the Adriatic," was at the zenith of her power, after a past that had been long and eventful.

In Roman times the site of patrician villas and the abode of fishermen and salt refiners, the cluster of islands off the northwest shore of the Adriatic was later a refuge from the barbarians invading from the north. Gradually the city became the center of the trade of the eastern Mediterranean and the Levant, and this commerce led to wealth, importance, expansion, and growing economic and political power, the last essential to the control and defense of what had been won by shrewd bargaining, guile, intrigue, and battle. Venice's government was unparalleled in Europe for its stability and permanence. Domination of the shores of the Adriatic led to empire, until the city on the sea ruled over a domain greater than had any state since the fall of Rome. This expansion inevitably led to clash and conflict with the rulers of the Byzantine Empire, of which Venice had for centuries been the vassal—a vassalage which had become increasingly an empty formality, the discord and dissension between the two powers ever more bitter and violent.

Finally, in 1204, the opportunity of severing definitely all ties of subserviency or fealty presented itself. The Venetians made the most of it, with the result that not only did they extend their political and economic sway, but for some decades they controlled the destinies of the Byzantine State itself, either directly or indirectly.

The Crusades, those recurring medieval waves of feverish war-like activity and fiery religious zeal, do not appear to have either inspired or encouraged the Venetians to emulate their fellow Euro-peans or join the hosts seeking the recovery of the holy places of Palestine from the infidel. They did not remain entirely aloof or uninfluenced by that strange ferment and unrest—part religious, part greed, part the love of adventure, part blind bigotry—which were to affect and finally to have a part in the reshaping of the social, political, and economic thought of the Occidental world. Close as they were to the frontiers where Eastern and Western commerce and exchange of ideas met, they recognized something of the sig-nificance of the crusading movement, and how it might effect their own future and that of their greatest commercial rivals, Genoa, Pisa, and Amalfi.

In 1201, with the blessing and active co-operation of Pope In-nocent III, a Fourth Crusade was preached, this time against the Saracens of Saladin, by Bishop Foulques of Neuilly-sur-Marne, in France.[1]

Although the organizers of the crusade were able to bring to-gether a large body of men willing to set out to the east, transporta-tion and sufficient funds for the expedition offered far more difficult problems. Because of the ever increasing weakness of the Byzantine State and its inability to control the overland route through the Balkans, transport by sea was necessary. Venice was the state to which they turned for ships, and to this end six envoys were dis-patched there to negotiate for a fleet.[2]

Fortune favored the Signory of Venice, for the request of the crusaders came at a most opportune time. Quietly and deliberately they laid their plans, taking advantage of the tumult and turmoil

[1] Foulques lost his influence when suspicion spread that he had misused cru-sading funds entrusted to him. He was the audacious cleric who called upon Richard Coeur de Lion to lay aside his pride, his greed, and his lust. In charac-teristic fashion Richard replied that he would bestow his pride on the Knights Templars, his greed on the Cistercian monks, and his lust on the bishops.

[2] Geoffroi de Villehardouin, an eyewitness of the Crusade and one of its chroniclers, was one of the envoys.

then existing in Constantinople. The weak, inept, and extravagant emperor, Isaac Angelos, had driven his courtiers to rebellion by maladministration and overtaxation. Finally, in 1195, his brother Alexius led a palace conspiracy which resulted in the dethroning, blinding, and imprisonment of Isaac. His son, also named Alexius, however, escaped to Germany, where he laid his case before Philip of Swabia, ruler of Germany, and Boniface of Montferrat, leader of the Crusade, who was visiting Philip. Since the King, whose wife was Isaac's daughter, was eager to restore his father-in-law to his throne, a pact was entered into by which Boniface, en route to the Holy Land, would lead his army to the city on the Golden Horn to restore the blind emperor.

There are few more stirring narrations in medieval history than that of the conquest and taking of Constantinople by the Crusaders and their Venetian allies, and few episodes in human history as base and shameful as that rape of a helpless and unoffending people.

Enrico Dandolo, described by Sansovino in his famous guidebook to Venice, published in 1581, as "*un huomo vecchio, ma pieno di meriti & di valore*," one of the most magnificent figures of his or any other age, was doge of the city-state.[3] He was a giant both mentally and physically, by turns merchant and ambassador, soldier and councilor, a typical upper-class Venetian of his time—shrewd, crafty, cautious, and infinitely resourceful. When the French messengers arrived with their petition in 1201, Dandolo was about eighty-nine years old (the exact year of his birth is not known) and though almost, if not totally blind, was still erect, handsome, and indomitable as ever. The Ulysses of his age, he well merited the characterization of Villehardouin—"*mult sages et mult preux*."

After eight days of hard bargaining the Venetians finally agreed with the Frenchmen on the terms of a contract, by which the

---

[3] (An aged man, but full of virtues and of courage.) He had served as Venetian ambassador in Constantinople. There, tradition relates, he had so angered Emperor Manuel by being too outspoken that the monarch ordered him to be blinded by passing a red-hot piece of iron over his eyes. Dandolo moved a bit and was not entirely blinded, but as a result his sight deteriorated so that at his election as doge when he was over eighty years old, he had lost his sight entirely. (Some historians have challenged the validity of the tradition.)

Venetians were to furnish transportation and provisions for the Crusaders. The French had not, however, reckoned with troubles at home and the oozing of both the courage and the enthusiasm of their fellows. The sum of money agreed upon failed to arrive at the time promised, and delay followed delay. Meanwhile, a large body of the Crusaders lay about the Lido for months, their camp "a den of gamesters, harlots, and mountebanks." Finally, when the Venetians saw that only a part of the contract money was forthcoming, they presented a shrewd and farseeing plan to the disappointed Crusaders, offering to cancel the unpaid portion of the sum due if the Crusaders would agree to aid them in regaining the rebellious city of Zara, across the Adriatic. The proposition was accepted by the Frenchmen with alacrity, and the expedition set forth. Dandolo, in spite of his years and infirmities, led the host in person, and thus for a short period of time he and his fellow citizens became, at least nominally, Crusaders.

A further agreement was made whereby, after the rebellious Dalmatians had been brought to terms, the allies should proceed to further conquests in the lands beyond the seas, where all spoils would be shared equally. Thus the Crusade was, through the wiles of the Venetians, converted from a religious expedition against the infidel to a military campaign against fellow Christians. All too willingly and quickly many of the followers of the Cross became more interested in loot and adventure than in the destruction of Saracen power, and moral and crusading fervor were largely set aside or abandoned.

The city of Zara fell to the allies, and thereupon the rapacious Venetians presented their plan to restore Isaac to his throne. They were not newcomers to the Greek Empire, for many Venetians had dwelt in Constantinople from very early times. In 1082 they had aided Alexius Comnenus in his struggle against the Normans and in return had been granted a quarter in the city for themselves together with an exemption from customs, imports, and excise taxes. But ever greedy for more, they readily consented to aid Alexius, and in the spring of 1203 they and the Crusaders sailed through the Dardanelles and the Sea of Marmora to Constantinople.

What the Eastern capital was like at the time is known to us from eye witness accounts. Rabbi Benjamin of Tudela (in Navarre), who traveled throughout the Mediterranean world and the Levant for thirteen years (1160–73), has left us a vivid account of the city in 1161, just forty-three years before it fell a prey to the grasping ruthlessness of the Latins and Venetians.

> The circumference of the city of Constantinople is eighteen miles. . . . Great stir and bustle prevail in Constantinople in consequence of the conflux of many merchants, who resort thither both by land and by sea, from all parts of the world for purposes of trade. . . . At Constantinople is the place of worship called St. Sophia. . . . It contains as many altars as there are days of the year, and possesses innumerable riches. It is ornamented with pillars of gold and silver, and with innumerable lamps of the same precious metals. . . . King Manuel has built a large palace for his residence on the seashore. . . . The pillars and walls are covered with pure gold, and all the wars of the ancients, as well as his own wars, are represented in pictures. The throne of this palace is of gold, and ornamented with precious stones. . . . The tribute, which is brought to Constantinople every year from all parts of Greece, consisting of silks, and purple cloths, and gold, fills many towers. These riches and buildings are equalled nowhere in the world. They say that the tribute of the city alone amounts every day to twenty thousand florins (100,000 gold francs) arising from rent of hostelries and bazaars and from the duties of merchants who arrive by sea and by land. The Greeks . . . are extremely rich, and possess great wealth in gold and precious stones. . . . They dress in garments of silk, ornamented with gold and other valuable materials. . . . The Greeks have soldiers of all nations, whom they call barbarians, for the purpose of carrying on their wars. . . . They have no martial spirit themselves, and, like women, are unfit for warlike purposes.

Robert de Clari, a French knight and an active participant in the siege and subsequent pillage of the city, indicates in his description of the division of the spoils what a magnificent place it must have been:

> It was so wealthy, and there were so many rich vessels of gold and silver and cloth of gold and so many rich jewels that it was a

fair marvel, the great wealth that was brought there. Not since the world was created was there ever seen or won so great a treasure or so noble or so rich. Nor do I think myself that in the forty richest cities in the world there had been so much treasure as was found in Constantinople. . . .

He then describes in fascinating detail the Great Palace and the magnificent churches with their many relics, the Hippodrome, the city gates, and the statues:

Now about the rest of the Greeks, high and low, rich and poor, about the size of the city, about the palaces and the other marvels that are there, we shall leave off telling you. For no man on earth, however long they might have lived, could number them or recount them to you. And if anyone should recount to you the hundredth part of the richness and the beauty and the nobility that was found in the abbeys and in the churches and in the palaces and in the city, it would seem like a lie and you would not believe it.

This magnificent city, capital of the Byzantine Empire and the repository of the wealth and culture of the ancient and medieval world, was presently destined to become the helpless prey of the greedy, unscrupulous, conscienceless marauders from the West. Villehardouin tells the sordid story with all its heroic exploits, its chicanery and trickery, its stratagems, and its cruelties. His was naught but a piratical expedition, masquerading as a pious mission bent on unseating a usurper. Dandolo was the leader; he had been the Venetian envoy to Constantinople and knew both the country and the people well. Victory came swiftly, and the capital threw open its gates to the invaders. The colorful pages of the old French chronicle tell how the proud city of a million souls, once mistress of the Western world, fell to the allies after a very brief struggle, and how the exiled blind Emperor was escorted from his dungeon to his ancestral throne and Alexius crowned as his coemperor, with the title of Alexius IV.

Immediately Dandolo and his Latin associates demanded fulfillment of Alexius' promises and full payment of what was due them. Part was delivered, but the Greek treasury was not able to meet all the demands on it. Heavy taxes followed, and Dandolo hastened the break with Alexius by unreasonable demands. Riots broke out in the city, Alexius was murdered, and his father Isaac died of ill-treatment and grief. Murzuphlus, son-in-law of Alexius III, who had fled the throne he had seized from Isaac on the first attack of the Greeks, succeeded him.

Dandolo thereupon saw this hour as auspicious for accomplishing his long-planned purpose and moved to the attack with his allies on April 6, 1204. Six days later Murzuphlus, who had reigned briefly as Alexius V, fled, the besiegers captured the walls and swarmed through the streets, their leaders giving the city over to their followers for three days of pillage and loot.

The inhabitants were powerless and the sack of the imperial capital was one of the most terrible in all history. "Humanity blushes with shame," writes Romanin, one of the historians of the siege, "and the mind shrinks from recounting the tale of the horrors committed." Nothing was spared. The magnificent church of St. Sophia was stripped of its priceless treasures, and the uncontrolled drunken soldiers of the Cross set naked women of the streets on the high altar of God to dance for their pleasure. Palaces and homes, churches and shrines were despoiled, and wanton destruction completed the rapine and pillage. The loss to art was incalculable, and books beyond all price vanished forever in the wholesale burning of public and private libraries. Precious manuscripts in untold numbers were thrust as fuel into the campfires of the soldiers. Even the tombs of the Christian emperors and the sarcophagus of Constantine himself were broken open and the bodies despoiled of their precious raiment and jewels, while the helpless women of the city, high and low, rich and poor alike, became the playthings of the conquerors. The Crusaders wrought more havoc in the ancient capital of the Christian world than had the infidels throughout the centuries. Villehardouin boasts that the plunder exceeded all that had been witnessed since the creation of the world.

The Greek government had been swept away like chaff in the wind. The Venetians had been not only the instigators but the real leaders of the conquest, and Dandolo was offered the crown by his allies. He wisely refused, and Baldwin of Flanders was elected emperor, the Venetians receiving as their share of the unholy bargain three-eighths of the loot of the once proud empire of the Caesars, as well as three-eighths of Constantinople, including the church of St. Sophia, together with parts of Greece, some of the Greek islands and ports of the Empire on the coasts of the Hellespont (the modern Dardanelles), the Sea of Marmora, and the Black Sea. The aged Doge who had received a new and greater title, that of "Despot and Lord of One Fourth and One Half of the Romanian Empire," lived but a short time to enjoy his triumph. Worn out by campaigning, disease, and old age, he died in Constantinople in June, 1205, and was buried in a chapel in St. Sophia where the remains of his monument may still be seen, although it was almost obliterated in 1453 by the conquering Turks.[4]

The Venetians had ventured forth in search of trade and had found themselves major sharers in the spoils of a fallen empire. They wisely shunned the precarious title to political power and assiduously devoted themselves instead to the developing and expanding of their far-flung commercial interests. The markets, factories, and mercantile establishments which they controlled in the eastern Mediterranean and the Levant, together with the lands which were part of their profits of the Conquest, constituted the greatest commercial domain that the world had ever known. In spite of the manifold weaknesses of the Latin Empire and its utter incompetence in governing its newly won state, the Venetians slowly consolidated their own gains and expanded their quarter in the Byzantine capital. Like the other Venetian colonies, it had its own administrative buildings, church, mills, and bake-ovens, its warehouses and wharves, and, in fact, constituted an *imperium in imperio* —a little Venice. To combat business dishonesty and cheating, as well as ill-treatment by the various states with which they traded, guilds and methods of insurance were developed.

---

[4] In the words of Villehardouin, "Henris Dandolo prist une maladie; si fina et moru, et fu enterrez a grant honor au mostier Saint Sophie." It was at this time that the four bronze horses, attributed to the Greek sculptor Lysippus and now adorning the façade of St. Mark's, were carried off as part of the Venetian share of the booty and at Dandolo's order were shipped to Venice.

Thus, with their interests protected and developed, their trade thoroughly organized on land and on sea, the Venetians made themselves as far as possible independent of the uncertain fortunes of the new rulers of Constantinople, and by conquest, treachery, and shrewd business enterprise, had become the greatest and most powerful maritime state in Europe.

In 1253, Constantinople, the ancient Byzantium, greatly enlarged and beautified by Constantine the Great and his successors, was no longer the proud metropolis pictured by Benjamin of Tudela, Villehardouin, and Robert de Clari. Following their successful assault on the walls of the city, the Crusaders and Venetians had set fire to the houses to drive out the citizens and prevent street fighting; two-thirds of the city had been laid in ashes as a result of these conflagrations, and innumerable structures, both public and private, had never been rebuilt. Of those still standing, many had been stripped of their copper roofs, bronze ornaments, lead, and tiles. Ruined walls and churches, public buildings and dwellings were on every side, and the imperial palaces themselves had been so neglected and befouled that they were no longer fit for human occupation. Essential public services, such as roads and the sewage system, had been entirely abandoned, many of the inhabitants had fled, and most of those who remained were of the poorest classes. Parts of the walled districts were a dreary wilderness, and the Arab geographer, Abulfeda, who visited the city in the fifteenth century, records that even then "in the interior of the city are sown fields,[5] gardens, and many houses in ruins."

However, despite rapine and destruction, dilapidation and ruin, Constantinople still remained the most important commercial city in the Western world. To it led the lanes of traffic from the uttermost corners of the earth. The great caravan routes of Asia converged upon it; the water-borne trade of the Eastern Mediterranean and the Black Sea sought its crowded harbor, and its coin was current wherever men bought and sold, from India to far-off Britain and from the shores of Africa to the Baltic Sea.

[5] One may see the same conditions in Nanking, China, where the T'ai P'ing rebels devastated vast areas within the ancient walls which were once covered with houses.

Such parts of the city as had been spared or rebuilt were crowded and huddled together, hovels and miserable tenements shoulder to shoulder with palaces, churches, and markets. The streets were narrow, the buildings had overhanging balconies, for the gregarious Greeks were ever inquisitive, finding great pleasure and food for gossip in watching their neighbors' daily lives and activities. The city's caravansaries, squares, and bazaars were the meeting places of Europe, Asia, and Africa. There men bargained and quarreled, bought and sold in a hundred different tongues and dialects. Her warehouses were heaped to overflowing with silks and spices, rare rugs and jewels, ebony and ivory. On the streets jostled freemen and slaves, Negroes and Tatars, Russians and Greeks, swarthy Egyptians and pale Englishmen. Mingling in the crowd were Jews and Mohammedans, Turks and Armenians, Italians and Ethiopians. On every side rose temples to a dozen faiths—churches, mosques, and synagogues, all dominated by the great mass of St. Sophia, built by Justinian in the sixth century. Within the city walls swarmed increasing thousands of refugees from the devastating and blighting advance of the Turks, who were already threatening what remained of the once vast and powerful Byzantine Empire. Constantinople still merited her proud title of "The City."

The temptation of lucrative trade attracted foreigners from every land in great numbers, and it is estimated that in the mid-thirteenth century more than 60,000 Westerners were engaged in commercial intercourse on the shores of the Bosporus, each nationality dwelling in a quarter assigned to it. Of the eight quarters of the city, the Venetians now possessed three, surrounded by walls—a necessary protection in a city rent throughout its history by frequent riots and insurrections.

Such was the capital of the medieval Greek world when the story of the Polos opens.

"One of the thinges most naturally desired of noble hartes is to heere reade or comon of straunge contreis and espetiallie of contreis that we have had no knowledge of being farre aparted from us, and of there comoditees, behaviour and customs wch are very straunge to owres." ——Roger Barlow to "the moste highe and myghtie prince our sovereine lord Henry the eight Kyng of England" (1541), *A Brief Summe of Geographie*

Rycharde Eden to the readers:

"Whereas in this Book (well beloued Reader) thou mayest reade many straunge thinges, and in maner incredible, except the same were proued most certayn by dayly experience, and approued auctoritie (as shall hereafter appeare) I thought it good for thy better instruction to make this Preface, whereby thou mightest more playnly and sensibly comprehend the reasons and causes, yf not of al, yet of some of the chiefest thinges, which are contayned in the same.

——Of the Newe India

"To al adventurers, and suche as take in hand great enterpryses . . .
What foles do fable, take thou no hede at all,
For what they know not they cal phantastical."

——Richard Eden, Of the Newe India

"Such other innumerable and marvueilous thinges, writeth *Paulus Venetus* that he hath sene and founde in his nauigacions into these partes."

——Richard Eden, Of the Newe India

"The book that he has made renders its author this service in return, that so long as the book survives, its author remains immortal and cannot die."

——Richard de Bury, Philobiblon

Contents

Preface   *page vii*
Introduction   *xiii*
I.   Prologue   3
II.   The Boy Marco   42
III.   The Journey   68
IV.   Cathay   113
V.   Homeward Bound   141
VI.   From Tabriz to Venice   163
VII.   Venice   170
VIII.   Genoa   181
IX.   Venice Again   210
X.   Epilogue   233
    1. Marco Polo, the Man   234
    2. The Tomb of Marco Polo   243
    3. Messer Marco's Family   247
    4. "Il Milione"   251
    5. Marco Polo's Wealth   252
    6. The Manuscripts and Printed Editions of
       Marco Polo's Book   254
    7. How Marco's Book Was First Received,
       and Its Later Influence on Geography,
       Cartography, and Other Sciences   258

8. Aftermath   262
Appendix: A Note on Ramusio   265
Bibliography   270
Index   301

Illustrations

Hulaku Khan of Persia, brother of
   Kublai Khan   *following page 36*
The will of Marco Polo
A detail of the famous *Atlas Catalan*
Kublai Khan presenting golden tablet of
   authority to Polo brothers
Part of the façade of San Giacomo di Rialto,
   oldest church in Venice
Return of Polo brothers to Kublai Khan
Map of East Asia from Ramusio's *Delle
   Navigationi et Viaggi*

Map of China from *Ptolemy's Atlas*   *following page 100*
Map of Asia from Ruscelli's *Expositioni
   ed Introduttioni Universali . . .*
Map of China by Ludovico Giorgio
Map of the world by Marino Sanudo
Map of the world by Fra Mauro
Map of the world by Johann Ruysch
Map of the world from *La Geografia
   di Claudio Tolomeo*

Page of the so-called "Paris text"   *following page* 244

Frontispiece of second volume of Ramusio's
   Delle Navigationi et Viaggi

Frontispiece of first printed edition of
   Marco Polo's book

Page of Francesco Sansovino's *Venetia,*
   Città Nobilissima et Singolare

Chinese paper money (A.D. 1368–98)

"Greek fire," from the Skylitzes Codex

MARCO POLO
Venetian Adventurer

·I·
Prologue

"... for I will tell you now
What never yet was heard in Tale or Song
From old, or modern Bard in Hall or Bowrie."
—Milton, Comus

I

THERE SET FORTH from the port of Venice in the year 1253 two
brothers, bound for Constantinople on a trading venture. Probably
neither of them believed that their voyage was to bring them fame,
and that through them and the son of one of them European geographical knowledge was to be enriched as never before. That
their adventures and those of the younger Marco Polo were to be
immortalized in one of the most famous books in all literature
could not have entered their minds, nor could they have known
how far from their home destiny was to guide them.

These merchants were Nicolo and Maffeo Polo, sons of one
Marco Polo, a descendant of an old Dalmatian family which had
come from Sebenico and settled in Venice in the eleventh cen-

tury.[1] The two men were probably not very wealthy, for they did their own traveling, buying, and selling instead of working through agents in the cities of the Levant where Venetian factories and colonies were to be found. Their elder brother, Marco, may have been living at the time in Constantinople, for his will, drawn in 1280, indicates that he once lived in that city, in the quarter of St. Severus.

Both men left their wives behind them in Venice, for traveling by either sea or land was dangerous, political conditions in the Greek Empire were none too stable, and they had no way of knowing how long the journey would last. Nicolo, the elder of the two brothers, left a wife with child when he departed.

As Venetian women of the upper classes were accustomed to remain in seclusion and did not go about the streets and canals, the Polos bade their families a last farewell at their door, where the lapping waters rose and fell, covering the steps with green ooze and trailing weeds. Their gondola swiftly found its way through wide canals and narrow, in and out of the shadows of high palaces and houses, many of which are still standing—for Venice has not greatly changed in its essentials since those adventurous days of the thirteenth century—and under the arches of numerous bridges spanning the canals. At last, after many twistings and turnings, the center of the city was reached—the Rialto, near whose old wooden bridge over the Grand Canal was the meeting place of all Venice. Mingling with the crowd that swarmed here, the busiest spot in the city, they greeted their friends and acquaintances, then continued on their way to the long quay where their vessel was berthed.

Long and narrow, built for both speed and fighting, with banks of oars on either side and a mast with lateen-rigged sail to take advantage of every fair wind, the galley lay heavily laden with goods—wood, iron, grain, woven stuffs, and salt meat—all much in

---

[1] The spelling of the names varies in the different manuscripts—Maffeo, Maffio, Nicholas, Nicolo, etc. "Maffeo" is the Venetian form of "Matthew," "Nicolo" that of "Nicholas," and "Polo" that of "Paul."

demand in the capital of the Greeks. It was one of a number sailing in convoy for greater safety in accordance with Venetian law. As was usual, armed escorts had been hired by contract to sail on the vessels. There were crossbowmen and slingers, and in the bows were platforms with catapults and ballistae with which to fight off the pirates who infested the sea. Trading was so perilous and vessels so liable to attack that they frequently entered port stern foremost, steered by great side-oars[2] so that the fighting men might gather on the high poop deck to guard against attack. By the ships' moving thus, moreover, precipitate flight, which was often necessary, was facilitated. In addition, a lookout was maintained in a crow's-nest on the mainmast top. The passengers themselves were expected to join in the defense of their ships and their goods, for there was peril at every moment from marauders both on sea and on land.

The crews were freemen, so many of them Slavonians from the Dalmatian coast that the long quay by St. Mark's was (and still is) known as the Riva degli Schiavoni. No seaman could be under eighteen years of age; each was to carry certain prescribed weapons and was under oath to obey the laws of Venice. They were hired for the shipping season—from March 1 through November 30—and were paid in advance every three months. So thievish were these men that passengers were always advised to deposit their valuables with the captain during the voyage. To ensure the keeping of accurate records, which were accorded official status, Venetian law required shipowners to maintain on board competent scribes, one to small ships, two to large vessels.

The ships were fitted out with trumpets, drums, and kettledrums, which were used for routine calls to duty, to mark the time, and, in case of fighting, to arouse and sustain the courage of crew and passengers. Each man on board was allowed to bring one trunk, bedding, and his own cooking utensils and firewood, also enough water, wine, and biscuits for the voyage. The food was simple—salt meat, vegetables, cheese, onions, garlic, and vinegar.

[2] Rudders did not come into use in Europe until the time of Columbus.

5

The frying of fish was forbidden by statute, however, in order to prevent fires at sea. The voyage to Palestine usually lasted from thirty to forty days, and passengers paid the equivalent of $45 to $125, according to their accommodation. The time and rates to Constantinople were probably approximately the same.

The accommodations on the ships were far from pleasant or convenient. Those who could afford it slept on deck under awnings; others had to make themselves as comfortable as possible below, a space declared by a pilgrim of the period as "right evill and smouldring hote and stynkynge." There was a permanent loathsome odor of bilge water, and the damp sand used as ballast was generally full of decayed matter thrown there. Daubed with pitch and tar, the sides of the vessel inside and out were sticky and slimy. The cabin below deck was one long room, infested with rats, cockroaches, and other vermin. At one side of the stern was a light basketlike privy overhanging the sea—a convenience not usable in rough weather. Add to these conditions the "feble bread, feble wyne and stynkynge water," and the hard black ship's biscuit that was given out, plus seasickness, and one cannot envy the lot of the medieval traveler on long voyages.

As soon as the passengers and freight were on board, the galley warped out, then glided slowly past vessels just in from Egypt and Palestine, from Greece, Crete, and the shores of the Black Sea. Along the quays and at anchor in the stream other ships were loading for Spain and France, the Low Countries, and England. After the ship passed low sandbanks and the Lido and finally reached the open sea, sail was spread and the long voyage began.

For many days the Polo brothers and their fellow travelers sailed toward their goal, steering by the recently imported magnetic "nedylle" and the stars. They headed southeast through the sunlit Adriatic, on past beautiful Corfu, rounding the southern coast of the Peloponnesus, then navigating among the Greek islands of the Aegean, past Tenedos and Lemnos, ever steering to the northeast.

As the ship passed through the Hellespont, to the left lay the long, low-lying sandy coast of the Thracian Chersonese, while far to their right were the storied plain of Troy and the high peaks of Ida, where Zeus sat and watched the struggle between the sons of Ilion and the wily Greeks. Here Xerxes had spanned the strait with his bridge of boats in the far-off days of the Persian wars, and here the fabled Hero and Leander perished. They continued into the Sea of Marmora, thickly peopled with legends and poignant memories from the beginning of time. Gods and heroes, generals and statesmen, builders of empire, world-conquerors—all had sailed its blue waters in their day. On the travelers continued, past the rounded hill of Lybissa, under whose cypress-crowned summit sleeps Hannibal, an exile in death as in life from the Carthage which he had loved and served so well. And ever they drew nearer to their goal, the city of the Caesars, heir to the mightiest empire of the Mediterranean.

At last, after weeks that must have seemed endless, weeks of seasickness, heat, bad food, sour wine, stale water, and cramped quarters, they sighted the city on the Golden Horn—Constantinople, with its great land walls and sea walls, the porticoes of the Great Palace, the curve of the Hippodrome, and the swelling domes of St. Sophia, all glittering afar in the sunshine.

2

Nicolo and Maffeo Polo sojourned in Constantinople for six years. Marco Polo's tale passes over their stay in absolute silence. Apparently they did not return to their homeland during all this time, but busied themselves in buying and selling, trafficking and bartering, ever adding to their store of wealth.

Meanwhile, politics, with all its plots and intrigues, was moving apace in the city. The Latin usurpers had never succeeded in ingratiating themselves with the Greeks, who rebuffed and rejected every advance at conciliation. Baldwin II (de Courtenay), on ascending the throne in 1228, found the Empire sinking rapidly into decay and abject poverty. To restore his fortunes, he spent much of his time abroad, begging in Western courts and at the foot of the Papal throne in Rome for financial aid. To support his family, he was even forced to strip off and sell what remained of the metal in the palaces, churches, and prisons of his capital and to order vacant buildings wrecked in order to obtain fuel. He received a few usurious loans from Italian merchants and once was so hard pressed for funds that he pawned his son and heir, Philip, at Venice to liquidate a debt. Finally, Baldwin was reduced to such dire extremities that his feudal barons pledged the crown of thorns of Jesus, which had been preserved in the imperial chapel, with Venetian bankers for a further loan, sending the priceless relic to Venice as collateral.

When the time drew near for its redemption and the repayment of the loan, Baldwin, realizing that he would not be able to raise the money to redeem and preserve it properly, dispatched agents to France to negotiate its sale to Louis IX (St. Louis). The King accepted the offer and forthwith sent two Dominican monks to pay off Baldwin's debt and convey the holy relic with proper ceremony to Paris. He went to meet the procession with its precious burden in Troyes, and "it was borne in triumph through Paris by the King himself, barefoot, and in his shirt, and a free gift of ten thousand marks of silver reconciled Baldwin to his loss." To house the crown in a befitting manner, the monarch caused to be erected within his palace precincts the most magnificent jewel box ever conceived or built by man—the Sainte Chapelle. It is empty now, stripped of its sacred treasure (though still possessing its glorious stained-glass windows), but the crown, broken into three pieces and bereft of many of its spines (which Baldwin had sold separately), is still preserved in the treasury of the Cathedral of Notre Dame.

Encouraged by the success of this transaction, Baldwin next offered to Louis for much needed cash another lot of holy relics—including "the baby linen of the Son of God, the lance that had pierced His side, the sponge and the chain of His passion, the reed of Moses, and part of the skull of John the Baptist."[3] The King eagerly bought them all, and on the delivery of these precious

[3] The Great Mosque of Damascus also claims possession of St. John's skull.

spiritual treasures, twenty thousand marks were sent from the state treasury to the necessitous Baldwin.

All these makeshift expedients failed either to prevent or to postpone for long the inevitable downfall of the Latin regime of Constantinople. Venice and Genoa were continually quarreling and disputing the mastery of the eastern seas and the rich commerce of the Levant. Finally Michael Paleologus, descendant of the Greek emperor deposed by the Crusaders, entered into an alliance with the Genoese to regain his throne, and a decisive struggle between Latin and Byzantine, each side with its Italian allies, was imminent in 1260.

All this activity became known to Nicolo and Maffeo Polo. Disturbing news and rumors were being constantly brought into the city by merchants and other travelers from every quarter, and the brothers, deciding that the situation was becoming unsafe for their persons and enterprises, turned much of their money into jewelry, purchased with the remainder easily transportable merchandise, and left the threatened city. Already there were continual clashes and riots on the streets, in the market places, and on the quays between Genoese, Venetians, Greeks, and Latins, and there was no time to lose.

The place which they selected for their new scene of operations was Soldaia (Sudan), in the Crimea. Members of their family apparently already had a branch business there, for Nicolo's brother in his will (dated 1280) left a house which he owned in Soldaia to be occupied by his sons and daughter during their lives, and to be deeded thereafter to the Franciscan friars of the city.

The Polos remained in Soldaia for some time, but affairs were not as satisfactory as they had been led to expect, for one of the manuscripts recites that they "saw after many days in that land that there was nothing for them, and decided to go farther afield." For the moment it was impossible to return to Venice—bandits on land, pirates at sea, marauding bands wandering everywhere—these were cogent reasons for continuing eastward. There the brothers hoped to engage in more lucrative trade with the Mongols and other tribes far from the beaten paths, for they felt that there was profitable business to be done in wood, pitch, skins, salt, grain —and, not least, in slaves.[4]

Thus the two Polos traveled for days on horseback, through country to them strange and unknown, occupied by groups of

[4] The number of slaves in the West had begun to diminish after the tenth century. Labor-saving devices were increasing, and the sources of supply were drying up with the growing number of conversions to Christianity, so that by the thirteenth century slaves were becoming a luxury possible only to the rich. However, the trade in human beings was still flourishing throughout the Eastern Mediterranean Basin and around the Black Sea and the mouths of the rivers draining into it. The Mameluke rulers of Egypt were continually in the market for slaves to enroll in their armies, and their harems necessitated large numbers of female slaves and eunuchs. Egyptian purchasing agents were to be found in every port which could supply their needs, and, as many European centers were also seeking slaves, the business was a thriving one.

The most prosperous regions of this nefarious traffic were the shores of the Black Sea and its hinterland, and the Byzantine Emperor Paleologus himself authorized the trade. Captives taken from the tribes which had refused to submit to the Mongol yoke were sold by them into servitude without mercy. Hungarians, Russians, Tatars, and peoples from the Caucasus were shipped like cattle throughout the Moslem world. Moreover, it was not uncommon for the little-civilized folk of Southern Russia to sell their children, especially their daughters, to slave dealers coming from the West.

The greater part of this traffic was in the hands of the Italians, who, we are assured, did their best (at least officially) to restrict the sale to non-Christians of both sexes. The business attracted many, for the profit was great—usually at least one thousand per cent on the investment—and often the despicable rascals engaged in it forced poor helpless Christians to renounce their faith so that they might be sold within the law. About two thousand female slaves were sold each year in Alexandria alone, Circassians bringing the highest prices, Serbs the lowest. One of the important centers of this nefarious traffic was at Tana, the present Azov.

Mohammedan slaves also were a profitable investment, and many, together with those of Tatar origin, were taken to Italy. As a result of the Crusades and business ventures in the Levant the numerous European merchants and other sojourners there became quickly accustomed to the service of slaves and conveyed them home to take the place of paid servants. A law of Florence of 1364 expressly permitted the importation of non-Christian slaves of both sexes for resale or gifts. From 1366 to 1397 there were recorded in the city of Florence alone 389 sales of female slaves, of whom 259 were Tatars, and Florentine dealers did a thriving business in Ancona and Lucca. Thousands were imported yearly into Genoa and Venice, and in 1364 there were so many slaves in the latter city, all shipped in from the Near East, that they temporarily threatened the tranquillity of the state. From the Italian seaports the slaves, sometimes entire families, were shipped throughout the country, and large numbers were re-exported to Spain and Germany, where Emperor Frederick III authorized the trade by law.

As males were sought after as soldiers in the slave markets of Egypt, so young girls were in demand throughout the West, some as domestic servants but the majority as concubines for their Christian masters. Some of the proudest names of Italy appear in contemporary documents as owners of Eastern slaves. Pretty

various nationalities, speaking divergent languages and dialects—
Prussians, Tatars, Goths, Greeks, Genoese, and many others—and
everywhere they bargained and bartered in salt and furs, wood
and slaves.[5]

Finally they entered the steppe country and encountered
wandering bands of Mongols living in round tents or *yurts*. Some
of these felt dwellings were twenty feet or more in diameter and
were transported from place to place on wheels, drawn by oxen.
The travelers now began to pick up Mongol words and phrases
and to make their way about unaided. They learned to drink
kumiss, the favorite beverage of the Mongols, made from fermented mare's milk. The wild horsemen whom they met had a
strange custom; when offering kumiss to a guest, they would, in

women brought as high as the equivalent of four thousand dollars each. No moral
stigma attached to either the slave trade or to the ownership of slaves—and one
wonders at those who argue for the purity of blood of any European nation!

This tremendous trade in Eastern slaves, although it came to a sudden end with
the fall of Constantinople in 1453, has left its deep permanent impress not only on
the population of Italy but on that of all those lands where such slaves were introduced. Every country from Scandinavia to the Mediterranean received a very
generous admixture of Russian, Tatar, Circassian, Turkish, and African blood, not
to mention that of the numberless small tribes which swarmed on the shores of the
Black Sea, in the Caspian Basin, and in Asia Minor.

Pero Tafur, the Spaniard, in his famous *Andanças y Viajes*, written in the
middle of the fifteenth century, describes the slave market of Kaffa, the center of
the trade in the time of the Polos:

In this city [Kaffa] they sell more slaves, male and female, than anywhere
else in the world. . . . I bought there two female slaves and a male, whom I
still have in Cordova with their children. The selling takes place as follows.
The sellers make the slaves strip to the skin, males as well as females, and they
put on them a coat of felt, and the price is named. Afterward they throw off
their coverings, and make them walk up and down to show whether they
have any bodily defect. If there is a Tatar man or woman among them, the
price is a third more, since it may be taken as a certainty that no Tatar ever
betrayed a master.

Again, speaking of the Venice of his time, Tafur states that "they say that there
are 70,000 inhabitants, but the strangers and serving-people, mostly slaves, are
very numerous."

We shall find that Marco Polo expressly manumitted a slave, "Peter the Tatar,"
in his will, leaving him as well a sum equal to five hundred dollars, and that later
the Republic granted Peter the full rights of Venetian citizenship.

[5] Europe by this time knew from travelers that beyond the Moslem nations lay
others where trade could be carried on in safety, for the *Pax Tatarica* was so widespread that, as a contemporary wayfarer wrote, "a young woman would have
been able to travel with a golden tray on her head with no fear."

their desire to assist him in drinking, seize and pull his ears with great force, in order, their interpreter told them, that his throat would open wider. They learned, too, to eat the tasteless dried meat with salt and water and to sleep out under the stars. What was repugnant was close contact with a people fanatically opposed to bathing or washing their clothes. One must not for a moment imagine Europeans of the thirteenth century to have been ultra-fastidious, either regarding bodily cleanliness or frequent changes of linen, but between them and the unwashed Mongol horde there was a vast difference.

Finally, near the junction of the Kama River and the Volga, they arrived at Bolgara, the chief town of Barka Khan, grandson of the great Genghis, whose custom it was to wander with his tribe in summer and to settle down in one of his towns for the winter. The Polos were so well received by Barka that, Marco Polo tells us, "they gave him freely, seeing that they pleased him, all the jewels that they had brought with them from Constantinople, beholding his greatness and gracious courtesy. And Berca Kaan took them very willingly and they pleased him beyond measure. And like a gentle lord he made for them other things which were well worth more than twice as much as the jewels were worth, and also very great and rich gifts."[6]

The brothers set about trading Barka's gifts, in this manner increasing their wealth. During the year of their stay with Barka they witnessed many strange sights—visits of desert tribes, the changing phases of the seasons, varying greatly from those of sunny Venice, outlandish heathen customs, different foods, and a social life like that of another planet. In their six years in the Greek capital Nicolo and Maffeo had adjusted themselves to the Orientalized life of Constantinople, with its peculiar manners and practices, where women were set apart from the men at home and in the church, and where the women's custom of veiling the face was prevalent, but here among the Tatars all was far different.

Business was excellent, and after a prosperous year the Polos prepared to return to Soldaia, and thence home to Venice. It was

---

[6] One wonders if the gifts of the Polos were voluntary or forced.

now the spring of 1262; they had been away for eight years, and probably were eager to be back with their families.

Just as they were about to depart, hostilities broke out between Barka, their host, and Hulaku, his cousin, a brother of Kublai Khan. The fighting continued for eight months, during which the brothers found it impossible to return to Constantinople and thence to Venice. Although in times of peace the Mongol powers maintained relative tranquillity and safety on the caravan routes, this strict supervision was perforce relaxed during their frequent wars. Bandits and highway robbers then took full advantage of the situation, and traveling merchants and caravans were at their mercy. Lawless bands of Russians, Tatars, and Hungarians roamed the country. Hiding during the day, they attacked at night with bows and arrows—their favorite weapons—killed, robbed, and stripped their victims, then vanished into the wilderness with their spoils. Driving before them herds of horses as both remounts and food, they were able to elude pursuit and remain far away from cities and towns. They were the dread scourge of the plains, and Nicolo and Maffeo Polo had good and sufficient reason to fear them.

The outbreak of the war rendered the countryside unsafe, especially in the west, and the two brothers, seeing that they could not go back, decided, "Since we cannot turn back to Constantinople with our merchandise, then let us go on proceeding farther until we go round the realm of Berca by unknown roads; so shall we be able to turn back at last to Venese by another way."

They loaded their goods—never for an instant did the elder Polos step out of their character as merchants—on arabas.[7]

They "went off in safety" to the ancient city of Oucaca, "which was at the end of the realm of the lord of the Tatars of the sunsetting." Thence, after several weeks of traveling over an exceedingly rough country, they entered a region which was a veritable desert. Its crossing lasted seventeen days, and never dur-

---

[7] The araba is still used in this region. It has two wheels of great diameter, in order to negotiate streams and mudholes, and a hood as shelter from sun and rain. Sometimes, in crossing extensive arid stretches, camels were harnessed to the carts in the place of the usual horses or donkeys.

ing the entire time did they sight a town or even a tiny village. They did, however, pass great numbers of Tatars on the move, living in tents and driving their flocks and herds before them from one grazing place to another.

On the seventeenth day they arrived at the city of Bokhara. It had been sacked by Genghis Khan[8] but was restored by Ogotai, the third son of the Mongol conqueror, and at this time was ruled by Barac Khan, a nephew of Hulaku. After the monotony of the long journey from Bolgara, Bokhara was a welcome sight. It was surrounded by ramparts above which rose the blue domes and tiled walls of mosques gleaming in the sunshine. Situated on the banks of the river Zaravshan, its castle rising from a hilltop in the city's center, Bokhara was one of the most attractive trading centers in the Mongol Empire. Its shops were overflowing with the merchandise of the East, for to the Tatar terror had succeeded peace, and commerce was safe and unhindered. There could be purchased silks, porcelains from China, ivories, spices, and cunningly wrought metalwork and rugs, and its streets, markets, and caravansaries were frequented by noisy, jabbering crowds from every country in Asia from the Yellow Sea in the east to the Black Sea in the west, drawn far from their own lands by the lure of profit.

Again the two Venetians began their trading, but ever with the hope of returning soon to their native city, from which they had been absent for so many years. But when they endeavored to move from Bokhara, they found themselves in even worse straits than before. Not only were they cut off from the roads leading eastward to China, but they found the route by which they had come likewise blocked by warring tribes. So, with that philosophical patience which comes with much traveling in Asia and dealing with her peoples, they settled down in Bokhara to await better times.

At the end of three years' sojourn in the city, peace finally

---

[8] Paul Pelliot, the greatest of French sinologues, believed that the correct translation of "Ghengis" (or Chinghis) is "Ocean Great," similar in meaning to the title "Dalai Lama."

settled on the embattled tribes, and with it came a change in the Polos' fortunes in a most unforeseen and unexpected manner. An envoy arrived in Bokhara, returning from a mission to Hulaku Khan to his brother, the Great Khan, lord of all the Mongols "dwelling at the ends of the earth, between the sunrise and the Greek [N.E.] wind, who had Cubli Kaan for name." Hearing of the presence in the city of two men from the Far West who had now fully learned the Tatar tongue, the envoy visited them, marveling much at them, their strange appearance and ways. On their part Nicolo and Maffeo saw that this visit might be the means by which they could not only leave Bokhara but eventually return to Venice, in the meanwhile transacting very profitable business en route. Trade—ever trade and the increasing of their fortunes—seems to have occupied their minds above all else.

This hope was encouraged by an invitation from the envoy (whose name never appears) to go with him to the capital of the great Kublai. "Sirs, [Marco quotes his words] if you will trust me you will have great profit from it and great honor . . . and you will be able to come safely with me without any hindrance from any evil people or fear that any attack will be made on your persons while you are with me."

And the Venetians, "like men of great spirit not counting the long journey they had to make," accepted with alacrity, for they were most eager to terminate their enforced stay in Bokhara. Curiously enough, Marco Polo's account states that "the great lord of the Tatars never saw any Latins and has great desire and wish to see some of them." Enough accounts of the thirteenth century have been preserved to indicate that there had been a number of travelers between Europe and the realm of the great khans during the Mongol domination, as well as sojourners at the court, and that the visit of the Polos was no unprecedented or unusual event. Friar John of Plano di Carpini had been in Karakorum, the ancient Mongol capital, in 1245, and had written an account of his two years' journey, still extant and printed many times. In 1253, William of Rubruck, another friar, had visited Mongka Khan at Karakorum as an envoy of Louis IX of France.

He describes meeting a Greek knight in the city, and a little later writes, ". . . a woman of Metz, in Lorraine, called Paquette, and who had been a prisoner in Hungary, found us out and prepared for us a feast of the best she had . . . she was fairly well off, for she had a young Russian husband who made her the mother of three children, and he was a carpenter . . . . Among other things she told us there was in Karakorum a goldsmith, named William, originally from Paris. His family name was Buchier, the name of his father Laurant Buchier. She believed, too, that he had a brother who lived on the Grand Pont and who was called Roger Buchier."

In a subsequent chapter, Friar William describes a great tree of silver with silver lions spouting mare's milk, made by the same Buchier for the Great Khan. The tree had branches, leaves, and fruit of silver, an angel with a trumpet on the topmost branch, and four gilded serpents twined about the tree spouting four different liquors into vases.

These references, together with many others, demonstrate that Europeans were not unknown or even a novelty at the Mongol capital in the middle of the thirteenth century, so it is impossible to accept Marco's statement that Kublai Khan had never met a "Latin"—but perhaps Marco really believed it, and it does make a better tale.[9]

Thereupon, "commending themselves to the care of God," they set out with the envoy on their journey to the East, "having Christians as their companions which they had brought with them from Venese."[10]

Their road led them across plains and rivers, deserts and mountains, all unknown to them, to the capital of the Great Khan, to that Kublai, whose grandfather Genghis had made the name

[9] The Polos were not the only Italians who at this time fared great distances from their homeland in search of lucrative trade. This fact is attested by many surviving contemporary legal documents, some referring to journeys as far as Delhi.

[10] The only manuscript referring to the Polos' "Christian companions" (*comites habentes quosdam alios Christianos, quos secum è Venetis duxerant*) is the Latin version of Father Francesco Pipino, a Dominican of Bologna. The translation was made probably in the lifetime of Marco Polo, and a number of editions have suggested (without evidence, however) that Pipino may have been a friend of the traveler and so received additional notes or other information from him in person.

"Mongol" a symbol of terror, destruction, and death in the West. They were to stand face to face with the monarch of most of Asia, before whose frown all men trembled and whose very whispered name struck fear and dread in all Europe, from the Pope and the Emperor on their thrones to the lowliest peasants in the fields.

3

Theodore Roosevelt, in his "Introduction" to Jeremiah Curtin's *The Mongols*, has well said that the most stupendous fact of the thirteenth century was the rise of Genghis Khan and the spread of Mongol power from the Yellow Sea to the Adriatic and the Persian Gulf: "Unheralded and unforeseen, it took the world as completely by surprise as the rise of Arab power six centuries before."

The Mongols make their first appearance in history as an obscure people dwelling south and east of Lake Baikal. They were a nomad race, wandering over the grasslands with their flocks and herds, hunting and fighting, stealing and carrying off cattle and women with equal coolness, daring, and dexterity. Believing only in the law of the strong against the weak, and acknowledging only the overlordship of their tribal leaders, they restlessly moved over the plains of northern and central Asia, and in the region of the Gobi.[11]

The life and campaigns of Temuchin, known to the world as Genghis Khan, have been the subject of many books, and a brief outline will suffice at this point. He was born about 1162; the exact date is not known. His father Yesukai, leader of his clan, died when the future conqueror was a mere boy. The clan's leadership passed to another group, hostile to Temuchin's family, and many of Yesukai's followers left his camp to join them. The dead man's widow immediately pursued them and brought them back by force, and by her iron will kept the clan intact and strong during her son's minority.

The young Temuchin, daring and ruthless far beyond his years,

11 "Gobi" means "desert," "Sha Mo" in Mandarin Chinese.

soon won and held the respect and admiration of his people by leading them fearlessly on raids and forays against their neighbors. Impressed, many of the other Mongol tribes joined him, and the confederation grew ever stronger. With growing confidence Temuchin next attacked his most powerful neighbors, the Naimans, who in their turn fell before his invincible generalship, and, as a result, many other tribes hastened to tender their submission and join his banner. Finally in 1206 he was acclaimed unanimously by an assembly of his chieftains as Genghis Khan, "the Universal Lord." Thereupon their leader ceased sending the tribute which his people had paid for centuries, first to the government of the Liaos, and subsequently to the Chins. The Chin emperor sent an envoy to demand immediate resumption of payment; the only answer of the Mongol ruler was to spit contemptuously toward the south, where dwelt the Chins. This gesture meant war.

Ghengis Khan attacked and won. By 1215 most of the Chin cities were in his hands. A chronicler of the period, when describing the capture of a town, remarks grimly and tersely, "The Mongol general butchered." This statement meant that the garrison and the greater part of the civilian population were slain, for the Mongols knew no mercy and no pity. Caught between the Sung Chinese forces in the south and the ever victorious Mongols in the north, the Chins were effectively and finally crushed. The termination of the campaign was left to the Khan's lieutenants, while he himself turned to further conquests.

The Mongol attack on the West had its origin and aim in a burning desire for revenge rather than lust for conquest, although the latter soon followed. The Khan of all the Mongols had sent a peaceful mission to Persia to negotiate commercial treaties with Mohammed, Sultan of Kivaresm, for apparently there was friendship between the two monarchs. Suddenly, by Mohammed's orders, several hundred Mongol merchants who had come to Otrar to trade were imprisoned and murdered. When the news was brought to Genghis Khan, he swore dire and full retaliation and vengeance and set out in person at the head of his warriors to punish the Sultan. It was a bitter and merciless struggle between savage, barbarous Mongol and semicivilized Moslem. Town after town was taken, pillaged, and burned, and their inhabitants, men, women, and children, were butchered like sheep, and all domestic animals, even dogs and cats, were slaughtered. When Termed was taken, it was reported that some of the people had swallowed their jewels in order to save them. The Khan immediately commanded that the entire population be ripped open one by one to find the jewels and to set an example. In Herat the looting, destruction, and murdering continued for an entire week, and when the horde swept on to further conquest, it left behind it one and one-half million corpses rotting in the ruins of the city.

At this time Genghis received at his headquarters China's most famous Taoist monk, Ch'ang Ch'un. During his invasion of the country of the Chins, the Khan had learned of the sage's great renown and sent him a cordial invitation to come to him and communicate at least a portion of his wisdom. The invitation was accompanied by a golden tablet shaped like a tiger's head, which granted Ch'ang Ch'un a free pass and the right of assistance everywhere in the Mongol realm. Fortunately the correspondence between the two men has been preserved.

Although seventy-two years of age, the monk set out on his long journey in February, 1220, planning to join the monarch in Karakorum, his capital. However, on his arrival at Yen (now Peking) with his retinue of priests and Mongol escort, he learned that the Khan had moved farther west on his campaign. Moreover, the monk expressed himself as being deeply disturbed at learning that the caravan was to be joined in Yen by a number of girls who had been gathered for Genghis' harem. Feeling that even his advanced age was not sufficient protection against the women (or perhaps fearing lest the morals of his fellow monks be corrupted), the old gentleman dispatched a vehement protest to the Mongol chief, saying, "I am only a mountain savage, but how can you expect me to travel in the company of harem girls?" The answer, if any, to his complaint is not in existence, but probably Ch'ang Ch'un was humored, for his caravan continued on its way from Yen, its Chinese chronicler telling of the people, habitations, manners, and customs of the regions through which it passed. Here we find descriptions of the black and white tents of the Mongols, their clothing of skins and furs, their diet of meat and fermented mare's milk (kumiss), the headdresses of both men and women, and their lack of writing. Scattered here and there in this serious account are to be found descriptions of miracles, all redounding to the great reputation of Ch'ang Ch'un, as well as some startling tales. We even discover a Mongol Tam o' Shanter, one Li Chia Nu, who told the Master that once, in the very mountains through which they were traveling, a goblin had cut off his back hair!

The caravan continued on its way over hills of sand "so numerous that they seemed to be rising and falling like ships on the crests of waves." At length, after many weary months, the monk arrived at Samarkand in the winter of 1221. Genghis Khan was again on the march, and Ch'ang Ch'un had to wait until spring to continue his journey. Then, with an escort which had been sent to greet and accompany him, he set out for the imperial camp near Kabul, in the present Afghanistan. There finally the two men met.

The monarch's first speech with the Taoist adept was a request for the elixir of long life. Although Ch'ang Ch'un could not supply this, the two became very friendly and had many discussions, we are told, on religion and philosophy—although the background and ability of the barbarian Mongol to debate on either is more than questionable. After several months' stay the Taoist departed for his faraway home, the narrator of the tale again noting in writing many things seen and heard on the road—all of it a most valuable contribution to our knowledge of central Asia and its peoples as they were in the early part of the thirteenth century.

Meanwhile, the all-conquering Genghis swept on his blood-stained way westward, leaving ruin and desolation behind him and ever pursuing the fleeing Sultan and his kinfolk. One Persian province after another fell to his horsemen. The fugitive Mohammed finally reached a small island in the Caspian Sea, where he died on January 10, 1221. His family was captured, all of his sons were killed, and his daughters were parceled out as concubines to various Mongol princes. Having drunk so deeply of the heady wine of conquest, Genghis became insatiable and continued westward, laying waste, burning, and slaying as he went. The story of his progress is almost too ghastly for repetition, for seldom has the earth run so red or been so soaked with human blood. No one was spared. At Nishapur, to make sure that none escaped, heads were cut from the dead and the wounded alike and heaped in great pyramids, and the city was so utterly demolished that the Mongols were able to sow barley on its site.

Genghis spent the winter of 1222 near the Indus River and in the spring started his return journey through Tibet to his homeland, arriving there in February, 1225. Meanwhile, two of his generals continued to campaign through Armenia and Georgia, overrunning the country between the Caspian and the Dnieper River. The tribes fleeing before them retreated into the lands of the Greek Empire and on into Russia. The Mongols followed ever closer on their heels across the Dnieper and swept through the Crimea and across the Volga, meeting nowhere with any effective resistance.

On his return to East Asia, Genghis Khan learned that both the once conquered Chin Tatars and the Sung Empire in China were again increasingly hostile and threatening. Efforts at negotiations between the Chin Emperor and the Great Khan failed, and the latter marched on Tangut, ally of the Chins. Before he had completed his conquest, replete as it was with sacking, massacre, and slaughter, he fell ill and died at the age of sixty-six, on August 18, 1227. Dreaming and planning of destruction and bloodshed to the very end, his last words were instructions to his sons for completing the subjugation of the Chins.

Thus passed from the earthly scene one of history's greatest conquerors, a man without conscience, to whom human life meant nothing, a ruler of supreme executive ability, of merciless cruelty, and with but one object ever his goal—absolute domination, at whatever cost, of his fellow men. Born heir to a handful of huts on the Kerulon River in Mongolia, at his death he was the monarch of more territory than any man before or since his day. To appease his insatiable ambition he had destroyed more than 18,000,000 human beings in Tangut and China alone, besides the uncounted dead left on the fields of battle and in the smoking ruins of cities and towns in the West. Not until modern times did such a monster appear again in the Austrian Hitler, awaking the world once more to the realization of what unbridled ambition, unrestrained force, and evil, homicidal mania can bring in their wake—the destruction of men and of human values, the suffering of millions, and an ominous threat to civilization itself.

At a gathering of the clans after the burial of Genghis, his son Ogedai was chosen as his successor, and immediately the temporarily suspended military campaigns were resumed. In the West the Mongols renewed their attacks in Mesopotamia and Syria with all the ferocity of their race. When Bagdad was destroyed by them in 1257, it was reported that over 800,000 of its inhabitants were slaughtered.

Meanwhile in the East the Chins had been crushed. In 1233, Ogedai demanded of the Sung Emperor that he acknowledge Mongol suzerainty and, upon his refusal, moved southward against him in 1234. In the midst of his campaigning, however, he died of acute alcoholism on December 11, 1241. After much quarreling and dissension at the *kuriltais* (great councils) of the Mongol clans, the supreme khanate was taken from Ogedai's line and bestowed upon that of Tuli, youngest son of Genghis, whose son Mengu succeeded to the throne. He, in turn, handed over the military command in part of China to his brother Kublai, who set to work at once to subjugate the country. In this objective he was most successful, winning the conquered people by his justice and humaneness. Kublai's success excited his brother's jealousy and suspicion, and, recalling him on the eve of complete victory over the Sungs, Mengu undertook in person the task of totally subduing the Chinese. He was, however, stricken with dysentery while besieging the city of Ho Chu and died in August of 1259. Kublai, after speedily concluding a truce with the Sung Emperor, hastened to the *kuriltai* which had been summoned to elect a new grand khan. There he engineered his election before others of the family could arrive from their distant capitals or army headquarters, and he was placed on the throne of Genghis Khan in 1260, at the age of forty-six.

No sooner had he assumed the khanate than civil war broke out between him, his brothers, and his cousins. The great empire of Genghis was too extensive and scattered for him to hold together, but he continued relentlessly to pursue his campaign against the Sungs. It was a long, wearing war, but the Sungs were pressed ever farther south until a last stand was made by them at sea, off the coast of what is now Canton Province. Surrounded by a superior Mongol fleet, Liu Hsiu Fu, the Chinese commander in chief, realizing that the end had come and that all was lost, forced his wife and children to jump overboard from the imperial war junk. Then, taking the little boy emperor in his arms and declaring that death was preferable to capture, he leaped with him into the sea, where both were drowned. When the death of the Emperor became known, all effective Chinese resistance came to an end, and Kublai Khan, who ascended the throne of China with the imperial title (*nien hao*) of Shih Tsu, first emperor of the Yüan ("Everlasting") Dynasty, soon ruled supreme over the Middle Kingdom and its dependencies.

He considered Karakorum[12] unsuitably located for effective control of the vast Mongol domain and removed his capital to Yen, on the ancient site of one of the chief cities of the Chin Tatars, renaming it Khanbaligh (called "Cambaluc" by Marco Polo), the present-day Peking.[13]

The principal land routes across Asia were two. The first from Little Armenia, the Empire of Trebizond, on the Black Sea, traversed Persia; this route was used by those planning to pursue their journey to India and the Far East by sea via the Persian Gulf.

[12] Karakorum, a Mongol word signifying "the Black Camp," was situated on the upper reaches of the Orkhas River. It was selected by Genghis Khan as his capital and was surrounded with a wall by Ogedai in 1235. In 1380 the Mings destroyed it. Never rebuilt, it was gradually engulfed by the desert sands. In recent years its ground plan has been reconstructed.

[13] The city of Khanbaligh lies slightly north of the present city, overlapping it on the south. The Bell Tower and Drum Tower are part of Kublai Khan's city, and north of them still exist mounds of ruins of the Mongol city.

The second began in southern Russia and crossed central Asia to the countries bordering the Pacific.

Thus it was that, when the elder Polos made their first journey to the Great Khan Kublai, the Western invasions of the Mongols had come to an end and the conquerors were engaged in consolidating and ruling the great territories which they had acquired,[14]

[14] Although we are not here concerned with the later fortunes of the Mongol rulers, it may be noted that the center of their control was by this move thrown off balance, and the deterioration of their empire set in shortly thereafter. The same shift of balance finally operated in like manner in the Roman Empire after the transfer of the capital from Rome to Byzantium.

The Mongols, continuing their conquest of the West under Batu Khan, overran and devastated Russia, taking and sacking Kiev in 1240. The next year they laid waste Poland, Silesia, and Moravia, and after a long siege captured Batu, pillaged, and burned Pest, capital of Hungary, and massacred its inhabitants. Pursuing the fleeing king of Hungary who had escaped the destruction of the city, the Mongol leader reached the shores of the Adriatic, where he took and sacked the city of Cattaro. Only the news of the death of Ogedai caused him to bring his campaign to a close and return to Mongolia.

The remarkable and swift success of the Mongols in their conquest of the West was largely due to the fact that the territories attacked were broken up into small, weak, impotent states, continually at war with one another. The Christian world was exhausted by the drain of its successive crusades to the Holy Land and was, furthermore, split into two bitterly opposed factions, those of the Pope and of the Emperor of the Holy Roman Empire who, not realizing the gravity of the situation and the necessity of uniting against the common foe, were forever quarreling among themselves. The West was thus largely at the mercy of the fierce warriors swarming from the steppes of Central Asia, and the Mongols rarely met with united or vigorous resistance. Moreover, the invaders were well organized and disciplined, and their feudal system bound all portions of their empire together, insuring a strict supervision over all its parts.

The merchants carrying on trade between the East and the Mediterranean littoral had been hampered for centuries by the continual wars of the many kingdoms and principalities which lay athwart the caravan routes. The coming of the Mongols, destroying these petty states and at least temporarily uniting their peoples under one mighty government, strong and at peace, was welcomed and supported most enthusiastically by mercantile interests.

When first the Mongols threatened the European frontiers, the Popes, one after another, preached crusades against the infidel invaders but, finding their invective and efforts in this direction of no avail, changed their tactics and began to send out emissaries to carry the faith to the barbarian hordes. Numerous monks journeyed east over the caravan routes to carry out the papal command, and brought back reports of the countries traversed and the peoples encountered. Unfortunately, most of their accounts were available and known to some of the clergy alone, and none of them was ever as widely read or as well known as the story told by Marco Polo.

With the passing of the years the Christian world seized upon the idea that in the Mongols they had a heaven-sent and welcome ally against the Moslems, who from the Pacific to Hungary and from the Arctic Ocean to the Indian frontier. The Pax Tatarica prevailed, and traders could travel unmolested from the capital of Kublai Khan to the shores of the Mediterranean and the Volga.

4

The two Polos traveled with the embassy north and northeast for a full year before reaching their destination. Unfortunately, the younger Marco recounts little of the journey in his book "because Messer Marco who saw all these things also will tell you about them clearly in the book which follows," dealing with his own subsequent journey. Therein his narrative gives his impressions of the various countries visited by the two brothers, and of the peoples whom they encountered.

The twentieth-century reader cannot adequately visualize the terrors and hardships of a journey of thousands of miles over central Asia seven centuries ago. Hunger, thirst, the crossing of snow-clad mountain ranges and long stretches of scorching desert country, threats and attacks (in spite of Mongol vigilance) of banditti and wild, savage tribes, discomforts of every kind—these were some of the physical deterrents to such an adventure. But even more terrible were the myriad superstitions and fears of the unknown, the incredible sensitiveness to tales of strange inhuman monsters and evil spirits which peopled plains and mountains, valleys, lakes, and watercourses. Travel then involved not only venturing in the regions of an unknown world but conquering

had not only held Spain for several centuries but were threatening the rest of Europe by land and by sea. Although this delusive hope was effectually shattered by the defeat of the Mongols at the hands of the Egyptian Khalifate and by the gradual fractioning of the Mongol Empire after the death of Ogedai, the changing attitudes of both infidel and Christian facilitated peaceful trading over the caravan routes of Asia for many decades. Moreover, the great Genghis himself had wisely decreed that nothing should be permitted to interfere with the caravan trade. In this connection it may be recalled that the first of his campaigns was actuated by his resolve to mete out punishment for the murder of the members of a Mongol caravan. To implement his decree, military posts were established along the main trade routes to protect traveling merchants, and the roads were regularly patrolled by police, for, even though the Mongols were merciless and rapacious in their military operations, they realized that when once the conquered countries had been pacified, trade was all important.

deadly fear of both real and imaginary dangers by sublime faith, stubborn courage—or both.

The simple tale of the Polos details nothing of all these hardships. There is no expatiating on the fears or sufferings of the brothers, nothing of their struggles, physical, mental, or emotional. Their journey is summed up in a few simple lines: They set out, they traveled a year from Bokhara to Cathay, they passed through many countries and observed many peoples and tribes—and finally arrived at their destination. Such an objective and unadorned narrative is unusual in the annals of travel and exploration. Perhaps, as Marco Polo himself tells us, he preferred to leave unrecounted the experiences of his father and uncle in order to incorporate them in his account of his own wanderings and observations. But the fact remains that only an indomitable will, remarkable physical resistance, infinite patience and an extremely shrewd and long view in making decisions and plans could have taken the Polos across unknown Asia and back to their home in Venice with no untoward accident—at least none that has been reported or handed down in either writing or tradition.

Even now, in the second half of the twentieth century, central Asia has been almost the last area on earth to be penetrated by external influences. Isolated by mountains and deserts, its people have changed but little, and their mode of life has not varied in many details. The situation of its plains far from the sea, the unreliability of its water supply, the everlasting snows on its mountains, its chill winds, its avalanches, its salt steppes and deserts —all had combined to mould its inhabitants into a people differing from any others encountered by the much-traveled Polos. Moreover their religions, their occupations, and their social life were all largely determined by their physical environment.

The winters in central Asia are cruelly cold, the summers likely to be intensely hot and dry, with terrific sandstorms that at times make mere breathing a torture. The autumns are bearable but brief. Spring, even though short, has always been the happiest season of the year for the Mongols. The snows melt in the warmth of the sun, the hurricanes die down and vanish, and streams thaw out in valley and plain. As by magic, flowers spring up everywhere. Indeed the expression "a meadow in full flower" is the highest praise that a Mongol can bestow on anything he admires, from a fine house to a young girl in her wedding attire, and many of the tribes indicate the lapse of years by the number of times that the flowers have bloomed. At this season of the year the tents are rolled up and their contents aired in the sunshine, the cattle and horses wax fat on the lush green grass, and all the people rejoice.

Everywhere on their journey Nicolo and Maffeo Polo perforce mingled with the natives, of whom it has been said that "their fatherland is the tent and the backs of their horses." By the roadside and beside the river banks, among the hills and in the valleys, wherever grass and water were available for their animals, rose the tents of the Mongols. Odd-looking, round or six-sided, with domelike roofs, the *yurts* dotted the landscape. They were made of black or grey felt, coated with tallow or cow's milk to keep out the rain, and tied with horsehair cords or thongs to well-fastened frames of light wood. The floors were of beaten cow dung, strewn with sand, sometimes boasting also a hand-woven rug or carpet. The furnishings were of the simplest, usually benches and a few chests, together with household implements hanging on the wall. The smoke from the fire, usually of *argols* (dried dung) in the center of the *yurt*, found its way out through a hole in the roof. The tent flap or door was usually placed on the south wall, to avoid the cold north and west winds. About the hut were placed the owners' carts.

The flocks and herds of the Mongols were at once their necessities and their wealth. The skins supplied clothes, rugs, and *yurt* coverings. From them were also made roughly tanned shields, belts, boots, shoes, and various vessels. The bones were used for innumerable purposes, the sinews and tendons twisted into bowstrings, threads, and cordage. Even the dried dung was carefully gathered and used as fuel, for wood was scarce on the plains and could not be wasted. The Mongols were forced by their environment to rely almost exclusively on an animal diet. As they themselves expressed it, "Grass is for animals, and animals are for man."

27

Nothing was thrown away, the tribesmen eating animals which had died of disease as readily as those killed for food. Cats, rats, dogs—all were welcome as long as they furnished meat. This they consumed in great quantities, roasted, smoked, or dried, biting into a large chunk of flesh and cutting it off at the lips with a knife. Then they wiped their fingers on their footgear, thus keeping the leather soft and flexible with a continual supply of grease. A cake resembling cheese was made from milk dried in the sun, and was eaten thus or dissolved in water or tea. Their only vegetable food consisted of millet (when obtainable) and wild garlic. And always they had their kumiss.

Cleanliness, far from being a virtue, was considered a definite vice by this people, who seemed to venerate filth with a religious awe. "They never wash clothes, since they say God would punish them for polluting the water; nor do they hang them up to dry in order not to pollute the air and they believe it would thunder if they did so, to show God's displeasure."

No one seemed to go afoot in Mongolia. Men, women, and children may be said to have lived astride their small but remarkably tough and wiry horses. In the wild century when the Polos traveled in their midst, war and the hunt were the two joys in life. Otherwise, they lay about in their huts and slept or drank.

The measure of material values was a head of cattle, a sheep, a camel, or a horse. Their moral values had but one standard: Is it useful? What was useful was good; what was not was bad. Loyalty to friend and ally was observed, but there their ethics appear to have stopped.

Their religion, conditioned as it was by their environment, could hardly have been highly speculative or idealized and was largely shamanism.[15] They held the hereafter to be a continuation

[15] Shamanism: A religious phenomenon found mostly in Central Asia and Siberia and among the Eskimos and North American Indians. The word (from the Tungusic *saman*—a monk or ascetic) covers the belief that the visible world is pervaded by invisible spirits and demons who can affect the lives of mankind. The shaman is a person who by his own power is able to put himself into such a state that he can communicate in mystic fashion with these external unseen forces and to influence or control them. He is not a priest in the strict sense of the word but uses his talents largely for ills, supposedly caused by the attacks of evil in-

of life on this earth and buried horses and implements with their dead to aid them in the afterlife. They believed in an invisible Supreme Being but called upon him for little. More attention was given their household gods, with whom they were familiar and to whom they made food offerings.

The family, under the control of the father, was the social unit of the nomads. Polygamy was common, but the first wife was entitled to prior rights in property and inheritance, as were her children. Often after a father's death, the sons married his widows, although no one espoused his own mother. So, too, a man often married his brother's widow. The women of the tribe, both married and unmarried, were respected, and sexual morality was relatively high, although on this point there are divergent opinions. On the other hand, the enemy's women, when captured, were violated and otherwise treated with uncontrolled brutality.

The women worked hard, were old at forty—and were even dirtier than the men; they performed most of the drudgery, reared the children, and bore the larger portion of the burden of the household and care of the flocks. In their scant leisure time they did fine embroidery. In return for all of these duties they were forced to sleep in the coldest parts of the *yurts* and received but little attention from their menfolk.

As the Polos traveled along the caravan track, they must have observed the Mongols at their daily occupations—little, if any, different from those of today. Some would be busy building *yurts*, others sewing at saddles or bridles, making bows or arrows, or hammering out rude metal ornaments. However, the majority lay idly about, for their recent wars had brought them an ample supply of slaves, who performed most of the men's work.

The women would be tanning skins, some using skim milk and salt, others ashes and salt. The skins were softened by rubbing in the putrid livers of cattle or sheep mixed with milk and salt or with sour cream. Other groups would be making felt, beating wet sheep's wool with sticks to tangle the fiber. After the strips thus

visible forces. The fullest discussion of shamanism is to be found in Mircea Eliade's *Shamanism*, English edition, 1965, and in Hastings' *Encyclopedia of Religion and Ethics*, "Shamanism."

made had been pressed and finished, they were tied to the grazing horses and dragged over the smooth grass to give them a final polish.

Both men and women amused themselves with racing and archery contests. The women developed great skill with the bow and often accompanied their men into battle.

Along the caravan roads were to be seen detachments of Mongol soldiers, on their way to or from encampments or military centers. Each man had slung on his back an ax and several bows and quivers full of arrows. They wore metal-topped leather helmets and wicker or leather shields, and carried long spears furnished with hooks below the spearheads, with which to jerk an opponent in battle from his saddle. Many also wore chain armor, made by smiths in the far-away Caucasus.

Visitors at Mongol campfires at night found entertainment in music of a kind, drawn from drums, fiddles, and guitars, with dancing to the clapping of hands—and in gluttonous eating and drinking. Wandering minstrels chanted long songs of war and love, or recited endless tribal legends, often horrible tales of rapine and butchery, cannibalism and the drinking of blood.

Frequently crowds could be seen surrounding shamans and necromancers at their weird rites, and fortunetellers reading a client's future from the marks on the shoulder blade of a sheep.

The Polos could not have failed to see the driving forth of evil spirits from the sick and the consecration of sacred white horses, nor could they have failed to witness marriage ceremonies—the bargaining for the bride and the feasting.[16]

---

[16] Among many of the Mongol tribes a man did not deem a woman his wife until she had conceived by him. Among others betrothed children or young people lived together several years before marriage—a practice accepted without comment. And in accordance with the custom of the country still in vogue, the traveler was offered a temporary wife when spending the night in an encampment or a Mongol village. Then, as now, a peculiar custom was followed—the ritual washings of a newborn infant. Seven days after birth the family teapot was rinsed, the water saved and salted, and the child washed in it. Seven days later he received a bath of salt water, and at the end of another seven days he was given a bath of diluted milk. Finally, twenty-eight days after birth, he was washed in his mother's milk, in the firm belief that it would ward off skin diseases. "And with these quadruple washings the Mongol is contented for the rest of his life."

Nomad burials were often in secret places to prevent grave robberies, and food, milk, and a horse were interred with the dead for use in the next world.

Since the two Polos were in the company of envoys to the Great Khan himself, travel must have been comparatively easy for them, even to the use of relays of horses awaiting at conveniently spaced post stations for those journeying on official business.

Now, during the six full years that had elapsed since the Venetians had departed from the great city of Constantinople, many momentous events were taking place in the world which they had left behind them. The Latin Emperor of Byzantium had been driven out, and Michael Paleologus the Greek once more occupied the throne of his ancestors. His allies the Genoese were again in the ascendancy, and Venice had begun a long life-and-death struggle with her commercial rival in the Levant and the Mediterranean world. The French Pope Urban IV had died and been laid to rest with imposing pageantry in Perugia's cathedral, and another Frenchman had been elected to the throne of St. Peter as Clement IV. He, in turn, was to be gathered to his fathers before the return of the Venetian brothers to their home in Europe, and his death was to affect their fortunes profoundly.

All these events were most probably unknown to the Polos as they slowly continued on their way. The days lengthened into weeks, the weeks into months until, when they had spent a whole year on the caravan route, they at last reached Cathay, goal of their desires and hopes. A few more days, and they stood before the Khakhan, the Great Khan Kublai, lord of all the Mongols and of China, undisputed despot of the East.

5

It is important at this point to review the relations of China and Europe prior to the visit of the two Venetian brothers. From the earliest period of human history, long before the keeping of written records, there had been trade intercourse between the Far East and the West. Millet of Chinese origin has been found in the remains of prehistoric lake (lacustral) dwellings in Switzerland—

perhaps 25,000 years old. Records of the Han Dynasty have preserved accounts of Chinese embassies and exploring expeditions to
the lands of the Occident. During the centuries of Greek and
Roman ascendancy commercial relations were maintained with
varying intensity. By camel caravan and junk, the spices, the silks,
and the precious stones of the Far East reached the great emporiums of the Western world, and the stuffs and glass of the
Mediterranean Basin were brought to the land of the sons of Han.
In desert oases, at the crossings and termini of the caravan routes,
and on rivers and natural harbors, great cities sprang up and
flourished, with thronged streets and market places, temples, and
palaces. Many of the trans-Asian paths of commerce remained
open for centuries; raids of nomad tribes and pirates or wars and
rebellion cut off all intercourse along other routes by land or by
sea. During such intervals of disorder, often lasting for many years,
certain trading centers were either abandoned by their inhabitants
or destroyed by ruthless chieftains. Increasing numbers of these
locations, containing precious records of past civilizations, are now
being excavated, while others still lie buried beneath the sands of
central Asia.

Some of the products of the Chinese were well known in the
Rome of the Caesars. Horace refers to the arrows and silks of the
Seres (the Chinese), and Pliny the Elder speaks in his *Natural
History* of the silk which the Chinese comb from the leaves of
trees. Lucan in his *Pharsalia* describes Cleopatra, "her baleful
beauty painted up beyond all measure. Her white breasts revealed
by the fabric of Sidon . . . close woven by the shuttle of the Seres."
Tacitus, in his *Annals*, refers to a law enacted by the Senate during
the principate of Tiberius "against men disgracing themselves with
silken garments" and speaks of a message from the Emperor to the
Senate urging restriction of the increasing commerce with the
East, which was draining the Empire of its gold. The *Historia
Augusta* records that in order to aid in defraying the expenses of a
projected Roman campaign against the Germans, Marcus Aurelius
offered at public sale in the Forum his wife's gold-embroidered silk
robes. Josephus, in his *The Wars of the Jews*, in describing a

triumph of Vespasian and his son Titus, states that they were both clad in silk. An epigram of Martial speaks of fine silk sold on the Vicus Tuscus, one of the most fashionable shopping streets of Rome, and there is preserved in the Vatican a fragment of a Roman tombstone inscribed with the name of a woman, "Thymele, dealer in silk," and the author has seen other stones erected to or by *siricarii*—sellers of silk—in various other museums in the Eternal City.

In the Roman markets many Chinese products (or shipments from various Eastern countries via China) other than silk were offered for sale, as well as commodities imported into China and re-exported to the peoples of Rome's wide-flung empire. In exchange the Chinese imported, over the caravan routes and by sea, glass, dyes, woven stuffs, lead, precious stones, and many minor articles. However, the balance of trade was always largely in favor of the Far East, so much so that among the causes contributing to the weakening and decay of the Roman Empire were the continual adverse trade balance and the draining of the precious metals into Asia to pay for the enormous quantities of goods imported to satisfy the extravagant tastes and insatiable demands of Rome's wealthy classes. Gradually the changes of the monsoons and problems of navigation were learned and understood by seafarers, and the maritime trade between East and West grew ever larger and more important, although the caravans' land routes continued to carry a large portion of the commerce.

As the power and prestige of Rome declined, the expansion, first of the Parthian Kingdom, then of Persia, lying athwart the caravan routes, threatened, diminished, and finally seriously interfered with direct intercourse between the East and the West, and the unending struggles of China against the nomad hordes on her frontiers served to make trade even more difficult.[17] The contest between the Chinese and the Mongols (often designated by different names, such as "Tatars" in English and "Hsiung Nu" in Chinese) lasted for centuries. At times the Chinese were able to

---

[17] These restless nomads were related racially to the Huns who swept in a great flood over Europe in the fifth century A.D.

repel the barbarian tide breaking on their borders; at times the invader was successful, even ruling portions or the whole of China for varying periods of her history.[18]

With the fall of the Eastern Empire, commercial relations between China and the West gradually declined almost to the vanishing point. Moreover, the new order of things in the Western world had elevated to power a rude and unlettered class, with but little knowledge and limited wants and desires. Their own lands produced enough to satisfy their physical needs, and under the feudal system commerce played but a secondary role in Europe. Neither the shrunken Empire and the new nations that were forged from its fragments nor their neighbors offered a very extensive or profitable market for Chinese goods—and they in turn had little to trade of interest or value to the Far East.[19]

In the cultural twilight which had settled over Europe after the breakup of the Western Roman Empire there was little place for active interest (except for religious endeavor) in far-away lands or people. The very memory of the early voyages to the East, and of Asia in general, had largely died out, and a real geographical knowledge was gradually replaced by a farrago of fantastic ideas and legends, some of them growing out of the reading—or rather misreading—of the Bible. Such interest as there was centered on Palestine, because of its religious associations. In Constantinople alone, where the arts and sciences survived, even though in an attenuated form, and where decadence never reached the depths that it did in Europe (always excepting Spain during its eight hundred years of Arab-Moorish domination), communication and some trade with East Asia were maintained. Scraps of information about the Far East were brought to the Greek capital from time to

[18] The Great Wall, largely built in the third century B.C., was devised by one of China's greatest rulers in an effort to keep the barbarians in check.

[19] Under the Emperor Justinian (535–65) sericulture was introduced (c.550) from the Far East and under him and his successors spread far and wide, establishing an industry quite large enough to satisfy the demands for the precious material in the West. So the East-West silk trade diminished rapidly from that time. The story is delightfully told by Procopius of Caesarea in *The Gothic Wars*, bk. VIII, chap. xvii (Loeb Classical Library; Procopius V, 227–31).

time by the rare Christian travelers[20] who ventured out upon the wastes of land and sea toward the regions of the rising sun.[21]

China herself had never lost touch with the peoples of central and southern Asia. In fact, during the flourishing centuries of the T'ang Empire (615–960) when China was all-powerful in the East, she was united to the important peoples of Asia by bonds of both commercial and social intercourse. Her merchants with their goods penetrated to the farthest corners of steppe and desert, mountain and valley. Her Buddhist pilgrims wandered afar to India and Ceylon and even to the islands of the southern seas. On their return several of them wrote accounts of their experiences. Some of these books have been preserved to our day—invaluable records of the life, politics, industries, and religions of the peoples of the East. Moreover, official Chinese embassies visited most of the important Asian cities, and treaties of amity and commerce were arranged with them. Printing was an art in China centuries before it was brought into use in Europe by Gutenberg.[22]

The use of the compass for navigation, one of the most valuable contributions of China to science,[23] spread rapidly in Europe,

[20] There were accounts, some of them detailed, by such Moslem travelers as Yaballah I, the merchant Suleyman, Maçudi, Ibn Battuta, Ibn Khaldun, and Rabbi Benjamin of Tudela, but these accounts became known to Europe very much later—and some of them have not yet been fully translated or annotated.

[21] Hennig in *Terrae Incognitae* observes that Jews from Spain and France went more than other Europeans to India and the Far East because of their linguistic talents.

It is noteworthy that despite the considerable trade between Asia and Europe at this period, little cultural influence appears to have entered Europe from the Far East until much later. It has been suggested that there was some religious reason for this. The Nestorian Christians in China were distinctly antagonistic to the Church of Rome, and Kublai Khan's mother was a Nestorian Christian. With the fall of the Yüan Dynasty, the conquering Mings were xenophobic; on land and on sea, foreigners went no farther than Java. Japanese pirates drove commerce from the China seas, the early Christian missions vanished, tolerance disappeared, vigor evaporated, and China became decadent and petrified in its traditions.

[22] Although printing flourished early in China, the earliest Chinese book, a scroll, still in existence (in the British Museum), "The Diamond Sutra," is dated A.D. 968. See Thomas C. Carter: *The Invention of Printing in China and Its Spread Westward*, 2d ed.

[23] See Joseph Needham: *Science and Civilization in China*, (Cambridge, 1962) Vol. IV, pt. I, sec. 26, p. 245ff., for a valuable discussion of China's priority in the use of the magnetic compass and its later appearance in the West.

making possible a very considerable extension of maritime trade. The T'ang emperors were the rulers of a country and a people more civilized than any the world had known since the fall of the Roman Empire.

Foreigners from every part of Asia came to reside and trade in Ch'ang An, the capital. In its streets men of every nation rubbed elbows, and every language and dialect from the Caspian to the Pacific could be heard in its market places. Its universities were crowded with students from Japan and Korea, from Tibet and the south. In the great cities and seaports were colonies of traders from far and near, including Arabs—and even Europeans. Some of these erected their own mosques and churches, so numerous were their inhabitants.[24] In the capital there stood for centuries a church erected A.D. 635 by a wandering remnant of the excommunicated Nestorian Christian sect.[25]

The ninth and tenth centuries witnessed the decline and fall of the T'ang Dynasty. Weakened morally by luxury and easy living, undermined by the rule of unscrupulous and venal eunuchs and women, this great period, often called the Augustan or Golden Age of China, ended in disintegration and a welter of blood. There ensued fifty years of disunion and chaos, known as the era of the "Five Dynasties." This period was finally terminated by an army revolt, which placed the imperial robe of yellow on the shoulders of Kuang Shun, the first ruler of the Sung Dynasty, which dominated China (960–1126) until its conquest by the Mongols.

Although not so powerful as the great epoch that had preceded it and with frontiers constantly under the increasing pressure and inroads of the Tatar tribes, the era of the Sungs was the mellow afternoon of Chinese culture following the brilliant midday of the T'angs. Its capital, K'ai Fêng Fu, was still the center of Far Eastern civilization, the storehouse of all that was rich and cultured and admired by the peoples of East Asia. Her very wealth and civilization, however, caused her to be coveted by the barbarian

[24] An Arab mosque, traditionally built shortly after the death of Mohammed, still stands in Canton.

[25] A large stone tablet reciting the story of the Nestorian church in Ch'ang An was excavated during the sojourn of Father Ricci in China.

Hulaku Khan of Persia, brother of Kublai Khan (?). From a Persian
manuscript of the sixteenth century. (Courtesy of the British Museum)

The will of Marco Polo, photographed from the original in the Marcian Library in Venice. (From the author's collection)

A detail of the famous *Atlas Catalan*, made in 1375 for Charles V of France, and now in the *Bibliothèque Nationale* of Paris. This section shows the Polo brothers on their journey. The inscription reads: "This caravan has departed from the Empire of Sarra to go to Cathay." The mountains beneath the caravan are designated "The mountains of Siberia, where the Volga River has its source." Cities are designated by walls and towers. (Courtesy of *Les Amis de la Bibliothèque Nationale*, Paris)

Kublai Khan presenting the golden tablet of authority to the Polo brothers, here, curiously enough, depicted as tonsured monks. From the Royal MS 19 D I, folio 59. (Courtesy of the British Museum)

Part of the façade of San Giacomo di Rialto, the oldest church in Venice, probably the fifth century, since moved and restored. The abbreviated Latin inscription reads: *"Sit crux Vera salus hius tua christe loco."* ("May Thy true cross, O Christ, be the true safety for this place.") The inscription below reads: *"Hoc circum templum sit ius mercantibus aequum, pondera nec vergant, nec sit conventio prava."* ("About this temple let the merchants' law be just, let not their weights be false, nor their covenant unfaithful.") (Courtesy of the University of California Library)

Return of the Polo brothers to Kublai Khan with the holy oil and letters from Pope Gregory X. Bodleian MS 264, folio 224. (Courtesy of the Bodleian Library)

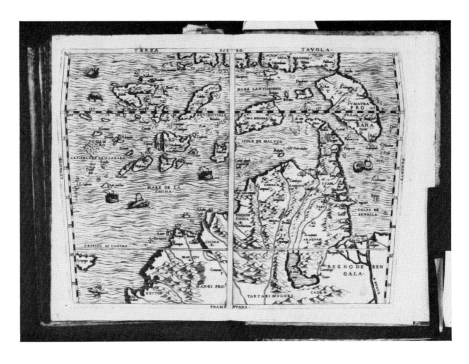

Map of East Asia from Ramusio's *Delle Navigationi et Viaggi* (Vol. I, Venice, 1613). (From the author's collection)

hordes. After many failures they finally had their way, and the highly civilized Sungs met their end, vanquished by the wild horsemen of the steppes. Khan succeeded Khan, as has been told above, and when the Polos arrived in Cathay,[26] the great Kublai sat upon the throne of China.

6

Such being the situation of China with respect to medieval Europe, what awaited the Polos on their arrival at the residence of Kublai Khan?

We have no information regarding where the Emperor was holding court on the arrival of the Venetian brothers from Bokhara. Khanbaligh (Peking) had been selected as his capital in 1263 and was in course of construction. He may have been there, or in Karakorum (the old capital), or at his summer palace at Shangtu, of which we shall hear more later. Wherever he welcomed the Polos, we are assured that the Grand Khan "beamed with the greatest graciousness" at the arrival of the strangers, and that he received them with great honor and joy, and feasted them well. He appeared consumed with curiosity concerning the West and asked all manner of questions about the Emperor of the Romans (the Emperor of the East, in Byzantium) and about other Western kings and princes and their administrative methods, their relations, peaceful or warlike, with each other, and their manners. Most of all, he appeared interested in "Master the Apostle"—the usual contemporary French designation of the Pope—and in the Church, its doctrines and practices.

The Emperor must have listened attentively to all that Nicolo and Maffeo had to tell of these various matters, and evidently gave much thought to what they recounted, for later he summoned his nobles and obtained their approval of his plan to employ the brothers as his messengers to the Pope, accompanied by Cogotal,[27]

[26] Cathay, more properly Khitai or Kithay—whence the modern Russian word "*Kitai*" for China—is a Tatar word, taken from the Kitans, a Manchu tribe, nearest the Mongols.

[27] For a discussion on the identity of Cogotal, see Louis Hambris, "*Le Pretendu Cogotal de Marco Polo*," in *VII Centenario della Nascita di Marco Polo*," Venice, 1954.

one of his "barons." The Italians were called before him, and the mission was offered them. They quickly perceived that this proposition presented a way to return expeditiously to their far-away home, and also, doubtless, they recognized the advantageous position in which this errand would place them for further trade with the Far East. They thereupon accepted and made preparations to leave with Cogotal.

On their departure they received their symbol of authority, a tablet of gold bearing his great seal and engraved with a declaration that the three men were his personal envoys and enjoining his officers everywhere to supply them en route with horses, escorts, and all other needful assistance and provisions.

The letter to the Pope which the Great Khan entrusted to the Polos was of the utmost importance, and its implications were many, for had the Church complied with its requests, the history of the Far East and perhaps of the entire world might have been profoundly altered. Kublai requested—some manuscripts read "commanded"—the Pope to send him one hundred men learned in the Christian faith and thoroughly acquainted with those seven arts which embodied the ideal of a liberal education for the medieval scholar—rhetoric, logic, grammar, arithmetic, astronomy, music, and geometry. Thus the monarch was asking that only men of the highest scholarly attainment be sent him. He specified, moreover, that the men be well trained in argument, capable of demonstrating to his people the superiority of Christianity over idolatry, and pledged his word that if they could prove their thesis to his satisfaction, he and all his subjects would become Christians and good sons of the Church.

The Great Khan also asked that, on their return to his realm, the brothers bring with them oil from the lamp which burned above the sepulcher of Jesus in Jerusalem.[28]

It was in no way strange that the Mongol ruler manifested such

---

[28] This oil, consecrated by the Patriarch, was a prized article of commerce in the Middle Ages, and Levantine Christians held it a sovereign remedy for all the maladies of both body and soul. The Armenian clergy had a monopoly of its sale in Jerusalem, and if we can accept the testimony of numerous pilgrims of the period, a most profitable business it must have been.

a keen interest in Christianity and the Church. Christians of various sects held influential positions at his court as ministers, physicians, and teachers, and marital alliances had united the family of Genghis Khan with the Christian Tatars of the Kerait tribe. In fact, some of the manuscripts inform us that Siur Kukteni, Kublai Khan's mother, was a Christian. This assertion is confirmed by contemporary Arab chronicles and by a statement in the *Yüan Shih*, the Chinese dynastic history of the Yüan Period. If true, it was only natural that the alert and intelligent Kublai should seek to learn more of his mother's religion and why it was so powerful in the West. Moreover, if it had potentialities—religious, political, or economic—for his people, he probably was determined to take advantage of them.[29]

Thus at last the Polos set out on their long journey of thousands of miles homeward to Venice. After only twenty days of travel Cogotal, their Mongol companion, fell ill—at least that was his claim—and could, or would, travel no farther. Nicolo and Maffeo, however, taking with them the imperial golden tablet of authority, continued on their way westward. There exists no information concerning their route across Asia nor their adventures, if any. Marco's narrative tells us simply that the journey lasted three years because of bad weather, floods, snow, ice, and the many difficulties of the road.

Finally they crossed the frontier of the Mongol territories into Armenia, and arrived at the coast town of Laias. Here they were returning to familiar scenes and encountered many Europeans, among them numerous Genoese, who were thriving mightily everywhere in the Levant as a result of their alliance with the Greek Emperor Michael.

The brothers took passage on the first ship available from Laias to Acre, the last port on the Syrian coast held by the Crusaders. It was destined to fall into the hands of the Turks in 1291 but was

[29] From what we know of Kublai Khan, he was shrewd enough to realize that imperial expansion and religious intolerance are contradictory terms. In general, only monotheistic religions are intolerant. Polytheism has no such limitations. Cf. the Roman altar to *"Deo ignoto."* Dokuz Khatun, wife of Hulaku, was a Christian, as were a number of Mongol officials.

still a flourishing seaport when Nicolo and Maffeo sailed in past the lighthouse and sighted its high walls and towers in April, 1269. Here they were able to get once more in touch with what had been transpiring in business and politics. To their dismay they learned that "Master the Apostle," Clement IV, had died in Viterbo, outside Rome, on November 23, 1268, and that his successor had not yet been elected. These developments altered all their plans for presenting Kublai Khan's letter to the Holy See and for a speedy return to Mongolia.

Fortunately the papal legate for Egypt, Teobaldo Visconti of Piacenza, was in Acre en route to Jerusalem. They sought and obtained an audience with the learned man, for they had heard that he was very influential in Church affairs and believed that his friendship and counsel might be of great value to them. The legate listened to the story of the Polos, which must have interested him, since the imperial letter gave promise of a great expansion for Mother Church—just as for the brothers it offered an unparalleled opportunity to increase their fortunes. But the return of the Polos to Cathay had to await events beyond their control. Teobaldo's advice was brief—to await the election of a new pope, then to return and carry out their mission.

The two brothers, realizing the wisdom of his words, decided to return at once to their families in Venice and to remain there until a new pope was seated upon the throne of St. Peter. They thereupon embarked at Acre and proceeded to Negropont[30] and thence home to Venice.

And now, after fifteen years of wandering, the brothers entered the familiar harbor. One may picture their emotions as the well-known landmarks came into view—San Giorgio Maggiore (not the great building of today, with its soaring campanile, but a smaller and far less pretentious building), then the two columns of the Piazzetta, the crowds of sailors at work loading and unloading vessels, the swift gondolas flitting in and out among the ships, under the bridges and into side canals, the striped mooring posts

---

[30] The contemporary name of the Greek island of Euboea, the center of Venetian influence in the East after the expulsion from Constantinople.

and lanterns, the swelling domes of St. Mark's, somehow reminiscent of that Constantinople where they had dwelt for so long, and, towering above all, dominating the whole seafront of the city, the great Campanile, built more than two hundred years before.

When Messer Nicolo arrived at his home, he found great changes. His wife had died during his absence, and the son to whom she had given birth after her husband's departure in 1254 was a fine lad of fifteen. He had been baptized Marco, after his uncle, Nicolo's oldest brother, "and it was that Marco of whom this book speaks."[31]

[31] An interesting discussion and analysis of the visit of Nicolo Polo and his brother Maffeo will be found in Olschki *Marco Polo's Precursors*, chap. iv.

·II·

The Boy Marco

"*Venise qui es orendroit la plus belle et la plus plaisant dou siecle; pleine de beauté et de tos biens. Les marchandies i corent par cele noble Cité, com fait l'eive des fontaines. Vos i poes trouver—li mariniers de totes guises, et les neş por condure en tos leus et les galies por damager lor enemis.*"

— Martino da Canale, *Le Cronique des Veniciens*

O F HIS BOYHOOD, or of what occurred in his life between his birth—most probably in 1254, the year of his father's departure for the Levant—and his departure from Venice on his own memorable journey, Marco Polo tells nothing in his book. We can, however, glean enough details from existing genealogies and other contemporary documents, as well as from careful reading between the lines of his book, to reconstruct at least part of it. Except in the cases of a few geniuses and infant prodigies, the life of a man to his fifteenth year, even though it be very significant from the psychological point of view, is seldom important with regard to his external experiences, so perhaps we have little reason to regret Marco Polo's reticence concerning his early years.

Although his mother had died at some untraceable date in his childhood and his uncle Marco was most likely away most or all of these years in Constantinople, his aunt Flora (on his father's side) was living in Venice with her child, and Marco had several cousins in addition. Three of the cousins were illegitimate, but bastardy appears to have been of little consequence in the Venice of the thirteenth century. In fact, he had still another cousin whose father and mother are both unknown and who, in his turn, had a natural child. With these relatives and perhaps others in Venice, and with the Italians' intense family loyalty through the centuries, there is little doubt that the lad was cared for by his family until the return of his father from Asia.

We may assume that his life was that of the other boys of his age. It included little schooling, and he acquired much of his education in the churches, on the canals and quays, the bridges and the open squares of the city. Formal education was reserved for the few, although one must believe, contrary to the opinion of many commentators, that Marco learned to read and write his own language. In the introductory chapter of his book he states that "he wrote only a few things in his notebooks" because he did not know whether or not he would ever return from China. In a later paragraph he remarks that when he traveled on missions for the Great Khan, he "would fix his attention, noting and writing all the novel and strange things which he had heard and seen."[1] Moreover, Ramusio, whose Italian edition of Marco Polo's book appeared in Venice in 1559, states that Marco found a way, while in prison in Genoa, to write to his father in Venice, requesting that he send his writings and notebooks which he had brought with him (from the East).[2]

---

[1] See page 127 below.

[2] *"Essendo astretto ogni giorno di tornar a referire con molta fatica, fu consigliato, che le dovesse mettere in scrittura. Per il qual effetto, tenuto modo che fusse scritto qui a Venezia a suo padre, che dovesse mandargli le sue scritture e memoriali che avea portato seco. . . ."* Ramusio, *Delle Navigazioni et Viaggi*, Vol. II, Venice, 1559, p. 7; reprint, Venice, 1954, p. xxiv.

We may therefore safely conclude that the boy, who, we are informed, learned four Asian languages, could read and write some Italian. Aside from his knowledge of letters—not enough, evidently, to enable him to write a long book unaided—nothing of his education is known.

With his companions he took part in the festivals of the Church —and there were many in Venice. With them he must have marched in the processions and joined in the pageants. St. Mark's, which has changed but little since the thirteenth century, was, and is, a school in itself for the unlettered and the learned alike, for its magnificent and extensive mosaics told in vivid fashion the story of the world. In the atrium was spread out the chronicle of the creation of the earth and of man—the tales of Cain and Abel, of Noah and the Ark, of the Tower of Babel, of Abraham and Joseph and Moses, among many others. Inside the church was unrolled on the walls the story of the New Testament, and young and old learned from the simple pictures in gleaming gold and richest colors the lessons of Jesus' life and ministry. In every corner and on every available bit of wall or column or arch was a picture from Scripture. Even the most ignorant could learn religious history as in a great picture book, its leaves those glowing mosaics which still look down on the visitor full seven centuries after the master workmen set them in their place, bit by bit, in fadeless colors and brightest golds.

Like every good Venetian down to our own day, Marco must have stood before the high altar and seen pictured and heard the legend of the bringing of the body of Holy Mark, the city's patron saint, from Alexandria in Egypt to Venice. That story, written down in quaint old French by Messer Martino da Canale during the very years of Marco Polo's boyhood, and still preserved, is well worth the retelling.

Tradition has it that Saint Mark was caught in a storm while on his preaching mission and made a forced landing in Venice. There an angel greeted him, "Peace to thee, O Mark, my evangelist," and foretold that someday his body would find its last resting place in a shrine of the city in the sea.

And in the time of Monsignore the Doge Giustiniano (827–29) there came to Venice the precious body of Monsignore San Marco. It is the truth that at that time there was a ship of the Venetians in Alexandria. In this city was the precious body of Monsignore San Marco, whom the unbelievers had killed.... Now in the ship of the Venetians ... there were three valiant men, one named Messer Rustico Torcellese ... and the second valiant man who was with Messer Rustico was named Messer Buono dal Malamocco, and the third was named Stauracio. These three valiant men had such great hope and devotion to convey Monsignore San Marco to Venice that ... they got into the good graces of him who was guarding the body of Monsignore San Marco and became his friends. And then it happened that they said to him: "Messer, if you wish to come with us to Venice and carry away the body of Monsignore San Marco, we shall make you a very rich man." And when the valiant man (who was called Messer Teodoro) heard this, he said: "Be silent, signori, speak no such words. This cannot be for anything in the world, because the pagans hold it the most precious thing in the world, and if they should spy out that we have such a desire, all the treasure of the world would not prevent them from cutting off our heads. And so, I pray you, do not speak such words to me." Whereupon one of them replied and said: "Then we shall wait until the blessed Evangelist commands you to come with us," and they spoke no more at that time. But it came to pass that there entered into the heart of this valiant man [the desire] to carry off the body of Monsignore San Marco from that place, and to betake himself with it to Venice. So he said to the valiant men: "Sirs, how can we carry off from here the Holy Body of Monsignore San Marco without the knowledge of any person?" And one of them said: "We shall do it well and wisely." And so they went to the sepulchre as quickly as they could, and raised the body of Monsignore San Marco from the sepulchre where it was, and they put it into a basket and covered it with cabbages and with pieces of swine's flesh, and they took another body and placed it in the same sepulchre and in the cloths from which they had taken the blessed body of Monsignore San Marco and sealed the tomb just as it had been sealed before, and the valiant men took the body of Monsignore San Marco and conveyed it to their ship in the same basket, as I have told you of before. And because they had fear of the pagans they placed the Holy Body between two slabs of pork and hung it (the basket) on the mast of the ship, and they did this because the pagans would in no way have touched the flesh of swine.

What shall I tell you? At the very moment that they opened the sepulchre there went forth throughout the city an odor so great and pleasing that if all the spice-shops in the world had been in Alexandria they would not have been sufficient to cause the like. And then the pagans said: "Now Marco is moving about," because they were wont to smell this fragrance every year. Nevertheless some of them went to the sepulchre and opened it, and saw the body of which I have made mention to you, which the Venetians had placed in the sepulchre in the cloths of Monsignore San Marco, and they were satisfied. But there were pagans who came to the ship and searched it in every part, for they believed most certainly that the Venetians had therein the body of Monsignore San Marco. But when they saw the flesh hanging from the mast they commenced to cry out "*hanzir, hanzir,*" that is to say "pork, pork," and departed forthwith from the ship. The wind was fair and in the right quarter, and they raised the sails to the wind and went out upon the high sea, and had with them one of the valiant men who had guarded the body of Monsignore San Marco, and the other remained in Alexandria and came to Venice a year later. . . .

What shall I tell you more? So the vessel continued on its journey from day to day until it had brought the blessed body of Monsignore San Marco to Venice. And it was so well received . . . that now that he was come to Venice the Venetians placed their hope in him and . . . carried before them the blessed figure of the precious Evangelist . . . and if any should wish to know the truth of the matter, just as I have told it to you, let him come to see the fair church of Monsignore San Marco in Venice, and let him look at all in front of the fair church, for there is written all this story as I have told it to you, and he will gain the great pardon of seven years which Monsignore the Apostle has granted to those who come into this fair church.

This story is not the only one which young Marco would have heard concerning the patron saint of Venice whose name he bore. He would surely have been told by the old men sitting in the sun in the great Piazza how, when the church built to receive the saint's body was to be consecrated in 1094, the body had vanished, for no trace of it could be found after the destruction of the older church in the great Venetian fire of 976. The Republic thereupon decreed a fast and public prayer to God, that He might reveal the holy body of Saint Mark. As the procession with the Doge at the head slowly wound through the church, a great light shone out near one of the pillars, part of the masonry crumbled, and a hand bearing a gold ring on the middle finger was thrust out through the hole, and at the same moment a sweet fragrance filled the entire edifice. There could be no doubt in the minds and hearts of the pious people that this apparition was the veritable body of the holy Mark, and solemn thanks were offered to God for the miraculous discovery of their lost saint.[3]

The Church of St. Mark's was, and is, among the most unusual in the world. Every pillar of the interior differed from its fellows, for not one was originally made for the church in which it stood. Each had a tale to tell of the pagan temple or an earlier church for which its sculptors had chiseled it. Every shipmaster was under orders to bring back with him loot from some ancient building— pillars, slabs of finest marble, statues, or other plunder which had once beheld the glories of ancient Greece or the Roman Empire. Many of the columns were sawed in half, the flat surfaces highly polished, and then the two smooth surfaces set in the walls, side by side, with the grain reversed. In this way their designs appeared much like those children make by putting a great blob of ink on a scrap of vellum or paper and folding it down the center while wet, so that the blot spreads, producing all kinds of queer patterns of imaginary plants or animals.[4]

On religious holidays great crowds, dressed in their best silks, velvets, and furs—but reeking of garlic and onions and fish, and none too clean beneath their holiday finery—came to catch a glimpse of the Pala d' Oro, that wonderful altarpiece of gold and

[3] The body was placed in a marble crypt, where it lay until 1811, when it was removed to its present resting place at the high altar of the church.

[4] To this day the imaginative visitor still traces dragons and trees, flowers and weird beasts, and even saints and angels on the slabs.

of silver gilt which, it was said, had been a hundred years in the making in Constantinople. There could be seen, when the curtains were drawn aside, wondrous scenes from the lives of Jesus, the Madonna, and the saints, all in multicolored enamels, set with six thousand pearls, garnets, sapphires, rubies, and emeralds, and the shrine itself was fashioned of thirty pounds of gold and three hundred pounds of silver.[5]

On the altar, before the Pala, were massive ritual vessels and candlesticks of gold, and behind it was the altar of the Holy Cross, adorned with two slender translucent twisted columns of alabaster.[6]

Marco must have also seen the master mosaic workers at their labors, for St. Mark's has been many years in the making, and work on it has not ceased even to this day.[7]

Outside, in the porticoes and on the steps, as well as on the seven arches of the entrance to the church, were other mosaics and pictures carved in stone—a mixture of the real and the fanciful—a child in the yawning mouth of a lion, an eagle about to eat a lamb, a farmer reaping corn, a man and woman astride dragons, men hunting, boys quarreling and stealing eggs, and the like. One carving of a little lame man on crutches, with his finger to his lips, was believed to be the portrait of the architect of St. Mark's, whose name is not known. A legend declared that he appeared from nowhere before the Doge Pietro Orseolo, who was eager to rebuild the edifice after its burning, and that the little man had offered to make the new church more beautiful than any other in the world if only his statue would be set up in a conspicuous place. Unfortunately, he was overheard saying that the church would, after all, not be as beautiful as he might have made it. The Doge did not

[5] This was before the masterpiece was looted by the French during the Napoleonic wars, when the great cabochons and other jewels were stolen and replaced by far cheaper cut stones.

[6] These columns, still in place, were reputed to have formed part of the furnishings of the temple of King Solomon in Jerusalem.

[7] The mosaic is made of real gold leaf laid on between two red-hot panes of glass, which when cool were cut into tiny squares and inlaid, tens of thousands of square feet of it, so that, with other mosaic bits made of glass and color, it gleamed from every wall and corner, setting forth the storied pageant of the ages.

forget the remark, and, so the story runs, the statue was made very small and was carved in a very inconspicuous position.[8]

In the time of Marco Polo's grandfather the four great gilded bronze horses were set high above the portico of St. Mark's, where they still stand after many wanderings.[9]

The Piazza in front of St. Mark's is no longer quite the same as when the Polos lived and walked there. The pavement has been raised and some new buildings have sprung up, but many landmarks still stand as they were in the thirteenth century. Against the southern sky near the water's edge could be seen then, as now, the two great pillars, the one of red, the other of gray granite. There once had been three pillars, brought from far-off Tyre with other spoil in the twelfth century. One had fallen into the sea and had never been recovered. The remaining two had lain for years on the shore, for no one able to raise them could be found. Finally, in 1172, one Nicolo Barattieri, an engineer from Lombardy, succeeded in raising the columns. On the top of one was placed the statue of St. Theodore, once patron saint of the Venetians, standing on a crocodile. There is still wonder that he stands facing the city, rather than the sea, whence Venice drew all her wealth and glory. It was only after the lifetime of Marco Polo that the second pillar received its fitting crown, the Lion of St. Mark.

In the thirteenth century, gaming tables, always crowded with patrons, stood between the two columns, the tradition holding that

[8] In like manner, Verrochio's equestrian statue of Colleoni was not placed in the great square where the *condottiere* had expected to stand but was relegated to a lesser place in the small square of the hospital.

[9] Some authorities claim that they are Greek, others that they were part of an arch erected in Rome in honor of Nero and that they had been transported by order of Constantine the Great to the imperial hippodrome of Byzantium. Dandolo had seized them as part of the Venetian spoils in 1204; they had been brought overseas and in triumph set high on the outer gallery of St. Mark's. By Napoleon's order they were carried off to Paris and were shipped back to Venice after Waterloo. During World War I they were transported to Rome for safekeeping and again, during World War II, taken there and buried in the Piazza Venezia until the cessation of hostilities when once more they were returned to Venice. It is regrettable that their artistic beauty and their age have not sufficed to protect them from the initials, names, and graffitti wantonly scratched on them by ignorant or stupid visitors who are able to reach them by ascending the very steep narrow stairway behind the gallery.

the engineer Barattieri had received the concession as a reward for his work. The pillars had another, grimmer attraction for the people of Venice, for with the granting of the gaming concession the city fathers issued a decree that thenceforth public executions were to take place between the columns. The stones of the Piazzetta about the columns could tell many a tale of men and women tortured or done to death there.

Venice was growing ever wealthier, and at every turn old houses were being torn down and new, rich, and luxurious palaces were being erected in their stead. Although the gondola was the favorite conveyance, horses were still being used in the streets and alleys, and beyond the Piazza where the Royal Gardens now flourish were located the Doge's stables.

The Rialto, on the Grand Canal, was the center of Venetian life. Thither converged bridges, canals, and streets, and it was crowded with shops and markets. There stood San Giacomo di Rialto, according to tradition built in the fifth century. In its colonnades adorned with frescoes merchants and brokers gathered to hear and exchange the latest news—arrivals and departures of vessels, political changes on the mainland, and all the multifarious gossip of metropolitan Venice. On its gable was carved the inscription now famous throughout the world, but probably as little heeded as are the sententious inscriptions on halls of justice and other civic monuments throughout the world. During Marco Polo's old age the church was moved when the Rialto was enlarged and a loggia built on its site. In the moving much of the ancient church was destroyed or renovated, but passers-by may still read the original inscription beneath the cross: "*Hoc circum templum sit ius mercantibus aequum, pondera nec vergant nec sint conventio prava.*"[10]

In the Campo of the Rialto swarmed Italians and visitors from every corner of the world—from Greece and the Levant, from Spain and France, and from cold northern Germany and England. Business was on everyone's lips, for Venice seemed to live only on business and for business. The canals and piazzas of the city were

[10] "About this temple let the merchants' law be just, let not their weights be false, nor their covenant unfaithful."

the crossroads of the mercantile world, where East met West, where Byzantine silks and satins rubbed shoulders with the furs and coarse clothes of visitors from Western Europe, and where faces and costumes from the four corners of the Mediterranean world mingled and jostled from dawn to dusk. From the ringing of the *marangona* bell, summoning artisans to their labors, until the *rialtina* sounded the curfew three hours after sundown, the narrow streets and campi were thronged, for the city was a great center of world trade, attracting every type of stranger, rascal, and adventurer.

Morals and manners were anything but strict, and the women of the city were notorious throughout Italy for their easy virtue, and contemporary chronicles read like the vitriolic lines of Martial, Juvenal, and Petronius. Women were not safe on the streets, or even in the churches.[11]

A decree of the Great Council, dated March, 1315, declares that *"multa inonesta et turpis committuntur in ecclesia et porticu et platea Santi Marci,"*[12] and Marco Grimiani, a patrician, was ejected from the Church itself for attempting to rape a young girl in its very atrium.[13] The archives of the period are replete with the trials and convictions of men of the finest families for abduction, bigamy, rape, and worse, all seemingly committed quite shamelessly in the open.

In an age when cursing and blasphemy were common—it is strange how many of man's curses have remained unchanged down the centuries—the Venetians were so notorious for their foul language that Petrarch complains of it, and the municipal records reveal formal decrees against cursing and blasphemy. One declared in the vile Latin of the lawbooks that any person, either man or woman, who injured another by calling him a *"vermum*

[11] A Latin document still in existence records that the Council of Forty tried and condemned Zanino Grioni, of the quarter of St. Eustacio, to three months' imprisonment (surely a light sentence!) for having assaulted and abused Moreta, one of Marco Polo's daughters, in the Campo San Vitale.

[12] "Many lewd and shameful acts are committed in the church and portico and place of St. Mark's."

[13] It is interesting to note that when he was tried and found guilty and fined three hundred lire, one third of the fine was turned over to the girl herself.

canem" should be penalized in the sum of twenty soldi. Gambling was so rife that laws were continually being enacted for its control. Among them was a statute prohibiting gaming in the portico of the Church of St. Mark, as well as in the courtyards, the chambers, or the doorways of the Doge's palace. Under its provisions professional gamblers were to be flogged and branded.

Simplicity and purity of life, incorruptibility in politics or commerce, or an exalted or rigid standard of morals was scarcely to be expected in thirteenth-century Venice, which was ever seething and throbbing with business and pleasure, passion and vice. As the city was on one of the most traversed routes to the Holy Land, pilgrims (men and women of every age and every condition—adventurers, honest men, thieves, priests, confidence men, prostitutes, merchants, slaves) forgathered on her canals, bridges, streets, and market places. The rich found lodging in her hotels and taverns, the poor in her hospices. A German bishop of Passau, Volger von Ellenbrechtskirchen, has left a vivid picture of the Venetian inns of the period. The travelers could admire beautiful marblework everywhere, but there were no stoves, no drainage, and absolutely no sanitary conveniences. The beds, or rather pallets, were miserable and the furniture rickety or broken. "But," he adds, "the Venetian innkeepers have the delightful custom of adorning the bedrooms with flowers."

In earlier days Venetians were evidently disturbed at the open way in which the inns offered feminine attractions to their guests, for they passed laws to abate the practice, but in vain. Finally, in 1226 the city fathers resigned themselves (one can almost hear them sighing virtuously) to the idea that "*le meretrici fossero omnino necessarie in terra ista.*" They thereupon simply forbade such women residence in the homes of private citizens and segregated them in a restricted area. By the same statute the women were permitted to mingle during the day with the crowds in the Rialto and in the vicinity of the taverns, but "when commenced to sound the first evening bell of San Marco," all had to retire to their quarter in Castelletto. The names of some of these bright-eyed ladies have been preserved, Maria Greca, Lena de Florentia,

Isabeta de Francia, and others, indicating plainly that ever and everywhere articles bearing labels of foreign origin have been more attractive and sought than home products.

The segregation laws proved ineffective, and the prostitutes scattered and plied their trade in many parts of the city. Quaint drawings of these women, modestly dressed but most assiduously engaged in seducing a very timid young man, have survived in the famous manuscript of *The First Decade of Livy*, and Carpaccio has pictured two of them richly dressed and bejeweled in the height of fashion, surrounded by pet dogs and birds, in his *"Due Cortigiane,"* now in the Correr Gallery in Venice.[14]

Venetian manners and morals were crude enough, but the strangers in the city with their uninhibited emotions and desires made them even worse. In that motley gathering were love and lust, religious fanaticism and atheism, charity and boundless greed, virtue and vice, courage and cowardice, hypocrisy and sanctity, blackest iniquity and spotless purity. The gradations and refinements of men's natures were not to be found in Venice where, in Marco Polo's lifetime, an old world was dying and a new one was passing through the painful travail of birth.

Crime was commonplace, although ever increasing numbers of statutes were enacted in efforts to eradicate it, statutes which throw a revealing light on thirteenth-century Venetian life and character. Crimes against property were punished with far more severity than those against the person, and theft was held the most heinous of offenses. For stealing the value of twenty soldi, a man was flogged and branded, and for a second offense, his eyes were torn out. If the amount stolen exceeded twenty soldi in value, the culprit was hanged. If a thief caught in *flagrante delicto* attempted to defend himself with weapons or wounded anyone, he was condemned to lose his eyes and his right hand. Murderers were decapitated, hanged on a gibbet between the columns of the Piaz-

---

[14] This picture Ruskin considered the finest painting in the world. "I know," he wrote, "no other which writes every nameable quality of painters and in so intense a degree—breadth with tenderness, brilliancy with quietness, decision with minuteness, color with light and shade. . . . I know no other picture in the world which can be compared with it."

zetta, or burned; a poisoner—and poisoning was much in vogue—
if his victim survived, had either one or both hands chopped off
or his eyes destroyed with a white-hot brazier. Before his execution
a particularly dangerous criminal was conducted on a long boat
through the Grand Canal from the Church of San Marco to Santa
Croce, stripped to the waist, being tortured with red-hot pincers
the while. From Santa Croce, after having had his right hand cut
off, he was dragged along the streets tied to a horse's tail. Arriving
in this fashion at the Piazzetta, he was decapitated between the two
columns, his body quartered and exposed to public view. Minor
offenders, especially if they were priests, were locked in wooden
cages hung from a pole part way up the campanile of St. Mark's,
fed on bread and water, and subjected to the jeers and insults of the
mob; in one case, a priest was thus confined for more than a year.
For petty misdemeanors, the culprit was compelled to wear about
his neck a board with an inscription setting forth his offense.

In these crowded streets, amid this open immorality, cruelty,
and inhumanity, this vice and crime, strangely mingled as they
were with beauty and pageantry, were molded the character and
mind of the boy Marco during the years his father, Messer Nicolo,
and his uncle, Messer Maffeo, were trading in Constantinople and
Bokhara, traveling across the deserts and steppes of Central Asia,
and sojourning with the Great Khan Kublai in his capital, Khanbaligh, many thousands of miles from Venice.

But all was not black and ugly in the Venice of Marco Polo. Its
people seem to have been then, as now, essentially light-hearted,
pleasure-loving, and blithe. Their calendar was punctuated with
many cheerful, colorful saints' days and festivals. Then the entire
populace would turn out in best doublet and hose, in silk and fur
and cloth of gold, to eat and drink, dance and make merry. They
would throw off the worries and dull gray cares of everyday life
and rejoice and revel under the intense blue skies and beside the
waters sparkling in the sun.

Many of these festivals passed away with the downfall of the
Republic, but some are still a part of Venetian life. The best-loved
one was "La Sensa," the great feast of Ascension Day, during

which the city was transformed into a pageant of blazing color and all the citizens poured forth to witness the wedding of Venice and the sea. This day, the greatest, most solemn and dignified of all the feast days of the Venetian year, had its origin in the conquest of Dalmatia by the Doge Pietro Orseolo II in the year 1000. On his triumphal return it had been decreed that the Doge, the clergy, and the people should, on each future Ascension Day (the day on which Orseolo had set sail on his campaign), assist in the benediction of the Adriatic Sea.

In that far-off time the ceremony was simple. The clergy in full and resplendent vestments and bearing water, salt for purification, and a branch of olive, were rowed out to the Lido, being joined on the way by the Doge in full regalia on the state barge. The procession then continued on to the Lido, chanting litanies and the psalm *"Exaudi nos Domine."* The bishop then intoned a solemn prayer to God, beseeching Him to remove all sin and to calm all troubled hearts, closing the prayer with the Latin invocation, "We pray Thee, O Lord, to grant unto us this sea, and that Thou wilt vouchsafe unto all who sail upon it peace and quiet." After blessing the water and chanting verse 7 of Psalm 51 ("Purge me with hyssop and I shall be clean"), the prelate asperged the Doge and his retinue with a portion of the consecrated water and poured the remainder into the sea. High Mass was then celebrated in the Church of St. Nicholas, and the Doge returned to his palace.

With the passing of the years the festival became much more of a pageant, and an additional ceremony, the *sposalizio*, or marriage, marked the day. Pope Alexander III, on the occasion of a state visit to Venice in 1177, presented a consecrated ring to Doge Ziani with these words: "Receive this as a pledge of the sovereignty which you and your successors shall have in perpetuity over the sea." Thenceforth the feast day of "La Sensa" took on more ceremonial than before and became the most magnificent of all Venetian pageants.[15]

The Doge, clad in his most gorgeous robes of state and rowed

[15] A most delightful description of the "Sensa" and the wedding of Venice and the sea may be found in *Coryat's Crudities*, Vol. I, 359ff.

in his barge, the *Bucentoro*, by young nobles, appeared with his retinue and was escorted to the Lido by thousands of crowded boats and gondolas. On his arrival he was met by the Bishop of Castello with offerings of peeled chestnuts and red wine, together with roses in a silver vase. After the usual prayers the Bishop blessed the gold ring provided for the occasion. The Doge then rose from his seat and threw the ring into the open Adriatic, pronouncing the solemn words: *"Desponsamus te, mare, in signum veri perpetuique dominii Serenissimae Republicae Venetae."*[16] After the customary Mass the Doge held a formal reception and a state dinner was served. St. Mark's Square was converted into an immense fair filled with booths erected for the occasion, and revel and merrymaking, eating and drinking continued without cessation for eight days. The day finally became the beginning of the great annual city fair, where all things were bought and sold. To it flocked folk from the neighboring cities and towns, for nowhere else in Europe could be seen so great a display of wares from East and West. To add a further attraction, indulgences were granted to all who came to the city's churches during this period of rejoicing.

Without doubt young Marco Polo witnessed, together with his companions and fellow citizens, the installation of Doge Lorenzo Tiepolo in 1268. The writer Martino da Canale was present, saw it all, and has preserved it for us in his *Cronique des Veniciens.* It is interesting to speculate that the future author of the most famous of all travel tales and Venice's medieval chronicler may have rubbed shoulders in the crowd on that occasion.

Canale begins the story of the day by informing his readers that the Doge's first act was to invite to meet him all those with whom he was not on good terms; these he embraced and admitted to his friendship. Then began the pageant proper. The first event took place on the water. Messer Piero Michele, captain of the state fleet of galleys, led his vessels in review before the ducal palace "and sang the praises of Monsignore the Doge in this manner: 'Christ

---

[16] "We wed thee, O sea, in token of the true and perpetual dominion of the Most Serene Venetian Republic."

conquers, Christ reigns, Christ rules; to our Signore Lorenzo Tiepolo, to God, be offered thanks, to you, O illustrious Doge of Venice, Dalmatia, and Croatia . . . salvation, honor, life, and victory, and may St. Mark aid you!' " Thereupon all the sailors raised their voices in cheers and cries of praise, and the galleys were rowed through the canals of the city.

Next came the boats bearing citizens of the other islands of the lagoon, the men of Murano, the island where are most of the glass factories, being especially noticeable with live roosters in their barges and great banners flying from their masts.

After the water display was ended, the one on land began. First came the craft guilds, the members marching two by two, in magnificent costumes, each guild wearing a different garb. Each guild, led by its master craftsmen in the van, marched past the new Doge and Dogaressa on foot. The smiths, wearing garlands on their heads and preceded by banners, trumpets, and other musical instruments, passed in review, saluting the Doge with shouted wishes for his long life, victory, and good fortune. Next came the furriers, marching two by two, clad in ermine and other rich furs, and in their turn shouting and cheering. They were followed by the weavers with their music and singing, together with ten master sailors dressed in white clothes decorated with vermilion stars. Behind them marched long lines of clothworkers with trumpets and silver cups, olive wreaths on their heads, and olive branches in their hands. After them came in turn the several crafts—workers in cotton and woolen cloth and quilt makers in white cloaks decorated with fleurs-de-lis, with garlands of gilt beads on their heads, the whole procession preceded by banners and music. Before this group marched, two by two, little boys and girls singing, while everywhere were heard cheers and cries of *"Viva il nostro Signore Lorenzo Tiepolo, nostro Doge!"*

"Now," continues Canale, "I shall tell you of the master workers in cloth of gold. Know then that they had robed their bodies richly in cloth of gold and they had arrayed their apprentices, some in cloth of gold and some in purple and taffeta, their heads wreathed with garlands of pearls with borders of gold."

The march past seemed endless. Following the clothworkers paraded the other guilds—shoemakers, mercers, and purveyors of provisions and cheese, all in scarlet and violet, the sellers of birds and fish in fur-trimmed robes. Then came the master barbers bedecked in garlands of pearls, in their midst two mounted men costumed like knights-errant, leading four women dressed in strange garments, two on foot, two on horseback. After them marched the barbers, then the master glassworkers in fur-trimmed scarlet robes and gold-trimmed pearl headdresses, bearing in their hands flasks, goblets, and other fine specimens of their handiwork, music playing the while before them. On their heels were the comb and lantern makers, the latter carrying lanterns full of birds of many varieties. "To rejoice Monsignore the Doge they opened the lantern doors and released the birds, which thereupon all flew out, and departed hither and thither, each according to its desire." The goldsmiths brought up the rear, richly dressed, "wearing garlands and necklaces of gold and silver, pearls and rich and precious stones, sapphires, emeralds, diamonds, topazes, jacinths, amethysts, rubies, jaspers, and carbuncles of great value."

Canale concludes, "I shall remain silent about the other crafts. ... Know ye that Monsignore the Doge was installed on a Monday, and until Sunday the people of Venice did nothing but go to see their Signore and their Lady in the manner which I have related."

It was a spectacle which Marco Polo probably recalled often, lying out under the stars in the deserts of central Asia, surrounded by ill-smelling, sheepskin-clad Mongols, listening by the flickering firelight to their interminable tales of foray and of love and their piping on their high-pitched Tatar flutes.

The boy and his companions must have heard of many a scandal, for the Venetians have been great gossips, and little could happen that was not discussed in street and market place. The rites of the Church were employed in Venetian weddings, but often women schemed to marry to escape payment of their debts, often seemingly without benefit of clergy and sometimes not even having met their future husbands before their union. Such marriages

58

could be and often were annulled, and many men thus had several wives. Some of these unsavory affairs ended in the law courts; reports of many have been preserved in their strange mixture of local dialect and bad Latin. A few sentences from two of the trials will bear repeating; although the incidents took place in 1443, they illustrate the frank ideas and practices of the thirteenth century as well.

A certain Pietro of Trent, a broom peddler, passing one evening through the parish of S. S. Gervasio e Protasio, stopped before the house of one Cataruzza, widow of Giovanni Banco. Seeing the lady at her window, he called out to her, "Madonna, find me a pretty girl."

"You beast, you drunkard! What are you trying to do, make a procuress of me?" she screamed.

"I'm not saying that at all. I mean that I want you to find me a girl for a wife."

"Good, if that's it," replied Cataruzza, thinking immediately of a girl of her acquaintance. "By the faith of God I'll get you one. Come back here tomorrow."

The next day Pietro returned and found at the house a pretty girl called Maria, together with a certain Domenico Moxe. The latter thereupon asked of both the man and the girl if they wished to be united "as commanded God and Holy Church." They answered in the affirmative, took each other by the hand, "*fecero colassion de brigada e poi consumaverunt matrimonium*"—and that was all there was to it!

Another musty old volume recites the tale of Beatrice Francigena. On her way home from a visit to Treviso she stopped at the house of a relative, Zanina, where by chance was a man named Falcon, an old acquaintance of Beatrice. The two appear to have come to an understanding very speedily, as Zanina states very naïvely in giving her testimony at the trial:

"While they were standing conversing, the said Falcon spoke thus to the said Beatrice: 'Beatrice, will you do me the great honor? You know that I offer you my hand, and are you going to give your hand to another?'

"And she replied: 'I thought you were making sport of me, and that you were jesting.'

"And the said Falcon answered: 'What I have promised you I wish to promise you again.'

"And both of the aforesaid persons went into the room of the house of the said witness and spoke there, saying: 'Beatrice, you know that you are my wife.'

"And she replied: 'But yes, by God.'

"And then he touched Beatrice's hand saying: 'I take no other wife but you.'

"And she replied: 'And as for me, I take no other husband but you.' " Thus concluded the match!

Marriage was cheap, lightly taken on, and as lightly put off by the good citizens of Venice, who did not seem to be guided by the contemporary dictates of European chivalry and idealized love. They appear rather to have had much of the older Asiatic (and ancient Greek) attitude toward women, selecting and treating their wives primarily as housekeepers and breeders of children. Fra Paolino, in an interesting document written in the early fourteenth century, gives his fellow Venetians advice on the selection of a wife: "She should not be under eighteen years of age, nor her husband under twenty-one. The husband should not be guided by the advice of his wife, who has not sound judgment, because she has neither a sound or strong constitution, but one poor and weak, and the mind naturally inclines to the disposition of the body."

The widespread ownership of female slaves with their lack of moral sense, together with their open intimate relations with their masters, perforce tended to drag or force the free women down to their level in their efforts to hold or recover the affections of their husbands. The chronicles of the time are full of lurid tales of domestic strife, revenge, stabbings, and poisonings caused by the intrigues of wives, slaves, concubines, and lovers. Madness caused by poisoning was so frequent that it received a name of its own—"*erberia.*" Much of this activity was common street talk in Marco Polo's time.

Funerals in the Venice of the thirteenth century were such exhibitions that children playing in the streets could not escape seeing and being affected by them. The ceremonies in many ways resembled the rites of Egypt and the ancient East. The dying person was removed from his bed to a floor covered with ashes. A bell was rung to summon the mourners, while priests intoned the *Miserere* and psalms in the street before the door. A surviving spouse was expected to exhibit the most extravagant display of grief in public, rolling on the ground, screaming, tearing out her hair by the handful, and howling and moaning unceasingly in true Oriental fashion. When friends started to carry out the corpse, wrapped in a sheet or matting, the husband or other chief mourner threw himself on the threshold as though to prevent its removal and had to be dragged away. The family and friends followed the body to the parish church, shrieking and wailing through the streets. They maintained their noisy lamenting during the entire funeral service and re-enacted the same senseless performance at the grave. Poor people often left their dead exposed for several days in the street so as to touch the hearts of passers-by and elicit alms from them.[17]

As today, many of the homes were dark, dank, and cold with but few narrow windows, and these often fitted with iron gratings. On many of the narrower canals scarcely any light penetrated into the rooms, so that they were chilly, gloomy, and damp. Few houses had any sanitary drainage but relied on the rise and fall of the tide for flushing. True, there were fireplaces and sometimes ovens, but the furniture was solid, hard, and unyielding, and the average home had few comforts. Therefore then, as now, the inhabitants of the city spent much time on the streets where they could find light and cheer.

Dress did not consume much time for ordinary folk. As nearly everywhere in the Europe of that period, the Venetians, both men and women, slept naked. Bathing was not a common practice, and,

[17] This barbarous custom was maintained for centuries, though the Church vainly struggled against it, and threats of excommunication had finally to be invoked before it was stopped.

if indulged in, men and women bathed together, or scrubbed each other in turn, with none of our present-day sense of modesty. Underwear was seldom in use, but if worn it was practically never changed. It was considered such a luxury that we find a widow, one Sofia Banbarigo, leaving in her will "one of her new chemises to Dona Reni and one to Donado." Elsewhere we find included in the pay of a maidservant "one chemise a year." Cleanliness was entirely subordinated to outward appearance, and the Venetians, both men and women, like their fellow Europeans, went about in gorgeous silks, satins, furs, and jewels, but underneath were unwashed bodies and either undergarments that were filthy or none at all.

Such streets as the city boasted were unpaved and muddy. The women wore high pattens or clogs to keep their skirts clear of the mud. Sometimes these clogs were more than three feet high— almost like stilts—and a fall was highly dangerous, especially if a woman were pregnant. As the women persisted in wearing them, the city government was forced to prohibit their use, declaring that such accidents caused expectant mothers to give birth to premature or deformed children. No efforts were made to keep the streets clean, and housewives threw their refuse out before their doors. The only scavengers were the pigs of the monastery of St. Anthony of Padua, which wandered at will throughout the city.

The glassworkers of Venice have been famous from early times. Although practically all are now located on the island of Murano, in the thirteenth century there were still open-doored factories in Venice proper. There the loiterer might watch the dexterity with which the master worker dipped his long blowpipe into the pot of glowing liquid, twisting and turning it as he blew and, swinging the incandescent bubble in the air, produced any shape he desired, as though by magic. By dexterous movements of their wrists they built complicated pieces, adding or clipping a lump or strip here or there with their steel scissors or pincers, until they had evolved pieces of every conceivable pattern and color. The work was all done by the corporation or guild of glassworkers, who guarded jealously the secrets of manufacture. Most of the guilds plied their trades in the open—the weavers of silk and cloth of gold and silver and damask, and the embroiderers, whose work was justly famed throughout Europe. There, too, were the goldsmiths and jewelers, working away at ornaments, rings, filigree, plate, and enamel panels, much in demand at home and abroad. Certain streets were clamorous from sunrise to sunset with the hammering of the armorers and makers of weapons and chain mail for the pilgrims and soldiers who were continually passing through the city on their way east or west. The best products of all these craftsmen were reserved for exhibitions at festivals and fairs, where they brought high prices and advertised to the world the magnificence and the eminence of the Queen of the Adriatic in commerce, in wealth, and in the arts and crafts.

Not only was Venice famed for her artisans and their work; its Arsenal[18] in the eastern part of the city was rapidly becoming the greatest industrial plant in the Western world. The centers of Venice's wealth and power were the Rialto, St. Mark's, and the palace of the Doge, but the source and backbone of that power and wealth was the Arsenal. Built on two islands, it had but one access to the lagoon, and in the thirteenth century massive protective walls were being built around it.

We boast of our mass production and consider the assembly lines of our great factories one of the wonders of modern industry. Yet all these methods were known and used by the *arsenalotti* of Venice more than seven hundred years ago. Pero Tafur, the Spanish traveler who visited Venice in 1436, has left the following vivid picture of the speed with which war galleys were equipped, once the hull had been built:

> And as one enters the gate there is a great street on either hand with the sea in the middle, and on one side are windows opening out of the houses of the Arsenal, and the same on the other side. And out came a galley towed by a boat, and from the windows they handed out to them, from one the cordage, from another the bread, from another the arms, and from another the ballistas and

18 From the Arabic *dar al sina'ah*, a workshop.

mortars, and so from all sides everything that was required. And when the galley had reached the end of the street all the men required were on board, together with the complement of oars, and she was equipped from end to end. In this manner there came out ten galleys fully armed, between the hours of three and nine. I know not how to describe what I saw there, whether in the manner of its construction or in the management of the workpeople, and I do not think there is anything finer in the world.[19]

The quays and wharves likewise were witnesses to the activities of the greatest European commercial port of the Middle Ages. Heaped high were the principal Venetian products for export—glass, salt, salted fish, wooden utensils, woven goods, and wrought iron. Together with them were goods for reshipment to the East, for Venice was the great entrepôt for goods from other Italian cities, Germany, Hungary, and Dalmatia, and even from France, Spain, and far-away England. Great galleys, both long and round, lay at the docks disgorging their cargoes newly arrived from the East—neatly stacked heaps of reddish sandalwood from Timor, filling the air with its heavy fragrance, bales of silk and cotton goods, cloth of every texture and color from Damascus, Bagdad, and Alexandria. Piled high were bags of drugs and medicines—gum arabic, cinnamon, cassia, rhubarb, and myrrh. Standing about were to be seen ship's clerks and warehousemen checking off goods, weighing and measuring, comparing and arguing, while shipowners and merchants were supervising the unloading of the more valuable cargo—precious stones, pearls, gold and silver bars, and specie. Heaped in profusion were sacks, boxes, and bales of sweet-smelling cloves and nutmegs, camphor in bamboo tubes, pungent pepper and ginger, ivory and satinwood. Lying all about were columns and architraves, pedestals, panels and blocks of

[19] The speed with which the Venetians could build ships was phenomenal. In 1570, during the Turkish War (culminating in the defeat of the Ottoman fleet at Lepanto in 1571), one hundred galleys were built and outfitted in as many days. Henry III, King of France, during a visit to Venice in the summer of 1574, inspected the Arsenal. A galley was shown him of which the keel and ribs alone were in position on the stocks. He then sat down to a two-hour banquet, during which, in his presence, the galley was fully constructed, completely equipped, and launched.

polished marble—loot from some long-fallen temple on Syrian, Greek or Egyptian shore, brought to embellish St. Mark or other churches in the course of construction throughout the city, or to beautify the palace of some noble or merchant prince. These stones made convenient seats for idlers, who would sit and watch the busy scene about them much as the young Dante sat a few years later on a rough-hewn block of stone hard by the old Baptistery and watched the Duomo, the cathedral of his beloved Florence, grow under the magic hand of the master builder.[20]

The picture of humanity at the quaysides was colorful and kaleidoscopic, with ever new sights and sounds. Here were moving slowly long lines of women, interspersed with fewer men, all of a strange aspect and in outlandish garb, looking fiercely and sullenly about them. They were slaves, just brought ashore under guard from the Levant, far from the lands where they were born, en route to the market and the auction block.[21] In the crowds wandered sailors from many lands, speaking many languages, and Jews from Spinalunga, the island across the channel from the Piazzetta.

The Jews of Venice were gradually becoming a very important element in the Levantine trade, and, although they were forced to live apart from their Christian neighbors, their value to the maritime interests of the Republic was fully realized and they were not molested.[22]

Venetian vessels penetrated into every sea and river of Europe, and the flag bearing the Lion of St. Mark was a familiar sight in every harbor worthy of the name. Religion did not interfere with

[20] Although Dante came to Venice shortly before his death in 1321, there is no evidence that he and Marco Polo ever met. One of them was to recount the undying tale of the most wondrous journey of all times by land and sea to the Golden East and back to Europe; the other was to become immortal as the poetical narrator of the great journey of the soul of man upward through the realms of the spirit.

[21] There was an extensive trade in both Mongol and Chinese slaves, mostly in women. Needham I, 189, states that they were domestic servants in Italian homes. Between 1366 and 1397 no fewer than 259 Tatars (i.e., Mongol and/or Chinese) were sold in the slave market of Florence.

[22] Cf. C. Roth, *History of the Jews in Venice*, chap. I, and J. Needham and W. Ling, *Science and Civilization in China*, III, Appendix, p. 681.

commercial dealings, and treaties and pacts bound the city in amicable relations with Moslems and Christians alike. Venice bought and sold, not only with her sister cities of Italy and the emperor of Germany but equally with the sultan of Egypt and the khan of Tatary.

Every shape and size of vessel came and went in La Serenissina's harbor, some under sail, some rowed by slaves or freemen. There were small boats for trade in the estuaries, larger ones which ascended the rivers, great galleys to fare out on the high seas, and ships of war, long and powerful, with their *castelli* amidships guarded by slingers and bowmen, their decks fitted with catapults, ballistae, and heaps of stone missiles, their bulwarks covered with *impavesata*,[23] and their prows armed with great metal beaks for ramming the enemy. All along the waterfront moved guard boats with armored men, ever on the watch for smugglers. Interspersed with the larger craft, moving swiftly hither and thither among the islands and beyond the lagoon, were gondolas and fishing boats, the latter flat bottomed and easily steered, their sails of red and burnt orange glowing in the sunlight and casting strange birdlike shadows on the water, their open decks often heaped high with freshly caught fish on the way to market.

Adding to the color of the scene were farm boats going to market, heavily laden with pumpkins, grapes, figs, pomegranates, and other fruits. Here along the wharves we may imagine young Marco and his companions listening to the sailors spinning their endless yarns of war and piracy, of smuggling and shipwreck, and tales of the strange lands and peoples in the far corners of the world. Little could the boy have dreamed that he, the Venetian youth who sat hugging his knees in wide-eyed excitement at the stories of these seafarers, would wander thousands of miles beyond the distance covered by the farthest-traveled man of them all and that his written story of what he saw and heard there would surpass anything that the tired old ears of the world had heard since the narrative of the widely traveled Herodotus of Halicar-

[23] Bucklers of heavy leather to protect them from the Greek fire which might be thrown by attackers—Molmenti, *op. cit.*, 230.

nassus, told over sixteen hundred years before. Still less could he have known that his tale, translated into the tongues of Europe and Asia, would hold men and boys entranced and breathless for more than six hundred years after he had gone to rest in the city of his fathers, and that never to this day would his name or his book be forgotten.

Such was the Venice into which Marco Polo was born in the year 1254; such were its men and women, its streets and its houses, its ships and its life, its manners and its customs, its excellences and its shortcomings.

And so Messer Nicolo Polo, arriving home with Messer Maffeo, his brother, after their long absence in the far lands of the earth, found his "son of fifteen years who had for name Marco," and saw that the boy was comely and good.

·III·

The Journey

"*Linque tuas sedes aliena litora quaere,*
O iuvenis: maior rerum tibi nascitur ordo,
... Maior in externas fit qui descendit harenas."[1]

—Petronius, *Fragment 79*

"*Quo modo lucem diemque omnibus hominibus, ita*
omnis terras fortibus natura aperuit."[2]—Tacitus, *Historiae*

"*Crowns in my purse I have and goods at home*
And so am come abroad to see the world."

—*The Taming of the Shrew*

THE ARRIVAL of Nicolo and Maffeo in Venice marked a turning point in young Marco Polo's life. All the evidence in his book marks him as alert, intelligent, observant, and insatiably curious.

---

[1] "Leave thy home, O Youth
And seek out foreign shores:
A broader range of things begins for thee.
... He who disembarks on far-off sands
Thereby becomes the greater man."

[2] "Just as she has given to all men the light of day, so has nature opened all lands to men of courage."

With what eagerness he must have listened to his elders' tales of the strange lands through which they had traveled and the many peoples with whom they had dwelt—their appearance, their dress, their manners and customs, and how their lives and habits differed from those of the Venetians! He probably even picked up a few words and phrases which his father and uncle in all likelihood used at times in their Venetian speech and stored up practical knowledge which was surely to prove invaluable in the days to come.

As every inveterate traveler can readily understand, Nicolo and his brother must have found it very difficult, after fifteen years of travel, to settle down to the comparatively humdrum life of their home city on the sea. Moreover, as a result of their promise, given to Kublai Khan, to return to take to him men to teach the Christian faith, together with their conversations with the Pope's legate in Acre, they felt that their stay in Venice was at best but temporary, pending only the election of a new pope, an election which seemed endlessly delayed.

Meanwhile, Nicolo took a new wife unto himself, and Marco found what he had never known before—two parents and a home in which he was more than a mere nephew or cousin or friend.

The chafing at the delays grew ever greater, and the patience of Messer Nicolo and Messer Maffeo grew ever shorter as month dragged after month until two long years had passed, with never an indication of agreement on the man who was to succeed the late Pope on the throne of St. Peter. Finally the brothers decided not to postpone their departure for the land of the Great Khan any longer. They feared his displeasure at their failure to return. Moreover, the greatest opportunity of their lives to increase their wealth would be lost if they delayed too long. Fortune beckoned insistently, and they obeyed her urging.

The men decided to take Nicolo's son Marco with them. He was now a man, for in 1271 a youth of seventeen was fully grown and ready to take his place in the world. In addition, the brothers very evidently believed that he would be an aid to them on the long journey across Asia.[3]

[3] It should be carefully noted by the captious critics of the shortcomings of

Marco Polo was one of the fortunate mortals of this earth—or perhaps one of the most unfortunate. He was fortunate because Fate granted travel, wealth, and distinction, unfortunate because all these came to him in youth and early manhood. The evening of his years, instead of being a glorious sunset after a brilliant day, seems, from the evidence we have, to have been a fading into a dull and gloomy twilight, deepening into night, far from the lands where he had found joy and excitement and prominence—and, perhaps, love. Destiny decreed that people were not to believe his later tales of wonder, that his townsfolk were to make a mock and a byword of him, and that his book, born of the ardor and fire of the adventures of his best years, was to be accepted as nothing more substantial than a romance and a pleasant tale to read or hear by the fireside of a cold winter's evening, along with tales of King Arthur, Huon of Bordeaux, and Tristan and Iseult. But all these developments were in the womb of time; the young Marco knew only the joy of living, the thrilling delights of travel, sight-seeing, new scenes, new peoples, new adventures.

Again the Polos prepared to travel toward the rising sun, and again Nicolo left his wife with child. Once more they must have made their round of visits to relatives and friends and, this time with Marco, heaped their luggage into their gondolas and, after last farewells, wound their way through echoing canals, between the shadowy high-walled palaces and tenements, past markets and dark shops, and under the arched bridges.

At last the familiar docks were reached. There were the Piazza and the Piazzetta, the stone masons still patiently in process of laying the pavement. There were the great bronze horses gleaming in the sunlight and the statue of St. Theodore smiling down from the top of his lofty pillar. As now on a warm summer day, so did the world seem to be singing, with Venice aglow with warm

---

Marco Polo's book that he left Italy at the age of seventeen, too young to have acquired the wisdom and culture of a well-educated and widely read elderly scholar which they would have him possess. It is doubtful in the mind of the author that any seventeen-year-old lad (unless he be a precocious scholar and an omnivorous reader) would have a bit more preparation for such a journey.

marbles, blue sky, and sparkling water, when Marco drew along-
side his ship, clambered up on her deck, and looked back upon his
beloved city and toward the south, beyond the Lido and the
lagoons to the new world to which he was faring forth. The
knowledge he acquired on his travels he was destined to bring back
to his fellow countrymen and the whole world after many long
toilsome years.

Never was the city which he was leaving to be so fair, so rich,
so powerful again as when Marco Polo left it that day in all the
impatience and insouciance of youth. Da Canale, who gave the
account of the installation of the Doge Lorenzo Tiepolo, has left
us his vivid impression of Venice at the beginning of his chronicle:

> Venice, today the most beautiful and the pleasantest city in all
> the world, full of beauty and of all good things. Merchandise flows
> through this noble city even as the water flows from the fountains.
> Venice is enthroned upon the sea, and the salt water flows through
> it and about it and in all places, save in the houses and on the
> streets, and when the citizens go forth, they can return to their
> homes either by sea or by the streets. From every place come
> merchandise and merchants, who buy the merchandise as they will
> and cause it to be taken to their own countries. Within this city is
> found food in great abundance, bread and wine, chickens and
> river fowls, meat, both fresh and salt, the great fish both of the
> sea and of the rivers, and merchants of every country who sell and
> buy. You may find in plenty within this beautiful city men of good
> breeding, old and middle-aged and young, much to be praised for
> their noble character, and merchants who sell and buy, and money-
> changers and citizens of every craft, and seafaring men of every
> sort, and vessels to carry [goods] to every port, and galleys to
> destroy their enemies. Moreover, in this beautiful city are fair
> ladies and damsels and young maidens in great number, and ap-
> parelled very richly.

A familiar sight in Marco Polo's time was a building on the Riva
degli Schiavoni, near the Doge's palace. Demolished long ago to
make room for improvements, it was known because of its two
high towers as the Palazzo delle due Torri. It was a prominent

landmark in its day and is pictured in a vividly colored miniature on a page of an early fifteenth-century manuscript of *The Book of Marco Polo* now in the Bodleian Library at Oxford. It represents the departure of the three Polos from Venice. In this palace in the year 1362, some thirty-nine years after the death of Marco Polo, dwelt the poet Petrarch. From it he dispatched to a friend, the secretary of the Pope, letters in which he describes the busy waterfront as he saw it and as it must have been a few short years before on that day when the Polos set sail:

> See the innumerable vessels which set out from the Italian shore ... one turning its prow to the east, the other to the west; some carrying our wine to foam in British cups, our fruits to flatter the palates of the Scythians, and, still more hard to believe, the wood of our forests to the Aegean and the Achaian isles; some to Syria, to Armenia, to the Arabs and Persians, carrying oil and linen and saffron, and bringing back all their divers goods to us. . . . Resting on their anchors close to the marble banks which serve as a mole to the vast palace which this free and liberal city has conceded to me for my dwelling, several vessels have passed the winter, exceeding with the height of their masts and spars the two towers which flank my house. The larger of the two was at this moment . . . leaving the quay and setting out upon its voyage. If you had seen it you would have said it is no ship, but a mountain swimming upon the sea, although under the weight of its immense wings a great part of it was hidden in the waves.

Even though the Mediterranean had been plowed by countless keels since man first dwelt on its shores, it and its storms were still feared. Not only were mariners in terror of its natural dangers, but they ventured forth fearsomely because of their dread of unknown or imagined monsters. Ludolph Von Suchem, a German churchman, has told of the perils of Mediterranean sea-travel in his *Description of the Holy Land*, written about A.D. 1360:

> I have often been in sundry storms at sea beyond all description. ... Indeed I know it to be true that there is no stone or sand at the bottom of the sea that is not moved, if it can be moved, when the sea rages and raves thus, and this is often proved among islands,

where the sea is narrow, where an exceeding great number of stones are cast from one shore to another in storms.

After describing strange winds and shoals and rocks and coral, he regales us with a tale of the "sea-swine":

... which is greatly to be feared by small ships, for this same fish seldom or never does any mischief to great ships unless pressed by hunger. Indeed, if the sailors give it bread, it departs, and is satisfied; but if it will not depart, then it may be terrified and put to flight by the sight of a man's angry and terrible face. . . . Howbeit, the man must be exceedingly careful when he is looking at the fish not to be afraid of it, but to stare at it with a bold and terrible countenance, for if the fish sees that the man is afraid it will not depart, but bites and tears the ship as much as it can.

Another fish men feared was the *melar*, which lurks near the coast of Barbary. Ludolph was told that one of these fish bit a certain ship, thinking it was good to eat:

And straightway the mariners, the servants of the ship, went down into the hold, wishing to see where the ship was broken. They found that a fish's tooth, as thick as a beam, and three cubits long, had pierced the ship. . . . As I was wondering at the length and breadth of such a fish, the same sailor told me not to wonder, because there is in the sea a fish a mile long.

And Ludolph saw whales spouting, and speculated about flying fish, and wondered how far they could maintain their flight:

I have diligently inquired of knowing seamen whence these fish come, and they have answered me that in England and Ireland there grow on the seashore exceedingly beauteous trees, which bear fruit like apples. In these apples there is bred a worm, and when the apples are ripe they fall to the ground, are broken in the fall, and the worms fly out, having wings like bees. Those of them who first touch the land become creatures of the air, and fly about with the other fowls of the heavens; but such worms as first touch the water become creatures of the water, and swim like fish, but yet sometimes wander into the other element and exercise themselves by flight.

Ludolph was a bit cautious, for he added, "Whether they do grow upon trees I do not know beyond having the story, but they are eaten like fish, and are seen to fly by men voyaging at sea." The "knowing seamen" certainly had much amusement at the expense of the simple, credulous pilgrim from far-off Germany.

These stories indicate how the sea was still feared by man. Marco must have heard many such tales and even taller ones from his friends among the sailors on the water front of Venice and on the very ship which took him to Syria. He must have drawn his blanket just a little closer over his head at night, when the wind rose and the tempest roared and the lightning flashed and the little vessel rocked and tossed as it was buffeted by the great seas and all the monsters of the deep reached up with greedy clawing hands from the depths or screeched and howled in the rigging, enraged at being cheated of their prey.

At last the voyage came to an end. The coast of Syria was sighted, and shortly thereafter Nicolo and his son and Maffeo arrived in the great city of Acre.

The same Ludolph, although he arrived in the city after it had been taken and sacked by the Moslems, describes it much as it must have appeared to the eyes of the Venetian travelers in 1271:

> This glorious city of Acre stands, as I have said, on the seashore, built of square hewn stones . . . with lofty and exceedingly strong towers. . . . Each gate of the city stood between two towers.[4] The streets within the city were exceeding neat, all the walls of the houses being of the same height and all alike built of hewn stone, wondrously adorned with glass windows and paintings. . . . The streets of the city were covered with silken cloths, or other fair awnings, to keep out the sun's rays.

The various kings, princes, and nobles of the Crusaders' kingdom were there, and they

> walked about the streets in royal state, with golden coronets on their heads, each of them like a king, with his knights, his follow-

---

[4] The walls of Acre still stand practically intact in their massive proportions, with little change.

ers, his mercenaries and his retainers, his clothing and his warhorse wondrously bedecked with gold and silver, all vying one with another in beauty and novelty of device, and each man apparelling himself with the utmost care.

The pilgrim describes in great detail the castles, palaces, and dwellings of the Knights Templars and other orders of chivalry. Fortunately Ludolph also speaks of the foreign merchants' quarters of Acre:

> There also dwelt in Acre the richest merchants under heaven, who were gathered together therein out of all nations; there were Pisans, Genoese and Lombards. . . . There dwelt therein also exceeding rich merchants of other nations, for from sunrise to sunset all parts of the world brought merchandise thither, and everything that can be found in the world that is wondrous or strange used to be brought thither because of the nobles and princes who dwelt there.

The Polos immediately sought out the papal legate, Teobaldo of Piacenza, whom the brothers had met on their return journey to Venice two years before, and consulted with him about their future movements. They desired to fulfill as many of the requests of Kublai Khan as possible, so as not to return to him empty-handed. They therefore asked Teobaldo's permission to proceed to Jerusalem to obtain some holy oil from the lamp ever burning above the sepulcher of Jesus. Having received his consent to the journey, the Polos again boarded ship and sailed south to Joppa and thence made the journey of thirteen leagues overland to the Holy City.

Jerusalem and the surrounding country were as a magnet to the medieval world. Sacred to three religions, the City of David had been the center of strife and pilgrimage for centuries. Crusader and Moslem were continually at war over it, and the poor townsfolk were seldom at peace. It was the goal of countless pilgrimages from all over Europe, and many of these pious travelers of the Middle Ages have left remarkable tales of what they saw and believed about the "sights" of the city. In their naïveté they accepted every tale or legend told them with unquestioning credulity. There was something to be shown to convince the visitor of the absolute truth of nearly every verse in both the Old and the New Testament, although most of the pilgrims took greater interest in the scenes of the life and passion of their Lord. Seemingly nothing had been lost or destroyed since the beginning of the world. Evidences of the veracity of every phrase of the Gospels were to be seen on all sides, and the city swarmed with guides eager to conduct the visitors from place to place.

Burchard of Mount Zion, a German Dominican monk, came to Palestine about 1282. At the foot of the Mount of Olives he visited the Garden of Gethsemane and there saw the imprint of Jesus' head and hair and knees on a rock so hard that a chisel could not remove even a little dust. Burchard has described also the place where Marco and his father and uncle obtained the holy oil:

> The cave wherein is the Lord's sepulchre is eight feet long and likewise eight feet wide. It is entirely cased with marble on the outside, but within it is bare rock, even as it was at the time of His burial. The doorway into this cave is entered from the east, and is very low and small.
>
> On the right as one enters is the tomb of the holy sepulchre, against the north wall. It is of gray-colored marble, and is three palms above the surface of the pavement and eight feet long, even as is the crypt or cave itself within, and is closed on every side. No light from without can be had inside, because there is no window to bring light into it; but nine lamps hang above the Lord's sepulchre, which give light within.

Burchard describes the stone at the entrance to the cave as part of the very one which was rolled away from the entrance after the death of Jesus. He also was shown the hole where the Cross was erected, still red with blood, and part of the stone pillar where Jesus was scourged, and the spot where St. Helena found the True Cross.[5]

[5] It is interesting to note that the Colonna family of Rome derives its name from the fact that one of its ancestors is supposed to have carried off a part of this same column to the Eternal City. St. Helena, mother of Constantine the Great,

Marino Sanudo, a noble Venetian who visited Palestine in 1321, wrote several chapters describing the country in a book with the quaint title *Secrets for True Crusaders to Help Them to Recover the Holy Land*. He had pointed out to him, among other things, the prison where Jesus was confined, the chamber of the Last Supper (still shown to tourists), and the basin in which the Disciples' feet were washed—and "hard by are the tombs of Solomon, David and the other kings of Judah." At the south of Mount Zion (where the so-called Tomb of David is still shown) he saw "the field that was bought for the thirty pieces of silver for which Christ was sold by Judas." He was taken to what was designated as Pilate's house, and "that of the traitor Judas, where he dwelt with his wife and children."

The same Ludolph who described the perils of a pilgrim at sea also visited the holy places in and about Jerusalem. He saw a pit in Bethlehem where

the Blessed Virgin lay hid for three days for fear of Herod, and suckled the child Jesus there. In her fear she chanced to let fall some of her milk upon a stone in that place, which milk is there even to this day. The milk oozes out of the stone like moisture, and is a milky color with a tinge of red. The more of the milk is scraped off, the more is restored in the same quantity, and no more. This is the milk which may be seen, and is shown in many different churches; for it is taken away hither and thither by the pilgrims.

He saw too, the rocky cave into which many of the bodies of the slaughtered Innocents were cast, and he tells us sadly that "this rock has been almost entirely carried away by the pilgrims."

Ludolph visited the tomb of Rachel and "the pit into which Joseph was cast by his brethren, and sold to the Ishmaelites." He also saw the Dome of the Rock, and believed that he was gazing upon the Temple of Solomon. He made a pilgrimage in his turn to the Church of the Holy Sepulchre and tells how the sepulchre itself is covered with white marble:

is supposed to have found the pieces of the True Cross, now in a church in Rome. In 325 she made a pilgrimage to Jerusalem and caused to be built the Church of the Holy Sepulchre and the Church of the Nativity.

The stone which covers it on the front side has three holes pierced through it, and through those holes one can kiss the true stone thereof. This stone wherewith the sepulchre is cased is so cunningly joined on to the sepulchre that to the ignorant it seems to be all one stone. . . . It is and ever has been kept most carefully guarded. Indeed, if Christ's sepulchre could be carried away in grains of sand it would have been so carried away long ago, even had it been a great mountain, so that scarce one grain of sand would have remained on the spot.

Ludolph gives us also a bit of interesting information about the exact place where the Polos bought their oil:

Now, as for the lamps and candlesticks which are said to be round about the sepulchre; but there dwell in the Church of the Holy Sepulchre ancient Georgians who have the key of the Chapel of the Holy Sepulchre, and food, alms, candles, and oil for lamps to burn round about the Holy Sepulchre are given them by pilgrims through a little window in the south door of the church.

A pilgrim of the twelfth century tells of seeing a beautifully adorned lamp which burned over the sepulchre, one which went out of itself at the ninth hour each Good Friday and lighted itself again on Easter Sunday at the hour of Jesus' resurrection. He was told that this lamp had been placed there by Martha and her brother Lazarus. Possibly some vague report of this miracle was the reason for Kublai's desire to possess some of the oil. It was evidently quite a usual custom for visitors to take away with them some of the blessed oil, for an early pilgrim who visited the sepulchre describes the lamp at its head as having been placed there when Jesus was laid in the grave and asserts that it has burned on the same spot day and night ever since. He also states that he took some of the oil away with him as a blessing and replenished the lamp with fresh oil.

After obtaining the oil, the Polos returned to Teobaldo, in Acre, and announced that, even though no pope had been elected and no early decision was indicated, they felt it their duty to proceed at once to the court of the Mongol ruler. At their earnest request the legate gave them official letters to Kublai, certifying that the brothers had made every effort to do his bidding but that the death of the Pope and the failure of the cardinals to elect a successor had prevented their earlier return. Moreover, Teobaldo, acting as the official representative of the Church, assured the Lord of the Mongols that he would be informed when a new pope had been elected, and that every effort would thereupon be made to comply with his wishes.

Upon receiving these valuable documents, the Polos packed their effects and set forth from Acre.

They had proceeded only as far as Laias[6] when they were delayed by a rebellion led by one of the Great Khan's grandsons, and troops and refugees blocked the caravan routes, making further progress temporarily impossible.

While the travelers were waiting for the road to clear, a courier arrived in Laias from Teobaldo with the news that Teobaldo himself had been elected pope and had taken the title of Gregory X.[7]

The message of the courier also contained a summons to the Venetians to return to Acre. The King of Armenia, regarding them as official papal ambassadors, sent them back to the city together with the courier on an armed galley. On their arrival they immediately presented themselves before the newly elected pontiff to felicitate him on his elevation to the throne of St. Peter and to receive any orders he might desire to give them.

Marco states that they were welcomed with great honor and

---

[6] "In this Province upon the Seaside, there is a Citie called *Gloza* [sic], whereunto is greate trade of merchandise, and all Merchantes that doe triffique thither, have their Cellers and Warehouses in that Citie, as well Venetians, and Ianoueys, and all other that do occupye into Levant."—Frampton, reprint 25. This is the modern small town of Ayas, on the Gulf of Alexandretta, on the Turkish coast. It was once an important port and entrepôt.

[7] Teobaldo de Visconti, Archdeacon of Lüttich, was elected pope on September 6, 1271, though he was only an archdeacon. His election eventuated after the longest balloting (34 months) in papal history. Although his reign was very short, 1271–76, it was the most outstanding papal reign in the second half of the thirteenth century. A conciliator of note, he helped end a civil war in Germany and initiated the fourteenth ecumenical council of the Church (the Second Council of Lyons), which effected the (temporary) union of the Greek and Roman Churches and established the modern form of the conclave by which popes are still elected. He was beatified in 1713.

feasting and that they received a special blessing, for Gregory hoped to spread the doctrines of the Church through them to the far-off land of Cathay. He evidently found a great dearth of priests capable of teaching and at the same time willing to venture into the little-known countries of the East, for he assigned but two to go with the Venetians.[8] Gregory conferred on the friars power to ordain bishops and priests, gave them jewels and other gifts to take to the Great Khan on his behalf, and so bade them farewell with his blessing.

The three Venetians and the two friars returned forthwith to Laias and finally set out on their journey toward the distant East. No sooner had they entered Armenia than they received information that Bibars "the Arbalester" was invading the land with his Saracen host, sacking, looting, and laying waste the country far and wide.[9] Although this development threatened a very real danger, the Polos determined to push on. The two friars, however, were terrified beyond all measure, fearing for their lives. They would not go farther and cast about for some means by which they could return to the greater safety of the seacoast. Very evidently they were not fired with that white-hot zeal which had impelled so many of their fellows to cross burning sands and snow-capped mountains to convert the heathen at the uttermost ends of the earth. Comfort, good food, and a pleasant life among their own people appealed far more to them, and even the fact that their fellow travelers were protected by letters of the Pope and the golden tablet of the Mongol Emperor did not allay their fears.

Very fortunately for the timorous friars, there was in the neighborhood a company of Templars planning a journey to Acre by sea.[10] The two friars seized the opportunity and threw themselves

[8] The two priests were Dominicans, one Fra Guglielmo di Tripoli, author of a book, *De Statu Saracenorum*, and other writings, the second Fra Nicolo da Vicenza. Ramusio states that the two men were *"gran teologi, molto letterati e savi."*

[9] Malik Dahir Ruknuddín Bibars Bundúkdári (user of the crossbow) was a Kipchak slave who rose to be the fourth of the Mameluke sultans of Egypt, reigning from 1259 to 1276.

[10] The Knights Templars, or the "Poor Knights of Christ and the Temple of Solomon," so called because of the grant to them by Baldwin I of Jerusalem of a

on the mercy of the leader of the Templars, pleading for permission to return under his protection to Acre. Permission was granted, and Guglielmo and Nicolo departed, after handing over to the Polos the letters and gifts entrusted to them by the Pope to be presented to the Great Khan. Campi, author of the *Ecclesiastical History of Piacenza*, with a malicious gleam in his eye, closes his account of the incident by stating that the priests returned without making any report to Pope Gregory, who believed them to be still on their journey with the Venetians.

The three Polos, undaunted by the defection of the two cowardly monks, continued on their way. The two brothers had crossed the Asian continent twice before, they could make themselves understood in the languages of the country, they bore letters and gifts from the Supreme Pontiff of the Western world to the most powerful monarch of the East, and, most important and valuable asset of all, they had in their possession the golden tablet sealed with the sign manual of the great Kublai himself. This signature in itself was a safe-conduct, an "open sesame," and a guaranty of food, shelter, and protection throughout practically all the territory which they were about to traverse.

palace next to the building called "the Temple of Solomon." Formed as a warrior group during the Crusades to protect pilgrims, the order grew strong and wealthy, its power spreading rapidly after recognition in 1128 at the Council of Troyes. After confirmation by Pope Honorius III, its establishments soon could be found in almost every important city in the West. Not only did the Templars fulfill their original aims—the guarding of the roads to the Holy Land and constant battling with the infidel—but during the thirteenth century they became a real financial power in both Europe and the Levant. Their commanderies were in constant communication, and their prestige and military power combined made them the natural depositories of wealth of many European nobles for safety and for transmission of funds from city to city—and finally even kings used them as their agents. A pilgrim who saw them in Jerusalem in 1185 described them as wearing "white mantles with a red cross, and when they go to wars a standard of two colors called *balzaus* [bauceant] is borne before them. . . . These Templars live under a strict religious rule, obeying humbly, having no private property, eating sparingly, dressing meanly and dwelling in tents." Hostility from the first to their military and financial strength from both laity and clergy gradually developed into hatred and jealousy. In 1307, Philip IV, King of France, in financial straits and coveting their wealth, seized it with the assistance of Pope Clement V and began an active persecution of the Knights. The order was finally destroyed, its properties confiscated, and, in 1314 the last Grand Master, Jacques de Molay, was, together with his leading knights, burned at the stake in Paris.

81

There have been countless arguments and many books written in an effort to trace the route followed by the three Polos from Laias to the place where they at last met Kublai Kahn. Marco does not outline the journey in the first part of his book, and one brief page covers the journey from Venice to Shangtu. He stated that he intentionally omitted making any mention of the places, peoples, and adventures met en route "because we shall tell it to you in order in its proper place below." However, he does say that they traveled through many perils and hardships with unflagging courage for three and a half years. They traversed burning deserts many days' journey in length and crossed many difficult mountain passes, "always in the direction of the Greek wind [the northeast] and the Tramontana [the polestar, hence the north]." He explains that the excessive length of the journey was caused by heavy snows and ice, the necessity of crossing great rivers, and by contrary winds which interfered with traveling. Moreover, he points out, they could in no wise proceed as swiftly or as easily in winter as in summer.

Even though we cannot follow with certainty the exact route of the travelers, references by Marco throughout his book and vivid descriptions of some of his personal experiences give us a general idea of the itinerary and of what he and his father and uncle encountered on their long journey to the East and back to Venice.

The first land through which they passed was "Little Armenia" (Cilicia), of which Laias was the port. It was the center of a very large and flourishing trade in cotton and spices. In his detailed description of the very first country of the domains of the Great Khan which he visited, Marco indicates his interests and gives us the attitude of mind that we shall find throughout his work. He discusses trade, hunting, the religion and politics of the country, and the manners and customs of the people. Of the last he sadly tells us that, although they are Christians, they are not good Christians, for they are not "as the Romans are." He asserts that once they were doughty and valiant warriors, but now "they are without any good qualities, but are the best sort of drinkers."

From Cilicia the travelers passed through modern Anatolia, which he calls "Turcomania." Marco informs us that the Turcomans weave the finest and most beautiful rugs in the world. One Latin manuscript of this chapter contains a most interesting and significant paragraph, contrasting as it does the bigoted, fanatical, narrow-minded religious ideas of thirteenth-century Europe with the tolerant, broadminded outlook of the Mongol monarchs, rulers of broad domains inhabited by peoples of most diverse faiths:

> Those Tatars have no concern as to what god is worshiped in their territories. As long as you are faithful to the Khan, and very submissive, and thus give the tribute which is fixed by decree, and justice is well served, you may do as you please about your soul. Nevertheless they are unwilling that you speak evil of their souls, or that you should interfere with their acts. Do whatsoever you will about God and about your soul, whether you be Jew or pagan or Saracen or Christian who dwell among the Tatars.

With such farseeing wisdom did the Tatars grant freedom of thought to all within their borders and keep religious peace and amity among the inhabitants of their dominions.

After passing through Turcomania the travelers reached Greater Armenia.[11] There, the Venetian recounts, stands Noah's ark on the top of Mount Ararat. According to the Armenian Prince Hayton, who, during the time he was prior of the monastery of the Prémontrés de Poitiers in 1307, wrote a history of his country, "this mountain is higher than any in the world." Both he and Marco tell the same tale—that the mountain cannot be ascended because of the heavy snows which blanket it in summer as well as in the winter, but at the top the black ark protrudes from the snow and is visible.[12]

[11] Greater Armenia corresponds roughly to the present-day Armenia.

[12] "*Haithoni Armeni Historia Orientalis*," etc., in Pipino, Cologne, 1671 . . . "*semper tamen apparet in eius cacumine quoddam nigrum, quod ab hominibus dicitur esse Arca.*" Josephus (A.D. 37–?100) in his *Antiquities of the Jews*, Bk. I, chap. iii, quotes earlier authors thus, writing of the Ark, "It is said there is still part of the ark in Armenia, at the mountain of the Cordyaeans [Mount Ararat]; and that some people carry off pieces of the bitumen [with which Noah coated the ark] which they take away and use chiefly as amulets." Ararat (16,953 ft.) was first ascended by Professor Parrot in September, 1829. Needless to add, no traces of the ark were found.

Among other phenomena observed by the travelers in this region, the most noteworthy was what Marco called "a fountain from which oil flows in such a great abundance that a hundred shiploads[13] of it may be taken at one time. This oil is not fit to use as food, but it is excellent for burning and for anointing camels which have the mange or the itch. People come from far distant places to obtain it, for in all the countries round there is no other oil."

This brief reference to petroleum, the use of which has revolutionized the industries of the entire world, is a striking example of the neglect of the Europeans of the Middle Ages of products and processes used extensively by the ancient Mediterranean peoples and then entirely forgotten until very modern times. Forms of both bitumen and petroleum had been used by the Egyptians, the inhabitants of Mesopotamia, the Persians, and the Romans. Their employment ranged from mummy preservation to burning for both heat and light, and much use was made of them for waterproofing and binding brickwork and on roads. Our deep-drilling methods were, of course, unknown except by the Chinese, who drilled as early as 200 B.C. and went to a depth of 3,500 feet with crude bronze drills and bamboo casings. Many of the classical writers mention both bitumen and petroleum and describe their properties fairly accurately.

Crude petroleum was an article of commerce in the Roman Imperial Era. In 624 the Emperor Heraclius invaded the Baku region and destroyed many temples where the Persians prayed before burning wells of natural gas. Agricola, in his famous *De Re Metallica*, so wonderfully translated by Herbert Hoover and his wife, speaks of the collection of "liquid bitumen" and gives a woodcut of the process. The ancient Babylonians used torches soaked in crude oil, and the Romans not only burned it in lamps but employed it as fuel in their central heating plants and in their enormous baths. Gradually, however, after the decay of the Empire and the destruction of great homes and public buildings, the use of petroleum as a fuel among the peoples of the Mediterranean

[13] The Zelada ms. gives *"mile cameli"* (a thousand camels).

area was discontinued and was not revived until the eighteenth century, in the district around Baku described by Marco Polo.

A limited use of petroleum did survive through medieval times in addition to its use in warfare. We are solemnly assured by Aethicus Istricus, writing in the eighth century, that if armor is dipped in a mixture of petroleum and the blood of a child, it will become impenetrable by any human weapon. "Mummy," a sovereign medieval medicine for many ailments, was obtained from the scrapings of the bitumen-saturated clothes and visceral cavity-fillings of mummies of the Ptolemaic era in Egypt.

Marco Polo must have been aware of the use of petroleum in battle—and he may have seen it in use. The famous "Greek fire" was employed in warfare for hundreds of years after its invention, or development, probably by a Greek architect, Kallinikos, who lived in Constantinople about A.D. 650. It is supposed to have been a mixture of petroleum and quicklime which ignited spontaneously by the simple addition of water, being projected against the enemy from pumps or siphon-like structures at the prows of war galleys.[14] It was also squirted through hand syringes. Its use spread rapidly as far as China in the eighth century—another evidence of the intercourse between East and West in the Middle Ages. A variant method of using the compound was to load it into pottery hand-grenades, to be flung upon the enemy's decks or into the midst of his advancing host. The Arab armies trained special *naffatyn* or "naphtha throwers," who, wearing fireproof clothes, threw jars of burning naphtha from catapults. Finally, because of the great suffering and useless loss of life entailed by Greek fire, the Second Lateran Council decreed in 1139 that it should no longer be employed in European warfare. This ruling was obeyed for several centuries, and after 1400 Greek fire is seldom mentioned in accounts of warfare—until *napalm* came into use by the armies of modern states.

The next city mentioned by the Venetian is Mosul, where "all the most beautiful clothes of gold and silk which are called 'mosu-

[14] Forbes, *Bitumen and Petroleum in Antiquity*, chap. vii, and Gibbon, chaps. lii and liii.

lin' are made." Mosul is situated on the western bank of the river Tigris, opposite the site of ancient Nineveh, and was so famed for the fine stuffs woven on its looms that we still use the word "muslin" to designate certain finely woven textiles.

In describing Mosul, Marco speaks of the Nestorian Christian church, which took its name from Nestorius, Patriarch of Constantinople, who had been deposed in 431 as a heretic by the Council of Ephesus. His heresy—and that of his sect—consisted in his belief that in Jesus there were two persons, one the divine, the other the man, the one dwelling in the other. After the deposition of their patriarch many of his followers wandered out over Asia, teaching, converting, and founding churches as they went. In A.D. 735 a group of them under one A-lo-pen reached Ch'ang An, the capital of the T'ang Dynasty. There they petitioned the broad-minded, tolerant Emperor T'ai Tsung for permission to erect a church in the city. It was granted, and for many decades they taught and made converts. Later they set up a tablet inscribed in both Chinese and Syriac—the language which they had brought with them—reciting part of the Old and New Testament versions of world history and Christian origins and describing the coming of A-lo-pen and his band to China.

During the religious persecutions of the later T'ang era (ended in 907), the community was evidently dispersed and its church destroyed. The so-called "Nestorian Tablet" was buried, perhaps by the priests, who hoped for better times, when they could restore the shrine of their faith. It was not heard of again until 1625, when it was unearthed during some excavation work on the foundations for a new viceregal yamên. News of the find, with rubbings of the inscription, was then brought to the Jesuits at Peking. Further investigations were made, and the inscription was translated. Although controversies raged for many years over the authenticity of the relic, scholars are now generally agreed that the stone is genuine and that it constitutes one of the unique religious monuments of the world. It still stands very near the place where it was brought to light over three hundred years ago.

It is not at all certain that the Polos visited Baghdad, as Marco's description of the city is quite vague. Baghdad had been destroyed by Hulaku Khan in 1268, and, as it was rapidly losing its commercial importance, it was perhaps no longer on the main caravan route. Be this as it may—and scholars are by no means in full agreement—Marco tells us the wondrous tale of a miracle which occurred "between Baghdad and Mosul."

It appears that about the year 1275 there was a very cruel Caliph ruling in Baghdad. He hated the Christians and wished to do them great evil. His wise men informed him that in the Christian Gospels was a passage which stated that if a man had as much faith as a mustard seed, he could command a mountain to move and it would move. The Saracens perceived in this statement the opportunity they had been seeking. The Caliph summoned the Christians and demanded that such a miracle be performed by someone among them under pain of extermination, "by an evil death," of all the worshipers of Jesus. He offered them but one alternative if the miracle were not performed—conversion to Mohammedanism —and granted them a respite of ten days in which to prepare. The Christians were terrified, and prayed strenuously that they might be delivered from such a cruel fate. They fasted and prayed, "both men and women, for eight days and eight nights." And at the end of that time an angel from Heaven appeared in a vision to one of the bishops, "a man of very holy life," and commanded him to seek out a certain one-eyed cobbler. After describing the cobbler and his dwelling place, the angel vanished; however, he reappeared in the same vision several times before the good Bishop accepted his message and bestirred himself.

The legend goes on to tell why this cobbler had but one eye. He was very honorable, and lived a chaste and pure life, fasted much, committed no sin, and had perfect faith. He attended services daily, prayed often, and gave of his earnings and food to the needy. Often while in church he had heard the admonition that if a man's hand sinned, he should cut it off and cast it from him, and if a man's eye sinned, it should be plucked out or blinded, "because," as one manuscript has it, "it is better to enter Paradise with one eye than hell with two."

It happened one day, continues the tale, that a comely and beautiful young woman entered the cobbler's shop to purchase a pair of shoes. The cobbler asked to see her foot in order to measure it and fit her properly. The young woman thereupon unhesitatingly lifted her robe, and in removing her shoe revealed her foot and part of her leg. One could not ask to behold anything more beautiful, and the simple cobbler, being after all a man, was seized with carnal desire at the sight and was sorely tempted to fall from grace and sin. But after a moment's weakness he recovered his self-control and purity of mind and let the woman go without even trying to sell her a pair of shoes. And then, alas, the poor man recalled the Gospel teaching as his naïve nature interpreted it. His conscience smote him sorely, for he felt that he had sinned with his eye. Thereupon he seized an awl from his work-bench, sharpened it to a fine point, and plunged it into his right eye, totally destroying its sight. Thus did the good man purge himself of his sin and regain his pristine virtue.

The Bishop and his flock summoned the holy cobbler and told him of the recurring vision. After many protestations of his unworthiness, the cobbler finally consented to pray for the miracle to take place. On the tenth day the whole congregation of the faithful went forth to the mountain, and the cobbler fell on his knees and prayed and cried aloud to the mountain to move. And, behold, the mountain moved forthwith of itself with a great roar and rumble and trembling of the earth, and betook itself bodily to the spot designated by the Caliph, a full mile from its original position, whereupon the Caliph was amazed, and many of his followers became Christians. In an epilogue Marco tells us that the Caliph himself was baptized, but in secret, lest the Saracens revolt. Moreover, when he died a gold cross was found hanging about his neck, and he was buried apart from his ancestors, who were heathens.

The travelers' next important stop was at Tabriz, a very large trade center, where men gathered from all parts of the earth and where the Genoese had a flourishing colony of merchants. The Spaniard, Clavijo, who visited Tabriz not long after the Polos, has left an interesting description of it. It was a city without walls, lying in a valley among mountains, some of which were snow-covered.

> The city has many beautiful streets and lanes and great market places whose entrances resemble shops. And inside the markets are houses and stores laden with goods, as well as passages and gates which lead from one street to the other, and there are sold there woven stuffs of silk and cotton, sandalwood, taffetas, silk, and pearls. In one of the arcades of the market place are merchants who sell perfumes and cosmetics for the women, who come themselves to buy these products. The women are wrapped in white veils and wear horsehair nets before their eyes. In the streets and squares of this city there are many wells and fountains. In the spring lumps of ice are put in these, and goblets of copper or pewter are placed on the well curbs, so that all who pass may quench their thirst.

Tabriz at the time of the Polos' visit was the world's greatest pearl market, and thither were brought the harvests of pearls obtained from the oyster beds of the Persian Gulf. There the gems were matched, bored, and strung, and thence they were distributed throughout the markets of the East and West. There the Venetians probably watched and were fascinated by the unusual method employed in selling pearls. After appraising them with the eyes of experts, the buyer and seller would squat opposite each other, throw a cloth over their hands and then argue quality and price by pressure of the hidden fingers and wrists, thus keeping bystanders in ignorance of the terms of the transaction.[15]

The Polos continued on their way, buying, selling, gathering profits, and making their stock of coin and merchandise which

[15] This method of bargaining is common in the Orient today. At the auctions of jade in Canton, from which most of the jade mined in Yunnan and Burma is distributed through China for carving and sale, something of the same procedure is followed. The auction is conducted in silence. After the piece of jade to be auctioned has been examined, each bidder steps up to the auctioner, thrusts his hand into the latter's wide sleeve, and by pressure of different finger combinations on his arm makes known his bid. After the bids have all been made and entered on paper, the auctioneer looks over the list and without further ado announces the successful bidder. The practice of silent, hidden bidding within the sleeve still obtains throughout China in many mercantile transactions where prices are not fixed.

they had brought with them from far-away Venice turn over and over to their advantage. And all along the road Marco, as numberless statements and comments in his book indicate, was learning the ways of men, of travel and of trafficking, at the same time acquiring enough of the Mongol tongue to express himself adequately. This knowledge, together with the words and phrases of Arabic, Persian, and local dialects, was to stand him in good stead in the service of the Khakhan. He was rapidly becoming a man of the world, no longer an immature lad, and his remarks show that women were no longer objects of indifference to his keen, all-appraising young eyes. His book also proves that hunting was a real joy to him, and he surely had his fill of the sport in a land swarming with game, to be pursued with bow and arrow and falcon when he was not assisting his father and uncle, who appear to have been ever busy with their trafficking.

Slowly the caravan wended its way along the well-worn, age-old road, leaving Venice and the sea ever farther behind them.

The next town visited was Saba,[16] in Persia. Marco speaks of seeing the tombs of the three Magi, the "wise men," Gaspar, Melchior, and Balthasar, of Matthew II, who had set out from there to pay homage to the infant Jesus in the manger in Bethlehem. He further states that he asked many questions about them, "but never one could he find who knew aught of the matter, except that these were three kings who were buried there in days of old." He assures us that the three bodies, in monuments side by side, were "still entire, with the hair and beard remaining."[17] According to Marco's story, "they carried with them three manner of offerings, gold, frankincense, and myrrh, in order to ascertain whether that prophet were God or an earthly king or a physician. For, said they, if he take the gold, then he is an earthly king; if he take the incense, he is God; if he take the myrrh, he is a physician.

So it came to pass when they had come to the place where the child was born, the youngest of the three kings went in first and

16 The present Savah.

17 An ancient tradition has it that Melchior was a very old man and Balthasar a vigorous bearded man, while Gaspar was young and beardless.

found the child apparently just of his own age; so he went forth again marveling greatly. The middle one entered next, and like the first found the child seemingly of his own age; so he also went forth again and marveled greatly. Lastly the eldest went in, and as it had befallen the other two, so it befell him. And he went forth very pensive. And when the three had rejoined one another, each told what he had seen and then they all marveled the more. They agreed to go in all three together, and on doing so they beheld the Child with the appearance of its actual age, some thirteen days. Then they adored and presented their gold and incense and myrrh. And the Child took all the three offerings, and then gave them a small closed box, whereupon the kings departed to return into their own land."

The story continues. "And when they had ridden many days, they would see what the Child had given them. So they opened the little box, and inside it they found a stone. On seeing this, they began to wonder what this might be that the Child had given them, and what was the import thereof. Now the signification was this: . . . that this faith which had begun when the Child had accepted all three [offerings] they had said within themselves that he was the True God, and the True King and the True Physician. And what the gift of the stone implied was that this faith . . . should abide firm as a rock. . . . Howbeit, they had no understanding at all of this signification of the gift of the stone, so they cast it into a well. Then straightway a fire from Heaven descended into that well wherein the stone had been cast."

And then, Marco continues, the Magi took of the fire and carried it to their country and placed it in their church and worshiped it. This, the traveler was informed, was the origin of the fire-temples of the Parsis.

We are told also by him of the industries of Persia, the fruits, the grains, the birds and beasts, and the cunning embroidery done by the women of the country. He also saw much turquoise ("the Turkish stone") brought from the mines in the Kerman region. It was a stone held in high esteem by the ancient Persians, and is still mined. The ignorant folk held it to be a stone of ill omen, believing that it came from the bones of people who had died because of unrequited love, and feared that wearing it would bring a like unhappy fate to them. Steel is also mentioned, the Venetian believing steel to be a different metal from iron, obtained from a different ore.[18]

From Kerman the travelers rode for seven days to the summit of a mountain pass, which required two days to traverse, where "the cold in winter is so great that you can scarcely abide it, even with a great quantity of clothing." Thereafter they crossed a vast hot rich plain where dates, pistachios, and other fruits were plentiful, and where Marco saw and described humped cattle and sheep whose "tails are so large and fat that one tail may weigh thirty pounds."

Now the three men and their caravan were entering an area fraught with great danger, for this part of Persia was infested by ferocious bandits called Karaunas,[19] who, according to Marco, when they start out on their forays, "have certain devilish enchantments whereby they do bring darkness over the face of day, insomuch that you can scarcely discern your comrade riding beside you."

The Polos' caravan was attacked by these banditti in one of the "dry fogs" prevalent in the region. The members of the expedition fled in every direction. Marco, his father and uncle, and seven of his men escaped to a village nearby. The rest were caught and put to death or sold into slavery. "So," says Marco in the simple, reserved, terse, and impersonal style with which he refers to so many of his most exciting adventures, "I have told you just as it happened. Now we shall go on to tell you of other things." Thus the three men nearly lost their lives and the world one of its most fascinating books.

Reorganizing their caravan, the indomitable Venetians pushed on toward their goal, the city of Hormuz, on the Persian Gulf, where, since that city was the terminus of the maritime trade between the Far East and Persia, they planned to embark for China.

[18] This was a common notion in the Middle Ages.
[19] The origin of the name is obscure.

The journey required seven days, of which the first part was a steep descent from the Iranian plateau through a mountain pass infested (as it is still) by bandits. The remainder of the route was over a beautiful, well-watered plain, where dates, pomegranates, oranges, and other fruits were grown, and where bird life was abundant. After two days of riding over this plain, the Venetians arrived at the port of Hormuz.

Hormuz, on the Persian Gulf, was situated on the mainland at the time of the Polos' visit. It was later destroyed by a raiding tribe and "the inhabitants moved their city to an island five miles distant from the mainland," as described by Odoric de Pordenone, who was in the city in 1321. It was an ancient city, where Nearchos, the leader of Alexander the Great's forces, had beached his fleet to allow his sailors to rest on the return from the great Indian expedition of 327–325 B.C. Long after Marco visited Hormuz it was captured (in 1507) by the Portuguese under Affonso de Albuquerque, the founder of Portugal's Eastern empire. With the discovery of new sea routes to India it rapidly lost its importance and became a tiny, obscure town.

The Polos found Hormuz, where they had planned to take ship for China, not at all to their liking. The heat was excessive and the land unhealthy. If a foreign merchant happened to die in the country, the king seized all his possessions for himself. The wine made from dates and spices was good to drink, but it acted as a violent purgative upon those who, like the Polos, were not used to it. "The people do not eat bread or meat when they are well, as it will make them ill. If they are ill, then only do they partake of meat and bread. Their customary diet consists of dates, dried tunny fish, garlic, and onions." Ibn Battúta, who visited the place about the year 1325, tells us that the people of the city had a proverb to the effect that "fish and dates make a meal fit for an emperor." But Marco and his companions found the diet monotonous and unwholesome.

He describes the people as black worshipers of Mahomet. He found the hot winds in summer intolerable, and tells of the way in which the inhabitants, when such a wind swept down upon them, stood neck deep in water until the wind passed by. Marco further recounts that during his stay in the city a force of 6,500 men sent by the King of Kerman arrived to enforce the collection of tribute. They were caught by the dread simoon or hot wind while encamped in the wilderness not far from the city, and every man of them was suffocated. He also recites the curious fact, corroborated by later travelers, that the bodies of people who die thus decompose so rapidly that it is almost impossible to handle them for burial.[20]

The light-hearted Italian was much disturbed by the elaborate mourning of the widows of Hormuz for their husbands, and notes that they met with their kinfolk every day for four years to indulge in loud wails and lamentations. In addition, they hired professional women mourners to help them.

Probably Marco Polo would not have expatiated as he did on the unpleasantness of Hormuz had it not been that all his plans and those of his father and uncle were upset by what they found in the city. Their abrupt return inland after arriving at the seaport and the consequent loss of months of time plainly indicate that something happened to cause them to renounce the journey to China by sea. The probable reason is to be found in the contemptuous description given by Marco of the ships in which trade was carried on in the Indian Ocean.

"Their ships are very bad and dangerous for navigation, exposing the merchants . . . to great hazards." He describes in some detail the way in which they were built. "No iron nails are used, as the wood is too hard and splits and breaks. The planks are bored with augers of iron at the ends and fastened together with wooden pegs. They are then sewn together with a kind of yarn made from the fibers of coconut husks, thick as horsehair. This fiber is soaked in water until the softer parts rot away, and the threads are then

[20] This strange fact is also stated by Sir John Chardin in *Travels in Persia* (1686). Additional information on Hormuz at the time of the Polos is given by Iba Battuta. His life and travels are fully treated in *The Travels of Ibn Battuta*, ed. by Sir Hamilton Gibbs, 4 vols., Hakluyt Soc., Sec. Ser. CXVII, etc. The Arab traveled far more widely than did Marco Polo and wrote on the countries visited more extensively and in detail. Milton, *Paradise Lost* (1667), opens Bk. II with a reference to Hormuz.

94

spun. These threads are not affected by seawater, but cannot weather a storm." These ships had one mast, one sail, and one steering oar. They had no decks, but the cargo was loaded on the ship and covered with hides. They used no iron anchors, so that in bad weather they were often driven up on the shore and lost. "And because of this it is a very dangerous venture to set sail in these ships, and I tell you that many of them are lost, for great storms often occur in the Sea of India." These stitched vessels of Hormuz have been described by many authors of the ancient and medieval world.[21]

Even though going to China by sea was perhaps less dangerous and more certain than the overland journey,[22] the Venetians evidently (though this is problematical, and no reason is given) came to the conclusion that the risks of a long voyage on such a frail craft, particularly as a number of horses were often carried on top of the hide-covered cargo, were too great, so they turned back into the country, heading northeast to the Pamirs.[23] The road led through a desert country with bitter green waters for over a week. Here there was no potable water and supplies for three full days had to be carried. No living thing was to be seen in this inhospitable stretch of country, which led to Cabinan, "the hill of the wild pistachio," then on across the desert waste to Tunocain,[24]

[21] See "The Travels of Friar Odoric" in Yule, *Cathay and the Way Thither*, 2d ed., Vol. II, 113ff. *Mirabilia Descripta* of Friar Jordanus (*ca.* 1330), ed. by Yule, London, 1863: "But the vessels of these Indies be of a marvellous kind. For though they be very great, they be not put together with iron, but stitched with a needle, and a thread made of a kind of grass. Nor are the vessels ever decked over, but open, and they take in water to such an extent that the men always, or almost always, must stand in a pool to bale out the water." John of Montecorvino (*ca.* 1291), Yule, *op. cit.*, III, 66: "Their ships in these parts are mighty frail and uncouth, with no iron in them, and no caulking. They are sewn like clothes with twine. And so if the twine breaks anywhere there is a breach indeed! Once every year therefore there is a mending of this, more or less, if they propose to go to sea." See also Hourani: *Arab Shipping*, with its full bibliography.

[22] Hambis suggests that the possession of Chinese southern ports by the Sungs would have caused difficulties for the Polos. *Description du Monde*, vii.

[23] Lofty mountainous country in central Asia whence the Hindu Kush, Himalaya, and T'ien Mountains radiate. Often called "the roof of the world," some of the peaks reach an altitude of over 24,000 feet.

[24] Tunocain was the name of two neighboring cities in the Kuhistan (hill country of Persia) area.

"where the towns and villages have great abundance of everything good, for the climate is extremely temperate. The natives all worship Mahomet, and are a very fine-looking people, especially the women, who are surprisingly beautiful." The spring of life must have begun to stir in the young Marco, for this is the first of his many observations about women. The impression made upon him by the maidens of Tunocain must have been profound, for when he wrote his reminiscences (if they may be so considered in part) some twenty-five years later, after doubtless meeting many women and mayhap having had more than one romance in his wandering life, he still could say that the Moslem women of Tunocain were beautiful beyond measure, or, as the good Ramusio's version has it, "in my opinion the most beautiful in the world."

At this point in his narrative Marco pauses to tell in some detail the strange tale of Ala- 'u-'d-Din Muhammad, "The Old Man of the Mountain," and his murderous band, the Assassins, which has given the English language its word "assassin." Since the Polos do not appear to have come into personal contact with the band, the story must have been told to him by inhabitants of the region—or more likely by his father and uncle.[25]

The Venetian speaks of the Assassins as though they no longer existed in his day. He was mistaken. After their stronghold of Alamut (the Eagle's Nest) had been destroyed in 1256 by Hulaku, the Tatar, they fled into the neighboring mountains and have maintained their existence, sometimes precariously, ever since, though their murders are a thing of the past. In fact the titular leader of one branch of the sect today is the Agha Khan.

The three travelers continued for many days on their journey

[25] Almagià 12, 38n. Assassins (Arabic, lit. "those who eat hashish") is the name given to the Ismaili sect of Moslems who indulged in political murders, which they looked upon as meritorious religious acts. Before going to fulfill a mission of assassination they were given hashish (Indian hemp—*cannabis indica*) to eat. Their headquarters was at Alamut, which was destroyed by Hulaku Khan in 1256–57, and their leader, Ruknu-'d-Din, the son of Ala-'d-Din Mohammed, was killed. See Olschki, *Marco Polo's Asia*, chap. ix; Marshall G. S. Hodgson: *The Order of the Assassins*; J. de Hammer, *Histoire des Assassins*, Paris, 1833, *Encyclopedia of Islam*, new ed., I, art. "Alamut."

across arid deserts and fertile lands to the city of Sapurgan (Shiburgan)[26] where Marco found plenty of game "both of birds and beasts."

From Sapurgan the caravan continued on to Balkh, in what is now northern Afghanistan. One of the oldest cities in Asia, it was once the capital of Bactria. Although it surrendered without resistance to Genghis Khan, its citizenry were ordered outside the city under pretense of counting them, its young people sold into slavery, the older members of the population done to death with unspeakable cruelty, and the city burned to the ground. The Polos found the place in blackened ruins, though such of its inhabitants as had survived the Tatar scourge had begun to creep back and settle in their old abodes.[27]

Balkh was the city where, according to the legend, Alexander the Great took Roxana, daughter of the Persian King Darius, to wife. Amid the charred ruins and calcined marble palace walls could still be traced the mocking words of an old Moslem inscription: "This city was erected to the glory of God. By the will of the sultan it was converted into a veritable paradise." A gloomy silence reigned in the once great city which was the meeting place of India, Tibet, China, and the Near East. Grass was growing in the deserted, debris-strewn streets, and wild goats and other animals browsed in the abandoned and desolate fields and orchards all about.

From Balkh the travelers continued for many days through a flourishing region teeming with game and rich in fruits, nuts, wine, and wheat. The road led northeast for twelve days, partly through mountainous country, whose inhabitants, Marco states, had all fled to hide from raiding banditti. There was an abundance of game, but because of the lack of habitants, provisions for the

26 This part of the route of the Polos is not clear and has been the subject of much inconclusive controversy.

27 Once known to the Arabs as "Mother of cities," Balkh never recovered any importance after the Tatar devastation. Ibn Battuta, who visited Balkh about sixty years after the Polos had passed through, states (*Ibn Battuta*, De Fremery and Sanguinetti, ed. IV, 58f.) that "it is in ruins and uninhabited. . . . Vestiges of its mosques and colleges still remain, as well as paintings on its houses, traced in blue."

twelve days had to be carried by the caravan. At the end of the twelve days the Polos arrived at the wheat market of Taican.[28]

From Taican the Venetians continued for several days through a fertile country with orchards of almonds and pistachios, where "the people are worshippers of Mahomet, and are an evil and a murderous generation, whose great delight is in the wineshop, for they are great topers; in truth they are constantly getting drunk." He also observed that there were a great number of porcupines in the region.[29]

Four more days of riding brought them into the Mohammedan province of Badakhshan[30] near the River Oxus, north of the Hindu Kush Mountains.

There the Polos learned of (and very likely saw) the mines of spinel called "balas rubies" from the name of the province, the sapphire deposits, and the veins of lapis lazuli, for all of which the district of Badakhshan has been famous through the centuries.[31] The Ramusio edition of Marco Polo and the Zelada Latin manuscript have preserved a passage which does not appear elsewhere, but which is admitted as authentic by later editors. It is one of the few passages in the entire book touching on Marco's personal adventures. In describing the mountains of Badakhshan, he mentions that the cities of the country are built in high places for protection. He then continues: "They [the mountains] are so high that a man must travel from morning even until evening to reach their summits. On the tops are broad plains and a great abundance of grass and trees, and abundant springs of the purest water which flow down through rocks and ravines. In these streams are found

[28] Present Talikan, in the vicinity of which are important salt mines. Polo states, "I assure you that there is so much of it that the whole world would have enough until the day of doom." See also Olschki, *op. cit.*, 173.

[29] He added the erroneous folk belief that when hunted with dogs the porcupines shoot their quills at them.

[30] The different mss. spell the name of the province in at least thirty different ways, mostly with a pronunciation approximating Badashan or Balashan.

[31] Darker red spinels (double oxide of magnesium and aluminum) are known as ruby spinels, the lighter, rose-red stones as balas rubies. Michael Weinstein (*The World of Jewel Stones*, p. 153) states that the mines mentioned by Polo had been worked for over five thousand years before his visit.

trout and many other delicate fish, and the air is so pure on these heights, and living there is so health-giving, that if the people who dwell in the city, on the plain, and in the valleys are seized with a fever of any sort, or by chance are afflicted with any other sort of sickness, they immediately ascend the mountain and remain there two or three days and find themselves well again, because of the excellence of the air, and Marco says that he proved this, because while in these regions he was sick nearly a year, and that after he was advised to ascend the mountain (and did so) he recovered his health at once."

This brief statement—all in one long sentence in Ramusio's Italian text—throws a tiny ray of light on the personal experiences of Marco Polo and indicates but one of the many hardships that he and his father and uncle must have suffered on that long thirteenth-century journey across Asia. It also accounts for a whole year of the three years consumed in going from Venice to Peking. The caravan was delayed either because of the sickness of the young man or because the Polos had decided to remain in the healthful climate of Badakhshan to assure his complete recovery.

Marco's illness, however, did not cause him to avert his eyes long from the ladies of Badakhshan. He was particularly taken with a certain peculiarity of their dress, one which was the fashion from ancient times, if we may accept the testimony of coins. The men of Badakhshan were enamored of women with amply developed buttocks. This predilection, which from time to time has brought the bustle into style in the West, caused the women of the region to make their customary breeches or trousers so voluminous that they often swathed themselves in from 250 to 400 feet of linen, cotton, or silk, thickly pleated and scented with musk, "and they do this to show that they have large hips to become beautiful, because in that region their men delight in fat women, and she who appears more stout below the waist seems to them more beautiful and more glorious among other women."

At this point Marco Polo digresses with a few paragraphs on Kashmir, which was not on the Venetians' route. He ends his very sketchy remarks on the country with the statement, as translated by Frampton:[32] "I Minde not now to passe further in this province, for in passing of it I should enter into the Indeas, whereof, for this time I wil not declare any thing, but at the returne, I wil declare of it largely, as wel of the commodities there, as also of their manner, and usages."

From Badakhshan the travelers continued on their journey northeast, reaching the summit of the Pamirs, which, Marco was assured by his guides, was the highest place in the world, and he added that "the region is so lofty and cold that you do not even see any birds flying."[33] His powers of observation, ever keen, and his memory of the ascent to "the roof of the world," as the Pamirs plateau is often called, so vivid, that he recalled, while preparing his narrative in far-off Genoa nearly thirty years later, that at these great heights "fire does not burn so brightly, nor give out so much heat as usual, nor does it cook food so effectually." Here also Marco saw and first described the great wild sheep which have been named *Ovis poli* in his honor. He describes them as having great horns, from four to six palms in length, from which the shepherds made bowls and other vessels. The sheep were so plentiful in spite of the depredations of wolves that the shepherds built sheepfolds and huts for themselves from the great horns, and bones were heaped in high mounds along the roads to guide travelers when snow was on the ground and hid the path from view.

Descending from the Pamirs through the Gez defile, the Polos reached the broad plains of eastern Turkestan, or, as it is now called, Sinkiang. The region is partly desert, partly rich oasis fertilized by the many rivers flowing from the south and west. Here they saw beautiful gardens and vineyards and fine estates.

The next city which the Venetians reached was Kashgar, where they welcomed the milder climate after the rigors of the Pamirs and which they found productive "of all sorts of necessaries to

[32] A lengthy note on John Frampton, whose birth and death dates are unknown but who translated *The most noble and famous travels of Marco Paulus* ... from the Spanish translation (1503) of Rodrigo Fernandez de Santaella y Cordoba in 1579, is in N. M. Penzer, *The Most Noble and Famous Travels of Marco Polo*, London, 1929, reissued in 1937.
[33] The tales of numerous early Chinese pilgrims and of modern explorers who have crossed this same country confirm this statement.

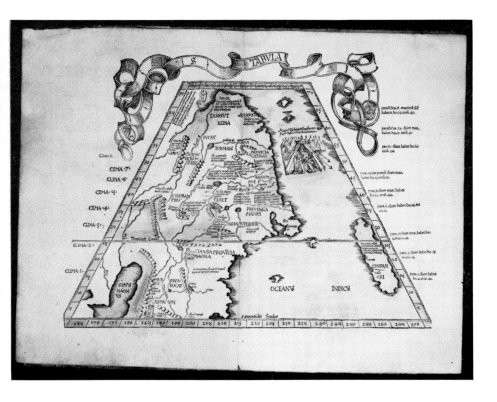

Map of China from *Ptolemy's Atlas* (1522 edition). (From the author's collection)

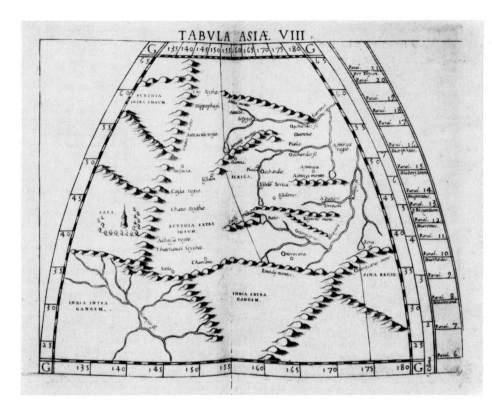

Map of Asia from Girolamo Ruscelli's *Espositioni ed Introduttioni Universali . . . sopra tutta la Geographia di Tolomeo* (Venice, 1573). (From the author's collection)

Map of China by Ludovico Giorgio, 1584. (From the author's collection)

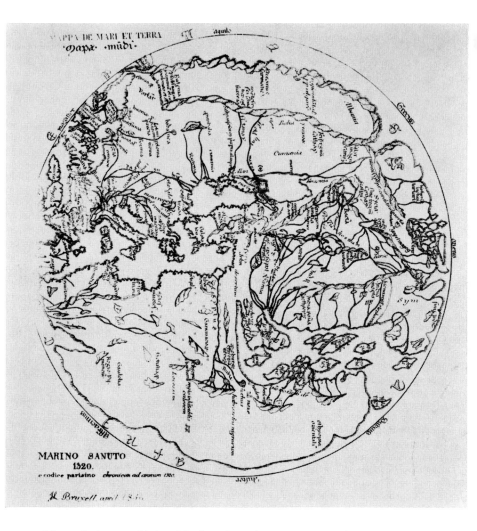

Map of the world by Marino Sanudo (*ca.* 1320), from Lelewel's
Geographie du Moyen Age. (From the author's collection)

Map of the world by Fra Mauro (middle of the fifteenth century), in the Marcian Library, Venice. (From the author's collection)

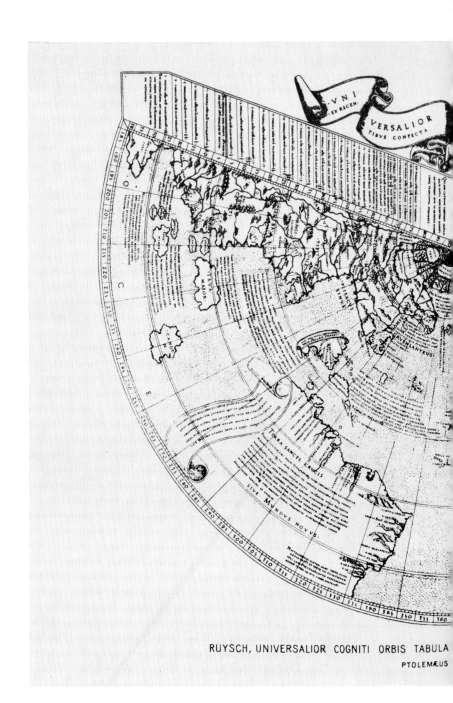

Map of the world by Johann Ruysch, from the *Nova Universalis Orb*
Cogniti Tabula (Rome, 1522). Reprinted from A. E. Nordenskiöl

EX RECENTIBUS CONFECTA OBSERVATIONIBUS

ROMÆ 1508

acsimile Atlas to the Early History of Cartography (Stockholm,
89). (Courtesy of the Library of the University of California)

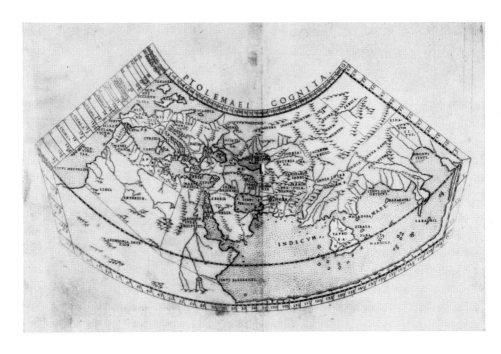

Map of the world, from *La Geografia di Claudio Tolomeo*, ed. by
Giacomo Contarini (Venice, 1574). (From the author's collection)

life . . . and cotton grows there in plenty and flax and hemp."
Marco observed also in the Kashgar region the presence of "many
Nestorian Christians, who have churches of their own."[34]

Perhaps in the belief that at this point his readers might enjoy
a short respite after all the foregoing geographical description, the
Venetian abruptly ends the material on Kashgar with the sentence:
"Now let us leave you this country and we will talk to you
of Samarkand."

Although it is generally conceded that Nicolo Polo and his
brother Maffeo had visited Samarkand on their previous journey,
there is no evidence whatsoever that young Marco visited the city.
Since he was not in a position to describe it with any degree of
accuracy, yet wished some mention of it in his book, he filled the
lacuna with another of his tales of Christian miracles. According to
the legend recounted by the Venetian, Chagatai,[35] lord of the
country, was converted to Christianity and baptized by mis-
sionaries in Samarkand. In their rejoicing over the conversion the
Christians of the city built "a very great and noble round church
. . . to the honor of Master Saint John Baptist." In its construction
they used as the base of one of the marble columns "a very beautiful and great square marble stone which belonged to the Saracens,"
and the church was so made that this column supported the whole
of the roof. This proceeding greatly angered the infidels who,
since they were obliged through fear to remain silent, hated their
Christian neighbors the more.

At his destined hour Chagatai was called to his fathers and his
minor son was placed upon the throne under the regency of
Chagatai's nephew, a Saracen. Thereupon his co-religionists, who
had patiently bided their time, raised a great clamor and demanded
the immediate return of their stone. They refused to compromise
for money, for they planned to tear out the stone and so cause the
entire church to collapse in ruins, that the hated Christians might
suffer grievously thereby. An order was issued by the regent that

[34] See Olschki, *op. cit.*, chap. vii.

[35] The second (1185–1242) of the sons of Genghis Khan, therefore the uncle,
not the brother, of Kublai, as stated by Marco; nor was he ever a Christian. See
Pelliot, *Notes on Marco Polo*, II, 250 ff.

within two days' time the stone was to be surrendered to the Saracens. Distraught, the good Christians "prayed devoutly and with many tears to Blessed John Baptist" to help them in this their great trouble. Now there came of it such a miracle "as I shall tell you, for when the Saracens came to the church on the appointed day to remove the stone, they found the column which rested on the stone lifted itself from its base—and was raised up quite three palms" and that it carried its weighty load suspended in the air with no apparent support below.[36]

From Kashgar the travelers proceeded through Yarkand, where the keen-eyed, observant Marco noted that a large proportion of the population was afflicted with goiter and hazarded the cause— the drinking water used by the inhabitants—an observation which has been corroborated by many later travelers.[37]

The next place noted on the route by Marco was the ancient city of Khotan, where there was a considerable trade in jade, found as boulders in the river beds. From Khotan the jade was taken by caravan across the deserts to Peking, Canton, and Soochow, there to be patiently "carved" into objects both sacred and profane. The Chinese have never been able to satisfy their demand for jade, to them the most precious substance in the world, the very quintessence in tangible form of the Yang principle in the universe.

Leaving Khotan, the Polos traveled on through miles of monotonous desert dunes, camping at the rare oases and wells. Marco was

[36] It is curious to note that a Chinese description of Sinkiang written in the fourteenth century states that "there is a temple [in Samarkand] supported by four very large wooden pillars, each forty feet in height. One of these pillars is in a hanging position, and [its base] is more than a foot from the floor." See *Chinese Recorder*, VI, p. 108. The story recalls the Corn Exchange which was built by Sir Christopher Wren at Windsor. The architect designed the building without interior columns supporting the roof, but the good people of the town insisted that columns be used. Sir Christopher acceded to their request; however, not only do the columns which run the length of the chamber bear no load, but there is a space of a couple of inches between the tops of the columns and the roof whose weight they are supposed to support. Mayhap some future credulous age will tell of some miracle which caused the roof of the Windsor Corn Exchange to lift and maintain itself with no visible columnar support.

[37] Both Sir Percy Sykes and Sven Hedin make mention of the prevalence of goiter in the Yarkand region, the latter ascribing it to the quality of the drinking water.

struck by the morals and manners of the desert folk, which have changed no whit since his day. We are informed that if a husband who finds it necessary to travel away from his home has not returned by the end of twenty days, his wife at once takes another "husband" until his return, and the man who is away is likewise permitted to take unto himself a temporary "wife."[38]

The region through which the caravan was now passing consisted of wide expanses of desert, sparsely sprinkled with oases inhabited by Moslem Tatar tribes, and it became necessary to carry sufficient food and water to last from one oasis to another. At Lop (the modern Charklik) travelers remained a week to refresh and prepare themselves for the crossing of the Gobi.[39] It was customary, Marco informs us, if the food was exhausted before the fertile land at the far side of the desert was reached, either to kill and eat the draft animals or to turn them loose to shift for themselves. He was informed, moreover, that it was unwise to travel in a company of more than fifty persons, as sufficient water to supply a larger number was not procurable anywhere en route, and that neither birds nor animals were to be found there because of the lack of food and water.

At this point we learn from the Venetian's narrative that in the

[38] One wonders why Polo, after all that he must have observed both in Venice and everywhere among the merchants en route, found this custom strange enough for even a brief comment. It may be of interest to notice a most valuable Florentine guidebook to Eastern countries written in the first half of the fourteenth century (and of which only one manuscript is extant) by Francesco Balducci Pegolotti, a much-traveled employee of the banking house of the Bardi, of which the father of Dante's Beatrice had been a member. Pegolotti distinctly indicates (Evans ed., p. 22) that he had never traversed the route to Cathay, but that he had his information "*secondo che si conta per li mercatanti che l'anno usato,*" that statement indicating that a number of merchants had made the journey. In chap. ii of this book the merchant who planned to travel to Cathay "to go there and to return with merchandise" was advised "to allow his beard to grow long, and not to skimp money in having a dragoman, and if the merchant wishes to take a woman with him from Tana, he may do so, and if he does not wish to do so it is not obligatory; but indeed if he does take one he will be cared for in a much better manner than if he does not take one. But if he does take one it would be advantageous if she as well as the servant were acquainted with the Cumanian tongue." If such was not an unusual proceeding for European travelers to the East, it is strange that the Venetian should have been surprised at this custom of an obscure Central Asian barbarian tribe.

[39] The desert is called Sha Mo (lit. "sandy plain"—desert).

Gobi dwell evil spirits, who devise illusions—mirages and the like—
to lead the unwary traveler to destruction if he lags behind or becomes separated from his companions. The spirits will surround
the luckless wight, calling upon him by name, and, speaking with
the voices of his companions, will lure him on to his death from
thirst, starvation, or exhaustion. This happens not only during the
night but even in the broad daylight. And not voices alone, but
the beating and throbbing of drums and the sounds of other musical instruments, are heard. To escape this calamity, all the caravan
animals wear bells that tinkle and announce the whereabouts
of each.[40]

After thirty days' journey the caravan reached Sha Chou
("Sandy District") on the edge of the desert. They were in what
is now Kansu Province, and here were first encountered essentially
Chinese modes of life.[41] Among these were the funeral practices—
the method of making coffins, the keeping of the coffined body in
the home (or funeral chapel), the offerings made to the spirit, the
burning of paper images and coins, and the like. These age-old
customs, unchanged since the days of the Polos, are still observed

[40] The Gobi's reputation as a place of terror and the abode of evil spirits is far
older than the tale of Marco Polo. The Chinese monk Fa Hsien, who passed
through the region in A.D. 399, records that "in this desert there are numerous evil
spirits and also hot winds. . . . Wherever one looks, as far as the eyes can reach,
the only guides in following the path are the decaying bones of men who have
died along the way." Hsüan Tsang, another Buddhist monk, while journeying
across the desert in 629, encountered "all sorts of demon shapes and strange goblins, which seemed to surround him behind and before." And in the night "the
demons and goblins raised fire-lights as many as the stars." See Giles, *Travels of
Fa Hsien*, p. 3, and Beale, *Life of Hsüan Tsang*, p. 20. Sven Hedin in *The Wandering Lake* states from personal experience that the storms in the Tarim Basin are
so loud that shouts and rifleshots cannot be heard, and the whirling sand, almost
like a thick fog, gives out a strange whistling sound. The description given by the
thirteenth-century Chinese encyclopedist Ma Tuan Lin states "you see nothing
in any direction but the sky and the sands, without the slightest trace of a road,
and travelers find nothing to guide them but the bones of men and beasts and the
droppings of camels. During the passage of this wilderness you hear sounds, sometimes of singing, sometimes of wailing, and it has often happened that travelers
going aside to see what these sounds may be, have strayed from their course and
been entirely lost, for they were voices of spirits and goblins."

[41] Sha Chou is better known as Tun Huang, the "Caves of a Thousand Budd-
has," made known by Sir Aurel Stein in his "Ruins of Desert Cathay" and by the
researches of Paul Pelliot.

and practiced in Chinese cities and towns on such days as have been designated as propitious by the *fêng shui* practitioners.[42] Here is also described the practice of breaking a hole through a wall of the deceased's house for the removal of the coffin, to avoid the bad luck that the Chinese believed would inevitably ensue if the coffin were carried out through the door. Although this custom is not universal in China, it is mentioned by several travelers and is still followed in many places.[43]

That Marco Polo passed through Kamul, the next province to which he devotes a chapter, is not certain, though perhaps his father and uncle had been there on their earlier journey. He digresses just long enough to discuss lengthily the moral laxity of its inhabitants, for he was informed that the generous hospitality of the good folk of Kamul included the free offering of the host's womenfolk. Moreover, says he, if a stranger came to a man's house to sojourn for some days, the host would leave and work elsewhere, leaving the field open to the traveler and not returning until the departure of the latter. This custom was believed to bring to the host much wealth, fine crops, and healthy children. We are told further that the Great Khan Mongka attempted to abolish this free and easy reception of the stranger, but met with such opposition that he angrily revoked his edict as follows, according to Ramusio: " 'Go, and live according to your customs, and so act that your women may be charitable gifts to wayfarers.' And with this response [to their petition] they returned home with the greatest rejoicing of all the people, and so they observe this custom up to the present time."[44] The whole subject is then dismissed with the words, "Now let us leave Kamul, and we shall tell you of the

[42] *Fêng shui* (wind and water): "The art of adapting the residence of the living and the dead so as to co-operate and harmonize with the local currents of the cosmic breath [Yin and Yang]"—Samuel Couling, *Encyclopaedia Sinica*, p. 175.

[43] The writer recalls seeing a hole thus cut in a second-story wall of a house and the coffin lifted through it and lowered by ropes to the ground, where it was received by the funeral cortege waiting on the street below. This occurred on Queen's Road, the main thoroughfare of the native quarter of Hong Kong.

[44] *"Andate, & vivete secondo i vostri costumi, & fate, che le donne vostre siano limosinarie verso i viadanti & con questa risposta tornarono á casa con grandissima allegrezza di tutto il popolo & cosi fino al presente osservano la prima consuetudine."*

others"—but not without adding (in one of the old French manu-scripts) that *"les femes sunt beles et gaudent et de soulas."*[45]

Following the account of Kamul is a brief description of the area which Polo calls Chingintalas (or Ghinghitalas), which has not been definitely located, but may well be the Barkul district. The principal product of this region was asbestos,[46] and Marco takes great delight in exploding the current medieval belief that the substance was the wool of the salamander, a lizard-like crea-ture. In his earnest desire to convince his readers he assures that *"io stesso ne fui testimonio"* (I myself was a witness)—and he sel-dom refers to himself in the first person. An interesting detail is added by him, one of his few direct references to the earlier jour-ney of Nicolo and Maffeo:

> And I shall tell you, moreover, that there is one of these napkins [of asbestos] at Rome, a magnificent gift sent by the Great Khan to the Pontifex when he sent as ambassadors the two Polo brothers, that it might serve to wrap the holy handkerchief (*sudarium*) of our Lord Jesus Christ. And on this napkin are written in gold the following words: *"Tu es Petrus et super hanc petram edificabo ecclesiam meam."*

Continuing the progress of the caravan through Kansu, the Venetian mentions rhubarb, a plant that has been used in medicine for many centuries.[47]

The next city of importance reached was Kan Chou, where Marco Polo saw a giant reclining Buddha (still existing) in a temple. He also observed (though this may have been later) the sexual attitudes of the inhabitants of Kan Chou, and tells how they salved their consciences when they fell from grace. In the words of the worthy Ramusio, *"Perché questa e la loro conscienza, che se la donna ricerca l'uomo d'amore, possino usare con quella senza*

[45] "And the women are beautiful and sprightly and wanton, and derive much pleasure from this custom."

[46] The subject of asbestos is covered at length by Needham in *Science and Civilization in China*, Vol. III, 655ff. It was known to Pliny the Elder, *Natural History*, Bk. XIX, who believed it to be a vegetable fiber.

[47] Although rhubarb may have been an important product in Kansu in the thirteenth century, it is no longer. See Laufer, *Sino-Iranica*, 547ff.; Olschki, *op. cit.*, 429f.; Taylor, *Plant Drugs*, chap. 10.

peccato, ma se essi sono primi a ricercar la donna, allora lo reputano a peccato."[48]

The three Polos subsequently had more leisure to study the manners and customs of Kan Chou, for Marco notes that later on he, his father, and his uncle Maffeo lived in the city about a year transacting their business, "which is not worth mentioning." Here we find the Venetian showing that same reluctance to disclose details of his private or personal affairs characteristic of his entire narrative.

Following the description of Kan Chou are several short chapters of digression and notes about Karakorum and other cities, the manners and customs of many central Asian areas probably not visited by the Polos, at least not on this journey.

Included in these chapters is a sketch of a war waged between Genghis Khan and a chief called by the Venetian "Prester John."[49] This historical dissertation—far from accurate—is followed by several interesting comments on Tatar (Mongol) life and habits as well as religion. As these chapters are found in every translation of Marco Polo's book, there is no need of referring to them here, with the exception of two—the making and drinking of *kumiss*, of which Marco remarks, "But I tell you, too, that they prepare it in such a way that it is like white wine." The other notation is the manner in which the Mongol warriors nourish themselves on the march when no food or drink is available. In the traveler's words, "in case their journey may chance to be delayed by cooking of food and without fruits, but often, for want of wine or water, they live on the blood of their horses, for each pricks the vein of his horse and puts his mouth to the vein and drinks of the blood till

---

[48] "For this is their opinion, that if the woman invites the man to love, they may lie with her without sin, but if they are the first to invite the woman, then they hold it for a sin." And in the very next sentence he speaks of the Buddhist saints' days, arranged "almost as we have ours," and "some of them do not eat meat all their time, these are the monks. . . . And the laymen take up to thirty wives, and more or less as their means allow. And many mortal sins are not held sins by them, because they live almost in the manner of beasts."

[49] The legendary and the real Prester John are treated in most encyclopedias, and fuller accounts are to be found in Yule, *Cathay and the Way Thither*, 2d ed., III, 15ff., and Jean Doresse, *L'Empire du Prêtre-Jean*.

he is satisfied; then they stop it up."[50] One paragraph, however, which appears in a single Venetian manuscript, is of great value. Since there are no contemporary documents which have preserved for us the physical and mental characteristics of Marco Polo, it is largely necessary to seek for such light as may be thrown on him by his own statements or by comments in his text. We must ever keep in mind that the book was dictated (or written) some years after his return to Venice, where he found the ways of life far different from those to which he had grown accustomed in nearly a quarter of a century of residence in East Asia. All was strange to him, and toward some of the social practices of his native city he appears to show a deep resentment, particularly the conduct of its women. The gentleness, self-discipline, reserve, and modest dignity of the women he had known or observed in the realm of the Great Khan contrasted sharply with the bold, impudent, flaunting manners of many of the Italian women of his day. The loose morals of Venice evidently distressed and disturbed him, as they probably never would have if he had lived all of his years there. We get a glimpse of his attitude of mind in the following passage:

> In my judgment they [the Tatar women] are those women who most in the world deserve to be commended for their very great virtue, and they are all the more worthy . . . because the men are allowed to be able to take as many wives as they please, to the very great confusion of the Christian women (I mean in these our parts). For when one man has only one wife, in which marriages there ought to be a most singular faith and chastity, or [else] confusion of so great a sacrament as marriage, I am ashamed when I look at the unfaithfulness of the Christian women, [and call] those happy who being a hundred wives to one husband keep [their virtue] to their own most worthy praise, to the very great shame of all the other women in the world.

From Kan Chou the travelers continued on their way to what is now the city of Liang Chou Fu. The yaks encountered on the

[50] The preparation and use of kumiss is referred to by as early an author as Herodotus, who states (Bk. IV, sect. 2) that "blind slaves [of the Scythians] prepare the drink," and by Strabo (Bk. VII, c. lv, 7).

route impressed Marco because of their size and economic value, and the valuable little musk deer, which is still found in great numbers in this region, was of such interest to him that on his return to Venice he carried with him the dried feet of one "and some musk in the musk sac, and pairs of little teeth."

The Venetians were now approaching regions where the inhabitants were of Chinese blood, whom he thus describes: "These people worship idols, and are fat, and have the nose small. Their hair is black[51] and they have no beards, except four hairs on the chin. The honorable ladies likewise have no hair except that of the head, and are white, of fair flesh, well formed in all their limbs, but very voluptuous." Our Marco has grown up, and appears to be more observant of the women at this stage of the journey than of trade and the profit therefrom.

The road now passed through territories belonging to the Great Khan, but believed to have been formerly the domain of the legendary Prester John. At this point in his narrative Marco writes: "Here also is what we call the country of Gog and Magog; they, however, call it Ung and Mungal."[52]

Now at last the Polos and their caravan were nearing the end of their journey across the plains, mountains, and deserts of Asia. They had been traveling for three and one-half wearisome years, and Marco had seen much and learned and experienced much. The callow lad of seventeen had rounded out physically in the outdoor life, as well as developing mentally. His faculties had ripened, and very evidently he appears to have missed but little of all that went on about him and to have registered all in a remarkably retentive memory. Moreover, he was constantly in the company of Nicolo and Maffeo, two older, wiser, shrewder, and much-traveled men, from whom he could not fail to learn. After all the hardships and

[51] "Li Min," the "black-haired people," is an epithet often applied to the Chinese people and used as early as one of the Confucian Books, the *Ta Hsüeh*, or *Great Learning*, chap. x, 141.

[52] Since the Venetian nowhere in his books mentions the Great Wall of China, many scholars believe that the above sentence refers to the region traversed by the Great Wall. The meaning of the reference is debatable. See also Andrew Runni Anderson, *Alexander's Gate, Gog and Magog,* and *The Inclosed Nations.*

vicissitudes of their travels all three men must have been thoroughly fatigued and sated with the seemingly never ending journey.[53]

What joy and relief were undoubtedly theirs when one day
they were met by an escort to accompany them the remaining
forty days to the presence of the Great Khan. Kublai must have
been informed of their coming, for Marco "tells you for truth that
when the Great Khan knows that his envoys Master Nicolau and
Master Mafeu were coming back from the lands of the Christians,
and how they were much toil-worn, he was very glad and he sends
his messengers quite forty days marches to meet them and had all
they needed prepared for them in every place, so that with the
help of God they were conducted at last to his court. And they
were very much served and honored with everything which they
could order, coming and going."

Thus the remainder of the journey from far-off Venice was
accomplished with ease, for at every stage all things awaited them
at the Khan's command.

On the fortieth day the city of Shang Tu,[54] the summer residence of Kublai Khan, was sighted, and ere long the travel-stained
caravan entered its gates. Marco undoubtedly visited the city often
during his seventeen summers in the service of the Khan, and the
palace especially impressed itself on his memory, thanks to which
an excellent description has been preserved. It was built of stone
and marble with halls and rooms gilded and painted with hunting
scenes and landscapes, birds and beasts, trees and flowers. The
great surrounding wall embraced an area of sixteen square miles,
which could be entered only by the palace gates. Therein were

[53] Several of the mss. state, "Moreover you may know that they hardly go
riding from Laias to where the great Kaan was on the return in quite three years
and a half before they could accomplish this their business, and this was for the
very great snow and ice and for the rain, for the bad weather which they had and
for the great cold and the great rivers, and for the great south-west gales which
were in the countries which they were obliged to pass, which much lengthened
and hindered their journey, and because they cannot ride by winter as by summer."

[54] Marco calls it by the older Persian name "Chemienfu," spelled in various
mss. in thirteen different ways, which represents the Chinese K'ai p'ing Fu. Later
the Venetian calls the city "Ciandu," an approximation of Shang Tu. Ciandu is
given thirteen different spellings in the various mss.

rivers and fountains and fair stretches of lawn and groves of beautiful trees. And in it were kept beasts for the chase, but only such
as were not dangerous to men, and there the Great Khan went
hunting at least once a week with his falcons or tame leopards. In
the middle of the park was set a palace or pavilion built of bamboo,
its columns lacquered and gilded, with dragon capitals, and its
lofty roof of gilded and varnished bamboo tiles. The pavilion was
braced against the wind with more than two hundred ropes of
twisted silk, and it was so constructed that the whole could be
taken down and moved hither and thither at the will of the monarch. The lord of the Mongols came from Cambaluc, his capital,
to dwell in one or the other of these palaces to escape the great heat
of the three months of summer. In order to insure perfect weather
during his sojourn at Shang Tu, Kublai employed "wise astrolo-
gers." At the first sign of storm cloud or mist they mounted the
roof of the palace and by means of their incantations drove off the
evil influences, so that, whatever bad storms might be all about,
the palaces and the surrounding park enjoyed nothing but the
finest weather, with warm suns and tempering winds.

Samuel Purchas, in his ponderous *Purchas His Pilgrimage*, written in 1613, paraphrased the description of Shang Tu (Xandu)
from the text of Ramusio. One day in the summer of 1798, Samuel
Taylor Coleridge, the English poet, who had taken a large dose of
laudanum to relieve the raging pain of an aching tooth, sat in his
garden at Porlock. On his lap lay a copy of *Purchas His Pilgrimage*,
open at the passage which begins, "In Xandu did Cublai Can build
a stately Palace, encompassing sixteen miles of plain grounde with
a wall, wherein are fertile Meddowes, pleasant Springs, delightful
Streames, and all sorts of beasts of chase and game, and in the
middest thereof a sumptuous house of pleasure, which may be
removed from place to place." As he was reading this chapter, he
was gradually overcome by the opiate, his head sank upon his
breast, and he slept profoundly for three hours, and dreamed. On
awakening, the images of his dream were still before him. Paper
was at hand; he seized his pen, and, while the vision was vivid and

etched clear in his mind's eye, he hastily scribbled the immortal
lines of "Kubla Khan."[55] The vision of the poet lives for us, and
will live on while Shang Tu and its palaces are naught but heaps of
ruins. During the rebellions against Mongol rule in China which
terminated in the establishment of the Ming dynasty, the magnificent summer palace of Kublai was looted and burned to the
ground. The summer capital has been deserted for centuries, and
the site of all the pomp and ceremony of the most magnificent of
the Mongol monarchs is "the abode of foxes and owls." The dilapidated walls of the city are still standing, together with the remains
of its six great gates. The Mongols of the region still cherish memories of the Great Khan and regard the place with awe and reverence, though they wander at will with their flocks and herds
over the plain strewn with the remains of palaces and temples.
Amid the tangled weeds and shattered stones a solitary broken
inscription stands, erected long ago by Kublai Khan, telling the
tale of a monastery which once reared its proud roofs there. All
else is forgotten in silence and decay, a mournful reminder of the
brief material glory of men that swiftly passes and is not.

Marco Polo closes his first book (in some editions there is no
break) with these characteristic words: "Now let us leave speaking to you of this, and we shall tell you of the very great deeds and
of the marvels of the very great lord of the lords of all the Tatars
of the world. That is the very noble great Kaan who is called
Cublai."

[55] The story of the writing of "Kubla Khan" is presented in one of the finest
monuments of American literary scholarship, John Livingston Lowe's *The Road
to Xanadu*. A description of the summer residence of the Great Khan, together
with much interesting material on the Mongols is to be found in Rashíd-u-din,
"Jamí-ut Tawáríkh," contained in Yule's *Cathay and the Way Thither*, III, 107ff.

·IV·

Cathay

"The superiour or high *India*, whiche is nowe called *Cathay* is a region exceedinge large and of greate power, whose Emperour is ye great Cham of Tartaria, hauinge under him many Prouinces, people and Princes, and innumerable Ilandes in the great East sea, called the greate Ocean. . . . In what pompe and triumphant magnificence he sheweth himself . . . he that desyreth to knowe, let him reade *Paulus Venetus*, in the second boke of hys nauigations into *India*, where he shal find thinges to marueyl at."—Sebastian Munter, *De Terris Asiae Maioris*, libr. v (trans. by Richard Eden)

"Marcus Paulus wryteth that the greate Chan is cauled Chan Cublai that is, the greate kynge of kynges: as the greate turcke wryteth hym selfe in lyke maner."—Paulus Iovius, Bysshoppe of Nuceria, *The Historie Written in the Latin Toonge* (trans. by Richard Eden)

Marco Polo's description of the travelers' reception is surprisingly simple and restrained. Whereas elsewhere he does not

hesitate to expatiate on the magnificence of the Great Khan's re-
ceptions, banquets, processions, and festivals, the welcome accorded the Venetians is given only one short unadorned chapter,
placed in the early part of the first book, but the description of the
reception begins with a device of which Marco—or his scribe, of
whom more hereafter—is especially fond:

> *Et que voz en diroie?* [And what shall I tell you about it?] When
> the noble brothers Master Nicolo and Master Maffeo and Marc
> were come into that great city aforesaid in which the great Khan
> was, they go off immediately to the chief palace where they find
> the great Khan with a very great company of all his barons. And
> they kneel before him with great reverence and humble them-
> selves the most they are able, stretching themselves out on the
> earth. The great Khan makes them rise and stand upright on their
> feet and receives them with the greatest honor and makes very
> great rejoicing and great feasting for them.

After the formal reception the monarch engaged the brothers
in a long conversation, for he was desirous of learning about their
adventures since they had left the Mongol court so many years
before. They then presented to him the gifts and documents with
which they had been entrusted by Pope Gregory (and by the two
timid friars who had turned back) and placed in his hands the
vessel of sacred oil which they had obtained at his behest from the
Church of the Holy Sepulchre at Jerusalem and had zealously
guarded through all the fatigues and dangers of the long journey
from the coast of the Mediterranean.

Kublai, after these various matters had been settled, looked
about him and spied the young Marco, who probably was standing
apart, silent and respectful while his elders conversed—one manuscript adding at this point in the narrative that "Marco was a young
bachelor of very great and noble aspect."

Upon his inquiring who the young stranger might be, Messer
Nicolo replied, "Sire, he is my son and your man, whom, as the
dearest thing in the world, I have brought with great peril and ado
from such distant lands to present him to thee as thy slave." "Let

him be welcome," said the Great Khan, and forthwith ordered the young man inscribed on the list of the members of his household,[1] "and," adds the same Venetian manuscript, "he was held of great account and value by all those at the court."

There was vast rejoicing and feasting at the court in honor of these distinguished foreigners from a distant land (or at least so writes the Venetian), and thereafter they held a high place in the esteem of the Mongol lord. Marco terminates this brief account of the reception of his elders and himself modestly enough with the remark, "And why should I make you a long story?"

Marco Polo has left a very interesting description of the personal appearance of Kublai Khan.[2] "The great lord of lords, that is of all those of his dominions, who is called Cublai Kaan is like this. He is of good and fair size, neither too small nor too large, but is of middle size. He is covered with flesh in a beautiful manner, not too fat nor lean; he is more than well formed in all parts. He has his face white and partly shining red like the color of a beautiful rose, which makes him appear very pleasing; and he has the eyes black and beautiful; and the nose very beautiful, well made and well set on the face."

This description is followed by an intimate and detailed account of the method of selecting his numerous wives and concubines, and of his marital and extra-marital relations. As all this is set forth at great length in Messer Marco's own book, it would be imposing

[1] The Mongols who conquered and ruled China with the title of the Yüan (everlasting) Dynasty were fighters, not administrators. Realizing the truth of the ancient Chinese proverb, "An empire can be conquered on horseback, but not ruled from horseback," Kublai Khan wisely sought help. Fearing to entrust important positions or tasks to the conquered Chinese, foreigners, either Asians or Europeans, when available, were pressed into government service. This may explain the enthusiasm with which the far-traveled and experienced Venetians were received.

[2] Kublai Khan, called in Chinese the Emperor Shê Tsu, born in 1214, was three generations removed from the steppes and had acquired some Chinese culture. He was more intelligent and benevolent than the earlier Mongol rulers, and more energetic, nobler, and more talented. It should be remembered that his mother (d. 1252, according to the Yüan Shih, the Chinese Chronicle of the Mongol Dynasty) was a Nestorian Christian of the Kerait tribe. He was a combination of warrior, sybarite, and carouser; he was greedy and generous at the same time, but always alert, and with an inquiring mind. Like all Mongols, he was a heavy drinker and suffered from gout."

on the reader's good will to recount it here—and so it is with the lengthy particulars of the Great Khan's palace and the magnificence of his capital of Cambaluc.[3]

The things which most impressed the Venetian were those which differed from what he had observed in his home city and in the places visited along the way. He marveled at the geometric pattern of the capital, the main streets of which "from one side to the other of the town are drawn out straight as a thread—and in this way all the city inside is laid out by squares, as a chess-board is." How different all this was from the narrow, twisting, dark streets with their overhanging houses which he had seen in the towns of Italy and the Levant! He describes the Bell and Drum Towers which are still standing in Peking, though to the south of the sites where they were erected by the Mongol emperor. Until very recent years they daily boomed out the curfew and the alarm, just as when Marco Polo trod the streets and lanes of the city. He informs us that when the curfew sounded three times from the Bell Tower no one might go forth nor dare leave his dwelling until daylight, "except the nurses who go for the needs of women in childbirth and physicians who go for the needs of sick men, and those who go for this good purpose must carry lights with them."

Messer Marco devotes many pages to a recital of Kublai's birthday, New Year's, and other feasts and great occasions, together with the overflowing riches and ceremonies of the court, as well as of his hunting with his barons. All this the Venetian wove into a brilliant tapestry of many bright colors, gold and silver, the like of which had never been revealed to Western peoples before. What could the dwellers in Europe make of such scenes as that of Kublai's dining, as described by Marco? "Those who do the service of food and drink to the great Kaan at the sideboard & at his table are many great barons, and I tell you that they all have their mouths and their noses wrapped in beautiful veils or napkins of

---

[3] Cambaluc, Khan-baligu, a pure Turkish word meaning the "royal city" and used for perhaps a century or more before Kublai made it his capital. It was situated north of the present city of Peking, whose Drum Tower and Bell Tower mark its approximate southern limits. Some mounds of ruins still remain.

silk & of gold, so that their breath nor their smell should not come into the vessels and cups, or into the food and drink of the great lord. And always when the great lord must drink, all those who wait on the king with the instruments of music, of which there are a vast quantity of all makes, begin to sound until he drinks. And when the great lord has his cup in his hand . . . all the barons and all the other people who are serving there kneel down and make a sign of great humility, and then the great lord drinks."

An interesting account is given of the women "*che servono gli huomini per danari*" (who serve men for money)—the prostitutes of Peking. Here he appears to compare the severe regulations of prostitution in the realm of the Khan with the open, flagrant promiscuity displayed in the Venice of his day. He tells us that these women numbered twenty thousand and assures us that they were indeed necessary because of the vast number of merchants and foreigners who entered the city every day. No such woman, however, dared live inside the city (unless secretly), all dwelling in the *borghi* (suburbs). And he naïvely adds that all twenty thousand of them "find a living." A "captain" was appointed for each hundred and each thousand, and all responsible to a "general captain." When ambassadors came to the court of the Great Khan and were lodged at his expense, this captain general was obliged to supply to an ambassador and to each of his retinue "one harlot each night, and they are changed every night, and they have no pay because this is the tax which they pay to the great Khan."

One may surmise that the numerous references to women—the intimate descriptions of their persons, their various aptitudes in sex relations and many other details not usually related even by hardy travelers of that or a later day (unless it be those having the profound knowledge and temerity of a Sir Richard Burton)—were largely, if not entirely, called forth by the frank curiosity and continual questionings of the stay-at-home Westerners for whom his tale was told and written. Travelers returning from foreign lands are still plied insistently with inquiries to which the answers are seldom set down in books written for the masses. We may be very sure that human nature has not greatly changed, and that not all, or even the greater number, of Marco's listeners were interested in the prices of musk and rhubarb or the dimensions of the palace of the Khan or the quality of the goods sold in the markets of far-distant China. They asked other questions, nearer their own interests and experiences, and Messer Marco accommodated them and set down for them the facts they desired most to know. As to his own diversity of interests, we may note that in this same long paragraph describing the *feme pecherise*, or "sinful woman," as a French manuscript has it, Marco tells of the burial places of Cambaluc, of the hunting and hawking of Kublai and his barons, of the precious merchandise brought into the capital for sale, and of the villages surrounding the city.

All of this calls to Marco's mind the matter of the Khan's mint and his paper money, which he tells us he will describe in his next chapter, with the assurance that he will not recount all of the wealth and spending of "the great lord," since no one would believe that he is speaking "truth and reason." This remark seems to be an intimation that Marco himself realized that his tale would not be entirely acceptable to his fellow Venetians. Not being able to conceive of the richness and magnificence of the Mongol ruler and his empire, they would dismiss simple statements of sober fact as staggering inventions of the author's active imagination.

The mint of the great lord of all the Tartars stood in Cambaluc, and there the Venetian saw the paper currency of the country printed and issued.

The Chinese were the first people to use banknotes. Setting aside the stories of the use of deerskin and other materials as currency, Chinese authorities agree that the Chinese Imperial Treasury issued the earliest paper money about the year 650. This currency bore the delightfully suggestive name of *fei chi'en* (flying money). It soon fell into disuse, and we hear no more of it until the tenth century, when it was reintroduced by banking guilds of Szechuan province. Shortly thereafter the state suppressed these private issues and printed its own notes. They were used through the Sung Dynasty, and the amount of paper currency in circulation was swelled enormously by the Mongols. Kublai Khan went so far as to prohibit the use of metal coin altogether, in order to accustom the people to accept his notes. At first the notes were partly guaranteed by metal reserves. When these were exhausted, however, more notes were issued without any metal backing whatsoever. This, of course, must have produced an enormous depreciation in their value, though Marco Polo, evidently having no grasp of the implications of such a financial system, makes no mention of it, assuming that the notes were equivalent to their face value in metal.

Polo was not the only medieval traveler who made mention in writing of the paper money of Cathay. Friar William of Rubruck, who was in the country some twenty-five years before the Venetians' arrival, recounts that "the common money of Cathay is a paper of cotton, in length and breadth a palm, and on it they stamp lines like those on the seal of Mongka [Khan]." Odoric de Pordenone, who was in China the year of Marco Polo's death (1324) speaks of a certain tax being paid in "five pieces of paper like silk," and elsewhere tells the reader not to wonder overmuch at the magnificence of the ruler of Cathay, "for there is nothing spent as money in his whole kingdom but certain pieces of paper which are there current as money." Ibn Battuta, the famous medieval Arab traveler (1304–78) states that "the people of China do not use either gold or silver coin in their commercial transactions. . . . They buy and sell by means of pieces of paper, each of which is as large as the palm of the hand, and bears the mark or the seal of the sultan." Pegolotti, in his guidebook, written about 1340, informs the would-be traveler to Cathay that there "the money is made of paper."

Polo's account of the use of paper money in China was rejected as one of his fables, and William of Rubruck's and Odoric de Pordenone's remarks remained long buried in ecclesiastical records, and no advantage of this method of state finance appears to have been taken by Italians of this period.

The Venetian has described in detail the method of manufacturing Kublai Khan's paper money, prefacing his description with the quaint observation that "the great lord has the alchemy perfectly." The most ingenious device in the financial scheme was in manufacturing the notes of such flimsy paper that they speedily wore out and fell to pieces. When the notes were torn or spoiled, they could be exchanged for new clean ones, a fee of 3 per cent being charged by the mint for the exchange. This method of redemption, which netted the imperial treasury a handsome profit —at the trifling cost of printing the notes—is confirmed by a document preserved in the Bibliothèque Nationale of Paris. It is a French translation (by John le Long of Ypres) of a lost Latin letter supposedly written by John de Cora, Archbishop of Sultanieh, about the year 1330. This letter, replete with interesting information, records, among other things:

> In Cathay, the Grand Caan there maketh money of paper. And this hath a red token right in the middle, and round about there be letters in black. And this money is of greater or of less value according to the token that is thereon . . . . The emperor above mentioned hath very great treasuries, indeed it is a marvel to see them, and these are for this paper money. And when the said money is too old and worn so that it cannot well be handled, it is carried to the King's chamber, where there be moneyers appointed to this duty. And if the token or the king's name is at all to be discerned thereon, then the moneyer giveth new paper for the old, deducting three in every hundred for this renewal![4]

Continuing his narrative, Marco describes some of the foods consumed by the subjects of the Great Khan. The statement is often made that the Venetian introduced macaroni (or spaghetti) into Italy on his return. This erroneous information is based (as far as the writer can ascertain) on the following paragraph found in complete form only in Ramusio's edition of Marco's narrative:

> As for foodstuffs, they have plenty of them for they use for the most part rice, panic, and millet. . . . They do not use bread, these

[4] Both the author and the Newberry Library of Chicago possess original notes of the very early Ming Dynasty, of flimsy blackish-gray paper showing signs of wear, and in the author's collection is a very old engraved plate for the printing of this money, made up of eight small blocks of buffalo-horn pegged together, with spaces left for the red imprint of reign, date, and value. The "letters round about" are of microscopic size interspersed with etchings of human figures.

people, but they simply boil these three kinds of grain with milk or meat, and eat them. . . . And wheat with them does not give such increase (as in the case of the three grains mentioned), but what they reap they eat only in strips of macaroni (lasagne) and other kinds of paste.

In like manner the claim that Marco brought the knowledge of ice cream to Europe is probably derived from his description of the use of dried milk by the Mongols, also told in detail in Ramusio:

Moreover they have dried milk like unto paste. And it is dried in this manner: They boil the milk and then the richest part which floats at the top is put into another vessel, and from this they make butter, for as long as it remains in the milk, it cannot be dried. They next place the milk in the sun, and thus it is dried. And when they go forth to war they carry with them about ten pounds of this milk. And in the morning each takes of it half a pound, and puts it in a small leather flask, made like a bottle, with as much water as he pleases. And as he rides his horse the milk in the bottle is churned up and becomes like syrup. This they drink, and it is their meal.

Coal was another product of China at which Marco Polo marveled greatly. Although coal was mentioned in Theophrastus[5] and was used by the Romans in Britain, its first general use as fuel is recorded in the Saxon Chronicle of Peterborough Abbey in 862. The Venetian had probably never seen it burned before his arrival in Asia, or he would not have recorded that "It is true again that through all the province of Catai there is found a kind of large black stones which are dug from the mountains as veins, which burn and make flames like logs . . . and keep up the fire and cook better than wood does. . . . And you may know that these stones are so good that nothing else is burnt through all the province of Catai as far as possible."[6]

[5] Theophrastus (*ca.*370–*ca.*285 B.C.), a pupil of Plato and Aristotle, a voluminous writer, author of, among other works, scientific essays on minerals.

[6] Aeneas Piccolomini (Pope Pius II, 1405–64) relates, as a "miracle" which he beheld with his own eyes in Scotland, that the beggars at the churches rejoiced when the monks gave them stones which they burned, for wood was scarce. Chinese records of the Han Dynasty speak of the use of coal for fuel at least 100 B.C.

The almanac used by the Chinese from very ancient times is described in great detail. Besides the usual astronomical data for the year drawn up by the Board of Astronomy, the official almanac contained a carefully compiled list of *dies fasti et nefasti*, similar to that of the ancient Romans.[7] It noted the days which were favorable to enterprises and the days when specified acts or undertakings should be zealously avoided. In Ramusio's version of Marco Polo's book we read:

> If anyone shall have proposed in his mind to enter upon some great work or to set out for some distant place for trade or any other things which he must do, or shall have planned to do anything, and wished to foreknow the end of the business, he will inquire of these. He will go to find one of these Astrologers and will say to him: "Inquire into your books how the sky is now, for I desire to go to enter upon such and such an affair or business transaction." The Astrologer will speak to him, informing him moreover that he should tell him the year, the month, and the hour of his birth, and when this is told him he will see how the constellations of his birth correspond with those which are in the sky at the hour of his request, and so he will predict what will happen to him in the future of good or of ill, according to the way in which the sky is disposed.

The Zelada manuscript adds that by this means the astrologer could advise his client whether or not he should await a more propitious moment for his business or his journey, by which gate he should go out of the city, where he might expect to meet with robbers, where he might encounter bad weather, where his horse would break a leg, and whether the business contemplated would result in a profit or a loss.

These almanacs with their forecasts of days good and evil are still in use in China, though the republican government made strenuous efforts to suppress them. However, until the fall of the Empire the government itself published the almanac annually in the name of the Son of Heaven, in several editions, large and small.

7 See Ovid, *Fasti*, in a remarkable translation with notes by Sir James G. Frazer, entitled *Publii Ovidii Nasonis Fastorum Libri Sex*, 5 vols., London, 1929.

Existing records of the Yüan Dynasty for 1328 contain a notation of the printing and sale of 3,123,185 copies of the almanac—and a further 5,267 especially issued for the *Hui Hui*, the Mohammedans of the Empire.

Following this interesting sketch, Messer Marco goes into more or less scattered details about the Chinese religion and the etiquette followed by the nobles when they appeared before their monarch. After describing their wearing of "certain beautiful slippers of white leather," which they carried with them and put on when they entered the audience chamber so as not to soil the handsome carpets of silk and gold, he makes an observation in which he seems mentally to compare the nicety of the manners of the Chinese with the vulgarities and grossness common in his own Venice: "Each baron or noble carries with him continually a vase, very small and beautiful, into which he spits while he is in the [audience] chamber, because no one would dare to spit on [the floor of] the [audience] chamber. And when he has spit he covers it and keeps it by him."

We are told in the same paragraph of the quaint decree by which Kublai Khan forbade gambling in his dominions: "I have vanquished you arms in hand, and all that you possess is mine. And if you gamble you are gambling with my property."

During his years in the administrative service of the Great Khan, Marco Polo had many occasions to use the roads and imperial traveling arrangements. And, as he remarks, "the manner of the great Kaan is wonderful." According to his account there was a different road leading to each province. At intervals of twenty-five or thirty miles (sometimes more) on each road were post stations shaded by trees planted for the purpose, "and at each post wherever they go the messengers find a very great palace and beautiful and rich where the messengers or envoys of the great lord may lodge with dignity, and these lodgings . . . have all the things which are right for exalted messengers and are required by them, [and] they find quite four hundred good horses at each . . . ready for his messengers and ambassadors when he sends them in any direction on his business, that they may be able to dismount there and leaving the tired horses to take fresh ones—And in this way it goes through all the principal provinces and realms." Ordinarily one or two stages (of about twenty-five miles each) would be ridden a day by the messenger, but for urgent dispatches messengers (with bells at their belts) would run between subsidiary posts placed three miles apart and hand on the dispatch to the next runner. The bells were to notify travelers on the road to make way for the imperial courier, and, even more important, that the runner at the next substation, on hearing the bells from afar, could get ready to take over the dispatches and start in his turn with no delay. If any military or other emergency arose, horses were at hand at the subsidiary stations to carry mounted couriers, also fitted out with bells, at a breakneck pace from post to post. We are assured by the Venetian that at such times and in such a manner men or messages could cover up to three hundred miles a day—using torches by night when necessary. Clerks at every post and substation kept a careful record of times of the arrival and departure of couriers, and their records were in turn examined monthly by officials appointed for the purpose.[8]

At this point in his narrative Marco makes an end for the moment of his desultory notes—which, strangely enough, fail to mention many common bits of Chinese daily life such as tea-drinking, foot-binding and printing—with the remark: "And now that there has come an end to telling of the government and administration of the province of Cathay, and of the city of Cambaluc and of the magnificence of the great Can, you will be told of the other regions into which Messer Marco went on the official business of the Empire of the great Can."

For (and here I quote from the Latin edition of Pipino, a contemporary and perhaps a friend of Marco Polo) "when the great Chan sent me, Marco, to remote regions on certain business of his realm (which kept me on the road for a period of four months), I observed all things diligently which came to my attention either in going or in returning." This statement definitely marks the end of one part of Polo's narrative, and a new section begins.

The mission to which the Venetian refers appears to be that of

[8] Cf. Herodotus, Bk. VIII, chap. 98.

which he speaks in the very brief outline of his travels at the beginning of his book. There he modestly says that he, Marco, was "of a very distinguished mind" and that he

> learned the uses of the Tatars and their language and their letters and their archery so well that it seemed a wonder to them all, for I tell you quite truly that before a great deal of time after he came to the court of the great lord, he knows several languages and four other different letters and writings so that he could read and write in any of those languages very well;[9] in virtue and noble manners, kindly and so that no other surpassed him in virtue and noble manners, kindly and gracious with all, loved and received by all. That noble youth being already come to a good age, he was wise and prudent beyond measure and much did the great Kaan above all men wish him great good for the goodness which he saw in him and the great valor.

Some manuscripts record that "Dominus Marco," while he was at Kublai's court, was "wise and prudent beyond measure." In all fairness it should be noted that these phrases may be interpretations of later copyists or editors, for, though Messer Marco nowhere seems to be eager to hide his light under a bushel, it is difficult to believe that he would use such fulsome praise of himself in his book. Moreover, the paragraph in question varies in different manuscripts in numerous details and phraseology, no two manuscripts seeming to agree on more than a phrase or two. What is brought out clearly, however, is that the young Venetian very speedily brought himself to the attention of Kublai by his keen wit and intelligence, as well as by the speed and facility with which he made himself thoroughly familiar with economic and political affairs at court and throughout the Empire. He had observed with what avidity the monarch seized upon any information about his

[9] I take issue with several editors who believe that Chinese was not one of the languages acquired by Marco Polo. He could hardly have sojourned in China for seventeen years, of necessity dealing with or at least living, traveling, and in administrative work among the people (for the Mongols constituted but a small part of the population) without acquiring some practical knowledge of the spoken language at least, for it is not too difficult. On the other hand, it was natural for him to use the Mongol or Persian words for names, places, etc., or his approximations of these words as he learned and used them at court.

subject states, their people, products, and ways of life, and had also noted his impatience with returned envoys who seemed to have carried out their missions successfully without noting or observing anything aside from the strict demands of their duties. Shrewdly making use of this knowledge, Marco set about acquiring and accumulating information and making note of each place he visited, and never hesitated to acquaint his master with these details. To his diligence and zeal in these investigations Marco owed his success at court, and to them the great value and interest of his book are largely due.

According to Messer Marco's own statement, the Great Khan decided to test his abilities as a "messenger" and sent him on a mission to the distant city of Caragian,[10] a place so far from Cambaluc that "he hardly goes in six months of marches." The young man carried out his assignment most satisfactorily, and on his return brought back in addition much information which greatly interested the monarch. His report was evidently accurate, detailed, and fascinating, for, according to some manuscripts "to the lord this noble youth seemed to have divine rather than human understanding & the love of the lord increased . . . until by the lord and the whole court there was nothing more wonderful told than of the wisdom of the noble youth." Several manuscripts add that the nobles told each other that if he, Marco, should live for long, "he could not fail to be a man of much sense and great valor." Then follows the naïve rhetorical question which Marco uses so frequently and so delightfully, as though to take breath before continuing his narrative: *"Et que vous en diroie?"* (And what shall I tell you of it?) We are told in the next sentence that thenceforth the young man was called "Messer" Marco Polo ("Mesere Marc Pol" in the French texts), "and thus our book will henceforth call him. And this is indeed very right, for he was wise and experienced."

"And for what reason should I make you a long tale?" we are

[10] The Mongol name is Qara-Jang, spelled in numerous forms in the various mss. It was in Chinese Yünnan, the southernmost province of the Empire, or a part thereof. See the note on Caragian in Pelliot, *Notes on Marco Polo*, Vol. I, 169–81, and Olschki, *Marco Polo's Asia*, 225n. The chief city was Tali.

asked, and are told in the same breath that after that Messer Marco remained in the service of the Great Khan for seventeen years.[11] The Elizabethan translation of a Spanish Polian manuscript (made by John Frampton in 1579) recites:

> He [Marco] was in the greate CANES Court XVIJ yeares, and when anye great Embassage or businesse shoulde be done in any of hys Countreys or Provinces, he was alwayes sente, wherefore, divers great men of the Court did envie him, but he alwayes kepte thys order, that whatsoever he sawe or heard, were it good or evill, hee alwayes wrote it, and had it in minde to declare to the great CANE in order.

The narrative takes occasion to point out that Marco's notes, investigations, and reports on these missions explain "why Messer Marco knows more of these things of this country than any other man, because he explores more of these strange regions than any other man who was ever born, and moreover because he gave his particular attention to learn this." And, adds Ramusio, "The things which Marco thus learned are those about which he has written so carefully and in order in his book."

Nowhere in the narrative is the reader informed specifically of the nature or the number of the missions on which Polo was sent at various times during the seventeen years of his service as an official of Kublai Khan, so it is impossible to reconstruct his itineraries, and it is not at all certain when or how information given about any particular country, province, or region was acquired. It may have been from notes jotted down during his journeyings back and forth on diplomatic or other missions, on expeditions perhaps made by him if and when engaged in his own private affairs, or from observations made during the long wayfarings from Venice to Cathay and back to his home. The information is usually given following the name of the particular place, with no indication of how it had been obtained. One must not cavil at

---

11 There is no intimation throughout the narrative of the activities of the elder Polos during this period. They, too, may have been in the service of Kublai, though the sequel would indicate that they had accumulated a goodly fortune—perhaps in trade. This is mere surmise.

Marco's failure to set down what was overlooked or evidently unimportant in his eyes—eyes which looked out upon the world with thirteenth-century selectivity and interests—for what he has given is a vast amount of precious material about Asia, a continent which is still replete with rich unexplored veins and pockets of golden ore. The accounts of the peoples and tribes of China and the adjacent lands, the strange ideas of the Tibetans in the realm of sexual morality, the descriptions of the primitive peoples of Yünnan and other remote provinces of the Middle Kingdom render his account curiously modern.

Although it is not certain that Marco Polo visited every place in East Asia discussed by him, the facts as he presented them in his book are accurate; e.g., the various notations on the customs of Yünnan province: the eaters of raw meat, the age-old use of cowrie shells for money, the crocodiles (which were held by the Venetian to be serpents with two legs), the method by which they were captured, the docking of horses' tails (so that they could not swish them and injure their riders)—all these add to the interest of the narrative.

Another custom that had existed among the Yünnanese interested Marco. If a handsome or "gentle" stranger or one "who had a good shadow and good influence and valor" came to lodge in the house of one of the natives, he was killed during the night by poison or otherwise; and "this they used to do, not for money or for any hatred which they had against him," but in order that his soul might remain in the house and give the dwellers therein some of "the goodly favor and wisdom and repute of the murdered man." But, adds our author, "indeed the great Khan, when he conquered the kingdom and brought it under his dominion, drove out that impiety and that exceeding folly."

We are told of the custom of the *couvade*[12] among the "gold-teeth people" of the Burmese frontier.[13] The conquest of Burma

[12] A widespread practice, both ancient (see Diodorus Siculus and Strabo) and modern among some primitive peoples, in accordance with which the father of a newborn infant takes to his bed and receives the attention and performs acts which among civilized peoples appertain to the mother.

[13] The use of a gold case fitting over the lower or both sets of teeth (sometimes

is related and a description is given of that country as well as adjacent Indian states. An interesting detailed account is included (more fully in some manuscripts than in others) of Burmese tattooing—how the victim was bound hand and foot and held motionless while the master tattooer, with an instrument holding five needles arranged in a square, pricked the pattern on him and then rubbed indelible ink in on the design. Marco adds that the person undergoing the operation suffers so that "it might be thought enough for them for purgatory" and that many die from loss of blood; and he ends by telling us that he will "leave you then from this province and from the men who are painted with flowers and animals."

After describing the countries bordering China on the south as no one had ever done before his day and as no other single traveler has since, Marco continues with China proper and describes some of its provinces. In the Zelada manuscript, lately discovered, is a unique and lengthy discussion of the manners and customs of the Chinese, many of which are identical with those of today.

The first is a tribute to the grace and virtue of the women of China, famous through the ages:

> You should know also that the maidens observe decorum. They indeed do not skip and dance about, or leap or burst into a passion. They do not hang out the windows scanning the faces of the passers-by or exhibiting their own faces to them. They do not lend a ready ear to unseemly conversation, and they do not frequent feasts or celebrations. And if it happens that they go to any decent place, such as by chance to the temples of the idols, or to visit the homes of their blood relations or other kinsmen, they go in the company of their mothers, not gazing boldly at people but wearing on their heads certain beautiful hats which prevent a glance upwards, so that always in walking they cast their eyes on the road before their feet. They are indeed demure in the presence of their elders, and never utter empty words, indeed none save when questions are asked of them; and they remain in their rooms at their tasks and seldom appear in the sight of their fathers and

indented to the shape of the teeth, but usually plain) and worn all the time is attested by Raffles, *Java*, I, 105; Marsden, *Sumatra*, 3d ed., 52, and others.

brothers and the elders of the household. And to suitors they give no ear.

It is difficult not to perceive the expression of Marco's personal attitude of mind in these sentences. After twenty-three years in Asia, most of them spent in China, he had learned to know and respect the Chinese. He had observed the position of women in Chinese society and was deeply impressed by their sweetness, dignity, modesty, and sobriety. On his return to Venice, thoroughly Orientalized as he probably was after his long sojourn in the Far East, he could hardly have avoided observing the daily life of his fellow citizens from a new point of view. His keen eyes must have made mental comparisons at every turn, and here, as in many other instances in his book, he appears by his comments to have reached the conclusion that his Venetian townsfolk had much to learn of gentility, breeding, and ethical attitudes from the people of the Middle Kingdom.

In the same manner he commented on the conduct of the Chinese boys and young men:

> And likewise we may say of the boys and young gentlemen that they never presume to speak in the presence of their elders unless they are asked. And what more? So great is the modesty among them, that is to say among blood relations and kindred, that in no way would two attempt to go together to the cold or hot baths.

Here follows a long and interesting discussion of the Chinese ways of marrying and giving in marriage, with guaranties, tests, and proofs of the virginity of the bride. In this intimate description, reminiscent of the customs of many ancient or primitive peoples and throwing light on certain age-old methods of practicing deceit, Marco may refer to the practice of foot-binding,[14] not otherwise mentioned by him, in the remark:

[14] Authorities do not agree about the date of the introduction of the practice, but it is at least as far back as the T'ang Dynasty, when an imperial concubine desired to have tiny feet (poetically called *chin lien*, golden lilies). The increasing of compression was acute torture and lasted for years. The psychological result was to cause the tiny foot to become an intensely erogenous zone and fetish, and it is so treated in Chinese literature and art. Chinese women are very modest about

And you should know that for the preserving of this virginity the maidens walk so gently in their progress on the road that one foot is never advanced before the other by more than the measure of a finger. . . . In like manner it is to be understood that this [custom] is of those whose origin is Cathayan, for the Tatars do not care for this kind of convention.

It may be observed that Marco is probably more nearly correct in his inference regarding the origin of foot-binding than are most of the dissertations written on it; and it is further to be noted that foot-binding appears to be entirely a Chinese custom, never adopted by their Mongol or their Manchu conquerors.

In this same section is a very interesting description of a temple erected to two "idols" who presided over the finding of lost things. These idols were small statues of boys, covered with ornaments, and the temple was presided over by an ancient dame whom Marco calls the "sacristan." "If a person loses anything, by theft or otherwise, he comes to the temple and tells his tale to the old woman, who orders him to burn incense before the gods. Then the sacristan asks the gods about the thing lost, and they tell her what will be the outcome. Then she directs the petitioner where to look if the article has been misplaced. If, however, it has been stolen, she tells him to whom to go, instructing him to warn the thief to restore the thing, with the admonition that 'otherwise I shall bring it about that he shall cut his hand or break an arm or leg by falling, or in some other manner he will come to harm, so that he will be compelled to restore it to you.' " We are assured that this always happens, be the thief man or woman; and "because by experience men now know that this happens to them because of denials of theft, they immediately restore the stolen goods." The old woman thanks the gods, and upon recovering the lost or stolen property the owner is expected to make an offering to the god. The Venetian closes the anecdote with the revealing remark, "And I Marco found in this way a certain ring of mine

their "golden lily feet," and they may not be exposed or touched—nor must one refer to them in any way. The practice was abandoned after the abolition of the Empire. See Couling, *Encyc. Sin.*, under "Foot-binding." The topic is fully discussed, with illustrations, in Matignon, *Superstition, Crime et Misère en Chine*.

which was lost, but not that I made them any offering or homage."

In the midst of his notes Messer Marco admonishes his reader not to "believe that we have treated of the whole province of Catai in order, not indeed of a twentieth part, but only as I Marco used to cross through the province, so the cities which are on the way across are described, passing by those which are at the sides and through the middle, to tell of which would be too long."[15]

As this part of Marco's account of China is to be found in every edition of his book, it is needless to go further into his descriptions. He traveled far and wide throughout the country, and in the course of his service under the great Kublai he may have reached the Irawaddy River in Burma and the confines of Tibet and Annam.

As a reward (we may assume) for his loyalty, administrative ability, and knowledge of the country, Messer Marco served in a post in Yang Chou, at that time a special province.[16]

Yang Chou was an important trade center until its destruction by the T'ai P'ing rebels in the nineteenth century and was evidently a rendezvous of many European merchants during the thirteenth and fourteenth centuries, for the monk Odoric de Pordenone informs us in his *Travels* that he found there "a house and a convent of our minor friars" and also that "in this city one finds all things necessary for the bodies [i.e., food, clothing, and lodgings] of Christians."

In view of the importance of Yang Chou and Marco's residence there, it is surprising that he devotes but one short paragraph to the city. We are informed tersely that its inhabitants "live by

---

[15] Almagià calls attention to the fact that this part of the description reads like a diary. It may well be that the traveler followed the notes which he had sent him from Venice to his prison in Genoa, where the book was written.

[16] See Pelliot, *op. cit.*, II, 833 (No. 338) and 875 (No. 383). Although some manuscripts state that Marco was a governor in Yang Chou for three years, this assertion is extremely doubtful. In fact, some of the manuscripts omit entirely any reference to his service in Yang Chou. As ably argued by Olschki, *op. cit.*, 174n., he was a foreigner, young (under thirty), and would not have been appointed governor of a newly conquered province—hardly pacified, and occupied by a garrison, probably under a high-ranking Mongol officer. Perhaps, as Pelliot and Almagià suggest, he was an inspector or comparable functionary, perhaps in the salt gabelle.

trades and crafts," especially in the manufacture of arms and armor. That is all, followed by the remark that "there is nothing else worth mentioning." This failure to give a more detailed description of a great city where an estimated 250,000 or more families lived at the time is one of the unexplained lacunae in the Polo narrative.

Continuing his account, the Venetian describes the Yangtse River most vividly as "the greatest river that is in the world . . . and it is in some places ten miles broad, and in some eight and in some (the most narrow) six, and pursuing its course it is more than one hundred and twenty days' journeys long before it enters the sea . . . moreover I tell you that by this river one goes so far and through so many regions, and there are so many cities upon it that I tell you truly that more boats loaded with more dear things and of greater value go and come by this river than go by all the rivers of Christians together nor by all their seas." It was, in fact, the greatest river ever seen by any European prior to the discovery of the Americas. Marco was amazed at its size, remarking that it was "so broad that it does not seem to be a river." He discusses the vast amount of shipping on the river, describes the river junks in great detail and the towing of boats upstream by means of ropes of twisted bamboo strips (he calls bamboo "canes")—a practice still followed on the upper reaches of the great river.

Several paragraphs are devoted to Soochow and many pages to Hangchow in Chekiang Province, perhaps the world's largest city in the time of Kublai Khan.[17] In fact, the space given to a discussion of Hangchow occupies about 4 per cent of Marco Polo's book, and one of the chapters devoted to the city is the longest in the entire narrative. The traveler obtained much of his information about Hangchow "according to the written statement which the queen of this realm (Manzi,[18] of which Hang Chou was the

[17] Yule, 3d ed., Vol. II.
[18] Cathay (spelled in many ways) indicates, in Marco Polo's book, North China, down to the region of the Yangtse River. Manzi (or Mangi) is the name he uses for South China, more properly the territory held by the Sung Dynasty in its later years, when it had been forced farther and farther south by the Mongol invasion—an invasion which finally resulted in the conquest of the entire country. *Man Tzu* means really "the sons of barbarians."

capital) sent to Bayan, the conqueror of the country, for transmission to the Great Kaan, in order that he might be aware of the surpassing grandeur of the city and might be moved to save it from destruction or injury. I will tell you all the truth as it was set down in that document, and that letter I Marc saw and read. For truth it was, as the said Messer Marco at a later date was able to witness with his own eyes."

After giving his description of the city, Polo states that "all this account was given me by a very rich merchant of Kinsay[19] when I was in that city. He was a very old man . . . and was pleased to be my guide over it."

The description of Hangchow, enthusiastic as it is, is but a faint echo of the praises voiced by generations of Chinese writers, who never wearied of singing the beauties and glories of both Soochow and Hangchow in prose and in verse, and one of the best-known Chinese sayings is *"Shang, T'ien t'ang, hsia, Su Hang."* ("Above, the halls of Heaven; below, Soochow and Hangchow.) The women of Soochow have been famed down through the centuries as the most beautiful in all China. Even the boatmen on its canals have been entranced by them, as in the "Song of Soochow" by Chang Min Piao:

> *A boat goes by,*
> *Poling slowly to the east.*
> *Another comes,*
> *Faring its way to the west.*
> *The passing boatmen*
> *Heed not each other;*
> *They have eyes only*
> *For the girls of Ku Su T'ai.*[20]

We are given a full description of the Western Lake of Hangchow and of its pleasure boats and the parties and feasts given

[19] Polo calls the city Quinsai. The origin and meaning of the word are obscure. See Pelliot, *op. cit.*, II, 817 (No. 323).

[20] Hart, *A Garden of Peonies*. Ku Su T'ai was the terrace at Soochow's waterside, where the "green houses" stood, and where the young women were wont to exhibit themselves, walk up and down, soliciting and enticing strangers into their abodes.

thereon. These are so detailed and vivid that the Venetian must have been there himself, and, too, seems to write of it all nostalgically.

The baths of the city and the cleanliness of the streets are also noted, and Marco surely was comparing them with the muddy, ill-kept streets of Europe when he wrote, "You may know quite truly that all the ways and streets in all this town of Quinsai are well paved with good hewn stones and with baked bricks, so that the whole city is very clean; and so are all the chief ways and streets and the causeways of all the provinces of Mangi paved so that one can ride at any time conveniently wherever one wishes quite cleanly both on horseback and on foot through all the lands of it without soiling the feet."[21]

Marco, too, pays his tribute to the beauty and gentility of Hangchow's women, as witness the testimony of Ramusio and some of the other editions of Marco Polo:

> And their ladies and wives are also most delicate and angelique things, and raised gently, and with great delicacy, and they clothe themselves with so many ornaments of silk and of jewels, that the value of them cannot be estimated. . . . And they love one the other in such a manner that a district of the city, because of the amiability which exists among the men and the women of the neighborhood, may be counted as a single household. So great is the familiarity that it exists among them with no jealousy or suspicion of their women, for whom they have the greatest respect, and he would be considered a most infamous person who would dare to address improper words to a married woman.

Ramusio has preserved an interesting note not appearing in other early editions:

> In other streets dwell the *donne da partido* (courtesans) in such numbers that I would not dare state it. . . . And they live in a most showy manner, with great perfumes and many maidservants, and the houses all adorned. These women are very clever and versed in

[21] Odoric de Pordenone, Ibn Battuta, and the Jesuit Martinus Martini, in his great *Atlas of China* (1654–55) unite with Marco Polo in their description and praise of Hangchow.

knowing how to flatter, and caressing with ready words, and suited to every kind of person, in such fashion that foreigners who have once partaken of their favors remain, as it were, in a sort of ecstasy, and so much are they taken by their sweetness and charm that they can never forget them. And from this it happens that when they return home they say they have been in Quinsai, that is, in the city of Heaven, and cannot [wait to] see the hour when they may again return there.

It is in speaking of Hangchow, too, that Marco gives us further interesting details of Chinese life, some of them customs peculiar to that city, others prevalent throughout the Empire. The Great Khan tolerated neither beggars nor vagabonds in Hangchow, for if the city guards "by day . . . see any poor man who because of being crippled cannot work, they make him go to stay in the hospitals, of which there is an infinitely large number throughout the city, built by the ancient kings, [and] which have great incomes. And if he be sound of body they compel him to do some work."

Another custom of the people of Hangchow, one which Marco asserted was followed throughout China, rendered the locating of any citizen comparatively easy and facilitated the taking of the census. Each person inscribed over the door his own name and the names of members of his family and slaves, as well as the number of horses owned by him. Names of deceased persons were erased and those of newborn children added. Another statute required innkeepers to write on the doors of their houses the names of all who came to lodge with them, with the date of their arrival and the day and the hour of their departure, so that the officers of the law could know the whereabouts of all travelers throughout the land. "And," adds Marco, "this is a good thing, and one that befits wise men."

After describing Hangchow and the surrounding district, many entertaining details are given of Fukien province. Of these the most interesting is the sketch of a numerous Christian sect then living in the province. It is not only of value in itself, but it throws light on Marco's extensive wanderings in the domain of the Great Khan which are not mentioned elsewhere. The description begins with the statement that the discovery of these Christians was made "when indeed Master Maffeo, uncle of Master Marco Polo, and Master Marco himself were in the said city of Foochow and in their company a certain wise Saracen."

That the Venetian was speaking, as far as China was concerned, largely from personal observation and experience is manifest in his frank and honest statement.

We have not indeed told you of all the nine kingdoms of Mangi but only of three, avoiding the weariness of long talking., these are Yangiu and Quinsai and Fugiu [Yangchow, Hangchow, and Foochow], and of these you have well understood. Of these three, however, we have told thus in order because Master Marc made his passage through them, for his way was directed thither. But of the other six he heard and learned many things, and we should know well how to tell you of them., but because he was not in any of them . . . and because he did not travel over them, he would not have been able to tell so fully as about the others. Wherefore because it would be too long an affair to mention, we shall be silent about them now. . . . For we have told you well and sufficiently of the province in general and of a portion in particular, namely of Mangi, and of the nature of the province of Catai we have told generally and in particular orderly enough, according to what we were able to learn, and of many other provinces as our book tells you of them all clearly and in right order and one after the other and without mistake, and of the people and of the beasts and of birds . . . and of the sorts of all the merchandise . . . and of many other things and of the manners and customs of the people, just as you have heard according to what you were able to understand.

At this point Marco Polo terminates his discursive description of China, its people, government, religions, economic life, manners, and customs.

His frequent journeyings to and fro in the land, his government service and traveling on his own or his relatives' behalf were apparently unceasing from the time of his first arrival at the court of the Great Khan. The boy who had left Venice had become a youth, and the youth had developed into a man, intelligent, alert, lf-reliant, and wise in the ways of the world. Seventeen long years had slipped by since they had arrived in the Mongol capital, and the Venetians began to long for home. After all, they were strangers in a strange land, and, happy though the years had been, bringing riches and high honors, memories of far-away Venice must have haunted their dreams.

Other, more material considerations which made a departure from Cambaluc advisable surely weighed heavily with them also, causing them to seek a plan by which they could leave the East and return to Italy and their families. They had found great preferment at the hands of the all-powerful Kublai and had waxed wealthy and powerful in his service, but the sunshine of the imperial favor must have bred envy of them and their good fortune, and the number of their ill-wishers could not have been small. Moreover, the great Kublai was growing older and more feeble, and they dreaded his approaching end. Their experience and observation had taught them that with his passing the strong wall of his protection would fall. They, especially as foreigners, would be helpless in the presence of their foes, and their accumulated or supposed wealth would mark them more certainly as victims, once their sovereign lord had "mounted on high on the dragon."

That this fear was not without good foundation is attested by Francesco Pegolotti, who in 1340 in his *Practica della Mercatura* warned the prospective traveler to China that one of the dangers of the journey was that "when the lord [Khan of the Mongols] dies, and until the other lord who should rule is proclaimed, in this interim sometimes irregular acts have been done to the Franks and to other foreigners. . . . And the road will not be safe until the other lord who is to reign in the place of him who is dead is proclaimed."

The departure of the Polos from the court of Cathay was not to be as easy as their arrival there after the difficulties and trials of their journey eastward, for now apparently a network of interests bound them close to the Mongol throne. On their way to Kublai's court the Tatar peace and an imperial escort guaranteed their safety. But now the Venetians feared, with good reason, that rebellion and chaos might sweep over all the dominions of the Mongols once the firm hand that controlled from Cambaluc was relaxed in death. Then the caravan routes would once more be beset with a hundred perils, and even if they succeeded in leaving the court, it would be very doubtful that they could escape the multiple dangers that would threaten on the long journey to the West. As Marco wrote in his book, "Though they found themselves very rich in jewels of great value and in gold, an extreme desire to see their native land again was always fixed in their mind, and even though they were honored and favored, they thought of nothing else but of this. And seeing that the Great Kaan was very old, they feared that if he were to die before their departure, they might never be able to return home, because of the length of the way and infinite perils which threatened them., though they hoped to be able to do this if he were alive."

Ever wise, ever shrewd, well versed in the moods of the aged Emperor, the elder Polos bided their time.

> And so Messer Nicolo one day, seeing the Great Khan in high good humor, seized the occasion, and, on bended knee begged him, in the name of all three, for permission to depart. At these words he [the Emperor] was much disturbed. And he spoke to him, asking him what reason moved him to desire to set out on such a long and perilous journey, during which they could all easily die. And if it were because of wealth [goods] or of anything else, he would gladly give them the double of what they had at their home, and heap upon them as many honors as they might desire. And, for the great love which he bore them, he refused them flatly the right to depart, saying, "On no condition in the world am I willing that you depart from my realm, but I am well content that you go about it where you please."

A Venetian manuscript records a further plea by Messer Nicolo. He assured the Great Khan that he did not desire to leave for want of gold, "but it is because in my land I have a wife and by the Christian law I cannot forsake her while she lives." This from the man who had remained away from home on his first journey fifteen years in the pursuit of gain, and who, after he had taken unto himself a second wife on his return to Venice, had left her after two short years to answer the call of the East, and who had bestirred himself with thoughts of his homeland only after a life of riches and honor for seventeen years in China—and then seemingly from motives of personal safety!

But the Great Khan was obdurate—perhaps he saw through the flimsy pretext—and refused again. We are given no reason for this harsh ruling except, as reiterated by Marco, that "the Great Khan loved them so much." Repeated petitions met the same refusal.

But again the good fortune which seemed ever to watch over the Polos rescued them in this dire emergency. It came in an altogether unforeseen and unexpected manner, and just at the right moment, too. When they could least foresee it, fate placed in their hands the long and eagerly awaited opportunity to return to Venice.

·V·
Homeward Bound

I believe that the earth is of vast extent and we who dwell between the Phasis and the Pillars of Heracles inhabit but a small portion of it . . . and I believe that many other men dwell in similar places.—Plato, *Phaedo.*

Such other innumerable and marueilous thinges, writeth Paulus uenetus that he hath sene and founde in his nauigacions into these parts: of whom also I have gathered thus muche, lettinge passe manye other things whereof he speaketh more at large. —Rycharde Eden, *A Treatise of the newe India.*

THE VAST EMPIRE of the Mongols was, in the latter part of the thirteenth century, very loosely knit, and the direct descendants of the great Genghis held only a vague sovereignty over many vassal states and virtually independent territories only through ties of marriage. The giving of a princess royal (in many instances adopted) was often the only political bond between outlying parts of the empire and the capital.

Death had robbed Argon Khan[1] of Persia, grandnephew of the great Kublai, of his wife Bolgana. According to a strange custom of the Mongol-Persians, the Khan on ascending the throne took his mother to wife. Thus the deceased Lady Bolgana was both mother and wife to Argon. Of Mongol lineage, "This Queene ordeyred in hir testamente, that hyr Husbande shoulde not marrie, but with one of hyr bloud and kynred." She died April 7, 1286, and shortly thereafter Argon dispatched three envoys, Uladai, Apusca, and Coja, to his great-uncle in Cambaluc with the petition that he select and send him a wife of the line of the deceased Bolgana.

> And when the three barons were come to the great Kaan then they told him their message and the reason why they were come from Argon. The great Kaan received them most honorably and made great joy and great feasting for them. Then since King Argon was his very great friend he sent for a lady who had Cocacin for name who was of the lineage which they desired of that queen Bolgana who was dead, who was a girl of seventeen, a noble lady fair and amiable.[2]

Cocacin was presented to the three ambassadors as the one designated to take the place of the deceased Queen Bolgana. The envoys were well pleased with Kublai's choice and prepared to depart overland with her on the long return journey to Persia.

Leaving the city of Cambaluc, escorted by a great retinue that Argon sent to do honor to his new bride, the caravan crossed the Great Wall and started with its precious charge on its long and arduous journey over the desert highway to Persia by which they had come to the court of the Great Khan. Many weary months dragged by en route, and the envoys were looking forward with joy to beholding their homes again when war suddenly flared up among the Tatar tribes of central Asia, and attacks on travelers

---

[1] Spelled in thirteen different ways in the manuscripts, the commonest variant being Arghun, son of Abaqa (son of Hulaku) and the Khatun (Lady) Bolgana, of the Bayant tribe, succeeded his father in 1284. See Wallis Budge, *The Monks of Kublai Khan*.

[2] Cocacin (also pronounced Cocachin), "the whyche was verye fayre," was a Bayant, like Bolgana. Her name is Mongol, from *Koke*—blue and *jin*—like. Thus the name means "like the blue of heaven" or "celestial."

and raids on towns along the caravan route inevitably followed. The ambassadors found it impossible to continue on their way, and were forced to turn back to China. After eight months' absence they again beheld against the sky the crenelated walls and high towers of Cambaluc. Once more the cortege wound its way through the streets of the capital city, which the Persians had not expected to see again, and a second time they sought and obtained an audience with the Khan of all the Mongols.

Kublai heard the tale of the dangerous journey and its unfortunate interruption and was sorely perplexed as to how he could send the maid, Cocacin, with speed and safety to his kinsman in distant Persia. By a stroke of good fortune Messer Marco had just returned from an expedition by sea to India "as the Lord's ambassador"—one manuscript states that he was accompanied by his father and uncle—and had made a detailed report to the Great Khan concerning his mission and all the peoples and things he had observed en route. At that time the three "barons" saw the Venetians "and had great wonder" because of their wisdom. They were particularly interested because they believed that the Polos must have knowledge of the sea route for at least part of the way to their own country of Persia.

A carefully devised scheme was speedily worked out between the Venetians and the Persians. The former were shrewd enough to see in the predicament of the envoys the long-sought opportunity to return to their home. The officers of Argon on their side perceived a way of reaching their home by sea, thus avoiding the necessity of waiting an indefinite time at Kublai's court until the land route should be safe enough for their return by caravan. They had already been on their journey three years, and had no stomach for further delays.

The Persians and the Polos thus found their interests were identical, and after much discussion it was agreed that the envoys and Cocacin should present themselves before the Great Khan and point out that it was far safer to proceed to Persia by sea than by land. Moreover, they were to point out that the journey would be both cheaper and shorter by water than by caravan. Finally,

143

and most important to the Venetians, the envoys were to ask that the Polos be ordered to accompany them "to the lands of the lord Argon" because of their knowledge and experience in sailing the southern seas, "and especially Messer Marco." Moreover, the sending of such prominent men as the Venetians would show that much honor was being paid Argon, lord of Persia, by his great-uncle, Kublai.

The Great Khan "showed great displeasure on his countenance" at their request, for the three Latins were of real value to him because of their ability and wide experience in his service. (Their usefulness to him is far more likely to have been the reason for his desire to retain them than "the great love" which Marco repeatedly says he bore them.) Argon, however, was a powerful ruler, one whom Kublai could ill afford to offend or neglect. In fact, Marco (in the Ramusio version) frankly admits that "as he could not do otherwise, he consented to as much as they requested of him, and had not the reason been so great and cogent that compelled him, never would the said Latins have departed."

Kublai then summoned to his presence Marco, his father, and his uncle, "and spoke to them many gracious words of the great love which he bore them, and that they should promise that when they had been some time in the land of Christians and at their home they would return to him, & gives them two tablets of gold[3] sealed with the royal seal with orders written thereon that they should be free and exempt from every burden & secure through all his lands, and wherever they might go they must have the expenses for themselves and for all their train, and an escort given them that they may be able to pass in safety. He entrusts them with many things on his own behalf & with an embassy to the Apostle and to the King of France and to the King of England and to the King of Spain and to the other crowned Kings of Christendom."

[3] It is likely that three golden "tablets of command" were possessed by the Polos, one given to the two brothers on their first journey by Kublai and the two mentioned here. They were, on the return of the travelers to Venice, given into the custody of Maffeo, who speaks in his will of "three tablets of gold, which were of the great Khan of the Tatars." There is reason to believe (Moule and Pelliot, I, 555) that they are listed in the inventory of Marco Polo's goods bequeathed to his daughters.

By command of the Khan, fourteen great ships were fitted out for the expedition, probably at Zaiton (Ch 'üan Chou), each having four masts and such a spread of sails that they were a marvel to Marco Polo as to all medieval travelers to the Far East. He was so impressed by "the great ships in which merchants go and come into India by sea" that he has given a full and very interesting description of them.

The ships were built of fir and pine, and, though they had but one deck, the larger vessels contained as many as sixty cabins "where in each a merchant can stay comfortably." In this description appears the first mention of water-tight compartments in ships, a device seemingly unknown to European shipbuilders until modern times. The larger ships had thirteen divisions in their holds, made of closely fitted planks, "so that if it happens by accident that the ship is staved in any place, namely that it either strikes on a rock or a whale fish striking against it in search of food staves it in. And this often happens, for if the ship sailing by night making the water ripple passes near a whale, the whale seeing the water glisten as it is moved thinks that there will be food for it, and moving quickly forward strikes against the ship and often staves the ship in some part of it. And then the water entering through the hole runs to the bilge, which never remains occupied with anything. And then the sailors find out where the ship is staved, and then the hold which answers to the break is emptied into others, for the water cannot pass from one hold to another, so strongly are they shut in, and then they repair the ship there and put back there the goods which had been taken out."

Polo then describes the methods of putting the ships together and caulking them. The ships were manned according to their size by up to three hundred sailors, and this and other statements made by him and by other travelers of the period indicate that these far-voyaging Chinese vessels were far larger than the ships then used in European sea-borne commerce and confirm similar information left by Odoric de Pordenone, Friar Jordanus, and other travelers. Ibn Battuta, in his description of Chinese shipping, states that the largest junks—the ships were called "junks" or "gonk" as early as his time—carried "six hundred sailors and four hundred warriors. . . . The sailors have their children who live in the cabins, and they sow kitchen herbs, vegetables, and ginger in tubs of wood. . . . The captain of the ship resembles a great emir; when he disembarks the archers and Abyssinians [African slaves?] march before him with spears, swords, drums, horns, and trumpets."[4]

Before describing the long voyage from China to Persia, with notes on the islands and countries visited en route, Marco devotes an entire chapter to Japan. He did not visit the islands himself, and his account of the country, which he called Cipingu, is a farrago of fact and fancy which need not detain us long here. Suffice it to note that he placed the islands on the high seas fifteen hundred miles from the mainland of China. "The people are white. They have much gold, in fact the roof of the palace of their king is covered with plates of gold and the floors within are of gold tiles two fingers thick. And great pearls of red and white colors abound, so that the dead are buried each with a pearl in his mouth." These are some of the stories which fired Columbus with such zeal for discovery that he carried a copy of Marco Polo (which is still in existence with copious marginal notes in his own handwriting) with him on his first voyage. Of course the incorrect distances noted by Marco Polo upset all his calculations and conjectures about locations and mileages.

Following the fantastic description of the islanders we are given a hasty sketch of Kublai Khan's historic efforts to subdue the Japanese in several successive expeditions, the last one terminated in its preliminary stages only by his death.[5] Again in this story of the defeat of the Mongols Marco weaves a tale of men who could not be wounded by the sword because of the magical protection afforded them by certain precious stones inserted in the right arm between skin and flesh. And this stone, "enchanted by the devil's art," rendered them immune from death or wound by iron. Their

---

[4] No rudders were used until the time of Columbus, steering being done by one or two large oars.

[5] A very full and interesting account of this unsuccessful effort of the Mongols to bring Japan under their domination will be found in Nakaba Yamada, *Ghenko: The Mongol Invasion of Japan* (John Murray, London, 1916).

precious stones availed them nothing, however, for "the barons caused them to be beaten with clubs of thick wood, and they died at once." Friar Odoric tells of the same custom in one of the islands of the Indies (Borneo?), where, he says, certain stones are found in reeds that grow along the ground: "And they take their sons and cut deep wounds in their arms, and in these wounds they place these stones . . . and by virtue of these stones . . . they know that iron cannot injure them."

The account ends with a characteristic note by Marco Polo: "Now henceforth we will leave this country so that I will tell you no more of this country . . . particularly because they are too much out of the way and also because we were not there . . . and so we will go back to Zaiton and from there we will begin our book again."

The first country described by the Venetian after sailing from China was the kingdom of Champa (in Vietnam), a tributary to Kublai Khan. He states that he had visited the kingdom[6] earlier in his Chinese career and learned that the aged king had 326 children of both sexes, of whom more than 150 were men capable of bearing arms.[7]

The account given of Java and the other islands passed on the voyage to Sumatra need not detain us. The ships made a lengthy stay at different ports of that island, called by Marco Polo "Java the Less," and several pages are devoted to it, his information indicating that he visited six of the many kingdoms into which Sumatra was then divided. He was astonished to find that the island lay so far to the south that the North Star "is not seen there neither little nor much." He found many of the inhabitants of the kingdom of Ferlek (Parlak) all converted "to the abominable law of Mahomet" and the pagans in the mountainous regions eaters of human flesh.[8] In Basman he saw the rhinoceros (which he, familiar

---

[6] Champa occupied the middle and lower part of present Vietnam.

[7] This statement is corroborated by Odoric de Pordenone (Cordier, *Odoric de Pordenone*, 187ff.; Yule, *Cathay*, II, 161 f.) The Chinese emperor K'ang Hsi had twenty-four sons, and Ch'ien Lung abdicated in favor of his fifteenth son.

[8] Azurara, II, 146 and 330n., used a ms. of Polo to corroborate his story of cannibals "in those Eastern parts."

with the bestiaries and pictures of mythical animals current in Europe, calls a unicorn). From his careful, detailed description he must have seen them personally and been close to them. He observed that the animal "always carries its head bent toward the ground."[9] We are assured that they (the rhinoceroses) "are not so as we here [in Europe] say and describe, who say that it lets itself be caught in the lap by a virgin girl."

At this point Marco Polo waxes so wroth over the deceptions of the Arabs and other traders who offered for sale in Europe preserved bodies which they represented as the mummies of a pigmy people that he describes the whole process of preparing them:

> And we shall tell the method. On this island there is a type of monkey which is very small, and they have faces like the faces of men. And when the men capture them, they remove all the hair from them with a certain unguent and fix certain long hairs on their chin in place of a beard, and while the skin is drying, the openings where the hairs are fixed shrink so that it appears as though they had grown there naturally. And the feet and hands and other members which do not conform to human members they stretch and shorten and by handling make conform to human likeness. And then they cause them to be dried, and then they treat them with camphor and other things so that they appear to have been men. And they sell them to merchants, who carry them throughout the world and cause men to believe that they are such small men. And this is a great deception [deceverie], for they are made in such fashion as you have heard. For not in all India nor in any other more savage parts were there ever seen men so small as those appear to be.[10]

From a description of Basman he passes to that of the kingdom

[9] This is particularly true of the "white," or square-lipped, rhinoceros of Africa. A grazing animal, it cannot raise its head as can its congener, the "black" rhinoceros, which has a prehensile, forward-curved upper lip, can hold its head erect, and is a browsing animal. The two types are not really different in color, "white" being probably a corruption of the Afrikaans "wyd moud" (broad-mouthed). The white rhinoceros, the scarcer of the two types, is a far gentler and more placid animal than its cousin. See Maberly, *The Game Animals of Southern Africa*, and J. Stevenson-Hamilton, *Wild Life in South Africa*.

[10] In his notes on Sumatra, Marco Polo gives us the place and the earliest date of the introduction of Islam into Indonesia. See Vlekke, p. 51.

of Sumatra, which name had not yet spread to the entire island. There the expedition was detained for five months because of bad weather and contrary winds. For fear "of beasts and of those bad beastlike men who gladly catch and kill and eat men," Marco and those with him built "five towers or castles of beams and logs, surrounded by ditches, and in those castles we stayed thus with our people for the greater part of five months." We are informed that the plentiful fish in the region "are the best which may be found in the world" and learn of the method of making palm wine, and of the coconut and its uses as food and drink.

The cannibalistic habits of the people of Dagroian are presented in gruesome detail, and an account is given of the tailed men (probably orangutans, the long-armed anthropoid apes of Borneo and Sumatra). More interesting is the description of the sago palm (or cycad) and the method of obtaining its flour. And, adds Marco, "we often ate them. And I took some of this to Venese with me."

The ships finally departed from Java the Less and passed near the Andaman Islands, whose inhabitants, according to the Polo account, had heads and features like dogs and indulged in cannibalism.[11]

Continuing on its route, the expedition reached Ceylon, where a landing was made and where Marco beheld "the largest ruby that is to be found in all the world."[12]

[11] The anthropophagy and other unpleasant traits of the Andaman Islanders are affirmed by Chau Ju-Kua, p. 147.

[12] The story of this ruby was current throughout the East in the Middle Ages. Friar Jordanus, who visited the Far East in 1321-24, tells of two rubies owned by the King of Ceylon: "He wears one of them hung around his neck, and the other [he carries] in the hand with which he wipes his lips and his beard. And it [the ruby] is longer than it is broad, and when it is held in the hand it can be seen a finger's breadth on either side." Hsüan Tsang, the Chinese pilgrim-monk, records that on the top of the pagoda of the Sacred Tooth of the Buddha in Kandy there was an arrow surmounted by a stone of great value, called "Padmarâga" (ruby). This precious stone, he stated, constantly gives forth a brilliant flashing light, and, gazing on it from afar by day or by night, one would believe that he was gazing at a luminous star. (Note: The present author, on a recent visit to Kandy, could learn nothing of such a ruby). It will be recalled by readers of the *Thousand and One Nights* that when Sinbad the Sailor visited Sarandib (Ceylon) on his sixth voyage, the king presented to him a ruby cup a span high, adorned inside with precious pearls.

He tells his readers that Kublai Khan desired to buy the ruby, and offered "the value of a city" for it. The king refused all offers. So, continues the Venetian, "with this answer and without the ruby the ambassadors returned to their master. And I, Marc Pol, was one of the ambassadors and saw the said ruby with my eyes, and when that lord was holding it in his closed hand it projected below and above the fist, the which lord put it to his eyes and to his mouth."[13]

Polo next speaks of Adam's Peak in Ceylon, and the chains, climbing which pilgrims reach the top of the precipitous cliff to visit the sepulcher of Adam.[14]

From Ceylon the ships proceeded to the mainland of India, touching first on the Malabar (southwest) Coast. There Marco visited and described the pearl fisheries in detail. The industry seems to have changed its methods but little since he wrote of it 650 years ago. The Hindu princes with their retinues and attendants, their wives and concubines, their practice of burning the dead, suttee, self-decapitation with a two-handled curved knife, the sacredness of the cow, and the noneating of beef—these and many more customs of the Indian peoples are described in fascinating detail, the more interesting since many of these customs still survive in whole or in part in various parts of India.

Interspersed with this more or less impersonal account are anecdotes of Messer Marco's own adventures among the people. One delightful remark is about testimony: "He who drinks wine is not accepted as a witness, nor is he who navigates upon the sea. For they say that [a drinker of wine] or he who navigates upon the sea is a desperate fellow and therefore they do not receive him as a witness or place any value on his testimony."

The detailed descriptions of some of the religions and super-

[13] "The King (of Ceylon) holds in his hand a jewel five inches in diameter, which cannot be burnt by fire . . . the king rubs his face with it daily, and though he were passed ninety he would retain his youthful looks."—Chau Ju-Kua, 73. See also *Cosmos Indicopleustes*, Bk. XI.

[14] The pilgrims use the links of the chains as stirrups by which to ascend the cliff. It is not known when or by whom the chains were placed. They are mentioned in the earliest records of Ceylon, also by Ibn Battuta (Gibbs, one-vol. ed., 258). The chains are still in existence. *Ibid.*, 364n.

stitions of the country, the nautch girls, the "brides" of the temples (many of these matters found only in the Zelada manuscript) have preserved most valuable records of medieval customs of southern India. One interesting paragraph describes the method of placating a god who is vexed or angry with his *sakti*.[15]

> Then indeed the aforesaid maidens [i.e., the nautch girls] go to the monastery in the aforesaid manner, and they are all of them naked except that they cover their natural parts, and they sing before the god and goddess . . . and then those maidens come thither to pacify them [the gods] and when they are there they sing, dance, leap about, and tumble and make various diversions . . . and the maiden [who has addressed the god] . . . will lift her leg above her neck and will execute a spin about . . . and when they (the gods) have been mollified enough they go home. . . . Indeed those maidens [while they are maidens] are so firm of flesh that none can in any way seize them or pinch them in any part. And for a small coin [denaro] they will allow a man to pinch them as much as he is able. When they are married they are then also firm of flesh, but not so much.

Messer Marco's eyes missed nothing.

In spite of his acute powers of observation and his shrewd judgment, the Venetian was sometimes "taken in" by weird tales, as in his sober explanation of why the skins of the natives of southern India are dark. According to one of the manuscripts, he solemnly asseverates that when the Indian infants are born they are fair, but their parents anoint them weekly with sesame oil, so that they become *"si noirs comme dyables"* ["as black as devils"].

Returning again to a discussion about Ceylon, Marco gives in some detail an account of the life and ministry of the Buddha, whom he calls Sagamoni Burcan (Sakyamuni Buddha).[16] He evidently found the tale most fascinating, for his account is lengthy and circumstantial, indicating a genuine interest on the part of the narrator. He is, moreover, most broadminded and generous (and

---

[15] *Sakti*: the wife or the female energy of a deity, especially of Siva—Dowson, *A Classical Dictionary of Hindu Mythology.*

[16] Sakya-muni—the sage of the Sakya clan or tribe. "Burcan" is Uigur and Mongol for "Buddha."

courageous in view of the religious ideas and beliefs of his age) in his estimate of the character of the great teacher. He speaks of him gently and with reverence, and declares (most boldly for a European of the thirteenth century): "For truly if he had been baptized Christian he would have been a great saint with our Lord Jesus Christ for the good life and pure which he led." The good Messer Marco did not know that a century before his time the Buddha had already been canonized in the Church under the name of Saint Josaphat of India, and that his date in the ecclesiastical calendar was November 27.

A chapter of Polo's book is devoted to the mythical "male and female" islands. The fable is one that is very ancient in origin and is seemingly a variant of the age-old legend of the Amazons, which was accepted even by Sir Walter Raleigh more than three hundred years later than Marco Polo and which is related extensively, with much of the same details as in the Polian tale, as truth in his "Discoverie . . . of Guiana." Indeed it was the story as told by him that gave the Amazon River its name.[17]

Ambergris is mentioned as one of the products of the islands of the Indian Ocean, and the statement that it is found in the belly of the whale—a fact proved correct by science—and the frequency of his references to it as an article of commerce indicate that there must have been a considerable traffic in it in his day. There is no early evidence of the employment of this pathological intestinal secretion of the whale in the manufacture of perfumes, but other medieval uses of it are well attested. The Chinese called it "lung yen"—dragon's saliva. It was in great demand among them as a medicine, chiefly as an aphrodisiac. The Hindus sought it for the same purpose, and Burton found it so taken by the Arabs of the African coast, mixed in their coffee.[18] Medieval Arab medicine held it also as a valuable heart stimulant as well as a distinct and

[17] Pelliot, in Vol. II of his Notes on Marco Polo, No. 23, devotes fifty-four pages to the subject. See also Rothery, *The Amazons*, a book devoted entirely to tracing the Amazon stories throughout the world, and Raleigh, *The Discoverie . . . of Guiana*, Argonaut Press ed., 26ff.

[18] Burton, *op. cit.*, VI, 69.

delectable flavor in their cuisine, and there was a time when Western medicine placed great faith in its therapeutic properties.

In Polo's chapter on the island of Socotra, placed by him about five hundred miles south of the "male and female" islands, the Zelada manuscript has preserved a long and very interesting description of the taking of whales by harpoon in the Indian Ocean. The methods of whaling seem to have differed in a few details only from those of modern times.

The next description of interest in the tale of what the three Venetians saw or learned is of a place they did not visit, the great island of Madagascar. Although it may be noted that Marco Polo is the first traveler who mentions and describes the island, the narration is full of errors, probably the result of the hearsay information on which he draws for his notes. He speaks of the entire population as "Saracens who adore Mohammed" and mentions lions, elephants, giraffes, camels, etc. Much of this information is either incorrect or an indication of a confusion in his mind of Madagascar with other African coastal regions about which he had been told. In discussing Madagascar he tells of the "grifons"—the mythical roc or rukh of the Arabian Nights—to which reference is made by numerous writers of medieval Europe, Asia, and Africa. Although the form of the tale would make it appear that Messer Marco had heard it, together with many others, from Arab seafarers, he informs us in all seriousness that the Great Khan himself sent messengers to inquire about the giant birds. He further states (according to one Venetian manuscript) that the messengers had brought a wing feather of the rukh to the Great Khan, and solemnly deposes that he, Marco Polo, measured it himself and found it ninety handbreadths long and two of his palms in circumference. What the object which he thus saw and measured with his own hands at the court of Kublai Khan actually was, we shall probably never know.

After the description of Madagascar and its wonders, the next notes of the traveler concern Zanzibar, a place most likely never seen or visited by him. It was a very important center of the ivory trade, as it still is. Marco's description of the African Negroes is so vivid that there is no doubt that he saw some of them in the course of his voyages:

> And they are all black and go naked (except for a small covering). . . . And they have their hair curly and black so like unto peppercorns that even with water could it hardly be straightened. They have so large a mouth and the nose so flat and turned up and the lips and the eyes so large and so bloodshot and so red that they are a very horrible thing to behold. . . . For whosoever should see them in another land would say of them that they are devils. And again I tell you that the women of this island are a most ugly thing to behold. For they have great mouths and large eyes and large noses. They have breasts four times as large as other ordinary women have, which adds the more to ugliness. They are black as a mulberry and of great stature.

Polo then bids farewell to Zanzibar with a most amusing, intimate, and altogether erroneous account of the love life of the elephant, a description of their employment in warfare, and how the natives make them drunk before taking them into battle.

The land next described is "Abasce [Abyssinia] which is called Ethiopia." Curiously enough it is designated as a part of "Middle India," a confusion which was common from the classic period down to the years when the various regions were finally explored and properly mapped.

In the discussion of Ethiopia there is a reference to "great ostriches not at all smaller than an ass." Since there is no more detailed description nor any indication of surprise, the Venetians of the period were probably well acquainted with the bird.[19]

The expedition (or what remained of it) was drawing near its destination, and the third division of Polo's book terminates with a summary sketch of Aden and the southern regions of Arabia.[20]

---

[19] There are references even in ancient times and in many lands to the ostrich. Job 39:13; *The History of the Earlier Han Dynasty* (*Chien Han Shu*), Chap. XCVI.; a drawing in the *Pên T'sao Kang Mu* (Chap. XLIX); a sixteenth-century Chinese pharmacopoeia, etc. See Bretschneider, *Medical Researches*, I, 144.

[20] Aden has been well known to Europe since ancient times, the earliest mention being in Ezekiel 27:23ff. Therein are mentioned its "merchants in all sorts

The final notation of the long voyage in Marco Polo's book consists of a short additional description of Hormuz,[21] the Persian seaport which the Polos had found distasteful and disappointing on the outward journey. Then follows (in some of the manuscripts) a fourth section of the narrative, introduced by the words "now I shall touch upon certain noble and especially fine provinces and regions which are in the farthest parts of the north, about which, for the sake of brevity, I omitted to tell in its proper place above in the first part of the book."

The opening pages of this section treat of several obscure wars of the Tatars, none of which adds much to the interest of the narrative or throws any light either on the Polos or on the lands visited by them. Following these pages is a description of Russia and Siberia.

Although there is no evidence whatsoever that any of the Polos visited these countries, the chapter is full of detail, partly accurate and partly quite erroneous. A large part of this account remained unknown until the discovery in 1936 of the Zelada manuscript. This source supplies (together with a rather scabrous story quite unworthy of Marco Polo, and perhaps not by his hand) some information on medieval Russian customs. After a further tale of some long-forgotten Tatar conflicts the Venetian ends his account very abruptly in all manuscripts except one early Tuscan version, which contains a long additional final paragraph possibly ascribable to some anonymous editor or translator. This paragraph reads:

> Now you have heard all the facts, as much as can be told of them, of the Tatars and of the Saracens, and of their customs, and of the other countries which are throughout the world, as much as is possible to search out and to know, except that of the Greater Sea we have spoken or said nothing, nor of the provinces which are around it, although we have visited it all well. Therefore I omit telling of it, for it appears to me that it would be wearisome to recount that which would be neither necessary nor useful, nor that which others know each day, for there are so many who explore

of things, in blue clothes." Many inhabitants of the region still wear clothes dyed blue with indigo.

[21] See pages 93 above and 157 below.

and navigate [on] it every day, as is well known, such as the Venetians and Genoese and Pisans and many other folk who make that voyage often, that everyone knows what is there, and therefore I remain silent and tell you nothing of that. Of our departure, how we took our leave of the Great Khan, you have heard in the beginning of the book in one chapter where it is told of the trouble and weary time which Messer Maffeo and Messer Nicolo and Messer Marco had in asking of the Great Khan permission to depart, and in that chapter is told the good fortune we had in our leaving. And know that if that good fortune had not come to pass, we should [not?] have ever gotten away [even] with great weariness and much trouble, so that hardly should we have ever returned to our country. But I believe that it was the pleasure of God, our return, in order that the things which are in the world might be known. For according to the account which we have given in the beginning of the book under the first title, there was never a man, either Christian or Saracen or Tatar or pagan, who ever explored so much of the world as did Messer Marco, a son of Messer Nicolo Polo, noble and great citizen of the city of Venice. Thanks to God . . . Amen, Amen.

Thus ends the story of Marco Polo's travels through Asia and the Indies, together with the descriptions of the people and countries visited by him or about which he heard.

For our knowledge of the arrival of the expedition in Persia and the subsequent adventures of the three Polos we must rely on the short and extremely meager account in the introductory chapters of Marco's book, supplemented by such information as may be gleaned elsewhere. He states: "I tell you that they sailed the sea of India a full eighteen months before the arrival there where they wished to go." The journey from China had consumed more than two years, and the travelers had suffered from adverse winds, storms, illness, and many other misfortunes which Marco, with his customary reticence about his trials and tribulations, omits to mention. These afflictions must have been many and grievous.

And I tell you without fail that when they entered into the ships in the land of the great Kaan they were between ladies and men

156

quite six hundred persons without the sailors. And when they reached the land [Persia] where they were going they made a count that they had all died on the way except only eighteen. And of those three ambassadors there remained but one, who was named Coja; and of all the women and girls none died but one.

The landing at Hormuz was far different from the earlier visit of the Venetians on their outward journey, when, for some un-revealed reason, they had changed their plans about sailing from Hormuz to China. Arriving now with the envoy from the Great Khan, they probably saw the city through rosier glasses. At this period there were constantly coming and going a great number of vessels—Chinese junks, Persian vessels of every kind and size, and swift Arab ships and dhows, which were gradually monopolizing the sea-borne traffic between the Red Sea, the Persian Gulf, and the African, Indian, and China coasts.

The streets of Hormuz were swarming with people from every corner of Asia, and now and then Europeans were to be seen—Genoese, Pisans, Venetians, and others. Every tongue of the East could be heard—Persian, Arabic, Indian, Chinese—for the main-land city, in these last days of its glory, was one of the busiest and most prosperous entrepôts of the sea trade between India, the Indies, and the Levant. Heaped high on the wharves and along the shores of the port, or drawn in carts and wagons with creaking wheels, slow-moving through the hot dusty narrow streets and market places were to be found the wares of Asia, the islands, Africa, and the Near East. There were spices, drugs and pepper, dates and raisins and sulphur, nutmeg and cloves, cinnamon and ginger, sandalwood and saffron, sugar, rice, mace, and camphor. The bazaars were heaped to overflowing with musk and rhubarb, turquoises and emeralds, rubies, sapphires and amethysts, topazes, hyacinths and zircons, porcelains, gum benzoin, and quicksilver. Traffic was brisk in brocades and silks, vermilion and attar of roses, pearls and chrysolites. From hand to hand passed rich cotton cloths and fine gauzes, daggers and knives and swords, all inlaid and decorated with gold and silver. And over the crowded streets and shops hung the acrid dust, the heavy odors of incense and sweltering humanity, of animals and garbage, which pervade every market town in the East—an odor once experienced never forgotten, an odor ever nostalgic to the traveler and the wanderer.

How the crowds must have amused him—the Persians, very white and fair, fat and luxurious, with their beautiful dark-eyed women, the dark Arabs from the Yemen and the desert, tall, thin, nervous, aquiline of nose, sharp of eye, often wearing proudly the green turban of a hadji, one who had made the ritual pilgrimage to Mecca. There were people of every color—tall tribesmen from Abyssinia, Copts from Egypt, Jews from every land, Hindus with their caste marks, Mongols from the steppes, and, to Marco like a glimpse from home, Chinese, as well as sailors gathered from every port between Canton and Alexandria, slaves, soldiers, water carriers, fruit vendors, and merchants.

The travelers were probably met by an escort of soldiers in long white cotton shirts, with thick sashes wound about their waists and wearing daggers and knives and heavy short swords. They were equipped with large round shields and powerful Turkish bows of hardwood, reinforced with laminated strips of buffalo horn. Some carried maces, others battle-axes, all inlaid or enameled.

Upon landing at Hormuz, the Venetians learned of many events which had taken place during their long absence. They were much distressed at the news that death had carried off Lord Arghun before they had sailed from Cathay, even that Arghun who had dispatched the three ambassadors from Persia to his kinsman Kublai to seek a wife to succeed Lady Bolgana. Princess Cocacin was bereft of her affianced bridegroom, and other disposition of her had to be arranged.

Arghun's brother Kaikhatu was ruling as regent in his stead for Arghun's young son, reportedly an insignificant-appearing youth but one well endowed with intelligence and energy. The remaining leaders of the expedition which had conducted Cocacin from China presented themselves before the sovereign "to whom it seemed right to send and to say how, having brought that queen by order of the king Argon, they would do whatever seemed to him right. He made answer to them that they ought to give her to

Casan (Ghazan), son of the king Argon." Ghazan was at the time away with his army guarding the passes on the Khorasan frontier. Indeed, the young girl was far more suited to be the wife of the youthful Ghazan than of his father. They were evidently satisfied with each other, for they were married shortly thereafter.[22]

There is a curious additional passage at this point in two of the oldest manuscripts of the narrative. This recites that (although there is no other mention of her in the tale), in addition to Cocacin, the Venetians had been entrusted with the daughter of the king of Manzi[23] (perhaps, it has been suggested, a daughter of the conquered Sung monarch) and that she, too, had been brought by them safely to Persia.

> Moreover I tell you that these two great ladies were in the care of these three messengers, for they caused them to be saved and protected as if they were their daughters and the ladies who were very young and fair took these three for their father and obeyed them so. And these three placed them in the hands of their lord. Moreover I tell you with all truth that the queen Cocacin . . . wishes so great good to the three messengers that there is not a thing she would not do for them as for her own father himself. For you may know that when these three messengers left her to return to their country she wept for grief at their departure. Now I have told you a thing which does well to rehearse, how much two such ladies were trusted to these three messengers to take to their lord from so far a place. Now we leave you this and will go on with your story.

So, in these few short, simple, unadorned, and dispassionate pages Marco Polo dismisses his account of what must have been a long and arduous voyage, one crowded with perils of shipwreck, hunger, thirst, heat, and the attacks of savage and unfriendly

---

[22] In 1295, Ghazan succeeded to the throne of his father after his uncle Kaikhatu had been slain in a revolt. His reign, though short, was one of distinction and progress for his nation. Cocacin unfortunately did not survive to enjoy her throne long. She died in 1296 just a short time after the time the Polos finally reached their home in Venice.

[23] Manzi—in Chinese, Man Tzu—southern barbarians, a name used also by Odoric de Pordenone, John Marignolli, and others. In the time of Marco Polo it probably referred to the Southern Sung people. See Couling, 326.

peoples. Nowhere else in the annals of discovery or exploration is there such a terse, impersonal record of so adventurous a journey by land or by sea. The entire story of the voyage with its vicissitudes and inconveniences is told in half a dozen pages, all in that quiet impassive fashion so characteristic of those portions of Marco's story which refer to his personal life or affairs.

This recital, which so briefly and so reticently tells of a journey with which many another traveler would fill a long, closely written volume—one probably plentifully sprinkled with the pronoun "I"—ends with the brief remark *"Et que vous en diroie?"* ("And what shall I tell you of it?").

After having safely delivered the Lady Cocacin into the hands of her future husband, Ghazan, the three Venetians returned to Kaikhatu, who was probably residing at the time in his city of Tabriz. The place was situated on their homeward route, so they most likely took advantage of its comparative security and comfort to recuperate from the trying sea journey.

We are nowhere informed why they postponed further their return to Venice, but we do know that their sojourn in Tabriz lasted nine months. One may make one or more of several conjectures. Perhaps they were retained by the regent Kaikhatu for reasons of state. Perhaps they were awaiting their goods or servants on other ships from China. Perhaps they were awaiting letters from Venice or elsewhere, or there was sickness amongst them. Mayhap the keenness of all three Polos for trade and bargaining made them unwilling to forgo another possible opportunity of adding to their capital or of exchanging bulky possessions for wealth which could be easily carried on their persons or more safely concealed from marauders. One may speculate on these or other reasons for the delay at Tabriz, but nothing certain is known, nor is the exact reason ever likely to be revealed after nearly seven hundred years.

One event of their stay has, however, been recorded. From a clause in Messer Maffeo's will we learn that his servant Marcheto died during the stay in the city and that he entrusted to Maffeo certain moneys to be taken by him back to Venice, a part for his natural son Mayço, a part for the boy's mother, one Juça.

Finally, however, the Polos decided to resume their journey toward Venice and appeared before Kaikhatu to bid him farewell. As part of the reward for their great services the regent presented to them "four golden tablets of authority," two decorated with gyrfalcons, one with the figure of a lion, and the fourth plain. And each "was a cubit long and five fingers wide, and weighed from twenty-four to thirty-two ounces." These tablets were worth far more to the Venetians than their mere weight in gold, for they bore inscriptions which notified all subjects of the Khan "that by the power of the eternal God the name of the Great Khan must be honored and praised for many years, and that every person who does not obey shall be put to death and his goods confiscated, and, moreover, that these three ambassadors should be honored and served throughout all the lands and countries as though they were his [the Khan's] own person, and that their expenses should be met, and horses given them, and such escorts as might be necessary."

These tablets proved to be of inestimable value to the Polos, for, adds Marco, "through the land they were treated most liberally, and were supplied with horses and all else required for the journey. Moreover, escorts, sometimes numbering over two hundred horse-men, accompanied them" through the parts of the country where danger threatened. This protection was the more necessary be-cause Kaikhatu's authority was not accepted unquestioningly in all parts of Persia and a strong guard was often needed to insure the safety of the merchants and their retinue.

It was perhaps during this part of their travels that the Venetians learned of the death of the great Kublai Khan. In the Ramusio version "while Masters Nicolau, Mafeu, and Marc were making this journey they learnt how the great Kaan was cut off from this life, and this took away from them all hope of being able to return any more to those parts."[24]

---

[24] That this information was brought to the Polos while on their homeward journey, or if they received it later, or ever, is questionable. Marco everywhere in

If this statement be true, the Polos must have congratulated themselves that they had escaped the evil fate which more than likely would have overtaken them had they remained longer in the Great Khan's service.

Their good fortune seems to have served them well once more and to have contrived their escape with their lives and property at a time when they had well-nigh given up hope of being able to return to the West again.

---

his book speaks of Kublai Khan as though he were alive when the book was compiled. It is one of the numerous difficulties in the Polo story which have not been elucidated, for the manuscripts differ and without doubt suffered the usual interpolations, excisions, revisions, etc., of the copyists and editors of the Middle Ages. Moreover, in some cases the statements of the manuscript reveal anachronisms which are at present inexplicable.

·VI·

From Tabriz to Venice

ONTINUAL PETTY WARFARE between Persia and Egypt rendered the caravan route from Tabriz to the Syrian coast impassable. The Sultan of Egypt at the moment held the Syrian seaports, from one of which the Polos had planned to take ship for Italy, and it would have been folly to proceed westward. They therefore chose the well-traveled caravan route which led through more northerly regions. This itinerary brought Marco into areas which he had not visited before, and his description of the country fills several interesting chapters of his book. As they progressed slowly toward the Euxine (the Black Sea), the Venetians crossed historic ground on each day's march—the battlefields of ancient empires and the sites of long-dead cities. They were now moving through lands (part of which were most likely familiar to the elder Polos) where, since the beginning of man's struggle against man, the East had come into contact—often accompanied by violence—with the West, and where one merged into the other.

Although Marco had probably never heard of Xenophon and the famous march of the Ten Thousand, he and his caravan were passing over the territory traversed by the ancient Greek mercenaries, and with the same aim in view—to reach their native land as quickly as possible and with whole skins. So, too, though he and his companions did not cry *"thalassa! thalassa!"*[1] when they beheld the sea from the mountaintops, they must have been uncommonly thrilled at the first sight of the waters of the Black Sea and at the realization that at last they were really drawing near the land of their birth, to which they had been complete strangers for nearly twenty-five years.

Finally, "they were come at last by the grace of God after much time and after many labors to Trebisond [Trebizond] which is set on the Greater Sea [the Black Sea]." This was the ancient Greek colony where Xenophon had rested his weary troops seventeen hundred years before. It was more nearly like a European city than any upon which they had laid eyes for many a year. Spread out on a tableland beside the sea, a Byzantine wall encircled both it and the hills behind it, and all about stretched fertile orchards and smiling fields. It had been the temporary dwelling place of the Greek emperors after their flight from Constantinople, when the city was stormed and taken by Baldwin and Dandolo, and was still cherished by them. Their Genoese allies had been granted a special quarter with a great castle, the whole surrounded by high walls, and Genoa's merchants controlled the greater part of the city's trade. Although under Greek rule the place was full of the encroaching Turks, whose influence could be everywhere seen in the people's dress, manners, and customs. Even the Greek emperor's garrison bore Turkish swords, bows, and shields, and rode their horses short-stirruped after the fashion of the Ottoman Turks. Venetian merchants, though in the minority, still dwelt and trafficked in the city, and the Polos probably met many on the great broad main business thoroughfare which skirted the seashore on the town's lower edge. Most likely it was here, too, that they learned from their fellow countrymen what had occurred in

[1] Xenophon, *Anabasis*, IV, 7ff.

Europe and in the Levant since they had left it all behind in 1271, when they had turned eastward to further their fortunes in Cathay.

The three travelers apparently remained for a time in Trebizond or in the adjacent Black Sea region, for Marco acquired considerable knowledge of the territory and told of it in his book. Perhaps another trading venture, or the delayed sailing of a ship, or political matters again postponed the resumption of their journey homeward. As before, in Tabriz and elsewhere, we are left with nothing but speculation and mere surmise. However, during their stay in Tabriz the Polos evidently became involved in some serious difficulty and suffered a heavy monetary loss. Marco makes no reference whatsoever to the affair in his narrative, and knowledge of it appears in an unexpected source—the will of his uncle Maffeo, which is still extant.

It will be remembered that the short-lived Latin kingdom of Constantinople had been established by Baldwin of Flanders, largely with the assistance of the Venetians, and that its overthrow had been accomplished by an alliance of the Greeks and Genoese, Venice's most powerful and hated commercial rival in the eastern Mediterranean area. Now the Genoese were in the ascendancy throughout the Levantine ports, and the ousted Venetians were probably as harshly treated by both Greeks and Genoese as they had treated the Genoese, the Pisans, and the merchants of Amalfi in bygone days. Perhaps, though there is no certainty, this unfriendliness was to blame for the undisclosed disaster and loss which befell the Polos. Messer Maffeo's testament, dated February 6, 1310, which designated his nephew Marco as one of his executors, records that he, Maffeo, had

> satisfied the aforesaid Marco Polo my nephew . . . finally with reference to those three hundred and thirty-three and one-third pounds which were owing to me from those thousand pounds which the aforesaid Marco Polo received from the Lord Doge and from the Commune of the Venetians for a part of the loss inflicted on us by the Lord Comnenos of Trebizond as well as in the territory of the same Lord Comnenos and also in others of our

transactions, and I testify with regard to all other accounts which I might have to adjust with the said Marco Polo that I have reimbursed him in full, and, as for the rest, that I ought to have a third part of all that which may be received or recovered in whatsoever way or title and I testify that the aforesaid loss inflicted on us as well by the aforesaid Lord Comnenos of Trebizond as in his territory was in the sum of about four thousand hyperpera.[2]

Thus the will of one of the travelers, written fifteen years after the return to Venice, and studied but recently, has brought new light to bear on the lives of the Polos, about which we even now know far too little.

The journey from Trebizond to Constantinople was made by sea, and after a brief stay at the Byzantine capital, where the Venetians were neither as powerful nor as welcome as in the days when the elder Polos had lived there over thirty-five years before, the travelers again embarked with their servants, their merchandise, and their numerous slaves. It was the last stage of their arduous journey from Cathay, begun in 1292. After a short stopover made by their vessel at the Venetian trading port of Negropont, in Euboea, the weary Polos continued on their way, past the foam-girt green isles of the Aegean, skirting the rocky headlands of the Greek coast, and on past Corfu, their prow pointed north, their keel now cleaving the home waters of the Adriatic.

At last the day of days arrived. There lay Venice before them, the home of which they had probably so long dreamed in the chill long watches of the night, under strange, bright stars and amid alien folk—Venice, most likely glorified and exalted in their homesick hearts by years of absence and seen through the golden mist of tender memories, Venice, their mother-city, which had given birth to them, and nurtured them, and set their feet upon the path. There she lay in the distance, a jewel set in a sparkling sea, proud and arrogant as ever, with her innumerable high palaces and tall towers, St. Mark's swelling domes reflecting the sun's hot glare, San Giorgio seen as though afloat on the water inside the Lido, the

[2] The hyperpera or solidus was a gold coin of the period, worth about $3.00 in United States money.

Campanile appearing to reach to the very heavens, and far away the faint blue mountains in the north. There was the harbor, now that they drew nearer and could distinguish things more clearly. It was as busy as ever, ships moving to and fro, coming in like their own or departing heavily laden for foreign lands, or rocking at their anchors as though impatient to be off. The same small boats and gondolas moved swiftly about the port or appeared and disappeared in the canals and about the quays, the same familiar odors, the same musical voices and cries borne to them on the soft wind. There she was, the same tight cluster of islands, bright in her blue and gray and silver garments, the same beautiful and seductive bride of the Adriatic, her vows renewed each year by her Doge, still undisputed mistress of the seas and of the hearts of men.

A quarter of a century had passed over the Polos' heads since last they had watched the unfinished top of the great Campanile of St. Mark's sink below the horizon. Nicolo and Maffeo had grown old and gray, and Marco, the narrator of their wanderings, had become a man past forty, without doubt made older and wiser than his years by all that he had seen and experienced in the far-flung lands of the East. He had beheld what was given to few human beings of his time, or of all time, to behold, and now he was returning a stranger to the home of his childhood. Many of his boyhood friends had probably forgotten him, had moved, or had died —how few of our companions at fifteen are still our friends at forty! The friends of his late youth and his mature manhood were many thousands of miles away, dwelling in strange lands, speaking strange languages, living strange lives. The men and the women, too, who had shaped his character and who had set his criteria of life and of action were but wraiths of the past. He was cut off from them forever; return to them was impossible.

Venice must have been strange to him, removed from all contacts with her and her people since boyhood, probably speaking his mother tongue with an accent born of constant use of the languages of the East. Venice in all likelihood was at first almost as foreign to him as was Cambaluc when first he rode in through its high gates and past its bastioned walls in the morning of his years.

He had to begin life anew at forty, to settle down among a people whose ways were no longer his ways, whose thoughts were no longer his thoughts, to live in a sea-girt city of small islands after wandering widely up and down on the winds of the world for many years. Now he had to draw the curtains irrevocably on the glittering pageant of the medieval East with all its vivid, and perhaps romantic, memories. Surely some such thoughts and questionings must have surged in upon the mind of Messer Marco Polo as he watched his vessel move past the Lido and finally drop anchor in the shallows.

The wearisome voyage was over, the longest journey ever made and recorded by any man in all the world's history. As that anchor sank to the bottom in the tidal channel of Venice, the gates of his life in Asia clanged to with its splash, even as the great city gates of faraway Cambaluc were swung shut when the drums boomed out the hour of twilight and the coming of the night, and just as the great bars were dropped in their sockets by the Mongol guards inside, so invisible bars dropped which locked out from his life forevermore that dreamworld of his youth which had become the real world of his manhood, and now was once more become a land of dreams, but this time irrevocable, irretrievable, all belonging to the past. One wonders if his joy at arriving at Venice in safety with a fortune in his hands was not shot through and made somber by an aching homesickness for the lands he had left in the Far East with his dead youth.

And so "they returned unharmed to Venice, with great riches and with an honorable retinue. Which was the year of the Lord 1295, giving thanks unto God, who had conducted them to their home safe, and rescued from many dangers."

DISILLUSIONMENT
Slowly and sadly
The river flows
On its long journey
To the sea.
A solitary wild goose
Calls under the moon,

168

And the night
Is agleam with frost.
If for ten long years
You have wandered
In the distant lands
Of the earth,
Be not in too much haste
To seek
News of your faraway home.[3]
        Wang Tso (fl. *c.* 1368)

[3] *A Garden of Peonies*, by Henry H. Hart.

·VII·
Venice

SOBER HISTORY has recorded nothing of the landing of the three Polos in Venice, nor of their reception by their family and fellow citizens. But legend, various editors and commentators have preserved some pretty stories and anecdotes to ornament the already wondrous, even fabulous, tale of the three wanderers. If not true, well then, as Giordano Bruno has it, *se non è vero, è ben trovato.* So let us recount the incidents as written down. They may have occurred. Who knows? The skeptic is not half so happy, nor perhaps half so wise, as he who accepts with reservation in lack of further or absolute proof of what is false and what is true.

Reputedly the arrivals were poorly and coarsely dressed, as was the custom of traders and others in Eastern lands, where exhibition of any external indication of wealth was ever dangerous.[1]

---

[1] This custom has been noted by all observers in China, where costly furs are worn not outside but as the lining of plain-appearing clothes, and when in the streets and *hutungs* one cannot know from the walls surrounding buildings whether there are palaces or slum dwellings thus hidden from the passer-by.

Followed by their slaves or servants carrying their gear and goods, Messer Maffeo, Messer Nicolo, and his son Marco disembarked and once again set foot upon the stones of their native city. As they did so, they may have recalled the ancient Venetian proverb: "Beware of three things in Venice—slippery steps of stone, priests, and women of easy virtue." No doubt, as with voyagers long at sea in small ships, their legs were stiff and aching from many days in cramped quarters. Once more seated in gondolas (how different from the sampans and "shoe-boats" of old China!) they were conveyed through the canals and under the low bridges (how unlike the high-arched and "camel-back" bridges that spanned the canals and streams of Soochow and Quinsai the magnificent!).

At last they reached their home, which was situated, in the words of Ramusio:

in the district of San Giovanni Chrisostomo, as today it can still be seen, which at that time was a most beautiful and very high place ... and when they arrived there the same fate befell them as befell Ulysses, who, when after twenty years he returned from Troy to Ithaca, his native land, was recognized by none.

They knocked at the door, for they had learned that some of their relatives had moved in and were dwelling there comfortably as in their own homes. Those who responded to their summons did not know them. The travelers had been away nearly twenty-six years, and, although vague reports of their wanderings may have drifted back to Venice during the earlier part of their protracted absence, as the years had rolled by and they had never returned, they had long been given up as dead.

The Polos found it almost impossible to convince their kinsfolk of their identity. The long duration of their absence, the many hardships and adventures that they had undergone, had changed their faces and their appearance entirely. "They had an indescribable something of the Tatar in their aspect and in their way of speech, having almost forgotten the Venetian tongue. Those garments of theirs were much the worse for wear, and were made of coarse cloth, and cut after the fashion of the Tatars." The dwellers in their house refused to believe that these rough men, who in no way resembled the handsome, well-dressed gentlemen who had sailed from Venice to Acre in 1271, were Messer Nicolo Polo, his brother Messer Maffeo, and his son Marco. No, they were too shabby, too down-at-the-heels, and all in all too disreputable to be taken at their word. One of these who met them at the door was most likely Maffeo, the young half brother of Marco. They had never seen each other, nor did Marco know that Maffeo existed, for Maffeo, like Marco himself, had been born after his father had left Venice. Finally, with much misgiving and doubt, the doors were grudgingly thrown open, and the three adventurers were hesitatingly permitted to set foot once again in their own house.[2]

"And what should I tell you?" For strange tales like unto those of *The Thousand and One Nights* are told of the homecoming of the three.

The story has been handed from father to son that the faded, worn, and tattered clothes of Messer Maffeo sorely irked his neat wife, who evidently recognized her husband. One day, even though he appeared to treasure and watch over them as something precious, she gave his Tatar rags in disgust to a beggar who had come to her door. When Messer Maffeo that day asked as usual for his clothes—for you must know that all his wealth of jewels was sewn in the lining and the seams and under the patches thereof —she confessed that she had given them to an unknown beggar.

---

[2] The elder Marco (the uncle of Marco, the author of the book) in his will, dated August 27, 1280, names in his testament his sister-in-law Fiordelsia and Giordano Trevisan his trustees "until my brothers Nicolo and Maffeo should be in Venice. And then they alone are to be my executors. [*In quo esse constituo meos fide conmissarios Jordanum triuisanum de confinio sancti antoninj Et flordelisam cognatam meam de confinio sancti seueri quousque nicolaus & matheus fratres mei fuerint veneciis Et tunc ipsi soli sint mei commissarii*]." The elder Marco, it would appear, did have or might have had some news, messages, or other information that his relatives in China were safe. On the other hand, it may be argued that his testament was dated fifteen years before the return of the travelers. It is another case in which only speculation and conjecture may be offered.

Messer Maffeo flew into a towering rage and became like one possessed, tearing his hair and beating his breast. For hours he paced the floor, trying to evolve some strategem whereby he might recover his lost riches. At last he hit upon one. Early in the morning he betook himself to the Bridge of the Rialto, where the crowded stream of Venetian life pulsed ceaselessly at every hour of the day, and where one could, if he waited long enough, be fairly sure of finding his man. He carried a wheel with him—some say a spinning wheel without wool—and, seating himself in a corner where all could see him, set about turning the wheel constantly and aimlessly, like unto one whose brain is addled. All the while the crowd milled about him and men cried: "What do you thus, and why?" His only reply seemed inane, meaningless, mad, the echo of an empty brain: "He will come, God willing." Thus he answered unto each of his questioners—only that, adding no more. From mouth to mouth and ear to ear the word flew through the canals of Venice, and into the squares and market places and the multitude of churches, and wherever men and women gathered to talk one to the other—for Venetians have been wont of old to gossip mightily, and scandal and tittle-tattle are the life breath of idle folk. So all of Venice flocked to see the strange sight at the Rialto. But Messer Maffeo was neither dolt nor idiot. Finally, on the third consecutive day of this performance one came in his turn to see the foolery of the madman spinning his empty wheel—and behold! it was the same beggar to whom Messer Maffeo's wife had shown charity, and on his back he was wearing the very Tatar garments that she had given him. With a cry of triumph Maffeo leaped up and seized the hapless man and so recovered his robe still intact and the treasure within it all untouched. Then indeed did Venice learn that in Messer Maffeo Polo they had no mad fellow citizen but one well versed in the ways of men and in wiles to ensnare them.

Thus runs one of the stories that have clustered about the return of the Polos to Venice.

But of all the fascinating tales of their homecoming the best known is that told by Ramusio. The preface to his Venetian edition of the book of Marco Polo, published posthumously on July 7, 1559,[3] states that it was a story told him

> by the magnificent Messer Gasparo Malpiero, a very old gentle-man, and of singular goodness and integrity, who had his house on the Canal of Santa Marina, at the corner of the mouth of the Rio di San Giovan Chrisostomo, exactly at the middle point of the said Corte di Milioni [where the Polos lived, as we shall learn later], and he stated that he had heard it in turn from his own father and grandfather, and from some other old men, his neighbors.

Ramusio, having thus valiantly defended his fair name from all imputation of fabrication or exaggeration, sets down the story as he received it.

The kinsfolk of the Polos were, it would seem, still skeptical of the identity of the returned travelers and, even if no longer in doubt as to who they were, appeared to be in no way proud of their seedy, sorry-looking relatives. So the two elder Polos and Marco contrived a scheme whereby they would secure immediate and unequivocal recognition from the family and at the same time win "the honor" (i.e., the honorable notice) of all the city—in other words, properly and profoundly impress their fellow Venetians.

They sent out invitations to their kinsmen—the most important, we may be sure—requesting them to honor the three returned travelers with their company at a banquet and an entertainment. In all this activity they were most particular, and all was prepared with great care and splendor, in fact "in most honorable fashion, and with much magnificence in that aforesaid house of theirs." At the appointed hour the canals about the house of the Polos were crowded with gondolas, filled with invited guests in their best finery. They were received with due ceremony, and each was assigned his place for the coming feast. All were curious and expectant, for perhaps the Polos were going to show some of the precious goods which they had brought back with them, or perhaps—who knows?—they were going to distribute gifts of value to their invited guests. You may be sure that none failed to come and

[3] A fire at his publishers' prevented its printing until 1559.

greet the two elder Polos and Marco, who were in the great hall to welcome each guest as he arrived. Then they vanished.

When the hour for seating themselves at the table was come, the three returned travelers came forth from their chamber, each clad in long satin robes of crimson hue, reaching even to the ground, as was the fashion in the Venetian society of the day. When the perfumed water for rinsing the hands had been brought and all the guests were in their proper places, Messer Nicolo and Messer Maffeo and Messer Marco rose from their chairs, and, retiring, divested themselves of the costly satin robes and donned others of similar cut but of crimson damask and reappeared thus clad before the assembled guests. Then, to the horror and dismay of the invited kinsfolk—what wanton waste, with deserving relatives so close at hand!—they gave the order that the costly robes which they had just doffed be cut in pieces and distributed among the servants, which action was forthwith carried out.

A short time later, after some of the viands under which the well-set table groaned had been consumed and the guests had tossed the bones under the table and wiped their hands on the fine tablecloth and after much wine had been drunk, the three rose once more and retired to their chamber. They emerged after a few moments, this time clad in expensive robes of crimson velvet. When they had seated themselves as before among the diners, they ordered the damask garments just removed to be brought out, cut to pieces before the whole company, and given to the servants. More indignation and shocked and protesting murmurs arose, to the accompaniment of more meaningful glances, for kinsfolk have been thus everywhere and in every age. The order was nonetheless obeyed forthwith, and each servitor received his piece of the precious cloth.

The meal proceeded, but by now the family party was full of wonderment about what might happen next. A buzz of excited conversation filled the room from end to end. Now each told his neighbor that it must be true, that these three men rich enough thus to throw away a fortune in clothes in a few short hours were indeed their long-lost relatives. There was no longer any doubt about it. The relatives were convinced, hailing the three by their names in heartiest fashion and trying to revive talk of old times and ancient intimate reminiscences. The Polos smiled in their beards, looked grave, but said nothing. The dinner drew near its close, and the time came to set forth the sweets and pastries on the table. Thereupon up stood the three Polos and retired once more to their chamber. There their velvet robes were removed, and they re-entered the banquet hall clad once more in the kind of clothes worn by their invited guests. Again the order was given to cut up and distribute the costly velvet fabrics, and again the order was obeyed. "This thing made [all] marvel, and all the invited guests were as though struck by lightning." The cloths were then removed and the servants were ordered to leave the room.

As soon as they had retired and the doors were closed, Messer Marco again rose from the table and entered his chamber. He returned without delay, bearing the well-worn garments of coarse cloth in which the three had been clad on the day when they had landed in Venice and sought admission to their home. All present held their breath, for none knew what these eccentric men might do next. Forthwith the three seized sharp knives and without more ado started to rip seams and linings,

> and to bring forth from them enormous quantities of most precious gems such as rubies, sapphires, carbuncles, diamonds, and emeralds which had been sewn up in each of the said garments with much cunning and in such fashion that none would have been able to imagine that they were there. For when they took their departure from the Great Khan, they changed all the riches which he had given them into so many rubies, emeralds, and other precious stones, knowing well that had they done otherwise it would never have been possible for them to carry so much gold with them over such a long, difficult, and far-reaching road.

This magnificent and wholly unexpected display of a seemingly inexhaustible amount of precious stones spread so carelessly on the table caused more stir and excitement than ever, and the guests stood about dumbfounded and seemingly bereft of their senses. The tale ends on a sarcastic note, for Messer Giovanni Battista

Ramusio appears to have had a rare sense of humor and to have known human frailties full well. His own words are best:

> And now they (the kinsmen) knew in truth that those whom they had formerly doubted were indeed those honoured and valorous gentlemen of the House of Polo, and they did them great honor and reverence. And when this thing became known throughout Venice, straightway did the whole city, the gentry as well as the common folk, flock to their house, to embrace them and to shower them with caresses and show demonstrations of affection and reverence, as great as you can possibly imagine.

Now that the folk of Venice realized how rich the three returned Polos really were, they outdid themselves in bestowing upon them public dignities and civic offices. They created Maffeo (who, according to Ramusio, was the elder of the two brothers) "a greatly honored magistrate." What was done for Nicolo, we do not know. We are informed in the same paragraph that "all the young men went every day continuously to visit and to converse with Messer Marco, who was most charming and gracious, and to ask of him matters concerning Cathay and the Great Khan, and he responded with so much kindness that all felt themselves to be in a certain manner indebted to him."

But a little time and the hubbub and stir and excitement that had been caused by the return of the Polos and by their extravagant banquet with its dramatic climax gradually died away. The Venetians went about their business, and no longer did passers-by in gondolas or on the bridges or *fondamenta* nudge each other and whisper about them or point them out to strangers. Life settled down again to its normal routine.

Within the city itself the physical changes during the years of absence had been many, though gradual. An earthquake had demolished a number of buildings, new ones were rising in their places, and new additions had been made to structures which had been weakened by floods caused by unusually high winds. Work on the great Campanile in the Piazza had been continuous, and it was higher than in 1271, when the Polos had sailed away. The exterior of St. Mark's was practically unchanged, but many more areas within had been adorned with mosaic in gold and gleaming colors. After his acquaintance with the cool shadowed temples of Cambaluc, set in courtyards surrounded by gnarled and ancient trees—temples silent, removed from the noisy chatter of the streets, and often empty save for the tablets of the gods and the sages, the only movement the lazy curl of smoke from the incense sticks ascending slowly from a bronze bowl to merge in a faint blue-gray mist about the blackened gilt inscriptions on the high walls, the bright ornamentation of St. Mark's, the confusion and bustle and noise, the hammering of workmen, the chatter of children and the gossip of knots of idlers within the edifice while masses and prayers were being offered in several chapels simultaneously—these surely must have evoked memories and comparisons in Marco's mind.

The Piazza which on his departure as a lad had seemed so vast must have appeared shrunken and diminished when he recalled the spacious courts of Kublai's capital. As with all who have sojourned in its market places, its palaces, and its streets, the Orient probably had laid slim and gentle but firm and irresistible hands upon his heart and brain and soul and had taken him to herself with her heady, potent magic. One reads it in the sentences and between the lines of the tale which he wrote. He must, too, have sorely missed the walls that encircled Chinese cities and the houses therein, shielding their lives and their beauties from strangers. In China one dwelt always behind walls, and life could be lived where houses did not crowd one against the other, and there was breathing space—quite unlike Venice, where land was limited and every square foot was needed for dwellings or trade.

The territories of the Republic had expanded, in spite of the debacle of 1261 in Constantinople, and the government, which had undergone some changes, was ever busy in Eastern Mediterranean politics, gaining here by a petty war, there by setting neighbors at each other's throats, and elsewhere by treaties of commerce and friendship.

In his boyhood Marco had never seen gold coins, but during his absence Venice in her pride had ordered struck ducats of fine gold at the Zecca (the Venetian mint). They had quickly gained currency throughout the East, where they soon became standard and where they were called zecchini. The word has remained, although the coin has disappeared, and "sequin" is known in all languages. The word "Zecca" in itself told of Venice's long commerce with the East, for the city borrowed for its mint the Arabic word "*sikkah*"—a "stamp," a "seal" or a "die."

Commerce with the West had expanded, too. The quarrels of European princes and kings, the oppression of the people, the scorn and disdain of the nobles for any profession but that of a soldier, all these situations offered a free field for the Venetian shipmasters and merchants, who had no serious rivals but the Genoese and the Tuscans. The ways of trade with the feudal lords of the West were strange, for they did not hesitate to rob and pillage whenever they could. Large escorts were necessary at all times. In order to put these feudal barons, their best customers, in good humor, the Venetians took with them on their trading ventures corps of musicians, clowns, acrobats, and rare animals and thus amused the hosts with whom they would do business or through whose lands they sought safe passage. They wandered everywhere. The Danube was visited from its mouth to its source. Venetian vessels were to be seen in every Atlantic port from the farthest north to the south. Venice bound itself by treaties to Marseilles, to Antwerp, to London, and to other cities where its citizens could sell goods. A curious provision in these treaties of Marco Polo's day was that which exempted the Doge from all customs duties on goods in which he was personally trading. In a time when trade was despised by nobles and kings, the head of Europe's greatest commercial empire was publicly taking advantage of his high office to satisfy his desire for personal profit.

Anxiety for trade linked Venice even with the infidel who was harrying the coasts and the Christian cities of Asia. Finally the Venetians went so far as to begin their written contracts made with the Saracens with the phrase "In the name of the Lord and of Mohammed." This concession was too much for Rome, and in 1307 Clement V forbade all trading with the Moslems. The bull was ineffective but had unexpected consequences. Though willing to violate the decree of the Church, many merchants of Venice repented of their sin at the point of death, especially as their confessor often refused absolution. In order to die in peace the sinner would then will his property to the Church, "so that in less than fifteen years the apostolic government was the creditor of all the commercial capital in the richest city in the universe."

Venice was busier than ever at home, too. For industries were springing up everywhere to satisfy the demand for her goods, and foreign workmen were being brought in, until Venice was one vast workshop, the names of her streets attesting the diverse occupations of their inhabitants. Her own citizens could not suffice for her ever-growing needs; Dalmatia furnished soldiers for the city and her colonies, while sailors from the islands manned her innumerable ships. The land in Venice itself had become so valuable that the glass factories, famous even when Marco Polo was a boy, had vanished under the pressure of progress, and, by order of the Consiglio Maggiore, had been removed to the island of Murano, across the lagoon from the city.

Gradually Marco settled down into Venetian life and activities, very different from those to which his adventurous years in the East had accustomed him. He was too young to retire, and, as we have seen, conditions in East Asia made a return there impossible, and ever since 1291, when the Saracens had routed the Christians at Acre, commerce in the eastern Mediterranean had become increasingly difficult. Yet evidently Marco was not the man to sit back and take no part in affairs about him, for we find him leading the life of a wealthy bachelor of the city, dwelling in the Ca 'Polo, the family residence, and engaging in buying and selling.[4]

---

[4] Only a fragment of the original Polo home remains. In 1596 the *palazzo* was almost completely destroyed by fire, and in the record of the deliberations of the Municipal Council on February 6, 1597, there is a note that there was *"una ruina fatto dal foccho nella contrà de San Zuan Grisostomo in una corte detta million"* (a ruin caused by fire in the quarter of Saint John Chrysostom in the so-called "Court of Il Milion"—a name applied to Marco Polo). The celebrated Teatro Malibran now occupies a portion of the palace area. The present "Corte del Milion" probably was a part of the *palazzo*, a small carved marble arch in one of the walls being pointed out as a part of the original building.

·VIII·
Genoa

Nor strong tower, nor walls of beaten brass
Nor airless dungeon, nor strong links of iron
Can be retentive to the strength of spirit.—Julius Caesar

SCARCELY HAD Messer Marco Polo begun to adjust himself to his new life in Venice than ominous rumblings of war began to be heard over sea and land. Ever since Genoa had aided the Greeks to recapture Constantinople from the hapless Baldwin, an ever-increasing tension fraught with great danger had been developing between the two rival Italian cities, and now the trouble appeared to be approaching a crisis.

Venice and Genoa had been foes for decades. Even though both cities were Italian, separated by but a few hundred miles of land, the paramount importance of their sea-borne trade and the fierce determination that each possessed to become the dominant power in the Eastern Mediterranean rendered lasting peace between them impossible. The center of the interests of each city lay in the East, and uninterrupted commercial intercourse with the Levant was the life blood of their prosperity. These interests clashed at every point. Each of the two rivals was isolated from the remainder of Italy, the one by her lagoons, the other by her mountains, and internal Italian politics and the squabbles of the various other city-states concerned them but secondarily, that is, only when they affected their interests.

Rivalry over trade and the control of the Eastern emporiums apparently made this enmity incurable except by a decisive war in which one would inevitably be forced to crush the other. It was all an unhappy repetition of the commercial warfare and tragic struggle between Rome and Carthage, enacted on the same stage, the Mediterranean Sea, nearly fifteen centuries before.

When the Latins and their allies had been circumvented at Constantinople, the restored emperor, Michael Paleologos, had presented to his Genoese allies the palace of the Pankratore, where the Venetian representatives had formerly resided in the city. This act was a direct and gratuitous insult to the Venetians, especially since the building was not in the Genoese quarter, and the Genoese, in order further to humiliate the Venetians and to heap scorn and derision on them, demolished the palace carefully and shipped its red stones to Genoa, where they were incorporated into the Palazzo del Capitano (now called the Palazzo San Giorgo) which was then in course of construction on the water front. Thus they were enabled to flaunt in the faces of their rivals a permanent trophy of victory—their communal palace, whose lions' heads, once carved for Venice's proud headquarters in Constantinople, still gaze down on the visitor in Genoa as they have for seven hundred years.

This incident, together with the numberless reciprocal offenses and quarrels, was productive of continual conflicts—sometimes nothing more than riots where Venetians and Genoese clashed in the Levant, sometimes naval engagements in which the Venetians came off more often the victors. No conclusive victory or decision had resulted from these encounters, the only abiding effect being a gradual sapping of the resources and energies of both contestants.

As a result of this constant dissension, the Polos, like other Venetian travelers, must have met with animosity and hostility whenever they entered the Genoese quarter of any Levantine city and, as has been suggested, they were perhaps the victims of some Genoese attack or intrigue while sojourning in Trebizond on the Black Sea.

As has been stated, Acre fell in 1291 before the attacks of the Saracens. This event brought already strained relations between the rival cities near the breaking point, for after the fall of Acre (the present Akko) Venice concluded a pact with the Moslems whereby she acquired the exclusive right to receive armed escorts for the pilgrims who were continually arriving in Palestine to visit spots sacred to the Christians. This treaty, bolstering as it did the diminishing Eastern trade of Venice, infuriated the Genoese, who in retaliation attempted to persuade the Greek emperor to exclude Venetians entirely from the Dardanelles. Aroused by this move to a fighting pitch, the Venetians hastily brought together a fleet of war galleys under the command of Marco Basegio. Setting sail on October 7, 1294, he fell in with the Genoese fleet under Nicolo Spinola at Layas (Lajazzo), on the south coast of Asia Minor, and attacked at once. Through bad judgment and a mistakenly chivalrous idea of not attacking the Genoese fleet with fire ships, the Venetians were decisively defeated, losing twenty-five ships and many of their men, including Basegio himself.

This victory encouraged the Genoese to prepare an even larger fleet, said to have consisted of 195 war vessels with a complement of 45,000 men, under the command of Uberto Doria. The first move of the fleet was to swoop down on Crete and seize and burn Canea. The next disturbing news heard on the Rialto, soon after Marco's return to Venice, was that the Genoese had persuaded the Greek Emperor Andronicus to imprison Marco Bembo, the Venetian *bailo* of Constantinople, together with all his fellow citizens resident in the city. These unfortunates were handed over to the Genoese, who first cast Bembo to his death from a housetop and then put the other helpless Venetians to death without mercy. This report spread like wildfire through the lagoons of Venice and brought a realization that some swift and decisive action was necessary to restore Venetian prestige in the East and to safeguard her shrinking commerce.

Rogerio Morosini was dispatched in all haste with forty war galleys to join the twenty already in Levantine waters. He boldly sailed through the Dardanelles, reached the Bosporus, burned all the Genoese and Greek ships he could reach, sacked the Genoese quarter, attacked a Genoese settlement near Smyrna, and returned in triumph to Venice. Another commander, Giovanni Soranzo, sailed into the Black Sea, destroyed the Genoese stronghold of Kaffa in the Crimea, and burned all the Genoese ships gathered there. The Byzantine chroniclers of the period speak bitterly of the cruelty and rapacity of Morosini and the other Venetian commanders, but war has ever been war, and in medieval times there were no limits to the cruelties inflicted by the conquerors on the conquered. For example, when a Venetian fleet was captured in 1262 by the Greeks and Genoese, the Greek emperor ordered all the captives to be blinded, and the order was executed. Moreover (though the dates in the contemporaneous chronicles are confused), it would appear that the Venetians felt that their acts were but a just retaliation for the murder of Bembo and his countrymen in Constantinople.

On the Rialto, in the squares, where men gathered in church or in the taverns on the quays, all was excitement. No vessel came in under sail or propelled by oars that did not bear a story of forays on land or sea. The mutual hatred of the two cities became more intense than ever, ships could no longer venture out on the sea except in convoy, and it became ever more evident to the citizens of Venice that the frequent truces between her and Genoa were but a prelude to an inevitable war to the death. As fresh news of disaster and destruction continued to pour into Venice, there was less talk of trade and a growing conviction that the city's back was to the wall, that her very life was at stake, and that the final decision was close at hand. Grimly the men of the proud "Queen of the Adriatic" turned to serious preparations for the threatened war. The Arsenal became a veritable hive of activity, and every blacksmith, every armorer, and every shipwright began to work at top speed. Food and munitions were collected and stored, and all Venice talked of nothing but war, war to the end against the hated and feared Genoese.

To Marco, war was by no means unknown. He could not have failed to have seen battles and sieges, sudden death, wholesale slaughter and loot during his many years in Asia. He seems not to have been perturbed by the feverish activity about him, and to have been absorbed in his mercantile dealings and his personal affairs. For some unknown reason he did not marry immediately on his return to Venice. Here one may speculate on the reasons, but no facts from which one might draw conclusions have come to light. His father had contracted one or more alliances in Asia, his two illegitimate sons, Stefano and Giovannino (or Giovanni), the results of one of these unions, having returned to Venice with the three travelers in 1295.[1] It is probable (we may assume it from the existing family records) that he resided with his father, his step-mother and his half brothers, in the Ca' Polo.

Stories appearing in various documents lead one to believe that he talked much about his travels and life in the East, stories which left many skeptical and looking upon much of what he told them as romancing—the product of a prodigal and fertile imagination. They must have wearied, too, of his constant comparing (as his book indicates) the splendor of the court of Cathay life and the enormous riches of East Asia with the narrow existence and diminishing grandeur of his own homeland.

Shortly after his return Messer Marco planned a trading voyage and in due time (the date is unknown) fared forth upon the sea with his merchandise, this time alone, leaving his family behind in

---

[1] See Orlandini, *op. cit.*, 3f: "*Da Nicolo nacquero due figli legittimi, Marco e Matteo, et due naturali, Stefano e Giovanni. . . . Essi devono essere nati certamente in Oriente e Matteo seniore ricorda il nome della loro madre, tale Maria.*" That their mother was "one Maria" is not necessarily an indication that she was Italian. It may have been given to an Asian woman if and when she was baptized, or one substituted by Nicolo in place of her native name. Orlandini adds in his notes that the name of Marco's mother is unknown, and that "the name of the second was most certainly Fiordalisa Trevisan," named in the elder Marco's testament as temporary trustee pending the return of Nicolo to Venice.

Venice. Again his galley drew slowly away from the osier palings that protected the Venetian quays from the constant scouring and eroding of the waters of the Adriatic. Once more he was on a heaving ship's deck, once more outward bound to trade, to meet new people, to see new sights, perhaps hoping to encounter more adventures to his liking. For pervading his whole book, sober as it is, he appears to be a man always searching and observing the unknown and the curious.

The good fortune which had guided him and watched over him all the twenty-six years of his wanderings in Asia seems to have deserted him the moment he set sail. His new adventure was not destined to bring him riches or new honors, even though in the end, all unknown to him, it was to bring him immortal fame, long after he had departed this life.

The seas were swarming with vessels of the Genoese, war galleys and armed merchantmen, the former ready to swoop down on any vessel flying the Venetian flag, the latter not averse to attacking and looting any luckless vessel which happened to come along offering itself as a prize.

From the time of Marco's return home in 1295 to the mention of his captivity in Genoa, the records are silent, except for a few scattered paragraphs. But those few notices are all-important, even in their baffling mystery, for we are here confronted with one of the many unsolved enigmas of the tale of the life and activities of Messer Marco Polo. At this point we find two widely divergent stories of the time and place of his meeting with disaster and captivity at the hands of the Genoese, and we are forced to choose between them.[2]

A little known Latin chronicle, the *Imago Mundi*, written by a contemporary of Marco's, the Dominican friar Jacopo d'Acqui, contains several paragraphs concerning the traveler. He recounts:

> In the year of Jesus Christ 1296 in the time of the Pope Boniface VIII a battle took place in the sea of Armenia at a place called Layas between fifteen galleys of Genoese merchants and twenty-

---

[2] Whether Marco Polo was captured during his first trading voyage or later is not known, nor is the field of his mercantile activities on record.

five of Venetian [merchants], and after a great battle the galleys of the Venetians were defeated, and all [the crews] were either killed or captured; among them is captured Master Marco Polo the Venetian, who was with those merchants.[3]

On the other hand, Ramusio's introduction to Marco Polo, written in 1553, over 250 years after the event, states that Messer Marco Polo was appointed a *sopracomito*, or commander, on one of the galleys of the fleet commanded by Andrea Dandolo, and that he sailed with him in 1298 to attack the Genoese. The fleets, Ramusio says, met off the Dalmatian island of Curzola and fought a battle on the day of Our Lady of September (September 7) and

[as is commonly the chance of war] our fleet was defeated and [Marco Polo] was taken prisoner, for having desired to press on with his galley into the vanguard to attack the enemy's fleet, and, fighting valorously and with great courage for his native land and for the safety of his people, he was not followed by the others; he was wounded and taken captive, and, having been immediately put in irons he was sent to Genoa.

No contemporary account contains these statements.

The question arises: Which of the two accounts is correct? Without exception every historian of Venice since Ramusio's time has accepted his statement, for which no support is found elsewhere, although a Frenchman, Paulin Paris, writing in the middle of the nineteenth century, judiciously remarks that Marco Polo was held prisoner by the Genoese for unknown motives. Another French biographer, Charles-Victor Langlois, writing in 1921, goes so far as to say only that "it is without doubt legitimate to *conjecture* [italics mine] that Ser Marco, still of military age, had been captured in this 'clean up.'"

Sig. Guiseppe Tucci, writing on the occasion of the seventh centenary of Polo's birth,[4] states only that "in circumstances not entirely certain, in any case in an encounter between Venetian and

---

[3] Quoted in Benedetto, *Il Milione*, p. cxciv.

[4] Tucci, *Marco Polo*, Rome, 1954, p. ii. Also Yule, *op. cit.*, p. 54; in his introductory essay Paulin Paris' account states, without proof, that "*Marc Pol gravement blessé tomba au pouvoir des vanqueurs.*"

Genoese merchantmen, he was made prisoner and conducted to Genoa."

The question should be approached from the point of view of the known facts and the logical conclusions possible from them.

A brief examination of the extract from the *Imago Mundi* shows that the good friar was confused in his dates in discussing the supposed battle of Layas. The actual battle was fought on May 22, 1294, and resulted in the utter rout of the Venetians. Marco Polo could not have taken part in the battle, as he, together with his father and his uncle, did not return to Venice until 1295. Moreover, if, as he states, the battle took place "in the time of Pope Boniface VIII," it could not have taken place in 1294, for Boniface was elected December 24, 1294, and was not installed on the papal throne until the beginning of the year 1295. However, as Luigi Benedetto, the great modern editor of Marco Polo, significantly remarks, "the paragraph of Jacopo d'Acqui should not be dismissed without consideration." There should be weighed in connection with it the recital of Ramusio that Marco sailed with the fleet *non molti mesi dapoi che furono giunti a Venetia* (not many months after they had arrived in Venice). This statement is inconsistent with Ramusio's account of the capture at Curzola, for the lapse of time from the unknown date of the return in 1295 until September 7, 1298, is surely far more than a few months.

On the face of these facts as presented, one is inevitably led to two definite conclusions. These are (1) that Jacopo d'Acqui knew of the capture of Polo in an armed merchantman but dated the event too early and confused an unrecorded obscure skirmish with the better-known battle of Layas; and (2) that either Ramusio is mistaken in speaking of the battle in which Polo was captured by the Genoese as having occurred very shortly after his return, or else his statement that he was wounded at Curzola and carried off to Genoa was an error and was perhaps merely repeating tradition or hearsay. Ramusio is clearly inconsistent and, if the statement of Polo's capture at Curzola is accepted, he is also contradictory of the paragraph written by Polo's contemporary d'Acqui.

Further considerations contribute to a probable solution of the problem. The manuscripts of *The Description of the World* (Polo's book) are almost unanimous regarding the date of its completion—1298. Jacopo d'Acqui, in speaking of Marco and the other Venetians incarcerated at the same time in Genoa, avers that *"ibi sunt per tempora multa"*—bad Latin but perfectly clear. "There they are for a long time." If Marco was captured on September 16, 1298, and arrived in Genoa with the other prisoners taken at Curzola on October 16, it is manifestly impossible for his long book with all its descriptions and anecdotes to have been written (and that, too, in a language not his own, necessitating considerations of translation and correction) and dated in the same year. This possibility allows less than two and one-half months for the preparation, drafting, and completing of the work. When we consider, too, that, as some of the manuscripts state, Marco sent to Venice for notes which he had made on his travels, in order to incorporate them in his book, we must admit that Ramusio's account is wrong.

The reasonable conclusions from these facts would then seem to be those presented so succinctly and so ably by Moule[5] in his monumental translation of Messer Marco's book. We must henceforth abandon Ramusio's account of the time and place of Marco's seizure by the Genoese, even though the error has been repeated through the centuries. The year 1296 is the more reasonable one to accept, and probably Marco was taken prisoner during some unrecorded conflict between armed galleys of Genoa and Venice. Many such clashes occurred throughout the long years of the bitter conflict between the two city-states, and it is in no way surprising that the chronicles of the period have not recorded every insignificant chance encounter. History had not yet singled out Marco Polo as one of the "immortals," so there was no reason why historians of his time should have made any special effort to record his every move. His capture would have meant little to his contemporaries, who have, with one or two exceptions, been silent about him and his activities.

Moule's analysis of the facts of the enigma and his conclusions

[5] Moule and Pelliot, *op. cit.*, 31 ff.

constitute an important milestone in our study of Marco Polo and are a brilliant refutation of such statements as that made as late as 1934 by an accomplished student of Messer Marco and his book, that "nothing new is likely to be discovered about the man." The tale of Marco is not yet complete. Little by little, missing pieces of the puzzle are being found and fitted into place. More will be discovered and one never knows when some hitherto unknown document or bit of information—even, perhaps, the original manuscript written in the prison at Genoa—may be unearthed and throw a flood of new light into many corners which still remain dark in the story of Venice's greatest son.

Thus the proud Messer Marco Polo, merchant of Venice, once a favorite of Kublai Khan, Lord of Cathay, was ignominiously taken prisoner by the Genoese, who had captured his galley in some obscure and unrecorded encounter at sea, which is not even mentioned in his book. We have no details. All of which we are certain is that he was carried off to Genoa, there to remain a prisoner of war until after the signing of a peace treaty between Venice and Genoa in May, 1299.

Genoa the Proud! So proud that often historians have spoken of her as "La Superba," omitting her name as superfluous. So proud that, as recounted in the fourteenth-century chronicle of the Catalan Muntaner, her admiral, Antonio Spinola, dared in 1305 to sail to Gallipoli with two galleys and order the famous Catalan Company "in the name of the Commune of Genoa, to get out of their garden, namely the Empire of Constantinople, which was the garden of the Commune of Genoa and of all the Genoese in the world."[6]

Genoa, seen from the sea, was one of the world's fairest cities. Lying at the foot of a backdrop of mountains, crowned with the bluest of skies and the snowiest of clouds, clad as in a soft gray-green garment by the broad olive orchards on the slopes about her, her feet bathed in the warm white foam of the Ligurian Mediterranean coast, she was a worthy rival in beauty to many-islanded Venice set in her lagoons in the Adriatic.

[6] Ramon Muntaner, *The Chronicle*, II, 537ff.

Like Venice she had a long history, reaching back even beyond the founding of Rome, if her chroniclers are to be credited. At her waterside had gathered the multitudes who first took ship for Palestine to regain the Holy City from the infidel. To her shores came the seven thousand children, led by Stephen of Cloyes, a French boy of thirteen years, seeking transportation to the city of Jerusalem—children doomed to death or slavery, the tale of whose futile Crusade is one of the most pathetic and tragic in all history. It was Genoa that gave to Richard of England, surnamed "the Lion-Hearted," the eighty galleys to convey him and his ally of Spain to the Holy Land. It was then that in his enthusiasm he took for his own the battle cry of the Genoese, "Vive San Zorzo!" ("Long live St. George!"), and brought it to England with him. It was of Genoa that Petrarch wrote in glowing words of "towers which seemed to threaten the firmament, hills clothed in olives and oranges, marble palaces perched on the summit of the rocks— where art conquered nature." And in Genoa the poet was amazed to find "men and women right royally adorned, and luxuries abundant in mountain and in wood unknown elsewhere in royal courts."

To La Superba came the Venetian, not as a happy visitor seeking his fortune but as a humiliated prisoner of war, a prisoner of Venice's hated rival and enemy. And probably, to make him feel his abasement all the keener, the captured galley was, following the usual custom, towed shoreward stern foremost and banners trailing, the supreme insult to a defeated crew. As the vessel approached the quays, it passed the great breakwater, the Molo Vecchio, then in course of construction as a safe shelter for the commune's great fleet of war galleys and merchant vessels.

To a man from Venice with its silent canals and swift-gliding gondolas, Genoa's water front must have seemed to be all noise and confusion. Long lines of heavy carts rattled and rumbled by on the rough stones, heaped high with bales, bags, and boxes from the vessels moored at the quays, while porters and sailors, peddlers and beggars filled the air with their shouts and cries, and here and there scraggy fowls scratched hopefully in the dust for food.

From the sea front, narrow steps zigzagged up the hillsides as they still do today. Many of them were called streets by courtesy, for in reality they were steep flights of stone steps, not unlike those rising from the Golden Horn in Constantinople. In such a maze one could speedily lose his way, particularly if he did not understand the strange Genoese dialect. On both sides of the narrow streets and lanes towered houses eight and nine stories high, making of the thoroughfares dark gloomy canyons where the sun seldom penetrated, and everywhere hung varicolored washing on long poles and lines stretched across the streets. Beautiful when seen afar from the galley's deck, Genoa resolved itself on landing into a city of ugly houses crowded on narrow streets, and it seemed as though the inhabitants were intent on shutting out the light of heaven from their homes and churches. And above all, like gaunt fingers pointing to the blue sky, rose numerous towers from the palace fortresses of the nobles of the city. Although in 1143 and again in 1196 strict laws had been passed limiting their height to eighty feet, they still menaced the surrounding buildings, some of them even dominating the Cathedral itself.

Without doubt the greatest humiliation came to Marco when his captors pointed out the building where he was to be confined. It was not seemly for a prisoner of Marco's wealth and reputation to be cast into a dungeon with the common sailors and fighting men of the Venetian ships. So he was conducted to one of the rooms of the Palazzo del Capitano del Popolo (now called the Palazzo di San Giorgio), that same building into which the Genoese had incorporated the stones of the Venetian palace which had once stood so proudly in Constantinople. Built by the Cistercian Fra Olivieri in 1270, it rose in all its splendor a short distance from the landing stage; of red stone and brick, square, with high crenelations on its roof, its arched windows and open arcades at the street level showed the light fantastic influence of the Gothic Venetian style, probably made necessary by the employment of the material taken from the Pantokratore. There it stood, visible to all comers, the dwelling of Genoa's Captain of the People, an enormous and permanent trophy of the triumph of Genoese intrigue and arms over the Venetian Republic. Its high-arched portals still stand after seven hundred years, the stone lions, once Venetian, grinning down in sardonic humor. When Marco entered he must have observed that between them was hanging a length of the harbor chain of Pisa, placed there as a memorial of victory after the destruction of Pisa's maritime power by Genoa in the year 1290.

Messer Marco was not alone in prison. He found the rooms crowded with men who, like himself, had been taken captive in forays or battles. There were, besides Venetians, Pisans by the score, and men of Leghorn and other cities who had dared to challenge Genoa's supremacy on the Mediterranean coasts. Not only was the prison crowded when Marco arrived, but hardly a day passed that he did not see additional long lines of men, chained together by leg irons, dragging their way past the Palazzo. Often the doors of his prison were flung open to admit more unwilling guests of La Superba. At first the prisoners had difficulty in understanding each other, for every city and every district had its own dialect. Dante and Petrarch and Boccaccio had not yet established the classic Italian language in their limpid verse and prose, and these prisoners, though often from towns but a few miles apart, were as foreigners to each other. All they had in common were the misery, the bad food, the vermin, the lack of all comforts, and the longing for freedom and for home.

Some were there who had traveled in the south and to France, and many of these could speak more or less French, which even then was the language of the courts of kings and the lingua franca of diplomats. Gradually the groups of prisoners became acquainted, exchanged stories, told of the battles which they had fought, grumbled together, and cursed the bad food and water. Some of them, developing real friendships, would sit apart and while away the long days in talk of their home and their wives or sweethearts. And as ever when men gather, there were doubtless the loudmouthed boasters of exploits, martial or amorous; and, as ever, they were in good time singled out and shunned by their fellows.

Marco probably soon became known to his fellow prisoners. Time was heavy on their hands, for ordinary topics of conversation were few and were soon exhausted. But here was a man who could spin fascinating yarns of adventure and peril for hours. Had he not traveled to the uttermost ends of the world? Had he not seen great marvels of nature? Had he not been the companion of kings and princes? Had he not traversed all the lands of the paynim and the seas that bound the world? Did they believe him? *Dio mio!* Why should they believe all the marvels which he unrolled before their eyes? The places he claimed to have seen were in reality peopled with monsters, some having but a single leg, some with heads in the middle of their breasts or carried under their arms. Did he not tell of the Isle of Males and the Isle of Females? Children of their age, knowing but little beyond their own narrow horizon, but few of them able to read or write, fed on fantastic tales of chivalry, going through the forms of religion often with little or no comprehension of the spirit or practice thereof, leading hard and often strenuous lives, giving blow for blow, cherishing but few illusions, if any—most of these men could in no wise understand or accept even half of what he told them. But he was a good teller of tales to while away the dull monotonous hours and days, one whose humor was broad enough for their thirteenth-century minds, one not too squeamish, a keen observer of women and with no hesitation to tell what he knew of them. So we may well believe that they rejoiced in their living storybook and that Messer Marco never failed to gather about him a goodly crowd whenever he was in the mood to tell of his exploits and of the far lands where he had dwelt for so many years.

Evidently the prison officials and jailers spoke of him in their homes and over their wine cups, for Messer Marco little by little became known throughout Genoa. In the quaint language of Ramusio, our source of information at this point:

> because, as may be understood, of his rare qualities and the marvelous voyage which he had made, the whole City gathered to see him and to talk to him, not treating him as a prisoner, but as a

very dear friend and a greatly honored gentleman, and showed him so much honor and affection that there was never an hour of the day that he was not visited by the most noble gentlemen of that city, and presented with everything necessary for his [daily] living.

This information cannot be mere tradition or the fancy of the good Ramusio, though he loved his hero well. The liberty which made it possible for him to prepare his book; the permission which was granted him to send to his father in Venice for his notes; the fact that his fellow prisoner, Rustichello of Pisa (of whom more anon) was to help him; moreover, the completion of his book and its circulation while he was most likely still in prison—all these facts indicate that Marco was not the prisoner chained in a dungeon as he has so often been pictured but rather a gentleman who had been captured through the fortunes of war but who, because of his talents and "qualities," was granted a generous amount of freedom.

Marco's only known motive in reducing his story to writing is found in Ramusio's "Prohemio Primo," the first preface or introduction to his edition of the book, wherein he states that ". . . Messer Marco, beholding the great desire that everyone had to hear of the things of the country of Cathay and of the Great Khan, and being forced with great weariness to begin [the story] all over again each day, was advised that he ought to put it in writing."

At this point something should be presented to explain the presence in the Genoese prison of Rustichello,[7] Polo's collaborator.

Pisa was one of the oldest cities of Italy, her proud citizens dating her foundation from the pre-Tuscan Era. Situated on the Via Aurelia, constructed in 241 B.C., one of the greatest and most important of all the Roman arterial roads linking the capital to the provinces, and still a much-used highway, Pisa was throughout the Roman era an important trading city, and a palace of the

---

[7] Although the name appears in various editions as Rusticiane, Rustuciano, etc., Benedetto, *Il Milione*, p. xiii, has proven conclusively that Rustichello is the correct name, the others being misreadings or variants.

emperor Hadrian once stood on the site of its twelfth-century cathedral and campanile, the famous "leaning tower."[8] She early developed a lucrative maritime commerce and established trading centers along the Italian coast. The attacks of the Saracens brought together the Pisans and Genoese as allies, but after the defeat of the common foe the two cities returned to their bitter rivalry and continual dissensions.

Increased wealth and influence accrued to Pisa from dealing in naval armaments and the extending of her markets, while her harbor, Porto Pisano, received and sheltered galleys, great and small, richly laden with precious stuffs from East and West. Growing ever more powerful, she gradually added to her crown more rich jewels—the overlordship of the Balearic Islands, Carthage, Elba, the Liparis, and Palermo. Her city walls could no longer contain her expanding population and were finally actually hidden by the houses crowding inside and out, so that an outer wall, enclosing a far greater area, was erected. Beautiful edifices sprang up everywhere, and stately palaces were mirrored in the waters of the broad-bosomed Arno, which flowed through the center of the city in a perfect crescent. Like many Italian towns, medieval Pisa was crowded with the inevitable high towers of the ever-bickering noble families. So numerous were these towers that Benjamin of Tudela, the famous Arab traveler of the twelfth century, viewing them from afar, likened them to a group of chimneys huddled inside a wall. So close were they one to the other, in fact, that in times of peace balconies and bridges connected some of them. Within the city four bridges spanned the Arno, and much of the history of the city was enacted on and about them.

The citizens of Pisa had many buildings of which to be proud, and none more wonderful than their Duomo (Cathedral) with its Baptistery and Campanile. The Duomo was planned in the eleventh century, when Pisa had risen to her height as a great

---

[8] The city was built on low marshy ground at the confluence of the rivers Arno and Serchio, once about two miles from the sea. The coastline has gradually changed, however, and at the height of its glory Pisa was situated about five miles inland. It was enclosed in a strong wall, long sections of which still remain intact, and was surrounded by extensive pine forests.

maritime power. Begun in 1063 in a corner of the city far from the danger of inundation, the great building was consecrated by Pope Gelasius II in 1118. Nearby, rising like the half of a giant bubble 190 feet above the walls of the city, was the Baptistery, begun in 1154 but not finished until 1278.

Near the Duomo stood one of the strangest buildings ever erected by man, the Leaning Campanile, famous throughout all Italy. In an endeavor to outdo the magnificent Campanile of St. Mark's in Venice, the architect Bonanno made his plans and laid the first foundation stones of the tower in 1174. He had erected hardly forty feet of the structure when it was discovered that the building was slowly sinking in the soft ground and was no longer perpendicular. In spite of the architect's efforts to place the succeeding three stories nearer the center of gravity, the subsidence continued. Bonanno ceased his work at this point, and no one would undertake the completion of the tower until 1234. In the interval the tower had inclined still farther, and all the next architect, Benenato, accomplished was the addition of one more story, the fourth. A third architect had but little more success, and again the work was abandoned and remained unfinished until well into the fourteenth century.

Well beloved of the Pisans were these sacred buildings, especially in the early evening when the fretwork of the ethereal white marble leaning tower was a mass of lacelike tracery, of light and shade in arch and columns, and the shadow of its great length made it like the gnomon of a giant sundial. And near it the alabaster and porphyry and rich bronze gates of the Duomo and the Baptistery glowed as rich gold in the radiance of the setting sun. Then all would pale to soft, subdued, delicate grays and rose, enshrined in the hazy curved background of bluish hills. As the sun sank slowly into the sea by Porto Pisano to the west, the sound of many full-throated bells would ring out the call to vespers, the faint odor of smoking incense would come on the softest of breezes, and imperceptibly the twilight shadows would change from gray to deepest black, and with the coming of night a heavenly peace seemed to cast its benison over the beautiful city.

Perhaps Monsignore Paolo Tronci, who wrote his famous *Memorie Historiche della Città di Pisa* in 1682, was correct when he remarked of the Leaning Tower that some people believed that "as sank the fortunes of the city to a lower ebb, so the fabric [of the Campanile] was caused to incline—and as great buildings fall of decline thus do also Republics." For all the wealth of Pisa, all her pride in handsome men, in beautiful women, in noble buildings and crowded warehouses could not save her from her fate as another victim of the suicidal internecine quarrels of the medieval Italian city-states. Nor could they rescue her once she came into grim, bitter, and deadly conflict with her powerful and greedy rival for trade, Genoa la Superba. From the first she was doomed, and Genoa finally stripped from her all her ancient glories and reduced her to ignominious servitude.

The final struggle between the two cities began in 1282. The fortunes of war alternated with no decisive action for two years. At one point the Pisan fleet, taking advantage of the absence of the enemy's war galleys, sailed into the port of Genoa and in derision fired silver-headed arrows into the town. In 1283 the Genoese won two naval battles. These defeats aroused the Pisans to greater efforts. Hearing that they had assembled a fleet of galleys under the command of Ugolino della Gherardesca, the Genoese armed 130 vessels, and, led by Uberto Doria, a scion of one of Genoa's noblest families, sailed into Pisan waters.

On August 9, 1284, Ruggiero, archbishop of Pisa, boarded a galley to invoke God's blessing on the fleet. At that moment the heavy iron ball surmounted by a silver cross, the standard of the Commune, fell into the river Arno. This evil omen "struck great terror into the hearts of all, as though it were a demonstration that His Divine Majesty had shown by this sign that He did not wish to be favorable [to the expedition]." It was fished out of the river and set up on its staff again, and after the prelate had bestowed his blessing, the people took heart once more and, with loud cheers from crews and crowds, the vessels, eighty-three in all, sailed out of the Arno, attacking the Genoese fleet off the islet of Meloria. The Genoese were victorious, capturing forty galleys and slaying a multitude of brave men, and between ten and fifteen thousand Pisans, officers and men, were carried off to prison in Genoa.

The seventeenth-century *Annals of Pisa* closes the tale with the bitter words: "... it is certain that the city lost almost all its nobility and the bravest soldiers that it had, and from this circumstance is derived the proverb '*Che vuol veder Pisa, vada à Genoa.*' (Who wishes to see Pisa, let him go to Genoa.) ... and there remained not a house in the city which did not have reason to grieve."

Buried in one of the vellum-bound musty tomes of another late seventeenth-century chronicler, Ludovico Antonio Muratori, is a piteous account of the sequel. Set forth in crabbed medieval Latin is the recital of how the women of Pisa went in great numbers as suppliants to the prisons of Genoa:

> ... for one had a husband there, another a son or a brother or a relative. And when these women asked the prison guards about their captives the guards answered them: "Yesterday the dead were thirty and today forty, the which we have thrown into the sea, and this we do each day with the Pisans." ... When the women heard such things about their dear ones, and could not locate them, they fell into consternation from too great anguish, and scarcely could they breathe from the pain in their hearts. When after a bit they had recovered their breath they lacerated their faces with their fingernails and tore their hair and wept with loud voices. For the Pisans in the dungeons were dying from improper food and starvation, want and misery, distress and sadness.[9]

The story is inscribed on the worn striped marble façade of the Church of San Matteo in Genoa, where many members of the Doria family were buried. There, chiseled in queer, debased, and much-abbreviated Latin, may still be read the old tale of the naval victory at Meloria and the humbling of the Pisans.

There, too, may be read on the old stones the story of the destruction of Porto Pisano by the united power of Genoa and Lucca: "In the year 1290, on the tenth day of September, Conradus Auria [Corrado Doria], Captain and Admiral of the Republic of Genoa, took and destroyed Porto Pisano." This battle marked

[9] Muratori, *Rerum Italicarum Scriptores*, VIII, 1162f.

the end of Pisa as a maritime power. The victors carried off the harbor chain of Porto Pisano as a trophy, and portions of it were hung in different prominent buildings of La Superba to celebrate the victory in perpetuity.

Ramusio knew of no aid received by Messer Marco in the making of his book except that "*d'un gentil 'huomo Genovese molto suo amico, che si dilettava grandemente di saper le cose del mondo, e ogni giorno andava à star seco in prigione per molte hore.*"[10] This simple statement, coupled with the fact that Ramusio's text contains no reference to any other collaborator, seems to indicate that the learned editor was ignorant of the name of the man who really assisted in the preparation of the manuscript. It may be he was correct in stating that some unnamed Genoese gentleman had been of material assistance to Messer Marco in the preparation of his tale, but the important collaborator whose name has been revealed in other texts of the book was not from Genoa.

Living as a prisoner in Genoa at the same time as Marco Polo was one Rustichello, a Pisan. He had perhaps been taken captive at the battle of Meloria and had already been confined for many years when Marco joined him as an unwilling guest of the Genoese Republic.

Although but little is known of the life of Rustichello of Pisa, a few facts have been preserved. The catalogue of manuscripts preserved in the Bibliothèque Nationale in Paris lists several manuscripts of Arthurian romances written by one Rusticien de Pise, some as early as the year 1271. That this Rusticien de Pise and the Rustichello of Pisa of Marco Polo's book were one and the same person has been established beyond doubt by a careful comparison of his writings with the texts of the Polo book. This comparison reveals incontestable proof that not only is the style in general the same but that phrases, sentences, and in some cases entire paragraphs of the *Description of the World* set down in the prison in Genoa are almost identical with those in various extant French

[10] Paulin Paris appears, in 1833, to have been the first to suggest the collaboration of Marco Polo and Rustichello; in *Nouveau Journal Asiatique*, Vol. XII (Paris 1833), *id. Manuscrits* iii55f.; Benedetto, *Il Milione*, xiiiff.

romances written by Rustichello. Even the opening paragraph of Marco Polo's book—those famous lines beginning "Lords, Emperors and Kings, Dukes and Marquesses, counts, knights and burgesses"—corresponds almost word for word with the opening lines of Rustichello's compilation of stories of the Round Table. From these opening lines to the very end of the *Description* are to be found so many close correspondences and similarities of expression—largely clichés—that there is no longer any valid reason to question the identity of the Rusticien of the romances and Rustichello, Marco's fellow prisoner in Genoa.

That the Pisan agreed to collaborate in writing the *Description of the World* is understandable. Rustichello had here an opportunity to return to his métier, that of a writer of noble tales. His heroes had heretofore been men of a dreamworld, impossible *preux chevaliers* who passed their lives in deeds of derring-do, killing giants, rescuing and paying court to fair ladyloves, and ofttimes succeeding in seducing the fair ladyloves of other less-favored knights. Here to his hand was a real flesh-and-blood hero, one who had spent the best years of his life traveling in wondrous lands and sailing unknown seas. Here was a living man who had himself been the companion of real emperors and princes and who could in a trice unroll his pack and display before the astonished gaze of his auditors the whole glittering, dazzling pageant of the mysterious East. Above all, here was a man with a keen eye to discern what was interesting, exciting, or stimulating, an unerring sense of the essential and the unusual, and blessed with a prodigious and accurate memory, so that the tale would not flag and would not fail to be full and rich and well spiced—in short, it would be a most attractive and savory dish to set before his readers. And he, Rustichello (one may imagine this passing through his thoughts) might gain great honor and renown, for this Venetian prisoner who had had such colorful adventures could speak no French and would have to rely on him to cast the tale in the language that would be read far more widely than any in the dialects of Italy.

It is evident that much preparatory work was done on the book —sketching its form and divisions, what should be included and what omitted, etc. Marco without doubt quickly realized that it would not be possible to prepare such a book, covering the geography, history, manners, and customs of a multitude of Asian countries, peoples, and tribes without recourse to some *aide-mémoire*. No man, however brilliant an observer or possessed even of a phenomenonly prodigious memory, could accurately and in detail recall all the strange facts and names of persons and places in the projected narrative without notes. He bethought himself of the notes and memorandums which he had taken during his years of sojourning in the East and which were at his home in Venice. It may well be, also, that, in what leisure he had on his return home or while in Venice, he had jotted down in what certainly appears to have been a methodical manner additional observations, names, anecdotes, weights and measures, notations of products, prices, and like material, perhaps intending to use them in future business transactions. That many of these notes were made during his residence in China may be inferred from Ramusio's first "Prohemio." After stating that the matters set forth in the narrative "are few compared with the many and infinite [number of] things which he might have been able to write if he had believed that he would ever have been able to return to these our parts [of the world]," he continues, "but believing that it would most likely be impossible for him ever to depart from the Great Khan, King of the Tatars, he wrote in his notebooks only a few things, about which he believed that it would be a great pity if they should pass into oblivion, being so remarkable, and that they had never been set forth in writing by any other person." In his introduction Ramusio furnishes the additional information that Marco contrived to write to his father in Venice, requesting him to send him his notebooks and other memorandums which he had brought with him (from the East). There are, moreover, a number of references in the body of Marco's book to his making notes in writing concerning matters which he considered important or of interest. In fact, he attributes the favor in which he was held by the Great Khan Kublai to his noting and reporting what he had seen and heard while on his official missions and deemed interesting to the monarch.

He must have laid by a vast number of these notes, and from the accuracy of his descriptions of little-known and seldom-visited places and people, we infer that they must have been extraordinarily full and complete.

Sir Aurel Stein, the great modern explorer of Central Asia, one who had followed the footsteps of Marco Polo on many an arduous journey, writes in discussing Agror (a district of Kashmir):

> One concluding remark bearing on the value of Marco Polo's own record will suffice. We have seen how accurately it reproduces information about territories difficult of access at all times, and far away from his own route. It appears to me quite impossible to believe that such exact data, learned at the very beginning of the great traveler's long wanderings, could have been reproduced by him from memory alone close on thirty years later, when dictating his wonderful story to Rusticiano during his captivity at Genoa. Here, anyhow, we have definite proof of the use of those "notes and memoranda which he had brought with him," and which, as Ramusio's Preface of 1553 tells us, Messer Marco while prisoner of war was believed to have had sent to him by his father from Venice. How grateful must geographers and historical students alike feel that these precious materials reached the illustrious prisoner safely![11]

When the notes finally arrived from Venice—and that they were delivered to the prisoner and that he was given the liberty to make use of them as well as the comparative freedom and leisure necessary to prepare the book indicates that his imprisonment was not too oppressive—the two men set diligently to work.

Marco states in the beginning of his book that he "caused Rustichello of Pisa to recount all these things." We can perceive that certain material was drawn up in writing or dictated to Rustichello (and others?) to be placed in the book in its proper order. Rustichello's contribution appears to have been that of an editor whose

---

[11] Sir Aurel Stein, in *The Geographical Journal*, Vol. LIV, 92ff.

duty it was to arrange the various portions of the tale properly, to insert such passages as were necessary for smooth transitions from section to section, to knit the different chapters and divisions into a harmonious whole, and, finally, to translate the entire book into French—for there is nowhere any indication that Marco Polo either spoke or read French—unless, a task difficult to imagine, he wrote directly into French from Marco's dictation in Venetian. His work was indeed to be a thankless one, for but few could read and most of those interested in Marco's work would receive it from the lips of those learned few. They would be intent on the adventure itself and the descriptions of strange places and peoples and would give but little attention to finely turned phrases and polished sentences. And even the barbarous French of which Rustichello was so proud was to be largely lost on readers of the tale, for the book was destined to be translated speedily into learned Latin, into the vulgar Italian dialects, and into all the tongues of Europe, even the Gaelic of far-off Ireland. Hence its writer was to be deprived of the vicarious immortality that might have been his reward by the very interest which his written version of the *Description* aroused. Marco's name appeared often in the book; Rustichello's appeared but once, and that in the beginning.

Rustichello performed his task well in view of his definite and unmistakable limitations as a writer. His clichés, his irrepressible tendency to introduce words and phrases of the romances of chivalry into a serious account of the countries of Asia, his descriptions of Asiatic battles in terms of Arthurian legends—all are obvious to the attentive reader. Toward the end of the book his interest in parts of Marco's narrative seems to have flagged, for the geographical descriptions grow briefer, and dull accounts of obscure battles, with but little of the freshness and detail that mark the earlier part of the work, take their place. Perhaps this result was not his fault. Perhaps much of it was due to the inaccuracies of nodding, weary scribes, whose quill pens faltered and stumbled and abbreviated or omitted passages in their eagerness to reach the end of a long narrative. We shall most likely never know, unless by some chance the original manuscript is discovered.

However, Rustichello succeeded, in spite of great prolixity, much repetition of detail, discursive paragraphs of little value or interest, and a stiffness of form which were the inevitable results of his earlier training and writing, in producing a piece of prose which is not altogether to be condemned from a literary viewpoint. As Benedetto has well said, the book is presented in a clear and simple form, the historical and the storytelling elements alternate in a pleasing manner with the dry geographical descriptions, and certain pages, such as the legend of the Buddha, have the primitive power of the finest Romance prose of the period.[12]

So we take our leave of Rustichello of Pisa, Messer Marco's most worthy collaborator. The little we know of him leaves him but a shadowy figure behind the more glamorous, insistent Marco the traveler. After he had written *"Deo Gratias, Amen"* at the end of his long task and had laid down his pen, we hear of him no more. No chronicle or history has recorded when or if ever he was released from his imprisonment in the Palazzo of San Giorgio in Genoa, or when or where or how he died. We shall never know how much more he contributed to the book of Messer Marco Polo than appears in the actual words thereof. We shall never be able to count the hours and days he spent working on the notes and dictation and sorting and arranging all in proper order. We shall never learn how much of what the book owes to Rustichello's questioning, or how much was changed, expanded, or modified on his advice. But we may be sure that without him and the magic touch of his hand on Marco's paragraphs the world would have been immeasurably poorer and that Messer Marco himself might have been for us but another empty name inscribed in the "Golden Book" of Venice.

There is no longer any serious doubt that the original manuscript of the *Description of the World* was in French, although

[12] "The book of Marco appears from one end to the other to be [in] the tranquil style of a man of letters who has before him suitable material and who seeks to make it into a work in the best manner." Benedetto, *op. cit.*, xxii. Momigliani in his *Storia della Litteratura Italiana*, 8th ed., 17, avers that "we should keep in mind that Rustichello had contributed to this book only the stylistic elements, but that the soul and the grandeur of the work that appear here and there derive from the personality of Marco Polo."

Ramusio, writing in the middle of the sixteenth century, believed that it was first written in Latin, while still others held that it was in the Venetian or Tuscan dialect. A Latin version was made by Francesco Pipino very early, probably, from the evidence, during Polo's lifetime, but convincing external and internal evidence points to French as the original language of the text prepared by Rustichello and Marco Polo. This Old French is none too good in grammar, vocabulary, or style and abounds in Italian or Italianate words and expressions, but French it undoubtedly was.[13]

During Polo's incarceration in the Palazzo Giorgio another great disaster befell the Venetians in their war with Genoa. When the news of Pisa's defeat at Meloria reached Venice, her citizens vowed to visit a terrible defeat upon her inveterate rival. After two years of desultory and indecisive warfare the Republic in the summer of 1298 assembled a great fleet (the recorded number of galleys varies from 90 to 220) under the command of Andrea Dandolo. The Genoese did not await this enemy fleet in home waters but boldly sailed their fleet, reportedly composed of sixty ships, into the Adriatic under the command of Lambia Doria, brother of Uberto, the victor of Meloria. On his way Doria wasted no time but thoroughly sacked and looted various Venetian towns on the Dalmatian coast. He had just finished plundering a settlement on the island of Curzola when, early on Sunday morning, September 7, 1298, the Venetian fleet was sighted.

Doria at once arranged the plan of battle for his fleet to meet the Venetian ships, far more numerous than his own. Fifteen galleys withdrew and hid as a reserve, and the remaining vessels were drawn up into a triangle with the flagship at the apex. As the ships closed in, the Venetians rained flights of arrows on the Genoese,

---

[13] Martino da Canale, an older contemporary of Marco Polo, and author of *"La Cronique des Veniciens"* (*ca.* 1268) states in the opening paragraph of his book, *"Et por ce que lengue franceise cort parmi le monde, et est la plus delitable a lire et a oir que nule autre, me sins ie entremis de translater l'anciene estoire des Veneciens de latin en franceis"* (And since the French language is current throughout the world, and is more pleasurable to read or hear [spoken] than any other, I have set myself to translate the ancient history of the Venetians from Latin into French.) (*op. cit.*, p. 268). This statement was equally valid when Polo's book was written.

rolled open casks of boiling oil up their decks, and followed with a deluge of sand, lime, and soap. Though the wily Doria had maneuvered his galleys so that the sun was in the eyes of his enemies, the advantage was at first offset by the Venetians' having the wind behind them, and they captured ten of the Genoese ships. However, excited and emboldened beyond caution by their initial success, they pressed on too rapidly and rashly, running several of their ships aground—in fact, one of these was captured and turned against them, manned by an enemy crew. During this phase of the battle the Genoese were hard pressed and on the point of flight.

At a most critical moment Doria, standing on his high poop deck, where he could best survey the struggle, glanced forward to the forecastle, where his young son Ottavio was bravely fighting in the forefront of the melee. At that moment a Venetian arrow struck the lad full in the breast, and he fell dying before his father's eyes. At the sight the whole ship's company for the moment ceased the defense. But Doria, hesitating not a moment between his love for his beloved son and his duty to his country, leaped down among his men and rebuked and rallied them again to fight even more fiercely than before. Then, turning to the sailors, he commanded in a hoarse, grief-stricken voice: "My men, throw my son overboard into the deep sea. What better resting place can we give him than this spot where, fighting gallantly for his country, his death will be atoned for by the victory which will soon be ours? Now back to your work. Let each of you do his duty and avenge his untimely death with deeds rather than with lamentations."

With set face and dry eyes Doria ascended again to his post and directed the struggle with more vigor than before. As his own ship was urged forward by its rowers toward that of the Venetian Admiral Dandolo, he gave the signal for the hidden galleys to attack. As they broke from cover and bore down on the Venetians, masts lowered for action, oars flashing in the sun, men lining their bulwarks with arrows fitted to bowstrings, and the crews shouting and singing, terror struck the hearts of the Venetians. Seized with panic, for they knew not how many fresh galleys were attacking them, some of the war vessels turned to flee. The Genoese followed in close pursuit, pressing every advantage. The battle had lasted all day, and as the sun lit up the west with its glory of red and orange and gold, the weary, battered Venetian fleet, now thoroughly demoralized and scattered, thought only of escaping. The proud galleys (far more numerous and powerful than those of the Genoese) which had sailed out only a few short hours before, confident that a swift victory would be theirs, were fugitives, and Venice had suffered her first great defeat at sea.

The Genoese, flushed with their victory over tremendous odds, resolved to crush the enemy, and orders were given to pursue the escaping galleys, many of which had been so badly shattered that they were but leaking, crippled hulks. Sixty-six were burned and eighteen were carried off to Genoa, to be towed into the harbor stern foremost and with defeated battle flags trailing in the sea. Among these was the flagship of Dandolo, on which he himself had been captured while fighting desperately. Seven thousand and four hundred prisoners were carried to Genoa.

The prisons were overcrowded and disease spread and many died, while starvation and neglect added their toll to the misery.

Meanwhile Marco and Rustichello kept at their task, finishing the book in 1298, the year of Curzola. It is well for the world that it was completed, for it is doubtful that it would have been carried through to the end once the prisoners were released, and the day of their liberation was approaching.

All the story of the battle the newly arrived prisoners recounted, and more. And when the tale had been told and retold, and the edge of grief was dulled, and the maddening monotony of prison life had seized upon newcomers and old captives alike, Messer Marco and Rustichello sharpened their quills, stirred the ink in their inkhorns, smoothed out their sheets of vellum, checked on their notes, and again fell to work on the narrative which had been interrupted on that sad October day.

Diligently they worked, for disease was abroad in the prison. Men were dying like flies, of starvation and disease and neglect, and none knew when his turn might come. And none could know what worse fate might befall them if the war were to be waged further and more fiercely between Genoa and Venice.

At last the task was completed and the book finished, in the year of grace 1298.

The day of liberation of Messer Marco and his fellow Venetians was at hand. In 1299 Venice, undaunted by the crushing defeat at Curzola, fitted out a new fleet of a hundred galleys and hired a large body of crossbowmen from Catalonia to man them. Meanwhile, however, Matteo Visconti, Captain-General of Milan, offered his services as mediator in an effort to negotiate a peace on honorable terms between the two rival republics. The Venetians, though convinced that the defeat of Curzola was entirely accidental and that they could easily win the war eventually, decided nonetheless, since things were going none too well in their other foreign relationships, to accept the offer of Visconti. Venice selected the cities of Padua and Verona to represent it, and Genoa chose Asti and Tortona. The parties met and concluded a "perpetual peace" at Milan on May 25, 1299. The provisions of the treaty were surprising in their equality of treatment of both republics. No indemnities or compensations were exacted by the Genoese, and the various clauses of the treaty indicate that the Venetians were by no means considered to have lost the war.

On July 1, 1299, a Genoese delegate was present in Venice at the solemn ratification of the treaty, and on August 28 the Venetian captives in Genoa were released and returned to their home city. At almost the same time, on July 31, a twenty-five-year truce was concluded between Genoa and Pisa—and perhaps, after many years of confinement, Rustichello obtained his freedom.

·IX·

Venice Again

"*Traveling makes a man wiser, but less happy.*"
—Thomas Jefferson *Writings*

W E DO NOT KNOW how Messer Marco returned home from Genoa to Venice. He may have made the journey overland, or he may have traveled by sea. There had been many changes in the affairs of his family since he had sailed on his last ill-fated voyage. His imprisonment had been a source of great worry to Messer Nicolo, his father, and Messer Maffeo, his uncle. According to Ramusio, they tried several times to ransom him but without success, and they were in no way reassured by the frequent tales they heard of the Genoese who were said to retain Venetians in their dungeons "for ten years." Ramusio further states that they had planned to arrange for him to marry immediately on their return to Venice, because Maffeo was childless and the two brothers desired to keep their wealth in the family. This statement can hardly be correct, for Marco had a number of cousins; moreover, his half brother, Maffeo, who had greeted him on his return from China, was evidently still alive.

The branches and twigs of the family tree of the Polos are extremely difficult to disentangle, for the facts known do not fit exactly into any rational scheme. The evidence we have indicates that Marco was the only child born to Messer Nicolo's first marriage. Maffeo was evidently younger than Marco, for he is named second in the will of their uncle, Marco, dated August 27, 1280. We may speculate that Nicolo perhaps returned home once or more during his six years' residence in Constantinople and that Maffeo was begotten before Nicolo and his brother left Constantinople for the East. If this conjecture was so, it is difficult to understand the failure of Marco to mention his brother in describing his father's return in 1269 with his uncle. Moreover, at least one manuscript states that on his return Nicolo took a second wife and had a child by her. No satisfactory solution of this puzzle has ever been offered, nor have any documents appeared which might tend to elucidate it. Some scribe may have copied the story of Marco's birth twice and the error may have been repeated inadvertently by others, as often happened in the days before printing.

We cannot take too seriously Ramusio's naïve explanation regarding the reason for Messer Nicolo's supposed remarriage during Marco's imprisonment: "And seeing that they could not ransom him [Marco] under any condition ... and having consulted together they decided that Messer Nicolo who, though he was very old[1] was nonetheless of robust constitution, should take a wife unto himself." Here we have the two elder Polos, their beards whitened with the frost of the years, consulting together just as they had throughout all the years of their travels. In all the annals of mankind there is no record of two brothers more closely associated for the greater part of their lives, and seemingly never making a move without solemnly putting their heads together. We met them thus in Constantinople when they took counsel together

---

[1] One German authority, Hennig, in *Terrae Ignotae*, III, 81, avers that he was in the late sixties or even seventies on this second (or, more likely, third) marriage.

before moving farther east, and now, in the late evening of their years Ramusio presents them again together in a fashion that seems most natural. Also, the sixteenth-century chronicler fully believed in the *"complessione gagliarda"* ("vigorous constitution") of the aged Messer Nicolo, for he continues, "and so he married and at the end of four years had sired three sons, one Stefano, one Mafio [Maffeo] and the third Zuannes [Giovannino]."[2]

We have noted (p. 211) that the young Maffeo, half brother of Marco, was born before August 27, 1280. As for Stefano and Zuannes, alas, unless the documents still in existence are untruthful, they were like Gloucester's son in "King Lear," "not got 'tween the lawful sheets," for their elder brother Maffeo, in his will dated August 31, 1300, leaves money "to my natural brothers Stefano and Giovannino." As the foremost and brilliant English translator and commentator of the *Description of the World* states: "It is not unlikely that these were born from some connection entered into during the long residence in Cathay, though naturally their presence in the travelling company is not commemorated in Marco's prologue."[3] In the elder Maffeo's will their mother's name is given as Maria.[4] Other existing documents prove that Zuannes (Giovannino) was born before 1291.

Thus, in spite of Ramusio's valiant effort to ascribe extraordinary prowess to Nicolo's old age, the veteran traveler must be absolved from a marriage after his last return from the Far East in 1295 or, in any case, from having any offspring from that supposed marriage. One may surmise that Giambattista Ramusio met with the names of Marco's three brothers and, not being able to find any documents at hand to explain their presence, accepted or invented a plausible tale to fit them into the frame of the Polo family.

To his father and this oddly assorted trio of half brothers came Messer Marco Polo on his release from prison in Genoa. Either during his captivity or shortly thereafter the Polos had purchased

[2] Nicolo was dead in 1300, so this marriage was impossible. See Gallo, *Marco Polo*, p. 74.
[3] Yule, *op. cit.*, I, 25f. Orlandini, *op. cit.*, 4n., goes further and insists that they must certainly have been born in the Orient.
[4] See Chap. VIII, n. 1.

a mansion in the parish of San Giovanni Chrisostomo, and there Marco dwelt for some time, living quietly and endeavoring to take up the threads of his life where they had been broken off on his capture by the Genoese galleys.

After the five years of captivity Venice must have seemed to Marco a haven of rest, a refuge from all that he had seen and undergone on shipboard and in dungeon. Hand-to-hand fighting at sea, filth, vermin, bad food and water, pestilence, the sight of death in its most horrible forms—all these had been his lot. And now here was his written narrative with him in Venice. So doubtless he paced the bridges and quays, watching the sea and the ships that were ever present, no matter where one turned or looked in Venice.

Perhaps Marco Polo had been married during his long sojourn in the lands of the East or had lived with some woman and even had children there, but of this possibility there is no evidence whatsoever. But now, on his return from Genoa, he was five and forty—well past middle age in thirteenth-century Venice—so, recites the chronicle, Messer Marco Polo, noble gentleman of Venice, took unto himself a wife. The story is found in Ramusio. No record of the date of the marriage has been discovered, and it may well be that the marriage occurred before the Venetian was made captive by the Genoese.

Messer Marco and Donata, daughter of Vitale Badoèr, without much doubt were married in true Venetian style. It may have been a love match or, as was often the case, it may have been arranged by matrimonial agents. As in all things Venetian, business entered even into arrangements for marriage. There had to be pledges from the future groom to his bride—usually a ring, as well as sureties that the contract would be fulfilled. On the day known as the *dies desponsationis* the formal promise to fulfill the contract of marriage was exchanged between the relatives of both parties, and the marriage was fixed for the next feast day.

In due time the marriage vows were exchanged (on the *dies traditionis* or *dies nuptiarum*) in the presence of the relatives and friends of Marco and his bride. The neighbors as well were invited to the ceremony. The day before the wedding the bridegroom paid a solemn visit to his bride and, after the custom inherited from the Romans, washed her head. Venetian tradition prescribed three solemn wedding rites, called by their old Latin names. The first was *transductio ad domum*, the conducting of the bride to her husband's home. This act was accompanied by much feasting and merrymaking, and the bridal pair were followed by the relatives. Next followed the *visitatio* to the church and the *benedictio* or presentation and blessing of the ring. The bride brought to her husband caskets and coffers containing her jewelry and trousseau of silks and linens. Donata Badoèr also brought with her to Marco a substantial *repromissa* or dowry of personal as well as real property. In fact, the first documentary information we have of Donata Polo is a legal paper of March 17, 1312, by which her uncle liquidated her dowry in favor of Marco.

Eight days after the wedding came the *reventalia* or ceremonial visit of the young matron to her father's house, where a great banquet was served and rich presents were given to all the guests. Thereafter a newly married couple settled down to routine existence.

Of this marriage contracted by Messer Marco in his forties were born three daughters, christened Fantina, Bellela, and Moreta. Fantina was named for San Fantino, a Venetian saint.[5] The name Moreta is perhaps another form of Marotha, the name of one of Marco's first cousins, while Bellela, with variant spellings, appears frequently in medieval Venetian documents. Of the three daughters, Moreta was possibly the youngest (again a surmise); the two others were married when Marco made his will on his deathbed— for therein he made a special provision by which she was to receive the same amount for her dowry as her two sisters had been given.

When Messer Nicolo Polo, Marco's father, the man who had been his guide, counselor, and companion from youth until middle age, died, we do not know. In the testament of Marco's younger half brother Maffeo, made in 1300, the testator describes himself as "*Matheus Paulo filius condom [quondam] Nicolai Paulo.*" In

[5] One of her grandsons bore the name Fantino.

the crude Latin of the period *quondam*[6] often meant *defunctus*, i.e., deceased. So Marco's father passed away full of years and adventures.

He had crossed the desert wastes and mountains of Asia three times and had traveled from East to West by sea. He had been one of Europe's pioneers in the Far East, and although his son Marco did not hesitate in his tale to relegate him and Uncle Maffeo to the background, he is to be saluted as the venturesome one who, "taking counsel" with his brother, dared the unknown with intrepid courage in Asia Minor, along the Tatar caravan routes, and in Cathay, as well as on the seas from China to Persia. He it was who in Marco's youth had set his feet upon the path of fortune and honor, who had guided him and taught him the ways of Asia and its peoples. And it was he who in those far-off days had presented the "young bachelor" to the mighty Kublai Khan as "my son."

Ramusio tells in his quaint text how

> . . . his father then being dead, he [Marco], as befits a good and pious son, caused to be made for him a tomb which was very much honored for the conditions of those times, which was a great sarcophagus of living stone that may be seen to this day, placed under the portico which is before the Church of San Lorenzo of this city, on the right-hand side as one enters, with such an inscription as indicates that it is the tomb of Messer Nicolo Polo of the contrata of San Gio. Chrisostomo.

Messer Marco and his uncle Maffeo, judging by every indication and record which have survived, carried on their business— buying and selling, importing, exporting, seemingly playing a considerable part in the commercial life of Venice. And they— Maffeo and his wife, Marco and his family—shared their house in San Giovanni Christosomo with Marco's brother Maffeo and his family, with the young unmarried Giovannino, and with Stefano and his wife and their five children.

The business was still a family affair, and, as suggested by Orlandini, it was most likely for them that Maffeo the younger

[6] Du Cange, V, 569.

made a voyage to Crete. The contemplation of this voyage and its uncertain outcome caused him to write his last will and testament on August 31, 1300. Therein, in addition to the information about the decease of his father Nicolo, we learn that his wife was one Caterina Sagredo, and that he had one legitimate child—a daughter named Fiordalisa, probably after Maffeo's mother—and an illegitimate daughter, Pasqua. It is interesting to note that Maffeo provided that his wife should receive certain moneys and "all her clothes just as they stand up to the present." This stipulation would seem to imply that a Venetian husband retained ownership even of his wife's clothes. To Pasqua, his natural daughter, perhaps either because life was really more difficult by reason of her birth out of wedlock or because of some expressed wish, Maffeo left four hundred lire "for her marriage, and if she herself should wish to become a nun, I desire that she shall have two hundred lire to give to the convent, and as for the other two hundred lire, I desire that securities shall be bought and that she should have the income from her securities during her life." But the most interesting clauses of the will are those which make Messer Marco his brother's residuary heir, failing the birth of a son after his departure for Crete.

Surviving documents indicate that Marco returned to business life, employing his talents together with the wisdom born of the rich experience which had been his during his travels and his residence in East Asia.

The medieval period has often been described as "the Dark Ages." True, a different set of values obtained and superstitions and many strange beliefs held sway, but although human activities were not all the same as those of later centuries, men's lives—and women's as well—were by and large rich and varied. In Venice, more than in most other places, the days were full and interesting, for the currents of commerce and industry that flowed through her canals and lagoons ever brought new ideas, new stimuli, new discoveries and processes.

Each year two galleys heavily laden with spices sailed as far as

England, bringing back great sacks of English wool to sell to Lucca, Florence, and Genoa. Germans from beyond the Alps sent their sons to Venice "to learn grammar, arithmetic, and the ways of trade." Basel in Switzerland bought much Venetian glass, and so much brocade was imported from Bagdad that it was called "*baldacchini*," "goods of Bagdad." Quantities were resold to France and England, where it was fashioned into canopies and drapes called by the same name, baldachino.

Other cities' misfortunes became Venice's opportunities. Shortly after the Polos' return from Tatary civil strife arose in Lucca, whose weavers were reputed most cunning in working silk and velvet. Many of them fled to Venice with the tools of their trade, were made welcome by the shrewd and farseeing Council of La Serenissima, as Venice was often called, and set up their looms near the Rialto Bridge. There they plied and taught their art, and through their industry the trade in Venetian silks and velvets waxed greater throughout the world. The authorities wisely encouraged, and in fact forced, the guild of weavers to maintain high standards of texture and color, and many a high plume and puff of smoke arose from the ancient bridge where defective textiles were burned in public as a warning and to prevent loss of trade through delivery of inferior goods. Venetian silks of themselves did not suffice to supply the growing trade, so Greek silks were imported and skillful weavers—and all these stuffs found their way into the coffers and raiment-chests of monarchs, prelates, and merchant princes.

And this barter and trade and the use of many foreign moneys were bringing strange innovations into Venetian business practices, such things, for instance, as "bills of exchange," by which one could transfer money by an order on another who dwelt in some distant city. And such were the strange ways in which religion was mixed with business that in the bill were inserted the words: "*e che Christo vi guarde*" ("and may Christ watch over you").

By Venetian law, trade with foreigners was a form of barter.

They were not allowed to receive cash for their goods, but had to take Venetian goods in exchange and sell them elsewhere. Thus cash profits were reserved to the merchant princes of the city.

Meanwhile, although events of import were afoot in the city and the government of the Republic was undergoing many changes, there is no evidence that Marco Polo concerned himself in any way with politics.

Besides his financial affairs, he seems never to have ceased to talk of his travels and adventures in Asia and of the wonders that he had seen. Family and friends must have wearied of his tales. He always appeared to them to speak in extravagant figures, so that finally he received a nickname which clung (and still survives in Italy)—"Messer Marco Milione," or simply, "Il Milione."

Perhaps he even tried to persuade fellow citizens to enter into or invest in trading ventures in Asia. If so, he was unsuccessful, for the Venetians had enough troubles at home and abroad and were in no mood to listen to schemes for getting rich quickly in Eastern trade. Although the Republic was growing ever more wealthy and powerful, quarrels with the Pope, hostilities with other cities and states, changes of doges and councils, and civil disturbances to boot would cause the merchants to be cautious and wary, and to invest only where their moneys were secure and the returns thereon quick and certain. Milione seemed, with all his weird and fantastic tales of the lands of East Asia, to be more than a little "touched" in the head.

The traveler had not forgotten the book written in his Genoese prison, and seems to have kept a copy or copies by his side during his later life in Venice. According to an inscription in a copy of a Polo manuscript preserved in Bern, Messer Marco presented a copy of the book to "Monseigneur Thiebault, chevalier, seigneur de Cepoy, whom God absolve." This inscription states that the chevalier, who was visiting Venice as the representative of Charles of Valois, requested a copy of Marco's book from the author. Whereupon Marco gave him the very first copy made of his book, in August, 1307. Though Thiebault was in Venice at that time and no doubt obtained a copy of the book, there is no way of proving that Marco presented it to him. In fact, the inscription states that the book in which we find it is no more than a copy of the original volume which Thiebault obtained; and this fact, together with the fulsome flattery of Charles of Valois contained in the inscription, leaves the matter of the gift by Marco of his first copy, or of any copy, open to grave question.

The city of Venice was passing through troubled times at home as well as abroad, and Marco saw much history made before his very eyes. But like most witnesses of historic scenes, he was most likely too close to it all, too much affected by it in his business and social life, to see it in its proper perspective and in its true relation to the past and future history of his fatherland. Not all Venetians were satisfied with the rule of Doge Pietro Gradenigo. The year 1300 saw the abortive conspiracy of Marco Bocconio, and when all was over, his body and those of ten of his henchmen were swinging on great gibbets between the high red columns of the Piazetta—strange landfalls to mariners coming home from the sea.

The crushing of Bocconio's rebellion was but the beginning of more dissatisfaction and internal trouble in Venice. The streets seemed never free from rioters or from the militia guarding palaces, churches, factories, and warehouses. A quarrel with the Church over Ferrara led to the excommunication of Venice and its people by a papal bull, issued March 27, 1309. All Venetian treaties were declared null and void, Venetian properties abroad were subject to confiscation, commercial relations with La Serenissima were forbidden all sons of the Church, and the clergy were summoned to leave the doomed city. News came pouring into the Rialto of the burning, sacking, and looting of Venetian banks, factories, and vessels abroad, even as far away as England. The city's trade began to suffer as though from creeping paralysis, and religious, civil, and social life on the lagoons began slowly to disintegrate. At first the Venetians faced the issue bravely, but when their garrison at Ferrara surrendered to disease and attacks of besiegers, and when the news came of the destruction of one of the Venetian fleets, growing hunger and unrest in the city finally forced Doge Gradenigo to send a mission to the Holy Father at

Avignon with a humble petition for peace. It was granted and the excommunication was revoked, but a large indemnity was exacted, and, as a result, Gradenigo became more unpopular than before.

The discontent of the people with their ruler was seized upon as the rallying point of many of the noble families who hated the Doge and his power. The two leaders were Marco Querini and Bajamonte Tiepolo. The conspirators plotted to seize the Rialto and assassinate the Doge and the leaders of his party, and the time set for the insurrection was the morning of St. Vito's Day, June 15, 1310. Rain was then falling in torrents, and a howling hurricane was blowing in from the sea. Thunder crashed and the lurid flash of lightning lighted up the narrow winding Merceria—then as now the main business street. The shouts of *"Libertà"* and *"Morte al Doge Gradenigo"* were drowned out by the screeching of the wind and the roar of the pelting rain. The various bands of rioters failed to meet as planned, and one of the groups was attacked and routed on the Piazza by the guards of the Doge, who had been apprised of the plot the previous night.

As Tiepolo with his contingent marched down the Merceria shouting and brandishing their weapons, the householders, who loved a brawl, began to pelt them with stones and any other missiles that came to hand. At that moment, as with Abimelech in the ancient days of Israel,[7] so was panic started in Tiepolo's ranks by the sudden death of his standard-bearer, for a woman, one Giustina Rosso, hearing the bloodcurdling cry *"Morte ai tiranni!"* under her window, threw open the casement and looked down upon the crowd—an action strictly prohibited by Venetian law. Taking in the situation at a glance, she recked not at all of the law, but seizing a stone pot in which were planted red carnations, she flung it with all her strength at Tiepolo's head. The heavy missile fell, striking not the leader but the head of his standard-bearer. He fell, spattering Tiepolo with his blood and brains. This unforeseen and sudden disaster struck terror into Tiepolo's men, for they were jammed tightly in the narrow street, and missiles began to rain

[7] Judges 9:53.

down from window and housetop. Terror grew to panic and the conspirators turned and fled to the wooden bridge of the Rialto, where Tiepolo was finally persuaded to lay down his arms and surrender. He and the other ringleaders were banished across the Adriatic to Dalmatia for four years, and their houses were demolished; others, less influential, were beheaded and their property confiscated.

Shortly thereafter Donna Rosso was summoned before the Doge to receive the thanks of the grateful Republic. Being asked to name her own reward for her brave deed, she refused recompense, asking only permission to hang a banner of San Marco out of her window each St. Vito's Day, and that her rent never be more than fifteen golden ducats a year. The story quickly went the round of canal and square, and the house was pointed out to all and sundry as the Casa Giustina, whose tenant would take no reward for her prompt and courageous act. To this day she and her house are not forgotten in Venice.

Another, a gentler, sweeter tale, one which long lingered in the hearts of all who heard it, was told in Venice, and passed from lip to ear wherever pious men and women forgathered. It was the story of *La Beattina*, "the little blessed one." One day in June of 1288 a little child was born to Countess Elena, wife of Count Pier Tagliapetra, a soldier of fortune, who dwelt hard by the Campo San Vito. The child was a girl, beautiful as a flower, gentle as the soft spring winds of Venice. She was called Maria Beata and grew up a sweet and saintly child. Every day at Mass and vespers the little girl would go to San Maurizio's Church, across the Grand Canal. All the ferrymen on the canal knew and loved her and were her willing slaves.

As she approached the age of marriage, her father decided to betroth her to a wealthy suitor. The maiden refused, and when he forbade her visits to her church, she disobeyed. Her father bribed, threatened, and cajoled the boatmen, so that finally one day she found no one who would row her across the canal for fear of him. Whereupon the beautiful Maria Beata knelt upon the paving stones and prayed to the Holy Virgin and San Maurizio to come to her assistance. Having received assurances of their aid, she untied her little apron and, throwing it on the water, set her feet lightly and gently upon it. Lo and behold! The flimsy fabric bore her weight, and wafted by a gentle breeze and guided by divine hands, Beata reached the other side in safety. Whereon all the boatmen cried "*Uno miracolo! Uno miracolo!*" and swiftly the news coursed down the narrow streets and sped across the bridges to the market places and quays, and no other thing was told but of the prayer of La Beattina and of her apron. Though many of Venice's noble sons thereupon flocked to offer their hands and hearts, Maria Beata would have none of them but became a "Bride of Christ," with a convent cell for her nuptial chamber. It soon was whispered about that life held no longer any attraction for her, and that she continually prayed for death. Heaven heard her prayers and supplications, for beautifully and with no pain she passed into the arms of the Father on the Eve of All Saints' Day of 1308, when she was in her twenty-first year of life. All Venice followed her bier to the Church of San Vito, and never did so many candles blaze or sweet incense ascend as on that day when La Beattina was laid to rest. Her tomb thenceforth became a shrine for pilgrimage and prayer, and each year the Doge and Dogaressa laid gifts upon her altar. In time a strange custom sprang up. Each All Saints' Day her coffin was opened, and mothers from far and near came to have their tiny babies touch the sacred bones, that they might never drown. This rite finally became such a scandal that after much time had passed the church sealed the coffin permanently. But even now La Beattina is remembered by Venetian mothers and their children, who each All Saints' Day throng the Church of San Vito to overflowing to receive the blessing of the saint.

The date of the death of Messer Maffeo, uncle of Marco, is so far unknown. It must have been later than February, 1310, for his will, still in existence, is dated the sixth of that month. On the other hand, it must have occurred before the middle of May, 1318, as attested by legal documents of 1328. Moreover, Pipino's introduction to his Latin version of the *Description of the World*, bearing the date 1320, speaks of Messer Maffeo as having made certain declarations to his confessor on his deathbed.

Maffeo and his wife had not been blessed with children, and he left the greater part of his estate to his nephews, Marco receiving so much that by the bequest he came into control of more than half of the Polo property. At about the same time his half brother Matteo died without male issue, and a large part of his property passed into Marco's hands. Indeed, through these and other legacies, Messer Marco was rapidly gathering unto himself all of the results of the commercial investments and travels of the older generation of Polos. But the concentration of this wealth in his hands does not seem to have sufficed him. He appears to have been a shrewd man of business, one who never missed an opportunity to add to his wealth, and in his later years we find from the evidence that he had become greedy and rapacious. He lent money to his uncle Maffeo and other relatives, always seemingly profiting thereby. When they did not pay, he pressed them hard, and when that did not produce the desired results, he did not hesitate to bring suit against them in the tribunals of Venice.

There is in existence a court judgment of July 2, 1319, whereby Marco recovered from his cousin Marcolino Polo a debt owed him by his father, the traveler's uncle Marco, since March 16, 1306. The decree granted Marco the right to seize his goods to satisfy the judgment, plus double the amount due as a fine and interest at twenty per cent for thirteen years during which the debt had remained unpaid. This was a "merchant of Venice," and the defendant was his own cousin! A later decree of September 10, 1319, transferred the title of two properties in San Giovanni Chrisostomo, belonging to Marcolino, to Marco to satisfy the July judgment.[8]

Several records are in existence which, if they do not refer to a member of another Polo family, throw light on other appearances of Messer Marco Polo before courts and other tribunals. On April 13, 1302, an entry was made in the "Great Book" of the Maggior Consiglio exempting Marco Polo from the penalty in-

[8] Orlandini, *op. cit.*, Doc. No. 3.

curred for failing to have a water conduit inspected as provided by law "since he was ignorant of the ordinance on the subject."[9]

An amusing appearance of Messer Marco is recorded in a resolution of the Maggior Consiglio, dated April 10, 1305. Therein it appears that one Bonocio of Mestre was tried and found guilty of smuggling wine (*vini per eum portati contra dampnum*). He was fined 152 lire, but this entry grants him a pardon on condition that he pay his fine in four annual installments and that any deficiencies in the payments be made good by him or his sureties. "And his sureties are the Nobiles Viri Petrus Maureceno [Pietro Morosini] and Marcus Paulo Milion and several others." On the stained and yellow entry some hand turned to dust these many centuries had written under Marco's name the single word "*mortuus*" [dead].[10] This could not be our Marco Polo.

That Marco did not cease his business activities after his return from Genoa is evidenced by a very interesting legal document which has survived the ravages and vicissitudes of the years. It is a written judgment (in Latin, as was customary in the Venetian records of the time) of the "Court of Petitions" in a suit brought by the "noble man" Marco Polo of the district of San Giovanni Chrisostomo against one Paulo Girardo of the district of San Apollinare. Marco had turned over to Girardo a pound and a half of musk for sale on commission. The musk was valued at about $110. Girardo sold one-half pound at the stipulated price and returned the remainder to Marco who, when he weighed it, found it short one-sixth of an ounce. Moreover Girardo failed to pay him for the amount sold. Marco thereupon filed suit for the amount of the sale and for the missing one-sixth ounce. The court found in his favor and added the costs of the suit, directing the defendant "to be seized and confined in the common prison of Venice" if the money was not paid within a reasonable time.[11]

---

[9] Venezia, *Archivio Generale-Maggior Consiglio-Liber Magnus 81*. There is some question about whether this reference is to Marco Polo the traveler.

[10] Venezia, *Archivio Generale-Maggior Consiglio Reg. M.s, Carte 82*. In this Latin document Polo is called Marchus Paulo Milion; this entry and others have led some writers to hold that Milion or Milione was part of his family name.

[11] Archivio, *Casa di Ricovero* (the Almshouse of Venice), *Filza 202*.

Very evidently Marco Polo not only brought a sample of musk back with him from Asia but later dealt in the commodity.

Marco's travels and his book had made him well known even beyond the frontiers of Venice. One day he received a visit from a famous man, and the two had friendly and profitable converse. The visitor was no less a person than Pietro d'Abano (*ca.* 1250–1316), professor of medicine at the University of Padua and renowned as both physician and philosopher.[12] He was a most liberal thinker and writer for his time and was consequently in trouble with the authorities more than once. Very proud of his acquaintance with the much-traveled Messer Marco, he was profoundly impressed by the breadth of knowledge and the keen powers of observation of the Venetian. On his return to Padua the doctor wrote a Latin treatise entitled *Conciliator Differentiarum Philosophorum Praecipue Medicorum.* Therein he discusses among other things the problem "as to whether or not it be possible to live under the equator." In this section of his work he describes a certain great star to be seen in Zanzibar and adduces as testimony part of a conversation he had with Messer Marco in the following words:

> About this, together with other matters, Marco the Venetian told me, [and he is] the man who has encompassed more of the world in his travels than any I have ever known, and a most diligent investigator. He saw this same star under the Antarctic Pole, and it has a great tail, of which he drew the figure, thus [here follows a drawing]. He told me also that he saw the Antarctic Pole at an altitude above the earth apparently equal to the length of a soldier's lance, and the Arctic [Pole] was hidden. He informed me furthermore that thence camphor, lignum aloes, and brazilwood are exported to us. He informs me that the heat there is intense, and the habitations few in number. These things indeed he saw on a certain island at which he arrived by sea. He says, moreover, that the men there are very large, and that there are also very great rams which have wool coarse and stiff as are the bristles of our pigs.

12 This is the same Pietro who is the subject of Browning's poem *Pietro of Abano.*

Furthermore, d'Abano refers to Marco in his discussion of a problem of Aristotle: "Because of what are those who are in hot places timid, and those who are, on the other hand, in cold places virile?"

On this subject he says:

> I heard from Marco the Venetian, who traveled across the equator, that he had found there men larger in body than [those] here, and he had found this because in such places one does not meet with the cold of the body which is exhausting and consequently tends to make them smaller.

The admiring manner in which Pietro d'Abano refers to Marco in his work, the way in which he cites him as the highest authority, and the evident pride with which he says "he told me" and "I heard from Marco" indicate that Messer Marco's knowledge and experience were recognized and estimated highly during his lifetime by some of the learned men of his day at least—and this apart from his book. Perhaps the professor of medicine had also read the Venetian's manuscript, and it was his appreciation of its contribution to the world's knowledge that made him accept the authority of the traveler without question.

Time passed, and his two elder daughters grew to womanhood. Fantina, the eldest, married Marco Bragadin, probably before 1318, and her father, as was the custom, provided her with a handsome dowry. His second daughter, Bellela, married one Bertuccio Querini and likewise was well provided for by her father.

A feud had evidently developed during Marco's later years between the various members of his family, which had hitherto appeared so closely knit and united in all its enterprises. We have seen that Marco practically drove his cousin Marcolino from the palace which the family seemed to have shared amicably for many years. Now, in his last years, we find Marco turning his back on his own kin and working in conjunction with his sons-in-law, especially with Marco Bragadin, who lived in the Ca' Polo. Strangers backed by Marco were usurping the house of the Polos, and bitter lawsuits followed one on another when he was no longer there to guide and control, browbeat and pacify.

In 1318, Marco was sixty-four, indeed an advanced age for a man of the thirteenth century, and he was ever more grasping, querulous, and quarrelsome. In that year he lost his natural brother Giovannino. The young man had evidently been engaged in business with or for Marco or for his brother Stefano and, like his half brother Matteo, had traveled to and from Crete.

The reference to Giovannino's [Zuannes'] death has been preserved in a most unexpected fashion. On September 18, 1318, Stefano Polo applied for and obtained a license to export one thousand measures of grain "from Puglia to friendly countries." The license, granted by the Maggior Consiglio of Venice, recites that "Stefano Polo has set forth in his petition that Giovannino *his late brother*, who was on a ship . . . coming from Tana, and had with him all his goods, beyond the value of four thousand lire, perished by an unhappy fate with the said ship, and, as is clearly known he [Stefano] lost all his goods and . . . he has been reduced to poverty, saying that he cannot sustain his own life and that of five very small children, of which the eldest has not yet passed beyond the age of six years." And Stefano therefore asks for the export license to aid "in indemnifying him for such a grave loss." He evidently could not consummate the deal speedily, for the Maggior Consiglio, on May 22, 1319, extended the time for completing the transaction.[13] We may excuse the exaggeration—if such it be—which Orlandini suggests may have been made to soften the hard hearts of the fiscal agents of the Republic. The question then arises concerning how a man so poverty-stricken could handle such a transaction in grain? Of course, there was Giovannino's share in the Polo real estate, which came, as a result of his untimely death, into the possession of Marco and Stefano.

Of Fantina's marriage to Marco Bragadin were born six chil-

[13] Orlandini, *op. cit.* Docs. 12 and 13. It may be noted that available documents list the children of Stefano (whose wife's name is unknown) as three—Jacobello and Andrea, sons, and Isabella, a daughter. That he had two other children is known only from the reference in the license.

dren, four boys and two girls. Bellela bore two children, but Moreta was not married during her father's lifetime.

In 1321 a man famous in his lifetime and now one of the greatest figures in world literature—Dante Alighieri—came to Venice on a political mission for Guide da Polenta, Podestà of Ravenna. There had been some speculation on the possibility that there was a meeting between him and Marco, but no evidence has been forthcoming to the present time. Undoubtedly Marco Polo heard of the great man's visit.

The years passed, and the traveler seems to have become an "institution" in Venice. There is a tradition that the little children used to run after him calling, "Messer Marco, tell us another lie." But there would seem to be no foundation for this assertion, nor for the legend that even before his death a character appeared at Venetian masques dressed as Messer Marco and told monstrous, unbelievable fables as though they were real happenings. True it is, however, that most of the contemporary readers of Marco's book and those who heard his tale from his own lips believed little or nothing of his story. Its horizons were too broad, its facts about a world entirely unknown to them were too novel, too far removed from their own experience, and from what they had read of the outside world in other books, for them to accept. Moreover, the Republic was absorbed in profound readjustments in her government and distracted by contests and animosities with her neighbors and her rivals. Marco's tales of East Asia fell on deaf ears, and his oft-told, longwinded tales were no longer welcomed or relished by his fellow citizens.

The winter of the year 1323 set in. Marco was now in his seventieth year and was growing feebler.

Probably a physician was summoned, but his ministrations could not have been more scientific or efficacious than those of the contemporary physicians of Cathay. However, the physicians of Venice were better than those of the other Italian cities, as they were under strict government regulation. They occupied a high social position and conducted themselves like lords. Dressed in velvets and with morocco leather shoes, their fingers heavy with rings, they received handsome fees for their services. Their tables were set with the best foods and wines, and they were of the few who ate with two-pronged forks. Their failures appear to have been many, for an early law of the Republic provided that when an illness was deemed serious, the patient must be warned, in order that he might make or revise his will and seek spiritual consolation and absolution.

Once the physician was called in, he examined a patient such as Marco with solemn mien and grave face and discoursed learnedly of the four humors and their condition. Perhaps bloodletting would do some good. He finally departed, to make a uroscopy in his home at his leisure, in consultation with a fellow physician. Then followed prescriptions to be taken by the patient. At first the medicines were simple—spices such as pepper and ginger, and sugar mixed with rose water and essence of violet. But when these prescriptions, which could do no harm even if they had no curative value, proved of no avail, more radical remedies were employed. An apothecary might be summoned and a theriaca ordered. It was an electuary of sixty-five ingredients mixed with honey, as compounded by the apothecaries' guild of Venice, and was famous throughout Italy as "Venice treacle." There followed noxious mixtures and decoctions of human and other animal organs, as well as of plants gathered during correct phases of the moon, and even such things as vipers' fat, powdered mummy, and ants' eggs.

Finally, the physician would advise the family both as a friend and as one instructed thereto by the law, that the members should see to it that a notary be summoned and a will drawn up while the patient's mind was still clear and well balanced. He would urge haste, as he had often seen men taken off so suddenly that they had had no time to make a testamentary deposition of their property or receive the last comforting sacraments of Holy Church.

From Marco Polo's will, which is still in existence,[14] we may reconstruct his last hours, at least in part.

[14] The writer has examined the original, on vellum, which is kept between the pages of a very large volume together with many other documents in the Marcian Library in Venice, across the Piazzetta from the Doge's palace.

It was sunset in Venice, January 8, 1324.[15] Marco was dying and desired to make his last will and testament. The family hurriedly summoned Giovanni Giustiniani, the priest of San Procolo, who was also a notary who was empowered to write a will at the dictation of a testator. Marco evidently had a very clear idea of how he desired to dispose of his property. Notes were made by the notary and he proceeded to engross the will in Latin on vellum. The patient must have been *in extremis* and haste was necessary, for the will which is in the barbarous Latin of the period, instead of being written clearly and legibly, is in a crabbed hand with many contractions.

The principal provisions of the will are, in translation, the following:

His wife Donata and his three daughters were appointed the executrices of his will.

The proper tithes were to be paid to the Church.

Twenty *soldi* of Venetian *grossi* were to be paid "to the monastery of San Lorenzo, where I wish to be buried."

"I cancel the debt of three hundred *lire* which my sister-in-law owes me."

Bequests were made to various persons, churches, monasteries, and sums "to every guild or fraternity to which I belong."

The debt owed to him by the Convent of San Giovanni and San Paolo of the Order of Preachers is canceled and the money bequeathed to the Convent, and a debt owed him by one Friar Benvenuto of the same order is likewise canceled.

Giustiniani, the Notary who drew up the will is given 220 *soldi*

[15] The reader may wonder why Marco's will is dated January 9, 1324, while the date of his death is given as January 8, 1324, apparently a day earlier. The explanation is simple. In Venice of the fourteenth century the legal day began at sunset, whereas the people's day ended at midnight. Thus the notary who was summoned by Marco's family drew up the will (a public document as soon as filed, and hence one to be framed in strictly legal form) after sundown on January 8, and therefore dated it January 9. The engrossing of the will must have taken some time, and since Marco's death took place on January 8, as is stated in the paragraph referring to his death in the record of Fantina Polo's suit, he must have died at some time between sunset on the evening of January 8, 1324, and midnight of the same day.

of Venetian *grossi* "for his labor on this my testament and that he may offer prayers to the Lord for me."

Marco evidently was much attached to his Tatar servant (or slave), for he included him in the will in the following words:

> Also I release Peter my servant, of the Tatar race from all bonds of servitude as [I pray] God may absolve my soul from all guilt and sin, and I likewise release to him all that he may have earned by his labors in his own house, and over and above this I bequeath to him one hundred lire of Venetian denari.[16]

Certain moneys are to be distributed "for my soul."

The next paragraph provided for his family. His wife Donata was to receive certain moneys annually "over and above a settlement" which had been arranged previously, together with all the linens and household furnishings, "including three beds and all that went with them." His three daughters were to divide all his remaining property among them share and share alike (*equaliter*). But a proviso is inserted that "before such division is made my daughter Moreta is to receive a sum equal to that given to each of my other daughters as dowry and outfit."

This is followed by directions that any part of the testament which might be illegal or contravene the laws of Venice be brought in consonance with them.

The document terminates with the imprecation that

> if anyone should presume to break or violate this will, may he bring upon himself the curse of almighty God and may he remain bound under the anathema of the three hundred and eighteen Fathers, and over and above this he shall pay over to my above-mentioned executrices five pounds of gold and may this document, my will remain in force. The signature of the above written [named] Messer Marco Paulo who requested that this [testament] be drawn up. [The text has "made."]

The signature of Marco Polo does not appear, although the will is attested thus:

[16] About five hundred dollars in United States money.

I, Peter Grifon, priest, have signed as witness.

I, Nufrius [Yule transliterates as "Humphrey"] Barberi, have signed as witness.

I, Giovanni Giustiniani, priest of San Proculo and Notary have completed and authenticated this will.

Giustiniani's signature is preceded by his *tabellionato* (paraph or flourish, adopted by each notary as his identifying mark, to prevent forgery).[17]

Before midnight, but a matter of short hours after the execution of his testament, Messer Marco Polo the Venetian had fared forth on his last great journey, the longest and most adventurous of them all, and he was not coming home again to Venice.

He was, as he requested in his testament, laid away in a tomb by the side of his father Nicolo, in the portico of the old Church of San Lorenzo, there to rest and sleep after as full and as rich a life as has ever been given to mortal man to live.

[17] That Marco Polo's testament does not bear his signature is not surprising. Probably the dying man was not able to affix his name. It was of no consequence, as the signature of a notary, even without any witness, sufficed to make a Venetian will valid at this period. The will was bought in 1794 by the Marcian Library from one Amadeo Svajer, together with other documents. How it came into Svajer's hands is not known. The Latin text of the will, with a lithographed copy in color, together with a partial English translation, is to be found in Yule, *Marco Polo*, I, 70ff., the Latin text alone in Cigogna, *Delle Inscrizione Veneziane*, Vol. III, 489ff., and in Moule and Pelliot, *op. cit.*, I, 539.

·X·

Epilogue

"*. . . qui . . . multorum providus urbes et mores hominum inspexit, latumque per aequor, dum sibi, dum sociis reditum parat, aspera multa pertulit, adversis rerum immersabilis undis.*"[1]–Horace *Epistularum Liber Primus*

"*What foles do fable, take thou no hede at all,*
For what they know not they cal phantastical."
 —Richard Eden, *The First Three English Books on America*

"*Marco Polo, il protagonista instancabile e imperterrito, sembra un personaggio degno d'esser messo vicino all'Ulisse dantesco.*"[2]
 —Attilio Momigliano, *Storia della Letteratura Italiana*

WHAT SORT OF MAN was this Messer Marco, who lived so adventurous a life, traveled so far, fought in the Genoese wars,

---

[1] "Who looked with discerning gaze upon the cities and customs of many men, and while for himself and his comrades he sought a return across the broad sea, endured many hardships, but never was he overwhelmed by the waves of adversity."

[2] "Marco Polo, the indefatigable and undaunted protagonist [of the book] appears to be a personage worthy to be placed near the Ulysses of Dante."

was a prisoner, wrote his book, returned to Venice, married, begot children, and died at the age of threescore years and ten? As Orlandini said, "*La figura di quest' uomo rimasto assai enigmatico.*"

Nothing is known of his stature or appearance, for no description of him appears in any contemporary book or document. We may surmise from his successful endurance of the arduous caravan journey to China (during which he was ill for an entire year), the long sojourn in East Asia with its strange foods, many diseases, and varying climate, the strenuous return voyage via Persia during which so many of his fellow travelers died, his survival of the confinement in the Genoese prison, and his active life in Venice for a quarter of a century thereafter, together with his death at an age very advanced for his time, that Marco Polo possessed an extraordinarily robust and rugged constitution. Remarks here and there in his *Description* indicate a sobriety and temperance which differed much from the loose living so prevalent among his fellow Italians. The scanty references to him in his own book—perhaps added by another hand than his—would seem to imply that he was well built and attractive of form and face, if not, indeed, handsome; at least, as may be inferred from phrases and sentences scattered throughout that same book, he had been found attractive by women of various races. Other than this, we know nothing of the matter and must reject all existing portraits of him as works purely of the imagination.

1. MARCO POLO, THE MAN

Aided only by the rare passages from contemporary writers which deal with Marco Polo, we must glean what we can of the character and the qualities of the man from his own book—sometimes reading between its lines for more enlightenment when such inferences appear to be warranted—and from other surviving documents in the archives of Venice and elsewhere.

The Venetian character has been described as a combination of "cleverness, dissimulation, patience, perseverance, greed for gain, and tenacious energy." It may be said that Marco possessed all of these traits to a high degree with the exception of dissimulation, which appears nowhere in his work.

That he was clever appears throughout his book, but as this characteristic is one which embraces many qualities within its definition, we may pass it by for a closer analysis of the others. Patience is one of the most evident virtues of Marco's character. Even a close reading of his book will reveal none of those impatiences with which the Westerner meets the Oriental and which are usually displayed in his dealings with them. Marco may have been impulsive, headstrong, and impatient in his youth. His long journey of three years, however, was made in the company of two men much older and wiser than he, and in caravans of Orientals, to whom, as to their descendants of today, time means little. Then his sojourn of seventeen years among the Chinese, most patient of peoples, and the trials of the long journey home served as an additional schooling in this virtue. By the time he had reached his forties and was preparing his book, Marco's nature had been tried and tempered in many fires, and nowhere does he appear annoyed or disturbed to the point of rebellion or even irritation. Of course, his book was written as a series of reminiscences of peoples and places, and its impersonal, objective qualities largely prevent the revelation of deep personal emotions.

Hand in hand with patience goes perseverance, and Marco was nothing if not persevering in all his endeavors, even to the day of his death. His tenacious energy was rewarded by the friendship of the Great Khan, and every line that has been written by or about him pictures a man of firmness of purpose and boundless energy of both mind and body.

In his greed for gain, Messer Marco is typical of the Venetian of his time. Though the trait is not so apparent in the paragraphs of his book, his quick eye is ever roving about, wherever he finds himself, to seek markets for buying and selling and making a profit. Inheritances from his father, his uncle, and his brother evidently did not satisfy his hunger for this world's goods, and the manner in which he pressed his relatives and others who were monetarily indebted to him is a blot on a character which otherwise seems for the most part to be singularly upright, manly, and dignified. It may be that resentful disappointment at being forced to remain in Venice after many years of free wandering throughout the world of the East, or chagrin at the rebuffs and disbelief which he and his book encountered, embittered him, drove him to seek escape in business, and aroused in him a pettiness and a grasping disposition which may have been absent or dormant throughout his earlier years of activity.

His courage is unquestioned. Although he was ill for an entire year on the journey to China, we learn it only from an oblique remark. From his recital he must have endured many hardships in East Asia and on the arduous voyage home but makes no comment on it all except to state most impersonally that of the six hundred travelers who sailed from China for Persia all but eighteen died on the way. What a saga—a whole volume of personal adventure, dangerous living, and endurance—most travelers would have made of that voyage alone! He had great difficulties in Trebizond, but we learn of them only from a line or two in a will made some years later in Venice by a member of his family. He was taken prisoner in a sea fight with the Genoese. What a marvelous introduction to his book a vivid description of his capture would have made! Yet we are informed only that he wrote his book while a prisoner in Genoa, to escape idleness and to give joy to readers.

That Marco was a tactful man appears throughout his book in his relations with Great Khan and slave, merchant and noble. He seems to have known just what to say and when to say it, and when to remain silent. A man to have acquired all that he had must have been an extraordinarily good listener—and questioner.

Some commentators, demanding all things from an author, complain that Messer Marco had no sense of humor. He may appear to have had a very serious face when recounting the most unbelievable tales which he had heard. But surely one can believe his tongue was in his cheek when he tells the story of the virtuous cobbler or expatiates on the preposterous love life of the elephant.

He had traveled too long and too far not to have shed some of the ignorant beliefs of the stay-at-home of the thirteenth century. In fact, his humor becomes Rabelaisian in his description of Russia and its gaming parties—if (and this is very doubtful) this description was in the original book prepared by him and Rustichello. No, Messer Marco Polo is far from being devoid of humor.

For a man of his century Marco was most broad-minded in his religious attitudes. True, he accepted many "tall stories" and believed many so-called miracles which we of the twentieth century would reject with a smile, and he tells many a tale of marvels wrought by saints and holy men as a matter of sober fact, without comment. He was not bigoted, however, and was most lenient in his attitude toward those whose beliefs were different from his own. If we try to approach him from the point of view of a European of the thirteenth century, we shall find him far ahead of his age in his calm, sober judgments of other men's faiths. His story, garbled though it is, of the life and works of the Buddha is most generous; not many travelers even of today would be tolerant to the point of saying with Marco that "most certainly if he had been a Christian he [the Buddha] would have been a great saint with the Lord Jesus Christ."[3]

The long descriptions of the feasts of East Asia, the accounts of food and wine and raiment and the life of the peoples he encountered there would all seem to indicate that he found great joy in the good things of life, though he gives the impression of having partaken thereof in moderation. At times he seems prudish, but his numerous, keen, intimate, and often amusing observations on women indicate that they interested him mightily. He was young when he left home, and his observation of Venetian life as a boy was not calculated to inspire him with a desire for the life of an anchorite or an ascetic. He lived for a quarter of a century far from his people, with little, if any opportunity of marrying a woman of his own race. But nowhere does he appear other than a

[3] A feeble effort has been made to try to prove that a certain ms. Bible in the Laurentian library once belonged to Marco Polo, but no definite proof has been forthcoming. See Szczesniak, "The Laurentian Bible of Marco Polo," in *Journal of the American Oriental Society*, Vol. 75, No. 3 (1955).

gentleman of the world who knows much and has experienced much but is extremely reticent as to his private affairs.

Marco presents a strange paradox in that he is modest and diffident about his personal adventures and makes but little of his hardships and dangers, yet he is egotistic in his narrative to such a point that he forces both his father and his uncle entirely into the background. After the introductory chapters they appear but seldom, and then only as dim shadowy figures, mere foils for the glittering exploits of Marco himself. Nowhere does the Venetian show himself fair-minded or generous toward them. Yet they are the real heroes of the tale. They had made the first journey and had laid the foundations for the second. The way had been prepared and smoothed for Marco, and all had been rendered easy for him. Kublai received him with open arms because he was his father's son, and even the few references to Nicolo and Maffeo indicate that they were far from lay figures in that long drama enacted at Kublai's court during their sojourn with him. It was perhaps Nicolo, together with his brother, who planned and executed the stratagem by which they were finally enabled to leave Cathay for Persia. Even after their return to Venice all the evidence indicates that they worked together with Marco. Yet his book gives them but scant credit for all they had done for him over a period of many years.

This treatment is inexplicable except as a strange form of conceit, divorced, it would seem, however, from personal vanity. He desired the tale to be his, the entire Cathayan adventure to be his— and so his book sets him at the front of the stage, with the spotlight ever on him, to the exclusion of the other characters, who are forced to hover in the shadowy background.

Here and there the book reveals some petty traits of its author. Such is the anecdote of the recovery of his lost ring through the offices of the sorceress in a Cathayan temple; Marco recovered the ring but boasted with pride that he did not make the usual offering of money or homage in return for the service. It may be that he was trying to impress his readers with the sincerity of his Christian faith, but inasmuch as he sought the old woman's assistance and through it had his property restored, it is more likely an unwitting revelation of that pettiness and miserliness in money affairs, however unimportant, which most certainly characterized his conduct during his later life in Venice.[4]

This same trait is evident in those quarrels and lawsuits of which records have survived in legal documents. Marco was certainly of litigious proclivities, sparing not even the members of his own family when he believed that his rights had been violated or that sums, no matter how small, were due him. He appears to have been quick to seize profits or legacies or other benefits moving toward him but an exceedingly difficult man with whom to deal when others sought to enforce what they were convinced were their rights as opposed to his. Despite the fact that the meager details at our disposal present him as a just and kind husband and father, there is to be detected in him an indefinable harshness in his dealings with others. Perhaps further documents may be found at some future time which might reveal softer, more pleasant aspects of his character, but all that have been produced thus far show him in the years after his return from captivity as an inflexible, exacting, grasping man. His business dealings were characterized by coldness and insistence on the enforcement of the letter of the law, combined with an inability or an unwillingness to see or understand the rights, personal problems, or sufferings of others, even though they were of his own flesh and blood. That they had been stricken by adversity was not his fault. So much the worse for them. Truly, Shylock was never so exacting and harsh as was this most excellent merchant of Venice.[5]

[4] "And when the lost things are found, then men reverently and devoutly offer to the idols perhaps an ell of some fine cloth, as it might be of sendal or silk, or gilded. And I, Marc found in this way a certain ring which was lost; but not that I made them any offering or homage."—Zelada ms. xxxlx.

[5] An instance of Marco's kindness and thoughtfulness toward those less fortunate has been preserved—his manumission on his deathbed of Pietro the Tatar. Marco not only remembered to release his faithful slave, even at an hour when the agony of death was upon him, but also bequeathed him the fruits of his labor and one hundred *lire* of Venetian *denari*. It is not known whether Pietro was a slave who accompanied him home from the East, or one acquired later. Since he alone of Marco's slaves was manumitted in the will and received in addition a handsome bequest, it may be presumed at least that he had labored long and

It is difficult to reconcile the sternness and stubbornness of the later Marco with the younger man as he appears in his book. Either Rustichello "dressed up" Messer Marco in preparing his text and the older Marco is the real one, or else, as suggested above, the profound changes in his life and his manner of living after his return to Venice so warped and frustrated him that the milk of human kindness had been soured within him.

Such an alteration is not incredible. Messer Marco had probably been thoroughly Orientalized by his twenty-six years of travel and residence in the land of the Great Khan. It was too late for him at forty to readjust himself to new conditions and ways without violent mental, emotional, and physical conflicts. Modern psychology recognizes such maladjustments as affecting profoundly both the individual and the group. An understanding of these considerations should temper our judgment on Marco Polo and his shortcomings as we find them recorded in the cold, impersonal documents which have lain in the dusty archives of Venice these six hundred years and more.

The great traveler's intellectual qualities have been highly respected and praised by every serious student of the man and his book. It must be remembered that he was not a man of science and must not be judged adversely because of this fact. How could he be? Even if he had had the best of educational advantages—and we know not what his schooling was—he would have been able to receive no really scientific training. An age which looked to Ptolemy for its geography and to Aristotle as the final arbiter in things intellectual, an age which accepted Dante's topography of the various parts of the universe as correct and Brunetto Latini's *Trésor* as one of its most reliable encyclopedias, an age that drew its ideas of nature and the physical world from such works as the anonymous *L'Image du Monde* and the "De Naturis Rerum" of

---

faithfully for his master and may well have returned with him on his long voyage from far Cathay. It is pleasing to learn from a document still in existence, dated April 7, 1328, that the Maggior Consiglio granted to Pietro, "once the slave of Ser Marco Polo of San Giovanni Chrisostomo, who was a long time in Venice, for his good deportment, that for the rest he should be a Venetian [citizen] and should be held and treated as a Venetian."

Vincent de Beauvais could hardly prepare a man for scientific exploration or scientific observations and notations of such explorations. Despite the unwarranted carping of various editors and critics[6]—too many of whom seize the opportunity to exhibit their own erudition, or lack thereof, rather than discuss the contribution of an author—the wonder is that Marco Polo has given an account as clear and accurate as he has done. He was a rapid, acute, and judicious observer of facts, particularly those having a practical application. Fundamentally, he possessed both the spirit and temper of a great explorer. Without emphasis on the unimportant or nonessential, without intruding himself into his discussions, he extracts what is of value from whatever he has observed and sets it forth clearly and succinctly for the reader. Neither a learned nor a well-educated man but one who very evidently received most of his schooling from travel and other experiences, he demonstrates time and again a surprisingly systematic grasp of his subject and an ability to separate the true from the false. For the most part, he presents things seen by him as actually seen, and hearsay as hearsay. When setting forth material with which he was not personally acquainted, he is frequently in error—at times even gullible—but regarding the knowledge which he acquired through personal observation and inquiry, modern exploration and investigation have proved him a true and careful recorder of facts. He learned rapidly, assimilated thoroughly, and forgot little.

Marco has been censured by several editors for his verbosity and "hammering reiteration." Here again such critics view the work wrongly through modern eyes. Though the accepted prose style of the time abounds in prolixity, bombast, and repetition, his work contains comparatively little of such redundancies. To explain what is found of such elements in his book, it must be remembered that the work was probably written not by Marco himself but by a professional writer of romance, who naturally employed the turgid idiom of the thirteenth century. Moreover, the book was designed as much to be read aloud (for the reading public was but

[6] *See* Charles-Victor Langlois, *La Connaissance de la Nature et du Monde au Moyen Age.*

241

small when the book was written) as for private perusal in one's study, and for such readings iterations were a help rather than a hindrance to both reader and audience.

In like manner, Marco has been accused of being inordinately fond of pomp and ceremony, whereas pomp and ceremony, parade and pageant were among the chief joys of medieval life, and Da Canale and Froissart and the other chroniclers of the period provide numerous long and detailed descriptions of them. Mayhap Marco loved them, as well he might, and surely here, too, we find the professional hand of Rustichello. Moreover, these descriptions of battle and feasting afford welcome periods of rest and sojourn in the long book of travel and description—and often preserve for us precious information of the life of the times.

Messer Marco has been charged with a lack of appreciation of the arts and letters. One cannot ask more from him than he has to give. Surely he brought home for us riches in full measure, pressed down and overflowing, and we are most ungrateful if we find fault with him because he is not, forsooth, a genuine connoisseur of the arts and a student of the letters of those countries where he traveled and lived. Indeed, only those who have studied through a lifetime the literature and the arts of the Far East can realize the unfairness of such commentators.

We must grant that Marco is not always discriminating in his estimate of the true value or importance of his topics. He tells us almost in one breath of the prostitutes of Cambaluc and the making of paper money, and later in a single paragraph on Zanzibar he describes, in order, the giraffe, the elephant, the lion, the Negroes and their dress (or lack thereof), the products of the island, and the ugliness of the Negresses. Nonetheless, this very lack of scientific discrimination, disturbing though it may be to our modern methods of writing and sense of proportion, has caused him to include in his book much invaluable information which might otherwise have been lost to the world.

It is true that, Orientalized as Marco seems to have been, he never appears to have grasped the fundamental philosophies of the Eastern peoples among whom he had lived so many years. Neither

Confucianism nor Taoism is mentioned by him. Yet, of an infinite number of foreign travelers who have visited and have lived long periods in China since Marco's time, few have been able to understand or appreciate these philosophies without much preliminary or subsequent study and reading. Even today, most of the many intelligent men and women who spend the best years of their lives in China return to the West possessing the scantiest knowledge of the ethical and religious systems and practices of the Eastern peoples. Marco was a most unusual combination of merchant, administrator, traveler, explorer, and writer living in an era where scant material on the Orient was available in Europe. So here again, Marco Polo should be judged in the light of the age in which he lived and of his own particular activities.

He charmed the people of Asia, among whom he lived and traveled for more than twenty years, by his personality—his ability, his tact, and his pleasing manner. On his return to Europe, he likewise enchanted and amused his fellow prisoners in Genoa and the people of his native Venice. His book has attracted, entertained, and educated countless millions of every generation in every land since it was written. In its simplicity, its frankness, and its wealth of material—anthropological, ethnological, geographical, historical, and commercial—it stands alone as a treasure house of fact and story. The book will likely hold its place in the libraries of all mankind as the greatest work of travel ever written, and in like manner will its author, with all his faults, continue to be loved both for himself and for the priceless gift which his imprisonment and boredom in Genoa caused him to write.

2. THE TOMB OF MARCO POLO

It is a matter of surprise that Marco Polo's death and burial appear to have passed entirely unnoticed by his fellow Venetians. It might be supposed that the demise of such a prominent citizen and the author of a book widely read even during his lifetime would have caused at least a ripple of interest, enough to have produced some written notation or comment by some chronicler or official of the time. No such information has as yet come to light.

The earliest existing indication of his place of sepulture is the request in his testament that he be buried in the Church of San Lorenzo, where his father lay, and there is no reason to question his interment there. The existing will of his daughter Moreta, dated May 1, 1348, contains the following directions: "I bequeath to the convent of the nuns of San Lorenzo, in which place I wish to be buried in the tomb of my parents, twenty *soldi*." This statement proves beyond a doubt that not only Messer Marco but also his wife Donata were actually buried in the church in which he had wished his bones to rest.

Ramusio relates that in his time (the first half of the sixteenth century) the sarcophagus of Messer Nicolo, Marco's father, was still to be seen in San Lorenzo, but he makes no mention of Marco's tomb. The next reference to the tomb is found in the delightful guidebook to Venice, *Venetia Città Nobilissima et Singolare* of Francesco Sansovino, published in Venice in 1581, about twenty-two years after Ramusio's volume appeared. In his description of the Church of San Lorenzo, the author notes: "Under the portico [*angriporto*] is buried that Marco Polo, surnamed Milione, who wrote the travels of the new world, and who was the first before Christopher Columbus who discovered new countries." Although Sansovino has slightly confused East Asia with America, his information regarding the location of Marco Polo's tomb need not be questioned.

In the Museo Correr in Venice is a manuscript work entitled *Compendio dell'Origine e Progresso del Monasterio Illmo. di San Lorenzo* by Tomaso Fugazzoni, written in 1685, with additions by later authors. This work states that in 1580 repairs were commenced on the Church of San Lorenzo, then "old and falling to pieces," and that the work "was finished most religiously in the year 1592." Continuing, Fugazzoni writes that "in the center of the portico was the burial place of the most famous Marco Polo, noble Venetian." The church "was renewed from its foundation, and was in a noble and spacious form." This renovation, which gave a new form to the church, perhaps involved a change also in the floor level of the church or the portico, which was two steps

Page of the so-called "Paris text" (MS 1116, Bibliothèque Nationale, Paris), used as the basis of the best modern editions of Marco Polo's text. Early fourteenth century, Old French, small folio. (Courtesy of the Library of the University of California)

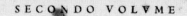

SECONDO VOLVME
DELLE NAVIGATIONI ET VIAGGI

NEL QVALE SI CONTENGONO

L'Historia delle cose de Tartari, & diuersi fatti de loro Imperatori, descritta
da M. Marco Polo Gentilhuomo Venetiano, & da Hayton Armeno.

Varie descrittioni di diuersi autori, dell'Indie Orientali, della Tartaria, della
Persia, Armenia, Mengrelia, Zorzania, & altre Prouincie, nelle quali si
raccontano molte imprese d'Vssumcassan, d'Ismael Soffi, del Soldano di Babilonia, di diuersi Imperatori Ottomani, & parti-
colarmente di Selim, contro Tomombei, vltimo Soldano
de Mamalucchi, & d'altri Principi.

Et il viaggio della Tana. Con la descrittione de nomi de Popoli, Citta, Fiumi, & Porti d'intorno al
Mar Maggiore, come si nominauano al tempo dell'Imperator Adriano, & molte altre narra-
tioni, cosi dello stato de Moscouiti, Scithi, & Circhasii, come d'altre genti barbare
a gli antichi incognite. Et il naufragio di M. Pietro Quirino gentilhuomo
Venetiano, portato per fortuna settanta gradi sotto la Tramontana.

Con l'Indice diligentemente ordinato, delle cose piu notabili.

L A

Con Priuilegio dell'Illustrissimo Senato di Venetia.

IN VENETIA NELLA STAMPERIA DE GIVNTI.

L'ANNO M D LIX.

Frontispiece of the first printed edition of Marco Polo's book, Nuremberg, 1477. (Courtesy of the British Museum)

scere il Vescouo con qualche censo. Di qui è che quelle donne mandano ogni anno al Patriarca, il dì della vigilia di San Pietro & di Santo Andrea,bozzolati & danari,i qua li gli sono portati da i Cappellani di San Seuero, a quali al-l'incontro sono donati alcuni pani della mensa Patriarcale. E adunque San Lorenzo luogo importante per l'origine sua & per la ricchezza ch'esso possiede ab antiquo.& anco-ra che la Chiesa non sia molto grande di corpo; il moniste ro è però larghissimo per ogni uerso, & habitato da buon numero di donne, & tutte nobili della città. Per fianco ui è l'Oratorio ò Cappella di San Sebastiano,ch'altre uolte fu parrocchiale. & è sottoposto alle monache,le quali danno una certa ricognitione al Patriarca, quando ua il giorno della festiuità sua a predicarui ò a celebrar la messa. & in questo è riposto il corpo del beato Giouanni,che fu Piouano di San Giouanni decollato. & si lascia uedere al popo-lo per la licenza che fu di ciò concessa da Papa Bonifatio Ottauo. Nella Chiesa di San Lorenzo sono i corpi de Santi Barbaro, Ligorio, Gregorio Vescouo nella Cappadocia, Paolo Vescouo & martire,Platone, & Leo che fu Vinitia-no,& della famiglia Bēba. Questo Sacrario è uisitato ogni anno dal popolo con gran frequenza, tutte le domeniche di Maggio: & ui uanno anco molti forestieri per l'indul-gentia, col cui mezzo si dice che si caua un'anima del Pur-gatorio. Sotto l'angiporto è sepolto quel Marco Polo co-gnominato Milione, il quale scrisse i viaggi del mondo nuouo, & che fu il primo auanti Christoforo Colombo, che ritrouasse nuoui paesi. al quale non si dando fede per le cose strauagāti che egli racconta, il Colombo aggiunse cre dulità ne tempi de nostri padri,con lo hauer ritrouata quel la parte,per inanzi giudicata da huomini singolari nō pun to habitata.

S. Giorgio de Greci.

NEl rio medesimo di San Lorenzo,apparisce la bella & honorata Chiesa fatta dalla nation Greca, la quale ri-
dotta

Page of Francesco Sansovino's *Venetia, Città Nobilissima et Singolare* (Venice, 1581), containing the location of Marco Polo's tomb. (From the author's collection)

Chinese paper money, of the first emperor (Hung Wu) of the Ming
Dynasty (A.D. 1368–98). (From the author's collection)

"Greek fire." From the Skylitzes Codex (*ca.* 1300)

blioteca Nacional, Madrid.

higher than the floor of the ancient church, first built in 809 by the Doge Angelo Participazio. Fugazzoni states that in the center was (*era*) the burial place of Marco. This would seem to imply that when he wrote Marco's resting place had already disappeared. During the succeeding centuries much remodeling and repairing was carried on in various parts of the church.

A record of the burials in San Lorenzo and San Sebastiano (a later chapel added to the original church), written in 1718, lists: "... in the Church [chapel] of San Sebastiano ... at the foot of the said altar, the burial place of the most famous and noble Venetian, Marco Polo Colombo Milione" (whence the "Colombo"?). This source would appear to indicate that in 1718 the place of the tomb or grave of the great traveler was known and perhaps even marked.

In 1765 there appeared in Venice a very interesting volume, illustrated with many engravings, entitled *The Foreigner Enlightened About the Rarest and Curious Things Ancient and Modern of the City of Venice and the Surrounding Islands*, by Giambattista Albrizzi. The author of this quaint guidebook describes the Church of San Lorenzo as it was in his day. Referring to the Chapel of San Sebastiano, he notes that there stood therein "three altars of not ordinary workmanship. . . . Here is buried Marco Polo, called Il Millione, so well known, and famous for the discoveries of new countries before Christopher Columbus." Albrizzi is evidently following Sansovino's erroneous note referring to Marco Polo's exploits but uses the expression *e sepolto*. The question then arises: Was the tomb or grave still known and marked as late as 1765? We have no answer.

Cigogna, in Volume II of his monumental and invaluable *Venetian Inscriptions*[7] (1827), discusses the disappearance of important tombstones and other inscriptions in the Church of San Lorenzo, a result of its many rebuildings. He states:

> As for the inscriptions, the [above] mentioned rebuildings and decorations have caused many of them to be missing, and certainly

[7] Emmanuele Antonio Cigogna, *Delle Inscrizioni Veneziane . . .*, Venice, 1827, 373, 381 ff.

some of them precious . . . and of the most popular [names] of the city. Among other lost memorials was that of the Polos, [the] celebrated Venetian traveler of the XIII century, whose tomb stood with many others in the portico of the ancient church, that is, of [the church] which was built after the fire of 1105.

In a footnote in the same section Cigogna refers to some inscriptions which had been found, adding that "those of the families of the Polo, Schiaveti, Guistiniani, Basadonna, Foscarini, and Biondi are still awaited." Thus in 1827 the tombs had disappeared, and no inscription remained to indicate the spot where Marco, his father, his wife, and his daughter Moreta lay buried.

An account has been published of more recent research and exploratory excavations in the Church of San Lorenzo. As a result of these studies, the last made in 1924, the director of the excavations came to the definite conclusion that it is useless to hope for the recovery of the remains of Marco Polo for reburial. He believed that when the church was rebuilt, the bones were removed and thrown into a common grave with those of victims of the plague and others, or else that when the church was partially razed before remodeling, they became, as have many other bones, part of the accumulated material used to bring the floor of the church to a higher level.[8]

[8] See article by Rodolfo Gallo, "La Ricerche della Tomba di Marco Polo," in *Rivista Mensile della Città di Venezia*, September, 1924. The author had occasion to visit again the places in Venice associated with the Polo family as late as the summer of 1938. The Church of San Lorenzo was then a dilapidated shell—the roof partly gone, the walls stripped and damaged, the pavements everywhere broken and torn up—with hardly a tombstone in place. Practically no undamaged evidence remained in the main edifice to indicate its former use for religious purposes. No priest was to be found, and when the ancient sacristan appeared with his keys, after a much rusted bell handle had been pulled again and again, he professed to know nothing of the tomb. The only information he could communicate was a hoary tradition that "the tomb stood over there, at the right of the door, and there were doves on it." By "doves" were perhaps meant the three jackdaws on the coat of arms of the Polos, referred to by Giambattista Ramusio in his introduction to Messer Marco's book.

Thus the exact burial place of Marco Polo is unknown at present. The very church where he asked to be buried near his father has been altered beyond recognition and is in ruins. Perhaps somewhere under the wrecked pavement of San Lorenzo still lies the coffin with the bones of the great traveler. It may be that

3. MESSER MARCO'S FAMILY

After hundreds of years of undisturbed repose in the dusty archives of Venice, several documents have recently been discovered which throw new light on the immediate family of Marco Polo. The tale is short but interesting.

Donna Donata Badoèr Polo, Marco's widow, first appears in the legal records of Venice on June 24, 1325, in a document whereby she and her three daughters delivered to Marco Bragadin, the husband of Fantina, a receipt for property which formerly belonged to Messer Marco.

Quarrels in the Polo family evidently continued after Marco's death, for his widow next appeared in the Venetian courts in a very unfavorable light. In some way not revealed to us, two bags of Venetian *grossi*, valued at $1,500, were left in her charge, tied up and sealed (*legati et bullati*), and placed in a sealed chest. When her son-in-law, Bertuccio Querini, Bellela's husband, took over the money and counted it, only $850 worth of the money was found. Relations between the two were evidently very strained, for Querini haled his mother-in-law before the Council of Forty, accusing her of abstracting the money "*non bono modo*" ("not in a goodly fashion"). She was found guilty, ordered to restore the money, and was fined an amount equal to $187.50. One may imagine the mutual attitudes of Querini and his mother-in-law.

Donata Polo figures once more in a document dated July 12, 1333, whereby she and her daughters were placed in possession of the property of Marco Polo, her late husband. The good woman died at some undiscovered date between July 12, 1333, and March 4, 1336, for on this latter date she is mentioned in a document as "the deceased widow of Marco Polo of the *sestiere* of San Giovanni Chrisostomo." Thus Donata survived her husband by at least ten years.

The dates of birth and death of the three daughters of the traveler have not been discovered, but a few facts about their lives have been preserved in Venetian documents, for the Polo family

proud Venice, which thus far has paid scant attention to the deeds of her greatest son, will some day erect to his memory that monument which is his due.

appears a number of times in open court and before other legal tribunals.

Fantina, the first-born daughter of Marco and Donata, was also the longest-lived of the three. She was married some time prior to 1318 to Marco Bragadin, who evidently enjoyed the confidence of his father-in-law. Fantina's name appears several times in extant documents pertaining to family affairs. One of the most interesting is an assignment, dated January 11, 1337, to Moreta, her surviving sister, of the household effects of their deceased mother. Therein is specific reference to those three beds, with their complete furnishings, which their father had also held sufficiently valuable to mention in his bequest to his wife, and which appear to have been prized family heirlooms.

On May 1, 1348, Fantina Bragadin again appears, this time as residuary legatee of her sister Moreta. By May 28, 1361, Fantina had become a widow, for on that date she appeared before the Court of the Procurators as the *"relicta nobilis viri Marci Bragadin,"* who seems to have died in Crete.

A lengthy decision of the Procurators of San Marco, dated August 4, 1362, would indicate further family difficulties among the Polos. It deals with certain properties which Fantina claimed were hers by inheritance from her father Messer Marco, and which her deceased husband had appropriated *"fraudulenter malo modo et violenter"* and against her will and consent.

Fantina Bragadin figures also in a court decision of July 13, 1366, in a lawsuit involving an inheritance claimed by her of property willed to her father Marco by his uncle Maffeo. The decision of the procurator in this case is one of the most valuable of recently discovered documents of the Polo family. Following several pages of an itemized list of properties bequeathed on his deathbed by Marco Polo, this notation appears in the handwriting of Marco Bragadin:[9] *"In nome de Dio 1323 die 8 zener mori miser Marco Polo."*[10]

[9] According to Orlandini, *op. cit.*, 4n.
[10] "In the name of God on the eighth day of January 1323 died Messer Marco Polo." The inventory was filed by Bragadin the month after Marco's death. See *Archivio di Stato, Procurati di S. Marco, 1323, Serie Misti, b. 152, fac. 2.*

248

The will of *"Fantina Polo, relicta nobilis Viri, domini Marci Bragadino,"* dated August 28, 1375, is still in existence, as is a bill of sale, found in the *"Ospitali e luoghi pii"* and dated December 18, 1380. By this document "Caterrucia Bragadin, daughter of the late Fantina Polo" sold a share of her maternal inheritance to one Fantino Marcello di Sant'Angelo. This evidence indicates that Fantina survived her father by at least fifty years and died at some unknown date between August 28, 1375, and December 18, 1380.

Bellela Polo, like her sister Fantina, was married during her father's lifetime, her husband being Bertuccio Querini. She survived her father Marco but a short time. She appears as living in a document dated June 24, 1325, but had died, childless, before October 16, 1326. On that date the Maggior Consiglio annulled her will on the ground that she was not of sound mind (*"non erat sane mentis"*) when she made it.[11]

Moreta, for whose dowry her father had provided in his will, was still unmarried at the beginning of 1326. This fact is attested by a legal document which has fortunately been preserved and which, besides giving another piece of information about the Polo family, reflects the social conditions of the Venice of the period. One Zanino Grioni assaulted Moreta Polo in the Campo San Vitale and, not content with the use of abusive language, laid violent hands on her (*verbis injuriosis et factis*). Neither the cause nor nature of the attack is recorded, but it must have been serious, for on February 26, 1326, Grioni was found guilty by the Council of Forty and sentenced to two months in jail. Justice was evidently speedy, for the document concludes with the note that "on that same day, before dinner, the said Zanino Grioni was arrested and placed in custody."

At some unknown date thereafter Moreta married Ranuccio Dolfin. In a document dated March 4, 1336, he appears as living, but in a later one, dated September, 1337, Moreta is referred to as his *"relicta"* or widow. Evidently another family difference arose, for she and one Baldovino Dolfin submitted their claims on Sep-

[11] It was her husband who two years after her death brought an action against his mother-in law to regain the money extracted from the two bags entrusted to her.

tember 12, 1337, for judicial arbitration "for the sake of peace and the avoiding of all scandal." On June 29, a decree was issued assigning property of her husband to Moreta. The case evidently dragged on for some years, however, as the final document in the file of the case is dated December 19, 1341. Nothing daunted by death or lawsuits, Moreta subsequently married Tomaso Gradenigo. We learn of this marriage from Moreta's will, dated May 1, 1348, in which she is mentioned as his wife and wherein he and her sister Fantina are named as her executors. The date of Moreta's death is unknown. It must have been before August 28, 1375, as Fantina's will of that date provides for money to be expended for prayers for Moreta's soul, among others. Moreta Polo, in spite of her two marriages, died childless.

Fantina, unlike her two sisters, had children—four sons and two daughters. Of these, Zanini and Nicoleto died unmarried before 1375. Steffano married Magdaluza Contareni and had by her two daughters, Cateruccia and Magdalucia, both of whom died unmarried. Steffano himself died before 1375, as his mother in her will of that year left money to be spent for prayers for his soul as well as for those of his two brothers. Another son, Pietro, married Ruzinella (surname not known) and was alive in 1403. The pair had a son Marco, who appears to have died unmarried at an unknown date. Of Fantina's daughters, Maria married Marcello (surname unknown) some time before May 1, 1348. She was still alive in 1375 and left two sons, Francesco and Fantino, who apparently died unmarried. The second daughter, Cateruccia, married a person whose name is not of record. By him she appears to have had a son Andriolo, although the reading is not clear. He was left forty *soldi* of *grossi* to outfit himself if and when he should become a priest. There is no further record of this Andriolo. Cateruccia appears in the latest document which has been discovered relating to Marco's descendants. On December 18, 1385, she sold her portion of the properties inherited from her mother to one Fantino Marcello di Sant'Angelo.

Thus the direct line of descendants of Messer Marco Polo and Donna Donata Badoèr Polo had no offspring after the third generation, and in the quaint phrase of Ramusio, "as the condition and the vicissitudes of human affairs brought it to pass, it became utterly extinct." In this way did the properties and wealth which the Venetian had labored so much of his life to accumulate become scattered and dissipated, and all finally passed into the hands of strangers.

4. "IL MILIONE"

The origin of the nickname "Il Milione" is uncertain as applied both to Marco Polo and to his book. In the contemporary work of Jacopo d'Acqui, Marco is referred to as "Master Marco the Venetian, who is called Millonus [or Milionus], which is the same as the wealth of a thousand thousands of lire, and so he is called in Venice." Ramusio, speaking of Marco's book in his Preface (1557), wrote:

> And because in the continual repetitions of the story which he gave more and more often when speaking of the magnificence of the Great Khan, he stated that his revenues were from ten to fifteen millions in gold, and in the same way in speaking of many other riches of those countries he spoke always in terms of millions, they gave him as a nickname, Messer Marco Millioni, and thus I have seen it noted in the public books of the Republic where mention is made of him, and the court of his house from that time to the present is still commonly called the Court of the Millioni.

When Messer Marco appeared as surety for the pardon of the smuggler Bonocio of Mestre he was set down as "Marco Polo Million." This event occurred in 1305, nearly twenty years before his death. In certain Latin papers concerning a lawsuit involving his daughter Fantina, dated September 5, 1362, he is referred to as "Marcus Polo Million." Sansovino, writing in 1581, states that "returning rich to his native country, he gained the cognomen of Milione through the riches brought back with him on his return." Cigogna, in a note written in 1827, expresses doubt and uncertainty concerning the origin of the name.[12] Thus through the centuries there has been no agreement of authority, and the matter must rest

12 While Yule and Orlandini incline to accept Ramusio's explanation, Benedetto has presented the novel theory that "Milione" is a form of "Emilio" and was part of Marco's full name.

undecided unless and until some hitherto undiscovered document reveals the true explanation.

The same strange uncertainty surrounds the title *Il Milione*, often given the book. Marco called the original, as far as is known, *La Divisement du Monde (The Description of the World)*. In describing the work, Jacopo d'Acqui, Marco's contemporary, states that it was entitled the *Book of Milione About the Wonders of the World*. Villani, another contemporary, refers to it as *Milione*. It is the title by which the book is commonly known in Italy today. The name may have been transferred from the book to the man as a nickname, or vice versa. No final decision is possible at present, and one surmise is as valid as another.

5. MARCO POLO'S WEALTH

The name Il Milione, as applied to Marco Polo, and the statement by some early writers that the appellation was based on his supposed great wealth, have given rise to much speculation regarding the real amount of that wealth. Fortunately, the researches of Orlandini have brought to light an inventory of at least a part of the property possessed by the traveler at the time of his death. The inventory is part of the record of the suit filed by Fantina Bragadin which revealed the date of Marco Polo's death. The list of goods covers several pages of the document. The property as catalogued therein consisted largely of various fabrics contained in boxes and coffers—one ironbound, another of walnut, etc. If one follows the calculations of Yule and those of Moule and Pelliot,[13] the value of the estate of Marco Polo appears to have been in the following amounts:

Gifts to charity in the will	$1,400.00
Investment value of the annuity left to Donata Polo (according to an estimate of Moule)	3,000.00
Goods as per inventory	6,865.00
Partial value of house (estimate of Moule)	3,500.00
Total	$14,765.00

[13] Yule, *op. cit.*, I, 71; Moule and Pelliot, *Marco Polo*, I, 31. The exact value of the various twelfth-century currencies is very difficult to estimate.

Even assuming, although there is no basis for such an assumption, that Marco had made gifts of portions of his property to various members of his family before his death, there appears nothing, in extant records at any rate, to warrant any belief that Marco's wealth attained more than very modest proportions. Though the sum total of the estate probably represented much more in actual value in the fourteenth century than in the latter part of the twentieth century,[14] there exists at present not a single fact which would lead to the conclusion that Messer Marco had accumulated that fabulous wealth so often attributed to him by writers of his day or later. The evidence that we have would, in fact, tend to cause one to be very skeptical, or even to reject Ramusio's account of the home-coming banquet of the Polos and their lavish display of jewels—unless, indeed, Messer Marco had been very extravagant in his living or had later sustained extraordinary and crippling losses in business or in the Genoese wars. There is no indication extant of either of these eventualities, and as the record stands today, the Venetian traveler seems to have lived modestly and to have died in comfortable but comparatively moderate circumstances.[15]

[14] An attempt has been made by Giuseppe Castellani to evaluate the various moneys mentioned in the will. See *Rivista Mensile delle Città di Venezia*, September, 1924, Anno III, No. 9.

[15] G. M. Urbani de Ghel, in *Bullettino d'Arti, Industrie, Numismatica e Curiosità Veneziane*, Anno III, No. 2, 1880, states that "a few months before" he had acquired a parchment document in Latin written in 1351, containing a list of objects "which are in the red room of the dwelling house of the very famous Messer Marino Faliero." (Note: The Doge Faliero was executed in 1355, convicted of plotting to overthrow the Republic of Venice.) This inventory contains, among other things, an enumeration of objects which appear to have been gifts from Marco Polo to Faliero, who was about forty years old when Marco died. A strongbox or casket is listed, containing objects in gold, among them a ring with the inscription "Ciuble Can Marco Polo" and a necklace in a pattern of wild animals, also a gift from Kublai Khan. There are also listed two chests of white leather, also containing gold and silver gifts to Polo by a barbarian king (*rege barbarorum*). There was a sword which the priest who drew up the list described as "*mirabilis*" and which had enclosed within it three other swords. "This sword," noted the same priest, "Marco himself carried with him in his travels." Another object was a "*tenturam*" (table service?) of Indian cloth "which Marco Polo had." Finally, the catalogue noted two books, one bound "in white leather with designs," entitled in Latin "*de itineribus*," and another copy "written by the hand of the aforesaid Marco," entitled "*de locis mirabilibus tartarorum*." The article by Ur-

6. THE MANUSCRIPTS AND PRINTED EDITIONS
OF MARCO POLO'S BOOK

It has been stated that the original manuscript of Marco Polo's book was written in Old French. Copies of this French text must have passed through many hands outside of Italy as well as within its borders. The story of the gift of a copy to Thiebault de Cepoy has been related. John of Ypres, Abbot of St. Bertin, also known as "John the Long," who compiled many valuable works of medieval travel and geography during the latter part of the fourteenth century, recounts the story of the Polos and their visits to the East and, speaking of Messer Marco, he adds, "And he afterwards composed a book about these things in the French vernacular, which book of marvelous matters, together with many similar [books] we have by us."

The French manuscript very evidently did not nearly satisfy the demand, and even during Marco's lifetime translations and abridgments were prepared. As early as 1520 an abbreviated translation was made into Latin (perhaps from a Lombard manuscript, not from the French original) "at the urgent request of many Brothers, Fathers, and Masters" by Friar Francesco Pipino of Bologna.[16] An Italian translation—in Tuscan, now in the Magliabecchian Library at Florence—can also be traced back to the lifetime of Polo. Other manuscripts gradually made their appearance in various languages—Venetian, Spanish, Bohemian, German, Aragonese,[17] Catalan, etc. In all, 119 manuscripts have been found to date, the latest in 1936, besides doubtful copies, compendiums, fragments, and extracts.

The book was very early used as a historical reference by the

---

bani adds "*delle reliquie di Marco Polo nulla rimase.*" Search by the present author has revealed no investigation or comment on this document or its authenticity in any authority on Marco Polo writing after 1880.

[16] See pages 16n. and 206.

[17] The archives of Aragon state: 1. In 1384 the Infant Joan presented to the Compte de Foix "*un llibre de Marco Polo*"; 2. On August 13, 1393, "being already king," he made present of another copy of "*mateix llibre*" to the Duc de Berry.

Florentine historian Giovanni Villani (*ca.* 1275–1348). In discussing the Tatars, Villani remarks:

> And whoever desires to learn fully about their deeds, let him seek out the book of Frate Aiton [Hayton], Lord of Colcos of Armenia, who prepared it at the instance of Pope Clement V, and again the book called *Milione*, which Messer Marco Polo of Venice made, he who recounts much of their power and their rule, inasmuch as he was for a long time among them. We shall leave the Tatars, and we shall return to our subject of the deeds of Florence.

That the tale recounted by Messer Marco found interested readers throughout Europe, even before the advent of printing, is attested by the large number of manuscript versions extant. One might assert that it began to circulate rapidly and was a sensational success; in the language of today it would certainly be called "a best seller," considering the small percentage of the population of Europe which could read. Its wide distribution is evidenced by a fragment of the work found by accident in Ireland, the westernmost civilized country of the known world (except Iceland) in the middle years of the fifteenth century. Its discovery is a romantic tale in itself.

In 1814 the Duke of Devonshire ordered repairs to be made on his ancient castle of Lismore, in Waterford County, Ireland. In the interior of the building the workmen found a doorway, sealed with masonry perhaps hundreds of years before the renovation began. The door was broken open, and a wooden box, containing a fine old crosier and a manuscript, was found. This famous manuscript, called the "Book of Lismore," remained virtually unstudied until 1839, when Eugene O'Curry, an eminent Irish scholar, investigated it thoroughly. It contained, among lives of the saints, legends, stories of Charlemagne, and the like, some incomplete extracts from the book of Marco Polo (about ten folios in all) written in Gaelic. This book had apparently been translated probably about the year 1460 "for Finghin McCarthy Reagh, Lord of

Carbery, and his wife Catherine, the daughter of Thomas, Eighth Earl of Desmond." The fragment, abridged and translated freely from the Latin version of Pipino, has been translated into English by Whitley Stokes.[18]

The interest in Marco Polo's work became ever greater, and it was one of the earliest books printed in Europe. It is strange that the text should have been compiled in French through the collaboration of a Venetian and a Pisan and still more unusual that the first printed edition should have been in the form of a German translation. This edition, bearing a fanciful portrait of Messer Marco on its title page, appeared in Nuremberg in 1477 and is one of the rarest of incunabula. The second edition was published, also in German, in Augsburg, in 1481. The first printed edition in modern French was issued in Paris in 1556. It was not the original work of Marco Polo but a French version from Pipino's Latin translation. The famous Italian edition of Ramusio[19] appeared in 1559. An abridged edition was printed in Italian in Venice by Marco Claseri in 1597.[20] And thereafter numerous editions have appeared in English (the first being a translation from the Spanish of Santaella by John Frampton, in London, in the early part of 1579), Spanish, Portuguese, Bohemian, Swedish, and other European languages and even in Chinese. Hardly any two of these editions are alike, as many of them have been derived from different manuscript versions. In fact, there is no assurance that we have as yet the complete work as prepared in the Genoese prison. The most authoritative version to date is that published by the Société de Géographie in Paris in 1824. A magnificent work on Marco Polo's text was published in 1928 by Luigi Foscolo Benedetto in Florence; it is a compilation and editing of all known texts (with copious notes) in an effort to produce what Sig. Benedetto calls an "*edizione integrale*." But, recent as this monumental work of scholarship is, it is incomplete because of later discoveries of manuscripts and other material.

---

[18] In *Zeitschrift für Celtische Philologie*, Band 2, 3 Heft (Halle, 1896–97).
[19] For information on Giovanni Battista Ramusio, see page 265 below.
[20] Copy in the author's collection.

An extremely valuable Latin text was recovered (though its likely location was known before) in 1932 after much search by Sir Percival David in the library of Cardinal Francisco Xavier de Zelada in Toledo, Spain. Cardinal Zelada (1717–1801), born of a Spanish family in Rome, had been "Librarian of the Holy Church" and secretary of state to Pius VI (1789–1796). He bequeathed his large library to the Casa di Gesù in Rome; part of it was obtained, however, at his death by Cardinal Francisco III Antonio Lorenzana and taken by him to the large Cathedral Library at Toledo, where he had been Archbishop from 1772 to 1800. An imperfect copy of the book had been made for the Ambrosian Library in Milan in 1795, but there were many errors in details. Handwriting experts judge the manuscript to have been copied in Italy in the fifteenth century, authorities differing as to the exact year. The transcription of the difficult manuscript was printed in 1935 and first published in London in 1938. This manuscript contains much new material, including several pages of information on Russia, which country, as far as is known, Marco Polo did not visit.

On the basis of Benedetto's work and the Zelada text, together with other records, the late Professor A. C. Moule of Cambridge University, together with the late brilliant French scholar Paul Pelliot, published what they termed "a composite translation." It was a prodigious and highly successful "attempt to weave together all, or nearly all, the extant words which have ever claimed to be Marco Polo's and to indicate the source from which each word comes." Volume I of the work contains an introduction, the translation, genealogical tables, pertinent documents, and lists of manuscripts and early printed editions. Volume II contains the Zelada Latin text. Other volumes of explanatory essays were to follow, but because of the death of Professor Pelliot, only two posthumous volumes of his notes have appeared, one in 1959, the second in 1963. An index, promised in Volume II, has not yet appeared.

For the general reader who is interested in Marco Polo's book rather than in the exact wording of the original text, the very fully annotated edition of Sir Henry Yule will be found the most satisfactory. No other edition contains more than a portion of the philological, ethnological, historical or geographical notes, and documentary material with which these volumes are replete, and they must ever be the starting point for any scholarly study of Marco Polo, his life, his travels, and his book.[21]

For the student with a knowledge of Latin and Italian, the rare pamphlet of the late G. Orlandini, *Marco Polo e la Sua Famiglia*, (Venice, 1926) will prove invaluable, containing as it does the texts of practically all the known documents relating to the Venetian traveler and his family.

7. HOW MARCO'S BOOK WAS FIRST RECEIVED, AND ITS LATER INFLUENCE ON GEOGRAPHY, CARTOGRAPHY, AND OTHER SCIENCES

Messer Marco Polo's reputation for veracity as an author suffered greatly during his lifetime, for his contemporaries (with very few exceptions) could not and did not accept his book seriously. Their ignorance and bigotry, their belief in and dependence on the ecclesiastical pseudogeography of the day, their preconceived ideas of the unvisited parts of the earth, as well as the inherited legends and utter nonsense to which the medieval mind clung with a blind persistence that is incomprehensible to modern man—all these factors combined to make it impossible to perceive or accept the truths contained in Marco's writings.

Jacopo d'Acqui, a contemporary of the traveler, records an anecdote which may be true. Marco's friends were evidently much concerned over the unfavorable reputation which he had gained by telling what were considered incredible exaggerations or downright lies. "And," noted Jacopo, "because [in Marco's book] there were to be found great things, things of mighty import, and, indeed almost unbelievable things, he was entreated by his friends

[21] Third edition, with a supplemental volume of notes and addenda, by Henri Cordier (London and New York, 1921). In spite of their excellence, however, extreme caution is necessary in using them, because of the results of research and finding of editions unknown to Yule, as well as much newly discovered material and documents. Moreover, a number of Yule's identifications have been found erroneous, and some of his theories have proven wrong.

when he was at the point of death to correct his book and to retract those things that he had written over and above the truth. To which he replied 'I have not written down the half of those things which I saw.' "[22] Whether the incident as reported occurred or not, every page of his volume attests to the truth of his statement concerning what he had himself seen.

This attitude of unbelief persisted for a number of years. The *Description of the World* was viewed as a creation of the author's vivid imagination by most of its readers—and, indeed, the manuscript was often bound in with manuscripts of romances and was usually classified as one. The compilation or fictional book of *Travels* of Sir John Maundeville, a spurious work, was very evidently more popular than Polo's truths, for five times as many editions of Maundeville were published in the fifteenth century as of Marco Polo's volume.[23]

Even as late as the end of the fourteenth century the veracity of the *Description* was often denied, doubted, or challenged. A Florentine manuscript of the work transcribed in 1392 is still preserved in the National Library of that city. Appended to it is the following curious note:

> Here ends the book of Messer Marco Polo of Venice, which I, Amelio Bonaguisi wrote with my own hand while Podestà of Cierreto Guidi to pass the time and [drive away] melancholy. The contents appear to me to be incredible things and his statements appear to me not lies but more likely miracles. And it may well be true that about which he tells; but I do not believe it, though none the less there are found throughout the world many very different things in one country and another. But this [book] seems to me, as I copied it for my pleasure to be [composed of] matters not to be believed or credited. At least, so I aver for myself. And I finished copying [it] in the aforementioned Cierreto Guidi on the 12th day of November in the year of the Lord 1392. And, the book being finished, we give thanks to Christ our Lord, Amen.

[22] "*O amici, vi accerto di non aver scritto neppure la metà di quanto mi fu dato vedere.*"

[23] See Malcolm Letts, *Sir John Mandeville: The Man and his Book.*

Bonaguisi's aspersions on Marco's veracity are not half so significant as is the revelation of the attitude of mind and lack of belief in
his book by those living in his own century.

Marco Polo's ill fortune pursued him even after men had begun
to accept his book as a real contribution to geography and the
other sciences. All knowledge of the man himself was lost, neglected, or ignored to such an extent that one historical writer of
sixteenth-century Spain (Mariana) referred to him as "one Marco
Polo, a Florentine physician," and an English author of the early
nineteenth century spoke of him as "a Venetian priest."

The demand of navigators for better maps finally resulted in the
production of more accurate charts for the use of seafaring men.
The first of these were the justly famous *portolani* made for practical navigation rather than for the general student. The *portolani*
reached their highest point of excellence in the products of a
family of Catalonian Jews who did their work on the island of
Majorca at the end of the fourteenth century. The greatest of
their atlases was that of 1375. It "differs from the ordinary
Portolans in that it has been expanded into a sort of world map.
Following the text of Marco Polo, it depicts eastern Asia, the
Deccan Peninsula and the Indian Ocean far better than any of the
earlier maps."[24] These charts were first made in the thirteenth
century and were used through the sixteenth century by seamen.
Before the compass came into general use, the names of the winds
were used to designate directions. "Legends were often inserted
referring to the products of the region bearing the legend, or to
the character of the inhabitants of the same. Much of this information appears to have been derived from Pliny, Solinus, Isador
(of Seville, in no way a reliable authority) or from travelers such
as Marco Polo."[25] There is an unsubstantiated tradition that the
world map of Marino Sanudo, made about 1320, was a copy of one
brought from China by Marco Polo.

Gradually the map makers of Europe recognized the validity of

[24] Erwin Raisz, General Cartography, New York and London, 1938.
[25] Edward L. Stevenson, *Portolan Charts*, Hispanic Society of America, New
York, 1911.

the geographical findings of Messer Marco, and a hundred years after his death the results of his book began to appear in their work. The influence of the Venetian's contribution became ever greater, in spite of many manifest errors in his location of various regions. Errera, the Italian historian, speaks of the writings of Polo as "a reliable fountain of truth" accepted by the end of the fourteenth century. The leaders of the European advances in science and discovery in that century and during the age of the great discoveries were often close students of Marco Polo's book. Fra Mauro's wall map of 1459, now in the Marcian Library at Venice, though it employs the fallacious theory of the disklike shape of the earth, appears to have taken place names and features from the book of Marco.

In 1426 (or 1428) Prince Pedro, the elder brother of Prince Henry the Navigator, visited Venice. While he was there, he was presented by the Signoria a copy of Marco's book and, according to tradition, a map copied from one made by Polo of his travels in the East.[26] Thus Marco Polo in all likelihood made a substantial contribution of valuable knowledge to the group of Portuguese geographers and navigators on the very eve of the discovery and exploration of a New World.

Contarini's map, published probably in Venice in 1506 (the earliest map known showing any part of America) contains names of places first mentioned by Marco Polo. Likewise the 1508 map of Johann Ruysch, published in Rome, contains for the first time the delineation of internal parts of East Asia, "no longer based on ... Marinus of Tyre and Ptolemy ... but on more modern reports, especially those of Marco Polo." The very important influence of Polo's book upon cartography need not be pursued further here, as later material is easily found in all histories of discovery, exploration, geography, or map making.

Marco Polo's contribution to his fellow men is not limited to his influence on the writings and maps of geographers. His prodigious memory, aided by the notes sent to him in his Genoese prison from

[26] See Francis M. Rogers, *The Travels of the Infante Dom Pedro of Portugal*, Harvard University Press, 1961.

his home in Venice, preserved aspects of the history, ethnology, sociology, physical geography, zoology, botany, economics, products, and politics of Asia such as have never been gathered into a single book by one man before or since. Even a short dissertation on each of the subjects discussed or mentioned by him would fill a small library. A list of the plants and animals named by him, excluding those which can no longer be identified from his descriptions, would fill pages. Yet carping critics complain that he has omitted much, instead of marveling that he has included so much precious information about the Asia of the thirteenth century which would otherwise have been irretrievably lost to the world.

8. AFTERMATH

In the middle of the fourteenth century darkness again settled over Asia. The trade routes became the prey of marauders. The "Everlasting Dynasty" of the Mongols fell after less than a century of diminishing glory, and the Ming Dynasty which overthrew it was antiforeign. Merchants and monks could no longer travel to and fro in safety from Europe to the Yellow Sea, and trade with the Far East faltered and died out. The ordinary man forgot Marco Polo and the strange new world which he had revealed, for internecine wars and the overwhelming victorious wave of Turkish conquest brought Europe new and serious problems. But Messer Marco's book lived on, passing from hand to hand, from country to country, from language to language, and was never entirely neglected. To some readers he brought the glow of romance, to others an escape from the everyday world about them to the unknown fabulous lands and peoples of Asia. To yet others his tale brought dreams—dreams of high adventure and of deeds of derring-do. To a few the book, written to while away long prison hours, brought stimulus to action, an urge to go forth and seek the unknown in their own day.

And when on that fateful third of August, 1492, Christopher Columbus sailed out from Palos to find another world, he carried with him a copy of the Pipino edition of Marco Polo's book in

Latin. That very copy, containing over seventy marginal notes in
the handwriting of the great discoverer, is still preserved in the
Columbian Library at Seville, Spain. It bears evidence of much
reading and study and must have been constantly at the navigator's
elbow during the difficult days and nights of the long voyage.
Thus in his book did the spirit of Messer Marco Polo, gentleman
of Venice, the first to write a rich and colorful description of
unknown Asia, fare forth over the seas with Columbus. It was
fitting that they should make this, the greatest and most momentous of all voyages, in one another's company—he who had revealed Asia to an incredulous Europe, and he who was, all
unwittingly, about to give a new world, a land of promise and of
high destiny, to mankind.

The greatness of Venice has vanished.

> *"Once did she hold the gorgeous east in fee,*
> *And was the safeguard of the west."*[27]

Now all that glory has departed. The spacious warehouses, heaped
high with the treasures of the East, the milling crowds of merchants and travelers on the Rialto, the wharves lined with richly
laden caravels, the proud and colorful pageants of the Doges, the
wedding with the sea—all these have passed away. Venice is fast
decaying. Her sunrises still clothe her in all their splendor of red
and gold, and the kindly twilight gently drapes her in blue and
gray and shimmering silver. The great moon still looks down on
her palaces, now deserted, dilapidated, and moldering, or become
the homes of humble laboring folk. The narrow waterways and
the Grand Canal still echo to the cries and calls of gondoliers and
the music of mandolin and guitar. But to him who knows her
history, her past prestige and glamor, Venice is sad—profoundly
sad and melancholy. She seems to dream of the days that were,
when she was mistress of the seas, and when conquest and glory
and the wealth of nations were hers. The waves softly lap at the
steps and bridges as aforetime, the stars shine down and are re-
flected in her waters as they have through the centuries, but the
days that were will return to proud Venice no more, and the spoils

[27] Wordsworth, "On the Extinction of the Venetian Republic."

of war and peace and commerce have passed from her. Indeed it seems at times as though the sea that once bore loaded argosies and galleys on its bosom is eager to take back unto himself what is really his—the lagoons and the islands of Venice, La Serenissima, his bride, whose greatest son was Messer Marco Polo, son of Messer Nicolo, who one day these many centuries past fared forth to unknown lands and on his return wrote a deathless book about it all, and who was neglected and forgotten by his own people and his own city.

Appendix: A Note on Ramusio

Giovanni Battista Ramusio, translator and annotator of the first important collection of accounts of discovery and exploration, was born in Treviso, on June 20, 1485, the son of Paolo Ramusio and Tamaris, nee Machachio. Taken to Venice when very young, he received a classical education there and in Padua, and then or later acquired a very competent knowledge of French, Spanish, and Portuguese.

This knowledge, together with honesty, courtliness, tact, and modesty, must have early attracted the attention of the heads of state, for when he was but twenty he was appointed clerk of the Chancellery of Venice and acted in this capacity for ten years. In 1515 he was advanced to the position of Secretary of the Senate, and from 1533 until his death in 1557 he served in the very important post of Secretary to the Council of Ten.

During his fifty years of public service he was dispatched on many missions for the Venetian Republic, among others as secretary to Alvise Mocenigo, envoy to the court of Louis XII in Paris, this task keeping him in France for eighteen months. During this sojourn he must have made considerable progress in French, for later he was appointed French interpreter to the Doge. Aside from this visit he does not appear to have traveled farther than to Genoa, to Switzerland, and perhaps to Rome.

On December 4, 1524, Ramusio married Franceschina Navagero, daughter of his relative and close friend Francesco Navagero, and had one son by her, Paolo, named for Ramusio's own father.

Throughout his life he never ceased his historical and literary studies. His notes and editorial comments, not always correct or faultless in the light of modern knowledge, give evidence of wide reading in the classics, ancient and contemporary, including among others Caesar, Cicero, Livy, Macrobius, and Ptolemy, as well as Oviedo, the Spanish historian, Peter Martyr, and Villehardouin. He translated the last into Italian.

Among his intimate friends and correspondents were the famous scholar-publisher Paulus Manutius Aldus, manager of the Aldine Press, the historian Andrea Navagero (whose work on Venice has unfortunately been lost), Girolamo Francastoro, and Cardinal Bembo, the Venetian historiographer. Though none of his own letters has survived, more than one hundred to him from these and other scholars testify to the diversity and profundity of his studies and interests. Moreover, several of these men and other associates were of valuable assistance to him in collecting material for his volumes. Navagero procured documents in Spain, unknown persons supplied him with Cartier narratives, and still another, perhaps Spain's envoy in Venice, is believed to have obtained for him priceless documents on the Coronado expedition.

Ramusio in his turn collaborated with these friends and others in their literary work. He aided Navagero in editing the Aldine editions of Cicero and Quintilian, and in the latter book, published before he had reached his thirtieth year, he was thanked by Aldus for his contribution. In addition, Aldus dedicated to him his edition of the *Third Decade* of Livy and the revised edition of the orations of Cicero. Ramusio also made translations of various Greek texts and assisted Cardinal Bembo in his official history of Venice.

His renown soon spread beyond Venice, and Donatus of Verona dedicated to him his edition of Macrobius, referring to him as *"doctissimus"* (most learned) in Greek and Latin.

The contents of the letters to him testify to the high regard in which he was held by his friends and the members of the scholarly circles in which he moved, and these, added to the fact that he refrained from appending his name to the two volumes of the *Viaggi* published during his lifetime, all reveal his scholarship, modesty, and frankness. His name appears in his posthumous Volume II of the *Viaggi* and in later editions of all three volumes.

Ramusio's friend and publisher, Tommaso Giunti, in the foreword introducing Volume II, printed in 1559, two years after Ramusio's death, wrote, in part:

> Two very serious events prevented me from satisfying your [the readers'] desire [for the projected Volume II]: one of these was the death of M. Giovan Battista Ramusio and the other the burning of my building establishment. And if the latter was a harsh blow for me, the former was most bitter for me, and how much grief and affliction this has brought me, every person to whom truly the great love between us two, which endured over such a long period of years, is known, can easily imagine. His was that remarkable intellect which, moved solely to benefit posterity by giving it information of so many and such distant countries—and in great part unknown to the ancients—gathered from diverse sources the two volumes with incredible diligence and judgment and, under his guidance and direction these were published by us on our press. He was able to do this most thoroughly, since he possessed besides the sciences and the knowledge which he had of the Latin and of the Greek languages, such as none other had, an expert's acquaintance with geography—which he had acquired partly from his continuous and diligent study of good authors with whom he was familiar, partly from having in his youth passed many years in various countries [having been] sent there in honorable service by this Most Illustrious Republic—whence it came to pass that he learned in like manner the French and Spanish languages, possessing them as well as [he did] his own native [tongue], and this [knowledge] served him in the translation of many narratives in the First and Third volumes. And if these [results of his] judicious and honorable labors did not make their appearance adorned with his name, it happened because of his

267

unusual modesty, which he was accustomed to employ continual-ly in his every action. He never conducted himself, wheresoever he might be placed, except as a man who was far from [having] any ambition, and had his mind directed solely at benefiting others, so that while he lived I loved him above everyone else and [now that he is] dead I shall love him as long as my life will last.

It is not known when Ramusio began to collect documents (though from his correspondence it must have been early) or when he began to translate the material for inclusion in the *Viaggi*.[1]

It is believed that a fourth volume was part of his project but that the documents were destroyed in the Giunti fire.

The original of the Polo narrative given by Ramusio in Volume II of his *Viaggi* has never been found. He appears to have known nothing of Rustichello of Pisa and to have held the belief that the original text of Marco Polo's manuscript was in Latin.

According to Cigogna's account, Ramusio died in Padua "at 1 P.M. Saturday, July 10, 1557, aged seventy-two years. His body was transported to Venice, and in this church [S. Maria] dell' Orto he was buried, according to his directions, in the tomb that he had erected to Tomaris his mother."

Cigogna further notes that "a portrait [of Ramusio] in conver-sation with Andrea Gradenigo, senator, was to be seen in the hall of the Maggiore Consiglio before the fire of 1577. We have an-other in the so-called Hall of the Shield, but it is rather the product of the imagination of the painter than a true [portrait]."

Ramusio's three volumes contain many narratives not found elsewhere before his collection was published. Unfortunately, none of his volumes has been reprinted since 1613, with the excep-tion of the Marco Polo account, which, with slight modernizations in printing, was published in 1954 by the Municipality of Venice

---

[1] It is noteworthy that in spite of his half century of service in the Republic's government, where he had the opportunity to examine countless documents, some of which might have been of value in his work, not a single Venetian paper ap-pears in any of his three volumes.

as part of the celebration of the seventh centenary of the birth of Marco Polo.[2]

[2] A reprint of the third edition of Ramusio's volumes has been announced (1966) in The Netherlands. The basic material on the life and work of Ramusio is the essay by Emanuele Antonio Cigogna in Vol. II, 315ff., of his *Inscrizioni Veneziane*, Venice, 1827. It contains (322ff.) a table of the contents of Ramusio's three volumes. A pamphlet, modestly entitled *The Contents and Sources of Ramusio's Navigationi*, compiled by George B. Parks, was published by the New York Public Library in 1955. It is an indispensable vade mecum for the student of Ramusio's volumes, containing as it does a list of the various editions of each volume with an analysis of the contents, and notes on variant readings as well as very valuable indications of Ramusio's sources.

Bibliography

Abd-er Rassak. Narrative of the Voyage of. *See* Major, *India in the Fifteenth Century.*

Ackerman, Phyllis. *Tapestry, the Fabric of Civilization.* New York, 1933.

Acton, Lord. *Lectures on Modern History.* London, 1906.

Adler, Elkan Nathan. *Jewish Travellers.* London, 1930.

Albrizzi, Giambattista. *Forestieri Illuminati.* Venice, 1765.

Almagià, Roberto. *La Figura e l'Opera di Marco Polo.* Rome, 1938.

———. "Marco Polo," in *VII Centenario della Nascita di Marco Polo.* Venice, 1955.

Amenti, W. S. *Marco Polo in Cambaluc.* Peking, 1892.

Anderson, Andrew R. *Alexander's Gate, Gog and Magog, and The Inclosed Nations.* Cambridge, Massachusetts, 1932.

Anon. *The History of Maritime and Inland Discovery.* 3 vols. London, 1830.

Anon. *Marco Polo, Venetiano.* Venice, 1597.

Anon. *Il Milione.* Turin, 1873.

Anon. *The Mongol Mission.* Ed. by Christopher Dawson. New York, 1955.

Anon. *Voyages de Benjamin de Tudelle, de Jean du Plan Carpin.* Paris, 1830.

Anon. *Wonders of Italy.* 7th ed. Florence, 1937.

Arrian. *History of Alexander and India.* Translated by E. Cliff Robson. 2 vols. Loeb Classical Library. London, 1929.

Asher, A. *Itinerary of Rabbi Benjamin of Tudela.* 2 vols. New York, n.d.

Azurara, Gomes Eannes de. *The Chronicle of the Discovery and Conquest of Guinea.* 2 vols. London, 1896–99.

Babinger, Franz. "*Maestro Ruggiero delle Puglie Relatori Pre-Poliano sui Tartari*", in *VII Centenario della Nascita di Marco Polo.* Venice, 1955.

Bacchelli, Riccardo. "*Marco Polo e la grande favola della Terra,*" in *Civiltà Veneziana del Secolo di Marco Polo.* Florence, 1955.

Backer, Louis de. *Extrême Orient au Moyen Age.* Paris, 1877.

Bagrow, Leo. *History of Cartography.* English ed., ed. by R. A. Skelton. Cambridge, Massachusetts, 1964.

Bailly, Auguste. *Sérénissime République de Venise.* Paris, 1958.

Baker, J. N. L. *History of Geographical Discovery and Exploration.* Boston and New York, 1931.

Balazs, Étienne. "*Marco Polo dans la Capitale de la Chine,*" in *Oriente Poliano.* Rome, 1957.

Ballesteros Beretta, Antonio. *Génesis del Descubrimento.* Barcelona, 1947.

Barckhausen, Joachim. *L'Empire Jaune de Genghis-Khan.* Trans. by George Montandon. Paris, 1935.

Barlow, Roger. *Brief Summe of Geographie.* London, 1932.

Barthold, V. V. *La Découverte de l'Asie.* Paris, 1947.

Barthold, W. *Geographische und Historische Erforschung des Orients, mit Besonderer Berücksichtigung der Russischen Arbeiten.* Leipzig, 1913.

Bausani, Alessandro. "*Religione Islamica,*" monograph in *Le Civiltà dell' Oriente.* Vol. III. Rome, 1958.

Beale, Samuel. *Life of Hiuen-Tsiang.* London, 1911.

Beazley, C. Raymond. *Dawn of Modern Geography.* 3 vols. Oxford, 1906.

———. *Texts and Versions of John de Pian Carpini.* London, 1903.

Benedetto, Luigi Foscolo. *Di una Pretesa Redazione Latina che Marco Polo Avrebbe Fatta del Suo Libro.* Florence, 1930.

———. *Il Libro di Messer Marco Polo Cittadino di Venezia detto Milione dove si raccontano Le Meraviglie del Mondo.* Milan-Rome, 1932–.

———. *Le Meraviglie del Mondo.* Milan, 1932.

———. *Le Meraviglie del Mondo.* Trans. into English by Aldo Ricci under the title *Marco Polo.* London, 1931.

———. *Il Milione.* Florence, 1928.

———. "*Tradizione Manoscritta del 'Milione' di Marco Polo*" (reprint of Part I of Benedetto, "*Il Milione*" *supra*). Turin, 1962.

Benjamin of Tudela. *The Itinerary*. Trans. and ed. by A. Asher. New York, n.d.

———. Translation, Bohn Library. London, n.d.

Bennett, Josephine Waters. *The Rediscovery of Sir John Mandeville*. New York, 1954.

Bensaude, Joaquim. *Histoire de la Science Nautique Portugaise*. Résumé. Genève, 1917.

Benz, Ernst. "*Cristianesimo d'-Oriente*," monograph in *Le Civiltà dell' Oriente*, Vol. III. Rome, 1958.

Berchet, Guglielmo. *Marco Polo ed il Suo Libro*. Venice, 1871.

Bergeron, Pierre. *Voyages Fatts Principalement en Asie*. La Haye, 1735.

Bernier, Francois. *Travels in India*. Oxford, 1914.

Bertholot, André. *Asie Ancienne . . . d'apres Ptolomée*. Paris, 1930.

Bettex, Albert. *The Discovery of the World*. London, 1960.

Blunt, Wilfred. *Pietro's Pilgrimage*. London, 1953.

Boccaccio, Giovanni. *Il Comento alla Divina Commedia e gli altri scritti intorna a Dante*. 3 vols. Bari, 1918.

Böhme, Max. *Grossen Reisesammlungen des 16 Jahrhunderts und ihre Bedeutung*. Amsterdam, 1962.

Boissonade, P. *Life and Work in Mediaeval Europe*. Translation with Introduction by Eileen Power. New York, 1927.

———. *Le Travail dans l'Europe Chrétienne au Moyen Age*. Paris, 1930.

Bonfadini, R. *et al. La Vita Italiana nel Trecento. (conferenze)*. Milan, 1941.

Bongi, Salvatore. "*Le Schiavi Orientali in Italia*," in *Nuova Antologia di Scienze, Lettere ed Arti*, II, 215. Florence, 1866.

Boni, Gio. Batt. Baldelli. *Il Milione di Marco Polo*. Florence, 1827.

Bonmarchand, Georges. "*Le Commerce de la Chine*," in Vol. III, *Histoire du Commerce*. Paris, 1953.

Bonvalot, Gabriel. *Marco Polo*. Paris, 1924.

Boulnois, Luce. *La Route de la Soie*. Paris, 1963.

Bourne, Edward Gaylord. "Voyages of Columbus and of John Cabot," in *The Northmen, Columbus and Cabot*. New York, 1953.

Bowle, John. *Man Through the Ages*.

Boxer, C. R. *South China in the Sixteenth Century*. London, 1953.

Boyle, John Andrew. "The Mongol Invasion of Persia, 1220–1223," in *History Today*, Vol. XLLL, No. 9. London, 1963. *See also* Juvalni.

Bradford, John. "The Nomad

Empires of Asia," in *The Concise Encyclopaedia of World History*. London, 1958.

Brady, Cyrus Townsend, Jr. *Commerce and Conquest in East Africa*. Salem, 1950.

Bragadin, Marc'antonio. *Histoire des Républiques Maritimes Italiennes*. Paris, 1955.

Bratianu, G. I. *Recherches sur le Commerce Genois dans la Mer Noire au XIII Siècle*. Paris, 1929.

Bravetta, Ettore. *Enrico Dandolo*. Milan, 1929.

Bretschneider, E. *History of European Botanical Discoveries in China* (reprint). 2 vols. Leipzig, 1962.

———. *Mediaeval Researches from Eastern Asiatic Sources*. 2 vols. London, 1910.

Brown, Horatio F. *In and Around Venice*. New York, 1905.

———. "Venice," in *Encyclopaedia Brittanica*, 14th ed., Vol. 23. London and New York, 1929.

Brown, Lloyd A. *The Story of Maps*. Boston, 1949.

———. *The World Encompassed*. Baltimore, 1952.

Browne, Sir Thomas. Works, 6 vols. London, 1926.

Brunetto, Latini. *Il Tesore, volgarazzato da Bono Giamboni*. Bologna, 1878.

Bryant, Arthur. *The Age of Chivalry*. New York, 1964.

Budge, E. A. Wallis. *The Monks of Kublai Khan*.

Burke, Edmund. *The History of Archery*. London, 1958.

Burton, Sir Richard. *The Thousand and One Nights*. 17 vols. London, n.d.

Burton, Robert. *The Anatomy of Melancholy*. 3 vols. (Bohn ed.). London, 1903.

Byrne, Eugene H. *Genoese Shipping in the Twelfth and Thirteenth Century*. Cambridge, Massachusetts, 1930.

Byron, Robert. *The Byzantine Achievement*. London, 1929.

Cady, John F. *Southeast Asia*. New York, 1964.

Cahun, Leon. *Introduction à l'Histoire de l'Asie*. Paris, 1896.

Campi, P. M. *Dell' Historia Ecclesiastica di Pincenza*. Part II. 1651.

Canale, Michel-Giuseppe. *Nuova Istoria della Republica di Genova*. Florence, 1860.

Candolle, Alphonse du. *Origin of Cultivated Plants*. New York, 1902.

Canestrini, Giuseppe. "*Mar Nero é le Colonie degli Italiani nel Medio Evo, II*," in *Archivio Storico Italiano*, N.S., Vol. V, Pt. 1a, p. 3.

Cange, Charles D. du. *Glossarium Mediae et Infimae Latinitatis*. 7 vols. Paris, 1845.

Cantrill, T. C. *Coal Mining*. Cambridge, Massachusetts, 1914.

Cantu, César. *Historie des Italiens*. Trans. by Lacombe. 12 vols. Paris, 1860.

Capecchi, Fernando. "*Livro das Maravilhas*" *de Marco Polo, O.* in *Sociedade de Geografia de Lisboa Boletim*, 73 série, Numeros 7–9. Lisbon, 1955.

Caramiñas, Juan. *Vinjes de Marco Polo*. Buenos Aires, n.d.

Carden, Robert W. *The City of Genoa*. London, 1908.

Cardona, Maria de, and Suzanne Dobelmann. *El Millón*. Madrid, 1934.

Carpine, Giovanni da Pian del. *Viaggio a Tartari*. Ed. by G. Pullè. Milan, 1929.

Carpini, John de Pian. Ed. by Raymond C. Beazley. London, 1903.

Carpini, Johann de Plano. *Geschichte der Mongolen und Reisebericht 1245–1247*. Leipzig, 1930.

Castellan, G. "*I Valori delle monete espresse nel testamento di Marco Polo*," in *Rivista Mensile della Città di Venezia*, Anno III, N. 9. Venice, 1924.

Cessi, R., and A. Alberti. *Rialto: l'Isola, il Ponte, il Mercato*. Bologna, 1934.

Chardin, Sir John. *Travels in Persia*. With introduction by Sir Percy Sykes. London, 1927.

Charignon, A. J. H. *Grande Java de Marco Polo en Cochinchine* (pamphlet). Saigon, 1930.

———. *Le Livre de Marco Polo*. 3 vols. Peking, 1924–28.

Charlesworth, M. P. *Trade-Routes and Commerce of the Roman Empire*. Cambridge, 1926.

Charton, Edouard. *Voyageurs Anciens et Modernes*. 2 vols. Paris, 1854.

Chatterton, E. Keble. *Sailing the Seas*. London, 1931.

Chau Ju-Kua. *Chu-Fan-Chi, the Chinese and Arab Trade in the Twelfth and Thirteenth Centuries*. Trans. by W. W. Rockhill and Friedrich Hirth. Chinese Text, Peking, 1914. Translation, St. Petersburg, 1912.

Chlovski, Victor. *Le Voyage de Marco Polo*. Paris, 1938.

Ciba Review. Basel, Switzerland, 1937–41.

Cibrario, Luigi. *Della Schiavitù e del Servaggio*. 2 vols. Milan, 1868.

Cicogna, Emmanuele Antonio. *Delle Inscrizioni Veneziane*. 5 vols. Venice, 1824–30.

La Civiltà Dell' Oriente. 3 vols. Ed. by Antonio Gargeno. Rome, 1956–58.

Clari, Robert de. *The Conquest of Constantinople*. Trans. by Edgar Holmes McNeal. Columbia University Press, 1936.

Clark, William. *Explorers of the World*. New York, 1964.

Classics Illustrated. *The Adventures of Marco Polo.* New York, n.d.

Clavijo. *Embassy to Tamerlane.* Trans. by Guy le Strange. Broadway Travellers' Series. New York and London, 1929.

Clifford, Sir Hugh. *Further India.* London, 1904.

Coedes, George. *Textes d'Auteurs Grecs et Latins Rélatifs à l'Extrême-Orient.* Paris, 1910.

Coletti, Luigi. *"Le Arti Figurative,"* in *Civiltà Veneziana del Trecente.* Venice, 1955.

Collins, W. W. *Cathedral Cities of Italy.* New York, 1911.

Collinson, Clifford. *Explorers All.* London, 1933.

Collis, Maurice. *The Grand Peregrination.* London, 1949.

——. *Marco Polo.* 2d ed. London, 1959.

Commynes, Phillipe de. *"Mémoires,"* in *Historiens et Chroniqueurs du Moyen Age.* Ed. by Albert Panphilet. Paris, 1938.

Comnena, Anna. *The Alexiad.* Trans. by Elizabeth A. S. Dawes. London, 1928.

Comune Di Venezia. *Marco Polo. Celebrazione del settime centenario della nascita.* Venice, 1954.

——. *Mestra dei Navigatori Veneti del Quattrecente e del Cinquecento.* Venice, 1957.

Conze, Edward. *"Buddhismo,"*

monograph in *Le Civiltà dell Oriente*, Vol. III. Rome, 1958.

Conti, Nicolo de. *Viaggi in Persia, India e Giava, a cure di Mario Longhena.* Milan, 1929.

Cordier, Henri. *Centenaire de Marco Polo.* Paris, 1896.

——. *Mélanges d'Histoire et de Géographie Orientales.* 2 vols. Paris, 1920.

——. *Les Merveilles de l'Asie.* Paris, 1925.

——. *Ser Marco Polo.* Notes and addenda to Sir Henry Yule's edition of Marco Polo. London, 1920.

——. *Les Voyages en Asie au XIVême Siècle du Bienheureaux Frère Oderic de Pordenone.* Paris, 1891.

Cordier, W. W. *"Extrême Orient dans l'Atlas Catalan de Charles V,"* in *Bulletin de Géographie Historique*, Vol. 10. Paris, 1896.

Coryat, Thomas. *Coryat's Crudities.* MacLehose reprint, 2 vols. Glasgow, 1925.

Cosmos, Indicopleustes. *Christian Topography.* Trans. by J. W. McCrindle. London, 18??.

Couling, Samuel. *The Encyclopaedia Sinica.* Shanghai, 1917.

Coupland, R. *East Africa and Its Invaders.* Oxford, 1956.

Crawford, Francis Marion. *Gleanings from Venetian History.* 2 vols. London, 1905.

——. *Salve Venetia.* 2 vols. New York, 1906.

Crawford, M. D. C. *The Conquest of Culture.* New York, 1938.

Crone, G. R. *The Explorers.* London, 1962.

———. *Maps and Their Makers.* London, 1953.

Crump, G. C., and E. F. Jacobs (eds.). *The Legacy of the Middle Ages.* Oxford, 1926.

Curtin, Jeremiah. *The Mongols.* Boston, 1908.

Dainelli, Giotto. *Marco Polo, celebrazione del settimo centenario della nascità* (pamphlet). Venice, 1954.

Daly, Charles P. "On the Early History of Cartography . . .," *Journal of the American Geographical Society,* Vol. II. New York, 1879.

Daniel, Hawthorne. *Ferdinand Magellan.* New York, 1964.

Darke, Richard. *The Quest of the Indies.* Oxford, 1920.

Daru, P. *Histoire de la République de Venise.* 5 vols., 4th ed. Paris, 1853.

Davies, C. Stella. *Exploring the World.* London, 1965.

Davis, William Stearns. *A Short History of the Middle East.* New York, 1922.

Dawson, Christopher. *The Mongol Mission.* New York, 1955.

Demiéville, Paul. "*Letteratura Cinese,*" monograph in *Le*

Civiltà dell'Oriente. Vol. II. Rome, 1957.

Demus, Otto. "*Oriente e Occidente nell' Arte Veneto del Duecento,*" in *Civiltà Veneziana del Secolo di Marco Polo.* Florence, 1955.

Derry, T. K., and Trevor I. Williams. *A Short History of Technology.* Oxford, 1960.

Desideri, Ippolito. *An Account of Tibet.* London, 1932.

Dickinson, R. E., and O. J. R. Howard. *The Making of Geography.* Oxford, 1933.

Diehl, Charles. *Histoire de l'Empire Byzantin.* Paris, 1924.

Doresse, Jean. *L'Empire du Prêtre-Jean.* 2 vols. Paris, 1957.

Douglas, Hugh A. *Venice and Her Treasures.* New York, 1909.

Dowson, John. *A Classical Dictionary of Hindu Mythology and Religion, etc.* London, 1914.

Duarte, Barbosa. *Book of Barbosa Duarte.* 2 vols. The Hakluyt Society, London, 1918–21.

———. *A Description of the Coasts of East Asia and Malabar in the Beginning of the Sixteenth Century.* Trans. by E. Stanley. London, 1866.

Dunne, George H. *Generation of Giants.* University of Notre Dame Press, 1962.

Ebersolt, Jean. *Constantinople,*

Byzantium et les Voyageurs du Levant. Paris, 1918.

L'École des Langues Vivantes Orientales. *Recueil d'Itinéraires et de Voyages dans l'Asie Centrale et l'Extrême Orient*. Paris, 1878.

Eden, Richard. *First Three English Books on America*. Ed. by Edward Arber. Birmingham, 1885.

Edrisi, Al-Sharif. "Geographie," in *Memoires de la Société de Géographie*. Vols. V and VI. Paris, 1836, 1840.

Eldridge, F. B. *The Background of Eastern Sea Power*. London, 1948.

Eliade, Mircea. *Shamanism* (trans. from the French). London, 1965.

Elliot, H. M. *Early Arab Geographers*. Ed. by John Dowson. Calcutta, 1956.

Embacher, Friedrich. *Lexikon der Reisen und Endekungen*. Amsterdam, 1961.

Enciso, Martin Fernandez de. *Suma de Geographia*. Seville, 1518.

Encyclopedia of Islam (new edition). Vol. I. Leiden, 1960.

Encyclopédie de la Pléiade. *Histoire Universelle*. 3 vols. Paris.

Errera, Carlo. *Epoca delle Grandi Scoperte Geografiche*. 2d ed. Milano, 1910.

Ferrand, Gabriel. "*Le K'ouen-Louen et les Anciennes Navigations Interocéaniques dans les Mers du Sud*," in *Journal Asiatique*. Paris, 1919.

——. *Relation de Voyages et Textes Géographiques Arabes, Persans et Turcs Relatifs à l'Extrême-Orient*. 2 vols. Paris, 1913.

——. *Voyage du Marchand Arabe Sulayman*. Paris, 1922.

Ferrari, Sante. *Per la Biografia e per gli Scritte di Pietro d'Abano*," *R. Accadèmia dei Lincei Roma*, Classa di Scienze Ser 5a, Vol. XV, p. 629. Rome, 1918.

——. "*I Tempi la Vita, le Dottrine di Pietro d'Abano*," in *Atti della R. Universitate di Genova*, Vol. XIV. Genoa, 1900.

Ficalho, Conde de. *Viagens de Pedro da Covilhan*. Lisbon, 1898.

Finger, Charles J. *The Travels of Marco Polo*.

Firestone, Clark B. *The Coasts of Illusion*. New York and London, 1924.

Fiske, John. *The Discovery of America*. 2 vols. Boston & New York, 1892.

Foord, Edward. *The Byzantine Empire*. London, 1911.

Forbes, R. J. *Bitumen and Petroleum in Antiquity*. Leiden, 1936.

——. *Studies in Ancient Technology*. Vol. VI. Leiden, 1958.

Foville, Jean de. *Gênes*. Paris, 1907.

Fox, Ralph. *Genghis Khan*. London, 1936.

Frampton, John. *The Most Noble and Famous Travels of Marco Polo*. London, 1929.

Fraser, Mrs. Hugh. *Italian Yesterdays*. London, 1914. Friedrich Hirth Anniversary Volume, London, 1923.

Freeman-Grenville, G. S. P. *The East African Coast*. Oxford, 1962.

Fresne, du. *Histoire de l'Empire de Constantinople sous les Empereurs Français*. Paris, 1657.

Gabriel, Alfons. *Marco Polo in Persien*. Vienna, 1963.

Gallo, R. "*Le Richerche della tomba di Marco Polo nella Chiesa di San Lorenzo*," in *Rivista Mensile dellà Città di Venezia*. Anno III, n. 9. Venice, 1924.

Gallo, Rodolfo. "*Marco Polo, la sua Famiglia e il suo Libro*," in *VII Centenario della Nascità di Marco Polo*. Venice, 1955.

Galvano, Antonio. *Discoveries of the World*. Hakluyt Society, London, 1852.

Gambier, Henri. *The Doges of Venice*. Venice, 1946.

Gardner, Edmund G. *Italy*. London, 1934.

Gaudio, Attilio. *Sur Les Traces de Marco Polo*. Paris, 1955.

Gibbon, Edward. *Decline and Fall of the Roman Empire*. 6 vols. Everyman ed. London, 1919.

Giles, Herbert A. *Adversaria Sinica*. Shanghai, 1914.

———. *A Chinese Biographical Dictionary*. London and Shanghai, 1898.

———. *History of Chinese Literature*. London, 1907.

———. *Travels of Fa Hsien*. Cambridge, 1923.

Giovio, Paolo. "Historie Written in the Latin Toonge" (extract), in Richard Eden's *The First Three English Books on America*. Birmingham, 1885.

Giudici, Paolo. *Storia dei Viaggiatori, dei e degli Esploratori*. Florence, 1936.

Glathe, Harry. *The Origin and Development of Chinese Money*. Shanghai, 1939.

Gonçalves, Julio. "*Mostras*" Italianas de 1254, etc., in *Boletim da Sociedade de Geografia de Lisboa*. July–December, 1954, 72-e Série, no. 7–12. Lisbon, 1954.

Goodrich, L. Carrington. "Notes on Marco Polo" (review of "Notes on Marco Polo," Vol. I), in *Journal of the American Oriental Society*. Vol. 81, No. 4. New Haven, 1961.

———. "Westerners and Central Asians in Yüan China," in *Oriente Poliano*. Rome, 1957.

Grantham, A. E. *Hills of Blue.* London, 1927.

Grekov, B., and Iakoubovski. *La Horde d'Or.* Trans. by François Thuret. Paris, 1939.

Grosvenor, Edwin A. *Constantinople.* 2 vols. Boston, 1900.

Grousset, René, *et al. Asie Orientale des Origines au XVe Siècle,* being Vol. X of *Histoire du Moyen Age.* Paris, 1941.

———. *L'Empire des Steppes.* Paris, 1960.

———. *Histoire de l'Extrême Orient.* 2 vols. Paris, 1929.

———, and Émile G. Léonard, eds. *Histoire Universelle.* Vol. II. Paris, 1957.

Gubernatis, Angelo de. *Storia dei Viaggiatori Italiani.* Leghorn, 1875.

Guerdon, René. *Vie, Grandeurs et Misères de Venise.* Paris, 1959.

Guillaume de Rubriq. "*Voyages en Tartarie et en Chine, on 1253,*" in *Voyages de Benjamin de Tudelle.* Paris, 1830.

Gusman, Pierre. *Venice.* Paris, 1907.

Haddon, Alfred C. *History of Anthropology.* London, n.d.

Hadi, Hasan. *A History of Persian Navigation.* London, 1928.

Hadjinicolaou-Marava, Anne. *Rercherches sur la vie des esclaves dans le Monde Byzantin.* Athens, 1950.

Haithon (*see also* Haiton and Hayton). *Armeni Historia.* Brandenburg, 1671.

Hakluyt, Richard. *Principall Navigations Voiages & Discoveries of the English Nation* (Originally published in 1589, reprinted for the first time by the Hakluyt Society, 1965.) 2 vols. Cambridge, 1965.

Hakluyt Society. *India in the Fifteenth Century.* Ed. by H. Major. London, 1857.

Halde, John Baptiste du. *General History of China.* 4 vols. London, 1736.

Hallberg, Ivar. *Extrême Orient dans la Litterature et la Cartographie de l'Occident des XIIIe et XVe Siècles.* Göteborg, 1907.

Hambis, Louis. "*Le Pretendu 'Cogatal' de Marco Polo,* in *VII Centenario della Nascità di Marco Polo.* Venice, 1955.

———. "*Voyage de Marco Polo en Haute Asie,*" in *Oriente Poliano.* Rome, 1957.

Hammer, J. de. *Histoire des Assassins.* Trans. from the German. Paris, 1833.

Hare, August J. C. *Venice.* London, n.d.

Hare, Christopher. *Dante the Wayfarer.* London, 1905.

Harff, Arnold von. *The Pilgrimage* (trans. by Malcolm Letts). London, 1946.

Harlow, Vincent T. *Voyages of Great Pioneers.* Oxford, 1929.

Harrisse, Henry. *The Discovery of North America* (reprint). Amsterdam, 1961.

Hart, Henry H. *A Garden of Peonies.* Stanford and Oxford, 1938.

——. *Luis de Camoëns and the Epic of the Lusiads.* University of Oklahoma Press, 1962.

——. *Sea Road to the Indies.* New York and London, 1950.

——. *El Veneciano Adventurero.* Buenos Aires, 1954.

——. *Venetian Adventurer.* Stanford, 1942.

——. *Venezianischer Abenteurer.* Bremen, 1959.

——. *Wenecki Podróznik.* Warsaw, 1963.

Havell, E. B. *The History of Aryan Rule in India.* New York, n.d.

Hazlitt, W. Carew. *The Venetian Republic.* 2 vols. London, 1900.

Hedin, Sven. *Overland to India.* 2 vols. London, 1910.

——. *The Silk Road.* New York, 1938.

——. *The Wandering Lake.* New York, 1940.

Hennig, Richard. *Terrae Incognitae.* 4 vols. Leiden, 1936–39.

Herodotus. *History.* Trans. by Rawlinson, ed. by H. Blakeney. London, 1910.

Herriott, J. Homer. "The Toledo Manuscript of Marco Polo," *Speculum,* Vol. XII (1937), p. 456.

Herrmann, Albert. *Das Land der Seide und Tibet im Lichte der Antike.* Leipzig, 1938.

——. *Die Verkehrswege, zwischen China, Indien und Rom.* Leipzig, 1922.

Herrmann, Paul. *Conquest by Man.* Trans. from the German, *Sieben vorbei und acht Verweht.* New York, 1954.

——. *Das Grosse Buch der Entdekungen.* Reutlingen, 1958.

——. *The World Unveiled.* Trans. of *Zeigt mir Adams Testament.* London, 1958.

Heyd, W. *Histoire du Commerce du Moyen Age.* (Reimpression) 2 vols. Leipzig, 1936.

Hickinbotham, Sir Tom. *Aden.* London, 1958.

Hirth, Friedrich. Anniversary volume. London, 1923.

——, and W. W. Rockhill. *Chau Ju Kua.* 2 vols. St. Petersburg, 1912.

——. *China and the Roman Orient.* Leipzig and Shanghai, 1885.

Hodgson, F. C. *Venice in the Thirteenth and Fourteenth Centuries.* London, 1926.

Hodgson, Masshall G. S. *The Order of the Assassins.* The Hague, 1955.

Home, Gordon. *Aong the Rivieras of France and Italy.* London, 1926.

Hookham, Hilda. *Tamburlaine the Conqueror*. London, 1962.

Horace (Quintus Horatius Flaccus). *Odes and Epodes*. Loeb Classical Library. London, 1925.

Horst von T. Scharner (ed.). *Der Mitteldeutsche Marco Polo*. Berlin, 1935.

Hourani, George F. *Arab Seafaring in the Indian Ocean* . . . Princeton, 1951.

Howorth, H. H. *History of the Mongols*. 4 vols. London, 1876–1927.

Hudson, G. F. *Europe and China*. London, 1931.

Humboldt, Alexander. *Examen*. Vol. V. N.d., n.p.

——. *Kosmos*. N.d., n.p.

Hutton, Edward. *Italy and the Italians*. New York, 1903.

——. *Ravenna: A Study*. London, 1913.

——. *Venice and Venetia*. London, 1911.

Hutton, Laurence. *Literary Landmarks of Venice*. New York, 1896.

Ibn Battuta. *Travels in Asia and Africa, 1325–1354*. Trans. by H. A. R. Gibb. London, 1929.

——. *The Travels of* . . . . Trans. by H. A. R. Gibbs. Vols. I and II of four to be published. Cambridge, 1957.

——. *I Viaggi*. Selections trans. by Francesco Gabrieli. Florence, 1951.

——. *Voyages*. Trans. by C. Defremery and B. R. Sanguinetti. 3d printing, 5 vols. in 4. Paris, 1893.

Al Idrisi, Al-Sharif. *Géographie d'Idresi*. Trans. from the Arabic by P. Amedée Jaubert. *See also* Edrisi. Paris, 1840.

Instituto Veneto di Scienze, Lettere ed Arti. *Nel VII Centenario della Nascità di Marco Polo*. Venice, 1955.

Ispizúa, Segundo de. *Historia de la Geografia y de la Cosmografia* . . . Madrid, 1922.

Iwamura, Shinobu. *Manuscripts and Printed Editions of Marco Polo's Travels* (pamphlet). Tokyo, 1949.

Jackso, G. Gibbard. *Boek der Ontdekkingsreizen*. 's Gravenhage, n.d.

James, David H. *The Rise and Fall of the Japanese Empire*. London, 1951.

Jarnes, Benjamin. *El Millon*. (Trans.) Mexico, D. F., n.d.

Jervis, W. W. *The World in Maps*. New York, 1937.

Jewish Encyclopedia, Vol. I. Article on "Benjamin of Tudela." New York, 1901.

John of Ypres (Johannes Iperii Abbatis). *"Chronicum,"* in *Thesaurus Novus Anecdotum*. Paris, 1717.

Johnson, Hildegard Binder. *Carta Marina*. Minneapolis, 1963.

Jordanus, Friar. *Mirabilia Descripta*. London, 1843.

———. *The Wonders of the East*. Trans. by Henry Yule. London, 1863.

Josephus, Flavius. *Wars of the Jews*. 3 vols. New York, n.d.

Josselin de Jong, P. E. de. "*Religioni dell' Indonesia*," monograph in *Le Civiltà dell' Oriente*, Vol. III. Rome, 1958.

Julien, Ch-André. *Les Voyages de Découverte . . .* Paris, 1948.

Julien, Stanislas. *Voyages des Pélérins Bouddhistes*. 2 vols. Paris, 1868.

Juvaini, 'Ala-ad-din 'Ata-Malik. History of the World-Conqueror. Trans. by John Andrew Boyle. 2 vols. Manchester, 1958.

Kammerer, Albert. "*Découverte de la Chine par les Portugais au XVIème Siècle et la Cartographie eds Portulans*," in *T'oung Pao*, Suppl. to Vol. XXXIX. Leiden, 1944.

Kerr, Robert. *General History and Collection of Voyages and Travels*. Vol. I. Edinburgh, 184?

Khaldûn, Ibn. *The Muqaddimah* (An Introduction to History). Trans. by Franz Rosenthal. 3 vols. 1958.

Kimble, George H. T. *Geography in the Middle Ages*. London, 1938.

Kingsley, Henry. *Tales of Old Travel*. London, 1890.

Kircher, Athanasius. *China Illustrata*. Amsterdam, 1667.

Kirchere, Athanase. *La Chine*. Trans. by F. S. Dalquié. Amsterdam, 1670.

Komroff, Manuel. *Contemporaries of Marco Polo*. New York, 1928.

———. *The Travels of Marco Polo*. New York, 1926.

Kreig, Margaret B. *Green Medicine*. Chicago, 1964.

Kretschmer, Konrad. *Geschichte der Geographie*. Berlin, 1912.

Kristeller, Paul Oskar. "*Petrarca, l'Umanesimo e la Scolastica a Venezia*," in *Civiltà Veneziana del Trecento*. Venice, 1955.

Lach, Donald F. *Asia in the Making of Europe*. 2 vols. Chicago, 1965.

Landstrom, Bjorn. *The Quest for India*.

Lane, Frederic Chapin. *Venetian Ships and Shipbuilders of the Renaissance*. The John Hopkins Press, 1934.

Langlois, Charles-Victor. *La Connaissance de la Nature et du Monde au Moyen Age*. Paris, 1911.

———. "*Marco Polo*," in *Histoire Litteraire de la France*, Vol. 35. Paris, 1821.

Latourette, Kenneth. *The Chinese, Their History and Culture*. 3d ed., revised. New York, 1946.

Laufer, Berthold. "China and the Discovery of America," a monograph. China Institute in America, New York, n.d.

———. *Jade*. Chicago, 1912.

———. *Sino-Iranica*. Chicago, 1919.

Lazari, Vincenzo. *"Del Trafico e della Condizioni degli Schiavi in Venezia nei tempi di mezzo."* Paper dated Giugno, 1862, journal of publication not located.

———. *"Del Traffico e della Condizione degli Schiave in Venezia nei Tempi di Mezzo."* Venice, 1862.

Leithaüser, Joachim G. *Worlds Beyond the Horizon*. New York, 1955.

Lelewel, Joachim. *Géographie du Moyen Age*. 4 vols. and Atlas. Brussels, 1852.

Lemke, Hans. *Die Reisen des Venezianers Marco Polo in 13 Jahr hundert*. Hamburg, 1908.

Leporace, Tullia Gasparrini. *Mostra L'Asia nella Cartografia degli Occidentali*. Venice, 1954.

Lessner, Erwin. *Cradle of Conquerors: Siberia*. New York, 1955.

Letts, Malcolm. *Sir John Mandeville, the Man and His Book*. London, 1949.

Leur, J. C. van. *Indonesian Trade and Society*. The Hague, 1955.

Li, H. L. *The Garden Flowers of China*. New York, 1959.

Libri, Guillaume. *Histoire des Sciences Mathématiques en Italie*. 2 vols. Paris, 1838.

Lister, Raymond. *How to Identify Old Maps and Globes*. London, 1965.

Lohuizen-De Leeuw, J. E. van. "Indonesia," monograph in *Le Civiltà dell 'Oriente*. Vol. I. Rome, 1956.

———. "Penisola Malese," monograph in *Le Civiltà dell 'Oriente*" Vol. I. Rome, 1956.

Lopez, Robert S., and Irving W. Raymond. *Mediaeval Trade in the Mediterranean World*. New York, 1955.

Lopez, Roberto Sabatino. *"Venezia e le Grandi Linee dell 'Espansione Commerciale nel Secolo XIII,"* in *Civiltà Veneziana del Secolo di Marco Polo*. Florence, 1955.

Löseth, E. *Le Roman en Prose de Tristan . . . et la Compilation de Rusticien de Pise*. Publication de l'École des Hautes Études. 82 fas. Paris, 1891.

Low, Charles Rathbone. *Maritime Discovery*. 2 vols. London, 1881.

Lowes, John Livingston. *The Road to Xanadu*. Boston and New York, 1930.

Luca, Giuseppe de. "Letteratura

di pietà," in *Civiltà Veneziana del Trecento.* Venice, 1955.

Lucan. *Pharsalia.* Loeb Classical Library. London, 1928.

Lucas, E. V. *A Wanderer in Venice.* 6th ed. New York, 1924.

Luzzato, Gino. *Breve Storia Economica dell' Italia Medievale.* Turin, 1965.

———. *L'Economià,* in *Civiltà Veneziano del Trecento.* Venice, 1955.

———. *Economic History of Italy* ... London, 1961.

———. "*Il Mercante Veneziano del Tempo di Marco Polo,*" in *VII Centenario della Nascita di Marco Polo.* Venice, 1955.

———. *Studi di Storia Economica Veneziana.* Padua, 1954.

———. "*Venezia e l'Oriente* (XI–XV secolo)," monograph in *Le Civiltà dell 'Oriente,* Vol. I. Rome, 1956.

Maberly, C. T. Astley. *The Game Animals of Southern Africa.* Johannesburg, 1963.

Macri, Christo M. *Des Byzantins et des Étrangers dans Constantinople au Moyen Age.* Paris, 1928.

McCrindle, J. W. *Christian Cosmography of Cosmos.* London, 1897.

McGovern, William Montgomery. *The Early Empires of Central Asia.* Chapel Hill, 1939.

McNeill, William H. *The Rise of the West.* Chicago, 1963.

Madariaga, Germán. *Amerigo and the New World.* New York, 1955.

Magnaghi, Alberto. *Precursori di Colombo.* Rome, 1935.

Major, R. H. *India in the Fifteenth Century.* London, 1855.

Major, Richard Henry. *The Life of Prince Henry of Portugal.* London, 1868.

Malcolm, John. *The History of Persia.* 2 vols. London, 1851.

Malte-Brun, V. A. *Géographie Complète et Universelle.* 8 vols. Paris, 1851.

Manly, John Matthews. "Marco Polo and the Squire's Tale," in *Publications of the Modern Language Association of America,* XI. Baltimore, 1896.

Mannix, Daniel P. and Malcolm Cowley. *Black Cargoes.*

Manuel II of Portugal. *Livros Antigos Portuguezes, 1489–1600.* 3 vols. London, 1929.

Maraini, Fosco. *Meeting With Japan.* London, 1959.

Marcello, A. "*Vicenda Climatica ed Avventura Poliana,*" in *VII Anniversario della Nascita di Marco Polo.* Venice, 1955.

Marci, Pauli Veneti. *De Regionibus Orientalibus.* Libri III. Brandenburg, 1671.

Marek, J., and N. Knízkova. *Jenghis Khan Miniatures from*

the Court of Akbar the Great. London, 1963.

Marsden, William. *The Travels of Marco Polo*. London, 1818.

———. *Travels of Marco Polo*. Ed. by Edward Wright. London, 1854.

Martial (Marcus Valerius Martialis). *Epigrams*. 2 vols. Loeb Classical Library. London, 1930.

Martin-Allanic, Jean-Étienne. *Bougainville Navigateur*. 2 vols. Paris, 1964.

Martini, Martino. *Atlas Extremae Asia sine Sinarum Imperii Geographica Descriptio*. Brussels, 1654–55.

Martins, J. P. Oliveira. *Filhos de D.João I, Os*. 7th ed. Lisbon, 1947.

Marvazi, Sharaf Al-Zaman Tahir. *China, the Turks and India*. Trans. by V. Minorsky. London, 1942.

Masefield, John. *The Travels of Marco Polo*. London, 1926.

Matignon, J. J. *Superstition, Crime et Misère en Chine*. 2d ed. Lyon and Paris, 1900.

Ma-Touan-Lin. *Ethnographie des Peuples Étrangers à la Chine (XIIIᵉ Siècle)*. Trans. by d'-Hervey de Saint-Denys. 2 vols. Geneva, 1883.

Maundeville, Sir John. *Voyages*. Ed. by J. O. Halliwell. London, 1869.

Maury, L. F. Alfred. *Croyances et Legèndes de l'Antiquité*. Paris, 1863.

Mayer, Anton. *6000 Anni di Esplorazioni e Scoperte*. Trans. by Rinaldo Caddeo. Milan, 1936.

Medard, M. *Ta-Ts'in, Province Romain en Asie*. Peking, 1936.

Meilink-Roelofsz, M. A. P. *Asia Trade and European Influence*. The Hague, 1962.

Mendoza, Juan Gonzalez de. *History of the Great and Mighty Kingdom of China . . .* Trans. by R. Parke and ed. by George T. Staunton. 2 vols. London, 1854.

Merrien, Jean. *Christopher Columbus*. English trans. London, 1958.

Meyer, Ernst F. *Geschichte der Botanik*. Vol. IV. Berlin, 1856.

Michiele, A. A. "*Gli Studiosi Veneti del Polo*," in *VII Anniversarie della Nascita di Marco Polo*." Venice, 1955.

Minorità, Fra Paolino. *De Regimine Rectoris*. Vienna and Florence, 1868.

Minorsky, Iran. "*Iran Islamico*," monograph in *Le Civiltà dell 'Oriente*. Vol. I. Rome, 1956.

Mirsky, Jeannette. *The Great Chinese Travelers*. New York, 1964.

Mitchell, J. Leslie. *Earth Conquerors*. New York, 1934.

Mitchell, Rosamund Jocelyn. *The Spring Voyage*. London, 1964.

Mollat, Michel. *"Le Moyen Age,"* in *Histoire Universelle des Explorations,* Vol. I. 4 vols. Paris, 1955–56.

Molmenti, Pompeo. *"La Grandezza di Venezia,"* in *Vita Italiane nel Trecente (conferenze).* Milan.

———. *Venezia: Nuevi Studi di Storia e d'Arte.* Florence, 1897.

———. *Vita Privata di Venezia.* 3 vols. Florence, n.d.

Momigliani, Attilio. *Storia della Letteratura Italiana.* 8th ed. Milan-Messina, 1963.

Montgomery, James A. *History of Yaballaha III.* New York, 1927.

Moore, E. D. *Ivory, Scourge of Africa.*

Monteverde, Angelo. *"Lingua e Letteratura a Venezia nel secolo di Marco Polo,"* in *Civiltà Veneziana del Secolo di Marco Polo.* Florence, 1955.

Morassi, A. *" 'Fondo or,' trecentesco e la predelle belliniana di Dignano,"* in *Rivista Mensile della Città di Venezia,* Anno III, no. 9. Venice, 1924.

Morris, James. *Venice.* London, 1960.

Mostaert, Antoine. *"Le Mot Natigay/Nacigay chez Marco Polo,"* in *Oriente Poliano,* Rome, 1957.

Moule, A. C. *Christians in China before the Year 1550.* London, 1930.

———. "A Lost Manuscript of Marco Polo," in *Royal Asiatic Society Journal.* 1928, p. 406.

———. *Quinsai, with Other Notes on Marco Polo.* Cambridge, 1957.

———, and Paul Pelliot. *Marco Polo.* 4 vols. London, 1938–64.

Muccioli, Marcello. *"Scienze della Cina,"* monograph in *Civiltà dell 'Oriente.* Vol. III. Rome, 1958.

Muirhead, Findlay. *Blue Guides: Southern Italy.* 1925.

———. *Northern Italy.* 1927.

Muntaner, Ramón. *The Chronicle of Ramón Muntaner.* Trans. by Lady Goodenough. 2 vols. Hakluyt Society. London, 1920.

Muratori, Ludovicus Antonius. *Rerum Italicarum Scriptores* . . . 25 vols. Milan, 1723–51.

Needham, Joseph. *Science and Civilization in China.* Vols. I–IV. Pt. II (all published to date). Cambridge, 1962.

Newton, Arthur P., ed. *The Great Age of Discovery.* London, 1932.

———. *Travel and Travellers of the Middle Ages.* London, 1926.

Nissen, H. *"Der Verkehr zwischen China und dem römischen Reiche,"* in *Jahrbücher des Vereins von Alterthums freun-*

den im Rheinlande, Vol. XCV. Bonn, 1894.

Nitsche, Roland. Uralte Wege, Ewige Fahrt. München, 1953.

Nordenskiöld, A. E. Facsimile-Atlas to the Early History of Cartography. Stockholm, 1889.

———. "The Influence of the Travels of Marco Polo on Jacobo Gastaldi's Maps of Asia," in The Geographical Journal, Vol. XIII, no. 4. London, April, 1899.

———. "Le Livre de Marco Polo." Fac. of the fourteenth-century manuscript. Stockholm, 1882.

———. "Marco Polo," in Periplus. Stockholm, 1897.

———. "Om det inflytande Marco Polos reseberättlse utöfvat pa Gastaldis partor öfver Asien," in Ymer. Arg, 1899.

———. Periplus; An Essay on the Earl History of Charts . . . Trans. by Francis A. Bather, reprint. Stockholm, 1897. New York, 1964.

Nougier, Louis-René, et al. Histoire Universelle des Explorations. 4 vols. Paris, 1955.

Nowell, Charles E. The Great Discoveries and the First Colonial Empires. Cornell, 1954.

———. Magellan's Voyage Around the World. Evanston, 1962.

Nunn, George E. Geographical Conceptions of Columbus. New York, 1924.

Oaten, Edward Farley. European Travellers in India. London, 1909.

O'Curry, Eugene. Lectures on the Manuscript Materials of Ancient Irish History. Dublin, 1873.

Odoric de Pordenone. Voyage. Ed. by René Grousset, 2d ed. Paris.

Okey, Thomas. Venice. Mediaeval Towns Series. London, 1925.

Oliphant, Mrs. The Makers of Florence. New York, n.d.

Oliver, Roland and Matthew, eds. "History of East Africa." Vol. I. Oxford, 1963.

Olivieri, Dante. Il Milione. Bari, 1912.

Olschki, Leonardo. L' Asia di Marco Polo. Florence, 1957.

———. The Genius of Italy. New York, 1949.

———. Guillaume Boucher. Baltimore, 1946.

———. "Marco Polo, Dante Alighieri e la Cosmografia Mediaevale," in Oriente Poliano. Rome, 1957.

———. Marco Polo's Asia. Berkeley, 1960.

———. Marco Polo's Precursors. Baltimore, 1943.

———. "Medical Matters in Marco Polo's Description of the World," in Bulletin of the History of Medicine, Supp. No. 3. New York, 1944.

———. *Storia Letteraria delle Scoperte Geografiche.* Florence, 1937.

———. *"1254: Venezia, L'Europa e i Tartari,"* in *VII Centenario della Nascita di Marco Polo.* Venice, 1955.

Olsen, Orjan. *Conquête de la Terre.* Trans. by E. Guerre. 6 vols. Paris, 1933.

Oman, C. W. C. *Art of War in the Middle Ages.* Oxford, 1885.

Origo, Iris. *"Domestic Enemy: The Eastern Slaves in Tuscany in the Fourteenth and Fifteenth Centuries,"* in *Speculum.* Vol. XXX, No. 3. 1955.

Orlandini, G. *Marco Polo e la Sua Famiglia.* Venice, 1926.

———. *Origine del Teatro Malibran.* Venice, 1913.

Orléans, Pierre Joseph. *History of the Two Tartar Conquerors of China.* Trans. by the Earl of Ellesmere. London.

Ortega Gasset, José. *"Medio Evo e l' 'idea' di Nazione,"* in *Civiltà Veneziano del Trecento.* Venice, 1955.

O'Toole, G. B. *John of Montecorvino.* Latrobe, n.d.

Ottin, Merry. *Land of Emperors and Sultans.* New York, 1962.

Outhwaite, Leonard. *Unrolling the Map.* New York, 1935.

Palestine Pilgrims Text Society. Vols. I–XIII. London, 1885–97.

Papanti, Giovanni. *Dante, Secondo la Tradizione* ... Leghorn, 1873.

Paris, Paulin. *"Extrait d'une Notice sur la Rélation Originale de Marc Pol, Venetian,"* in *Nouveau Journal Asiatique,* Vol. XII. Paris, 1833.

———. *Manuscrits Français de la Bibliothèque du Roi,* Vols. II, III. Paris, 1838–40.

———. *"Nouvelles Récherches sur les premières rédactions du Voyage de Marco Polo."* Extract from the *Transactions of the Institute National of France.* Paris, n.d.

Parker, E. H. *A Thousand Years of the Tartars.* 2d ed. London, 1924.

Parkinson, C. Northcote. *East and West.* Boston, 1963.

Parks, George B. *Contents and Sources of Ramusio's Navigationi.* New York, 1955.

———. *"Ramusio's Literary History,"* in *Studies in Philology.* Vol. 52. Chapel Hill, 1955.

———. *Richard Hakluyt and the English Voyages.* New York, 1930.

Parr, Charles McKew. *So Noble a Captain.* New York, 1953.

Pasini, Lodovico. *I Viaggi di Marco Polo.* Venice, 1847.

Patmore, Derek. *A Traveller in Venice.* London, 1951.

Pauphilet, Alfred. *"Robert de Clari Villehardouin ... ,"* in

Historiens et Chroniqueurs du Moyen Age. Paris, 1938.

Pauthier, M. G. *Cérémonial Observé dans les Fêtes . . . à la Cour de Khoublai Khan.* Paris, 1862.

———. *Description de la Ville de Quinsay* (Hang-Tcheou Fou). Paris, 1863.

———. *Le Livre de Marco Polo.* 2 vols. Paris, 1865.

Pegolotti, Francesco Balducci. *Pratica della Mercatura.* Ed. by Evans Allan. Cambridge, Massachusetts, 1936.

Pelliot, Paul. *Notes on Marco Polo.* 2 vols. Paris, 1959–63.

Penzer, N. M. "Marco Polo," *Asiatic Review,* XXIV, 657; XXV, 49.

Pepe, G. *Italiani del Medioevo in Estremo Oriente.* Milan, 1942.

Percheron, Maurice. *Genghis Khan.* Paris, 1962.

Peregrin, Felix. *Marco Paolos Reise in den Orient.* Ronneburg and Leipzig, 1802.

Pereira, Francisco M. E. *Marco Paulo.* Lisbon, 1922.

Peretti, Aurelio. *Per la Storia del Testo di Marco Polo.* Florence, 1930.

Pereyra, Carlos. *La Conquista de las Rutas Océanicas.* Madrid, 1940.

Perroy, Édouard, *et al.* "*Le Moyen Age.*" Vol. III of *Histoire Générale des Civilisations.* 4th ed. Paris, 1965.

Petech, Luciano. "*Asia Centrale,*" monograph in *Le Civiltà dell 'Oriente.* Vol. I. Rome, 1956.

———. "*Cina,*" monograph in *Le Civiltà dell 'Oriente,* Vol. I. Rome, 1956.

Petit, Joseph. *Un Capitaine du Règne de Philippe le Bel (Thibault de Sepoy),* in *Le Moyen Age, 2 ème Série, 1.* Paris, 1897.

Pettis Della Croix, Padre. *Istoria del Gran Genghizcan.* Venice, 1737.

Phillips, George. "The Seaports of India and Ceylon," in *Journal of the Royal Asiatic Society* (North China Branch), Vols. XXI and XXII.

Pigafetta, Antonio. *Magellan's Voyage Around the World.* 3 vols. Cleveland, 1906.

Pinkerton, John. *Voyages and Travels.* Vol. XII. London, 1808.

Pipino, Francesco. *Marci Pauli Veneti . . . de Regionibus Orientalibus.* Cologne, 1671.

Pirenne, Henri. *Histoire du Moyen Age.* Vol. VIII. Paris, 1933.

Pires, Tomé. *The Suma Oriental.* 2 vols. Trans. by Armando Cortisâo. London, 1944.

Plato. *Dialogues.* 5 vols. Trans. by B. Jowett. 3d ed. 1892.

Plinius, Gaius Secundus. *Natural History.* 6 vols. Bohn Library. London, 1855.

Pohl, Frederick J. *Amerigo Ves-*

pucci, *Pilot Major.* New York, 1944.

Polo, Marco. *La Description du Monde.* Ed. by Louis Hambis. Paris, 1955.

———. *Le Devisement du Monde.* Text ed. by A. t'Sersteoens. Paris, 1963.

———. *Itinerarium.* Fac. of the Antwerp mss., pub. 1845. Tokyo, 1949.

———. *Kniga Marko Polo.* Russian text. Moscow, 1955.

———. *Il Libro di Marco Polo Detto Milione (nelle versione trecentesca dell' "ottimo").* Prefazio di Sergio Solmi. Turin, 1954.

———. *Livre de Marco Polo, on le Devisement du Monde.* Ed. in modern French by A. t'Sersteoens. Small folio, ltd. ed. Paris, 1942–44.

———. *Livro, O . . .* (reimpression of the first Portuguese edition [1502] of Valentim Fernandes). Ed. by Francisco M. E. Pereira. Lisbon, 1922.

———. *Marci Poli Veneti . . . de Legionibus Orientalibus Libri III.* Trans. by Pipino. Brandenburg, 1671.

———. *Il Milione.* Ed. by Ramèri Allulli. Verona, 1954.

———. *Il Milione.* Ramusio text, ed. by Renato Giani. Rome, 1954.

———. *Most Noble and Famous Travels . . . of . . . .* Trans. by John Frampton, reprint ed. by N. M. Penzer. London, 1929.

———. *Die Reisen des Venezianers M. P. im 13 Jahrhundert.* Ed. in German by Hans Lemke. Hamburg, 1907.

———. *"Relation des Pais Orientaux,"* in *Voyages faits principalement en Asie dans les XII, XIII, XIV, et XV Siècles,* by Pierre Bergeron. The Hague, 1735.

———. *The Travels of . . . .* Trans. by Ronald Latham. London, 1958.

———. *The Travels of . . . .* Ed. by F. W. Mote. New York, 1961.

———. *The Travels of . . . .* Trans. from the text of L. F. Benedetto by Aldo Ricci. London, 1931.

———. *The Travels of . . . .* Ed. by Milton Rugoff. New York, 1961.

———. *The Travels of . . . .* Trans. by Marsden, Ed. by Thomas Wright. London, 1854.

———. *"Voyage de Marc Pol."* Old French and Latin texts in *Recueil de Voyages et Mémoires par la Société de Géographie.* Paris, 1824.

Pons, R. Giorgi de. *I Grandi Navigatori Italiani.* Florence, 1929.

Ponti, Giovann. *Giovanni da Pian del Carpine.* Turin, 1953.

Power, Eileen. *Mediaeval People.* London, 1924.

Powers, H. H. *Venice and Its Art.* New York, 1930.

Prawdin, Michael. *The Builders of the Mogul Empire.*

———. *Genghiz Khan.* Trans. by Franz Glaentzer. Florence, 1936.

———. *The Mongol Empire.* New York, 1940.

Prestage, Edgar. *The Portuguese Pioneers.* London, 1933.

Procopius of Caesarea. *Anecdota, or Secret History,* Vol. VI. Loeb Classical Library. Cambridge, 1935.

Psellus, Michael. *Chronographia.* Trans. by E. R. A. Sewter. London, 1953.

Puini, C. "*Il Ta-thsin o l' Impero negli storici Cinese,*" in *Atene e Roma,* Anno II, No. 9. Moggio-Guino, 1899.

Purchas, Samuel. *Hakluytus Posthumus* or *Purchas His Pilgrimes.* MacLehose reprint, Vol. IX. Glasgow, 1905.

———. *His Pilgrimage.* 3d ed. London, 1617.

Puschmann, The., *et al. Handbuch der Geschichte der Medizin.* Jena, 1902.

Rabelais, François. *Oeuvres Complètes.* Paris, 1951.

Ragg, Laura M. *Crises in Venetian History.* London, 1928.

Ragg, Lonsdale. *Dante and His Italy.* New York and London, 1907.

Raisz, Erwin. *General Cartography.* New York and London, 1938.

Raleigh, Sir Walter. *The Discoverie . . . of Guiana.* Vol. IV of *Hakluyt's Voyages.* 6 vols. London, 1811.

———. *The Discoverie of the Large and Bewtiful Empire of Guiana.* Argonaut ed. London, 1928.

Ramusio, Giambattista. *Delle Navigationi et Viaggi.* Vol. II. Venice, 1559.

Ramusio, Giovanni Battista. *Delle Cose de' Tartari e dell 'Indie Orientali.* Reprint. Venice, 1954.

Ramusio, Giovan Battista. *Il Milione.* Ed. by Renato Giani. Rome, 1954.

Ravenstein, E. G. *Martin Behaim, His Life and His Globe.* London, 1908.

Read, Bernard E. *Chinese Materia Medica, Dragon and Snake Drugs.* Peking, n.d.

Reinaud, M. *Géographie d'Aboufeda.* Vol. II. Paris, 1848.

———. *Relation des Voyages faits par les Arabes et les Persans dans l'Inde et à la Chine.* 2 vols. Paris, 1845.

———. *Rélations Politiques et Commerciales de l'Empire Romain avec l'Asie Orientale.* Paris, 1853.

Reischauer, Edwin O. *Ennin's Diary.* New York, 1955.

——. *Ennin's Travels in T'ang China*. New York, 1955.

——, and John K. Fairbank. *East Asia: the Great Tradition*. Boston, 1960.

Rem, Lucas. *Tagebuch*. Ed. by B. Greiff. Augsburg, 1861.

Remusat, Abel. *Nouveaux Mélanges Asiatiques*. 2 vols. Paris, 1829.

Renaudot, Eusebius. *Anciennes Relations des Indes et la Chine de Deux Voyageurs Mahometans*. Trans. Paris, 1750.

——. *Ancient Accounts of India and China by Two Mohammedan Travellers . . . in the 9th Century*. English trans. London, 1733.

Renouard, Yves. *Hommes d' Affaires Italien du Moyen Age*. Paris, 1949.

——. "*Mercati e Mercanti Veneziani alla Fine del Duocento*," in *Civiltà Veneziana del Secolo di Marco Polo*. Florence, 1955.

Reparaz, Gonzalo de (son). *La Epoca de los Grandes Descubrimientos Españoles y Portugueses*. Barcelona and Buenos Aires, 1931.

Ricci, Matthew. *The Journals of . . . .* Trans. by Louis J. Gallagher. New York, 1953.

Richardson, H. E. *Tibet and Its History*. Oxford, 1962.

Richardson, Mrs. Aubrey. *The Doges of Venice*. London, 1914.

Richthofen, F. von. *China*. 2 vols. Berlin. 1877.

Riesman, David. *The Story of Medicine in the Middle Ages*. New York, 1935.

Risch, Friederich. *Johann de Plano Carpini . . .* Leipzig, 1930.

Riverain, Jean and Roncière, Ch. de la. *Découverte de la Terre*. Paris, 1963.

Rivista Mensile della Città di Venezia. Several articles. September, 1924.

Roberts, Frances Markley. *Western Travellers to China*. Shanghai, 1932.

Robertson, Alexander. *Discourses on the History, Art and Customs of Venice*. London and New York, 1907.

Robertson, William. *Historical Disquisition Concerning the Knowledge Which the Ancients had of India . . .* Basil, 1792.

Rocca, Raimondo Morozzo della. "*Cronologia Veneziana del' 300*," in *Civiltà Veneziana del Trecento*. Venice, 1955.

Rockhill, William W. *The Journey of William of Rubruck*. London, 1900.

Rockhill, W. W., and Friedrich Hirth. *Chau Ju-Kua*. 2 vols. St. Petersburg, 1912.

Rodrigues, Francisco. *The Book of . . . .*

Rogers, Francis M. *The Quest for Eastern Christians*.

———. *The Travels of the Infante Dom Pedro of Portugal.* Cambridge, Massachusetts, 1961.

Roncière, Charles de la. *La Découverte de l'Afrique au Moyen Age*, 3 vols. Le Caire, 1925–27.

Ross, Janet, and Nelly Ericksen. *The Story of Pisa.* London, 1909.

Ross, Sir E. Denison. "Marco Polo and His Book," in *Proceedings of the British Academy*, Vol. XX. London, 1934.

Rossi, Ettore. "*I Turchi*," monograph in *Le Civiltà dell 'Oriente.* Vol. I. Rome, 1956.

Roth, Cecil. *History of the Jews in Venice.* Philadelphia, 1930.

Rothery, Guy Cadogan. *The Amazons in Antiquity and Modern Times.* London, 1910.

Rousseau, Pierre. *Histoire des Transports.* Paris, 1961.

Runciman, Steven. *Byzantine Civilization.* London, 1933.

———. *A History of the Crusades.* Vol. III. Cambridge, 1954.

Ruskin, John. *St. Mark's Rest.* New York, 1884.

Saint-Martin, Vivien de. *Histoire de la Géographie et des Découvertes Géographiques.* Paris, 1875.

Samhaber, Ernst. *Knaurs Geschichte der Entdeckungsreisen.* Munich, 1955.

———. *Merchants Make History.* Trans. by E. Osers. London, 1963.

Sansovino, Francesco. *Venetia, Città Nobilissima et Singolari.* Venetia, 1581.

Sanudo, Marino. *Diario de Marino Sanudo (1466–1535).* 57 vols. Venice, 1879–1902.

Sarton, George. *A History of Science.* Cambridge, Massachusetts, 1959.

Sastri, K. A. Nilakana. "Marco Polo on India," in *Oriente Poliano.* Rome, 1957.

Saunders, J. J. "Islam and the Mongols," in *History Today.* Vol. XI, No. 12. London, 1961.

Saviano, Renato, and Ernesto Rech. "*Missioni Cristiane in Oriente*," monograph.

Schafer, Edward H. *The Golden Peaches of Samarkand.* Berkeley, 1953.

Schafer, Ernst. "*Zur Erinnerung an Marco Polo*," in *Mittheilungen der Geographischen Gesellschaft in Hamburg.* Vol. XV, 1899. Hamburg, 1899.

Schaller, Michael. *Marco Polo und die Texte seiner "Reisen,"* pamphlet. Burghausen, 1889.

Schauber, Adolf. *Handelsgesch-*
Schauber, Adolf. *Handelsgeschichte der Romanischen Völker.* Munich, 1906.

Schevill, Ferdinand. *History of Florence.* New York, 1936.

Schindler, A. Hontouni. "Marco

Polo's Camadi," *Journal of the Royal Asiatic Society*. 1898.

———. "Notes on Marco Polo's Itinerary in Southern Persia," *Journal of the Royal Asiatic Society*, 1881.

Schneider, Wolf. *Babylon Is Everywhere*. London, 1960.

Schoff, Wilfred H. *The Periplus of the Erythraen Sea*. New York, 1912.

Schreiber, Herman. *The History of Roads*. Trans. by Stewart Thomson. London, 1961.

Schuman, K. *Marco Polo, ein Weltreisender des XIII Jahrhunderts*. Berlin, 1885.

Scriptores Historiae Augustae. 3 vols. Loeb Classical Library. London, 1921–32.

Seguso, L. "Casa dei Milioni, o l'Abitazione di Marco Polo," in *Venezia e il Congresso Geografico*. Venice, 1884.

Selfridge, H. Gordon. *The Romance of Commerce*. 2d ed. London, 1923.

Serristori, Conte. *"Documenti Spettanti al Commercio dei Veneziani con Armenia e Trebisonda,"* in *Archivio Storico Italiano*, app. Tomo IX.

Severin, Timothy. *Tracing Marco Polo*. London, 1964.

Shaffer, Michael. *Marco Polo und die Texte seiner "Reisen."* Burghausen, 1890.

Sherwood, Merriam, and Elmer

Mantz. *The Road to Cathay*. New York, 1928.

Simon, Edith. *The Piebald Standard*. A biography of the Knights Templars. London, 1959.

Simond, Charles. *Un Venetien Chez les Chinois*. Paris, n.d.

Sinica, Franciscana. Vol. I. *Quaracchi*. Florence, 1929.

Skelton, R. A. *Explorers' Maps*. London, 1958.

Slaughter, Gertrude. *Heirs of Old Venice*. New Haven, 1927.

Smith, Adam. *The Wealth of Nations*. 2 vols. Ed. by Edwin Cannan. London, 1930.

Smith, Frederick P. *Contributions Towards the Materia Medica and Natural History of China*. Shanghai and London, 1871.

La Société Asiatique. *Paul Pelliot*. Paris, 1946.

La Société de Géographie. *Receuil de Voyages . . . .* Vol. I. Paris, 1824.

Sottas, Jules. *Messageries Maritimes de Venese aux XIVe and XVe Siècles*. Paris, 1938.

Spilhaus, M. Whiting. *Background of Geography*. London, 1935.

Sprenger, A. *Die Post-und Reisenrouten des Orients*. Amsterdam, 1962.

Spuler, Bertold. *The Muslim World*. Part II, Mongol Period. Leiden, 1960.

———. "Le Situation de l'Iran à

l'Epoque de Marco Polo," in *Oriente Poliano.* Rome, 1957.

Staley, Edgcumbe. *The Dogaressas of Venice.* London, n.d.

Stange, Hans O. H. "Where Was Zayton Actually Situated?" *Journal of the American Oriental Society,* Vol. 69, No. 2, July–September, 1949.

Stange, O. H. "Ein Kapitel aus Marco Polo," in *Studia Sino-Altaica.* Wiesbaden, 1961.

Stein, Sir Aurel. *Ancient Khotan.* Oxford, 1907.

———. *Innermost Asia.* 4 vols. Oxford, 1928.

———. "Marco Polo's Account of a Mongol Inroad into Kashmir," in *The Geographical Journal,* Vol. LIV, No. 2. London, August, 1919.

———. *On Ancient Central-Asian Tracks.* New York, 1964.

———. *Ruins of Desert Cathay.* 2 vols. London, 1912.

———. *Serindia.* 5 vols. Oxford, 1921.

Stevens, Roger. *Land of the Great Sophy.* London, 1962.

Stevenson, Edward Luther. *Genoese World Map, 1457.* New York, 1912.

———. *Portolan Charts.* New York, 1911.

———. *Terrestrial and Celestial Globes.* 2 vols. New Haven, 1921.

Stevenson, William. *Historical Sketch of the Progress of Discovery* ... Edinburgh and London, 1824.

Stevenson-Hamilton, J. *Wild Life in South Africa.* London, 1957.

Stokes, Whitley. "Gaelic Abridgment of the Book of Ser Marco Polo." in *Archivo für Celtische Philologie,* I Band, 2 u.3. Heft. Halle, 1896, 1897.

———. "Lives of Saints from the Book of Lismore," in *Anecdota Oxoniensia,* Part V. Oxford, 1890.

———. "Translator of the Celtic fragment of Marco Polo," in *Zeitschrift für Celtische Philologie,* I Band, 2–3 Heft. Halle, 1896–97.

Strabo. *Geography.* 3 vols. Bohn Library. London, 1912.

Strachan, Michael. *Life and Adventures of Thomas Coryate.* London, 1962.

Stuebe, A. *El Libro de Marco Polo.* Leipzig, 1902.

Suchem, Ludolph von. "Description of the Holy Land," in *Palestine Pilgrims Text Society,* Vol. XII. London, 1885–97.

Sykes, Sir Percy. *A History of Exploration.* New York, 1934.

———. History of Persia. 3d ed. 2 vols. London, 1930.

———. *The Quest for Cathay.* London, 1936.

Symons, Arthur. *Cities of Italy.* New York, 1907.

Synge, M. B. *A Book of Dis-*

covery (rev.). Edinburgh, 1962.

Szczesniak, Boleslaw. "Laurentian Bible of Marco Polo," in *Journal of the American Oriental Society*, Vol. 75, No. 3. New Haven, July–September, 1955.

———. "Recent Studies on Marco Polo in Japan," in *Journal of the American Oriental Society*, Vol. 76, No. 4. Baltimore, 1956.

Tacitus. *The Annals of Tacitus.* 5 vols. London, 1874.

Tafur, Pero. *Travels and Adventures, 1435–1439.*" Trans. and ed. by Malcolm Letts. New York and London, 1926.

Tassini, Giuseppe. *Curiosità Veneziane.* 4th ed. Venice, 1886.

Taton, René, ed. *La Science Antique et Médiévale (des Origines à 1450).* Paris, 1957.

Taylor, Henry Osborn. *The Mediaeval Mind.* 2 vols. London, 1911.

Taylor, Norman. *Plant Drugs That Changed the World.* New York, 1965.

Teggart, Frederick J. *Rome and China.* Berkeley, 1939.

Teixeira, Pedro. *Travels.* Hakluyt Society. London, 1902.

Thayer, William Roscoe. *A Short History of Venice.* Boston, 1908.

Thompson, James Westfall, *et al. The Civilization of the Renaissance.* Chicago, 1929.

———, and Edgar N. Johnson. *An Introduction to Mediaeval Europe.* New York, 1937.

Thorndike, Lynn. Articles on Peter Abano, in *Speculum.* Vols. I and II.

Timkovski, G. *Voyage à Peking à travers la Mongolie,* 2 vols. and atlas. Paris, 1829.

Tiraboschi, Girolamo. *Storia della Letteratura Italiana.* Vol. IV. Milan, 1823.

Tolkowsky, S. *Hesperides: A History of the Culture and Use of Citrus Fruits.* London, 1938.

Tong-kien-kang-mou. Trans. from the Chinese into French by Joseph-Anne-Marie de Moyriac de Maille. 13 vols.

Tooley, R. V. *Maps and Map-Makers.* 2d ed. London, 1922.

T'oung Pao. Vols. XV, XVI. 1914–15.

Toussaint, Auguste. *Histoire de l'Océan Indien.* Paris, 1961.

Toynbee, Paget. *Dante Alighieri: The Life of Dante.* 4th ed. London, 1910.

———. *Dante, Studies and Researches.* London, 1902.

Trapier, Blanche. *Les Voyageurs Arabes au Moyen Age.* Paris, 1937.

Tronci, Paolo. *Memorie Istoriche della Città di Pisa.* Leghorn, 1582.

T'Serstevens, A. *Le Livre de Marco Polo.* Paris, 1957.

———. *Les Précurseurs de Marco Polo*. Paris, 1951.

Tucci, Giuseppe. *Marco Polo*. Instituto Italiano per il Medio e Estremo Oriente. Rome, 1954.

Urbani de Gheltof, Giovanni M. D. *"Collezione del doge M. Faliero e i tesori di Marco Polo,"* in *Bullettino d'Arti . . . et Curiosità Veneziane,"* Anno III, No. 2. Venice, 1880.

Vacca, G. *"Documento Cinese sulla Data del Ritorno di Marco Polo,"* in *Rendiconti delle Sedute dell' Accademia Nazionale dei Lincei, Classe di Scienze Morali . . . .* Sez VIII, Vol. II. Rome, 1947.

Van Den Wyngaert. *Jean de Mont Corvin*. Lille, 1924.

Vasiliev, A. A. *History of the Byzantine Empire*. 2d Eng. ed., rev. Madison, 1952.

Verlinden, Charles. *"Colonie Vénitienne de Tana, centre de la traite des esclaves,"* in *Studi in Onore di Gino Luzzatto*. Vol. II. Milan, 1950.

———. *L'Esclavage dans l'Europe Médiévale*. Bruges, 1955.

Vernadsky, George. *A History of Russia*. New Haven, 1929.

Vignaud, Henri. *Toscanelli and Columbus*. New York and London, 1902.

Villani, Giovanni. *Istorie Fiorentine*. 5 vols. Milan, 1802.

Villehardouin, Geoffroi de. *"Conquête de Constantinople,"* in *Historiens et Chroniqueurs du Moyen Age*. Paris, 1938.

———, and J. de Joinville. *Memoirs of the Crusades*. Everyman ed. London, 1908.

Villiers, Alan. *Monsoon Seas*. New York, 1952.

Viscardi, Antonio. *"Lingua e letteratura,"* in *Civiltà Veneziana del Trecento*. Venice, 1955.

Vissering, W. *On Chinese Currency*. Leiden, 1887.

Vladimirtsov, B. Ya. *The Life of Chingis-Khan*. Trans. by D. S. Mirsky. London, 1930.

Vlekke, Bernard H. M. *Nusantara*. Cambridge, 1943.

Volte, Gioacchino. *"L'Italia e Venezia."* in *Civiltà Veneziano del Trecento*. Venice, 1955.

Wagenführ, Horst. *Handelsfürsten der Renaissance*. Stuttgart, 1957.

Waldman, Milton, ed. The Omnibus Book of Travellers' Tales. New York, n.d.

Waley, Arthur. *Ch'ang Ch'un, Travels of an Alchemist*. Trans. London, 1931.

Walsh, James J. *The Thirteenth, Greatest of Centuries*. 5th ed. New York, 1912.

Walsh, Richard J., ed. *Marco Polo*. New York, 1948.

Walter, Gérard. *La Ruine de*

Byzance, 1204–1453. Paris, 1958.

Walton, John. *Six Explorers.* London, 1942.

Warmington, E. H. *Commerce Between the Roman Empire and India.* Cambridge, 1928.

Weinstein, Michael. *The World of Precious Stones.* London, 1959.

Welch, Sidney R. *Europe's Discovery of South Africa.*

Wendt, Herbert. *"À la Découverte des Peuples de la Terre."* Trans. from the German by Ugné Karvelis. Paris, 1962.

———. "It Began in Babel." Boston, 1962.

Wheatley, Paul. "The Land of Zanj," in "Geography and the Tropics." Liverpool Essays. University of Liverpool, 1964.

White, Lynn, Jr. *Mediaeval Technology and Social Change.* Oxford, 1962.

Whitlock, Herbert P. *The Story of the Gems.* New York, 1926.

Wiel, Alethea. *The Navy of Venice.* London, 1910.

———. *Venice.* The Story of the Nations Series. New York, 1894.

William de Rubruquis. *The Texts and Versions of* .... Ed. by C. Raymond Beazley. London, 1903.

William of Rubruck. *The Journey.* Trans. by W. W. Rockhill. London, 1900.

Williams, Harry. *Ceylon, Pearl of the East.* London, 1956.

Williamson, George C. *The Book of Ivory.* London, 1938.

Williamson, James A. *Cabot Voyages on Bristol Discovery Under Henry VII.* Cambridge, 1962.

Witsen, Nicolaas. *Father Pereira's Journey into Tartary* ... Trans. by the Earl of Ellsmere.

Wittkower, R. "Marco Polo and the Pictorial Tradition of the Marvels of the Earth," in *Oriente Poliano.* Rome, 1957.

Wood, H. J. *Exploration and Discovery.* London, 1951.

Wright, John Kirtland. *Geographical Lore of the Time of the Crusades.* New York, 1925.

Xenophon. *Anabasis.* Loeb Classical Library. London, 1921.

Yaballaha III. *The History of* .... Trans. by James A. Montgomery. New York, 1927.

Young, George. *Constantinople.* London, n.d.

Yule, Sir Henry. *The Book of Ser Marco Polo.* Three editions, each in 2 vols.: 1st ed., London, 1871; 2d ed., rev., London, 1875; 2d ed., rev., Tokyo, 1894; 3d ed., rev. by H. Cordier, London, 1921.

———. *Cathay and the Way Thither.* 2d ed. 4 vols. Hakluyt Society. London, 1915–16.

Zanelli, Agostino. *Le Schiave Orientali a Firenze nei Secoli XIV e XV*. Florence, 1885.

Zingarelli, Nicola. *Vocabulario della Lingua Italiana*, 7th ed. Milan, 1938–39.

Zurla, Placido. *Di Marco Polo e degli altri Viaggatori Veneziani piu Illustri*. 2 vols. Venice, 1818–19.

———. *Il Mappamondo di Fra Mauro*. Venice, 1806.

Index

Acre (Syrian port): 39–40, 79f., 171ff., 180, 183ff.; description of, 74 & n.; merchants' quarters in, 75; Knights Templars in, 75; Polos in, 78–80
Adam's Peak, Ceylon: 150
Aethicus Istricus: 85
Agha Khan, the: 96
Alamut (the Eagle's Nest): 96 & n.
Ala-u-'d-Din Muhammad: 96 & n.
Albuquerque, Affonso (Portuguese leader): 93
Alexander the Great: 93, 96
Alexander III, Pope: 55
A-lo-pen (a Nestorian): 86
Almanac: 122–23
Ambergris: 152–53
Anatolia: 82
Arabas (carts): 13 & n.
Ararat, Mount: 83 & n.
Argols (dried dung): 27
Argon (Arghun), Khan of Persia: 142–44, 158–59
Armenia, Little (Cilicia): 23, 82
Arsenal, The (in Venice): 63 & n., 64n., 185; *see also* Venice
Asbestos: 106 & n.
Ascension Day: 54–56
Asia, Central: 20, 24n., 25, 29n., 32, 35, 54, 95n., 103n., 107, 142, 203f.; travel in, 25–26; climate of, 26–27
Assassins, The: 96 & n.

Babylonians: 84
Badakhshan (Asian city): 98 & n., 99f.
Bagdad (Baghdad): 22, 64, 86f., 217; miracle in, 87–88
Baku (region of Persia): 84f.
Balas rubies: 98 & n.
Baldwin of Flanders (Baldwin II): 7, 9, 164–65, 182
Balk (Balkh, Bactria), Afghanistan: 97 & n.
Barka (Berca) Khan: 12, 13ff.
Benjamin of Tudela (rabbi): 35n., 196
Bodleian Library, Oxford: 72
Bokhara: 14–15, 26, 37, 54; Polos in, 14–15
Bolgara (city on the Volga River): 12; Polos in, 9
Bucentoro (a barge): 56
Burchard of Mount Sion (German monk): 76
Byzantine Empire: 37, 184

Cabinan ("hill of the wild pistachio"): 95
Cambaluc (Mongol capital): 111, 118, 124, 139ff., 142f., 167f., 178ff., 242ff.; towers of, 116; *see also* Khanbaligh
Canale, Martino da (historian): 44, 56f., 206n., 242ff.; quoted, 42, 71
Cathay: 26, 31, 37, 40, 80ff., 103n., 113, 119f., 127ff., 129ff., 138, 177, 185ff.,

190 ff., 212 ff., 215 ff., 228, 238 ff.; origin of name, 37n.; travel in, 123–24

Chagatai (lord of Samarkand): 101

Ch'ang An (Chinese capital): 36 & n., 86

Ch'ang Ch'un (Taoist monk): 19–20

Charkhlik: see Lop

China: 21 f., 23, 37, 43, 89n., 92f., 97, 119 ff., 123 ff., 125n., 133n., 138, 143, 156f., 170f., 172n., 178f., 202 ff., 215, 236 ff., 260 ff.; relations with Europe, 31–36; relations with Asians, 35 & n.; women of, 129, 135; boys of, 130; marriage in, 130, description of, 137

Chinghitalas (region of Asia): 106

Chins: 18f., 21

Chin Tatars: 21, 23 ff.

Church of the Holy Sepulchre (Jerusalem): 76n., 77–78, 114

Cilicia: see Little Armenia

Clavijo (Spanish traveler): 88

Clement IV, Pope: 31; death of, 40; letter to, 40

Coal: 121 & n.

Cocacin (princess in Cambaluc): 142–43, 158, 159 & n., 160

Cogotal (travel companion of the Polos): 37 & n., 38; illness of, 39

Colleoni, statue of: 49n.

Commerce, Venetian: 63 ff., 64–66, 179–80

Compass: 35 & n.; see also magnetic needle

Constantinople (modern Istanbul): 3f., 7 ff., 11 n., 12–13, 31 ff., 34, 40n., 41 ff., 43, 48, 54, 85 ff., 178, 181 f., 190, 192 ff., 211; Latin usurpers in, 7, 9, 164–65

"Coryat's Crudities": 55n.

Cronique de Veniciens: 56, 206n.

Crusades, the: 10n.

Dante Alighieri: 65n., 103, 193, 233n., 240 ff.

"De Re Metallic" (Agricola): 84; see also oil

Diamond, Sutra The: 35n.

Doge (magistrate): 44, 47–48, 50, 63, 71 ff., 167, 179, 219f., 245, 253n., 263 ff., 265; installation of, 56–58

Dome of the Rock: 77

Erberia (poisoning): 60

Europeans, in the East: 15, 16n., 157 ff.; relations with Chinese, 31–36

Fêng shui (wind and water): 104–105 & n.

Fire-worship: 91

Fortunetellers: 30

Frampton, John (translator): 79n., 100 & n., 256

Funerals in Venice: 61; see also Venice

Genghis Khan (Mongol ruler): 12 ff., 14 & n., 16 ff., 23 ff. & n., 39 ff., 101 n., 141 ff.; birth of, 17; conquests of, 18–20, 97, 107; death of, 21

Genoa, Italy: 9 ff., 10 n., 11 ff., 43, 100, 181, 188f., 195 ff., 198f., 201, 205 ff., 210, 212f., 217, 224, 236 ff., 265 ff.; skirmishes, wars of, 182–86, 189, 198–201, 206–208; description and history of, 190–93; prison of, 132n., 192–93, 209 ff., 212 ff., 232 ff., 256 ff.

Genoese: 9 ff., 31, 39 ff., 88, 157, 164f., 179, 182f., 188f., 196, 206f., 212, 233 ff., 236, 253 ff.; fleet of, 183f., 186 ff., 198, 207 ff.

Gez (mountain pass in the Pamirs): 100

Glass and glassworking, Venetian: 57, 62, 180, 217; see also island of Murano

Gobi Desert: 17 & n.; evil spirits in, 103, 104 & n.

Golden Tablet(s): 19, 38, 80f., 144 & n., 161

Great Wall of China: 34n., 109n., 142

Greek fire: 85; see oil

Greek wind (northeast): 15, 82

Gregory X, Pope: 79–81, 114; see also Teobaldo and Visconti

Grioni, Zanino (citizen of Venice): 51n., 249

Hayton, Prince, of Armenia: 83

Henry III, King, of France: 64n.

Hoover, Herbert and Lou Henry: 84

Hormuz, Persia: 92, 94n., 158; history of, 93; conditions in, 93; people of, 94; ships and shipping of, 94–95, 157–58; see also Persian ships

Horses of St. Mark's Church: 49 & n.

Hulaku Khan (Mongol leader): 13, 14 ff., 15 ff., 96 & n.

Ibn Battuta (merchant): 35n., 93, 94n., 97n., 119, 135n., 145, 150n.
Ibn Khaldun (merchant): 35n.
Ice cream: 121
Impavesata (leather bucklers): 66 & n.
Indigo: 155n.

Jade: 89n., 102
Japan: 146–47
Jerusalem: 80n., 191 ff.; oil from, 38 & n., 75, 78, 114; holy places of, 75–78 & n.
Jews of Venice: 65; *see also* Venice
Josephus, Flavius (Jewish historian): quoted, 32, 83n.

Kabul, Afghanistan: 20
Kallinikos (Greek architect): 85
Kamul (Chinese province): 105–106
Kan Chou (Asian city): 106–108
Kansu (Chinese province): 104f.
Karakorum (Mongol capital): 15, 16ff., 19, 23 & n., 37, 106f.
Karaunas (bandits): 92 & n., 93
Kashgar, China: 100f.
Kashmir, India: 99–100, 203ff.
Kerman, Iran: 91–92, 94ff.
Khanbaligh (Mongol capital): 23 & n., 37, 54ff.; *see also* Cambaluc
Khotan (ancient city): 102
Kiev, Russia: 24n.
Kublai Khan (Cubli Kaan, Mongol ruler): 13ff., 15–16, 22–24, 31, 37, 39 & n., 54ff., 69, 75, 78f., 90ff., 101n., 108f., 112 & n., 115n., 127 & n., 133, 138f., 142f., 145f., 150, 156f., 162, 176, 178ff., 191 ff., 202, 215, 235f., 238, 240, 251 ff., 253n.; mother of, 35n., 39; letter to Clement IV, 40; summer home of, 110–12; description of, 115 & n.; birthday of, 116; mint and money of, 118–20 & n.; death of, 161
Kumiss: 11–12, 20, 107, 108n.
Kuriltai (Mongol council): 22

Laias (port of Cilicia): 18, 39, 79f., 110n.
Lapis lazuli: 98
"La Sensa" (Ascension Day): 54–55 & n.
Lepanto, Turkey: 64n.

Lion of St. Mark: 49, 65
Lop (modern Charkhlik): 103
Louis IX (St. Louis): 8, 15
Lucan: 32
Ludolph Von Suchem (German churchman): quoted, 72–75, 77

Maçudi (merchant): 35n.
Magi, the: 90–91 & n.
Magnetic needle: 6; *see also* compass
Manzi (Mangi, southern region of China): 102ff., 159ff.; cities of, 133–37
Marcus Aurelius: 32
Melar (mythical fish): 73–74
Mengu Khan: 22
Millet: 31, 120
Milton, John: 94n.; quoted, 3
Ming Dynasty: 112, 120n., 262
Mongka Khan: 15, 105
Mongols, the: 9ff., 10n., 11, 13ff., 15ff., 18–20, 23–24n., 25n., 33, 36, 58, 65n., 78f., 83ff., 107, 111, 114–15n., 118, 125n., 126n., 138f., 141f., 151n., 158, 262ff.; first appearance of, 17; tents of, 27; life among, 28–31
Moravia: 24n.
Mosaics in St. Mark's Church: 48n., 178ff.; world story in, 44; legends in, 44, 48; biblical scenes in, 48 & n.; work in, 48 & n.
Mosul (city on the Tigris River): 87ff.; description of, 85–86; Nestorians in, 86
"Mummy" (a medicine): 85; *see also* oil
Murano, island of: 57, 62, 180; *see also* glass and glassworking
Musk: 99, 109, 118, 157, 224
Mythical Isles: 152–53, 194

Naphtha: 85; *see also* oil
Negroes, African: 154, 242ff.
Nestorian Christians: 35n., 36n., 86, 101
Nestorian Tablet: 86
Nestorius: 86
Noah's Ark: 44ff., 83 & n.

Odoric de Pordenone (friar): 93, 119, 132, 135n., 145, 147 & n., 159n.
Ogedai (son of Genghis Khan): 22, 23n., 24n., 25n.

Oil: 75, 207; sacred, 38 & n., 75–78, 114;
in Armenia, 84–85; in Rome, 85; use
in war, 84–85; other uses of, 84–85;
see also Jerusalem
Old Man of the Mountain: *see* Ala-'u-
'd-Din Muhammad
Oucaca (Tatar-held city): 13 & n.

Pala d' Oro (St. Mark's altarpiece):
47–48
Palazzo della due Torri in Venice:
71–72
Paleologus, Michael (Greek emperor):
9, 10 n., 31, 39, 182
Pamirs ("Roof of the World"): 95, 100
Pearls: 48, 57f., 64, 149n., 157; market
of, 89
Peking, China: 23, 37, 99, 102ff., 117ff.;
compared with Venice, 117; *see also*
Khanbaligh
Pelliot, Paul: 14n., 104n., 132n., 257
Persia: 23, 33ff., 92, 142f., 161, 215,
234ff., 236ff., 238ff.; industries of,
91–92
Peter, the Tatar: 11 n.
Petrarch, Francesco: 51 ff., 72, 191 f.
Petroleum: *see* oil
Petronius, Gaius: quoted, 68
Piazzetta (in Venice): 50, 54, 65ff., 70
Pietro of Abano (Padua professor):
225–26 & n.
Pietro, Orseolo II (Doge): 55
Pillars on Piazzetta: 40, 53f., 219
Pipino, Francesco (Dominican of
Bologna): 16n., 124, 206, 254, 256,
262ff.
Pirates, Japanese: 35n.
Poland: 24n.
Polo, Bellela (Bellela Querini, daughter
of Messer Marco Polo): 228, 247ff.;
birth of, 214, 247ff.; marriage of, 226,
249
Polo, Donata Badoèr (wife of Messer
Marco Polo): 213–14, 230f., 244,
246f., 250; death of, 247
Polo, Fantina (Fantina Bragadin,
daughter of Messer Marco Polo):
birth of, 214, 247ff., 248; marriage of,
226–27, 248; death of, 249; family of,
250
Polo, Maffeo (half brother of Messer

Marco Polo): 172, 211f., 214–16,
227ff.; children of, 216
Polo, Maffeo (Venetian merchant): 3,
4n., 9ff., 12–13, 41n., 69, 70f., 72ff.,
86ff., 88f., 96f., 98, 100f., 109f., 137f.,
156, 160f., 163, 210f., 216, 238ff.;
trade of, 4, 7, 9–14, 54, 89, 160ff.,
177ff., 215; route of, 6–7; in Constantinople, 7; in Soldaia, 7; in Bolgara, 9; in Bokhara, 14–15; with
Mongols, 27–30; messenger for Kublai Khan, 37, 40, 69; return to Venice,
39–40, 67–68; in Acre, 74–75, 78–80;
bound for East, 80; in Anatolia, 83;
in Hormuz, 93–96, 155; in Kan Chou,
106–108; received by Kublai Khan,
113; return planned by, 143–45; in
India, 150–52; in Tabriz, 160–61, 165;
home to Venice, 166–69; identity
questioned, 171–72; clothes given
away, 172–73; banquet of, 174–77,
253ff.; death of, 222–23
Polo, Marco (uncle of Messer Marco
Polo): 43ff.; will of, 4, 172n., 185n.,
211
Polo, Messer Marco: 3ff., 7ff., 11 n., 12,
15, 16ff., 23ff., 24n., 25, 26ff., 39, 42,
47f., 49, 51 n., 54, 56, 60 ff., 65n., 69f.
& n., 72ff., 82f., 86f., 88f., 94n., 96f.,
98 & n., 100f., 109f., 121 f., 125n.,
129f., 131, 135, 138, 146f., 149, 153,
156, 158, 159n., 160 f. & n., 163, 170,
179f., 183ff., 185, 210–11, 214f., 222ff.,
226f., 233n., 250; will of, 11 n., 214,
229–32 & n.; birth of, 41–42, 67, 211 ff.;
boyhood of, 44, 48, 54, 56, 60, 67–68,
74, 178; in Acre, 74–75, 78–79; travel
East, 80; in Anatolia, 83; in Hormuz,
93–96, 155; illness of, 99, 229, 236ff.;
in Kan Chou, 106–108; received by
Kublai Khan, 113; presented to Kublai Khan, 114, 215ff.; missions of,
124–28; reward to, 132–33; Yangtse
river described by, 133; return
planned by, 143–45; in India, 150–52;
in Tabriz, 160–61, 165; home to
Venice, 166–69; identity questioned,
171–72; banquet of, 174–77, 253ff.;
nickname of, 180n., 218, 224 & n.,
244, 251–52 & n.; prisoner of Genoese,
186–94 & n., 200f., 206ff., 213, 236ff.,

243ff.; book of, 200–206 & n., 208–209, 212ff., 218, 225, 237f., 240ff., 254–59 & n., 262–63; release from prison, 212; marriage of, 213–14; legal matters of, 223, 239; will of, 230ff.; death of, 232; character of, 233–43 & n.; tomb of, 243–46 & n.; quarrels in family of, 226–27, 247, 249–50; estate of, 252–53 & n.; influence on geography, cartography, science, 260–62

Polo, Moreta (Moreta Dolfin, Moreta Gradenigo, daughter of Messer Marco Polo): 51n., 228, 244, 246, 248; birth of, 214, 247ff.; marriages of, 249–50; death of, 250

Polo, Nicolo (Venetian merchant, father of Messer Marco Polo): 3, 4n., 9ff., 12–13, 41n., 69, 70f., 72ff., 86ff., 88f., 96f., 98, 100f., 109f., 137f., 139, 156, 160f., 163, 171, 210f., 238ff.; trade of, 4, 7, 9–14, 54, 89, 160ff., 177ff.; route of, 6–7; in Constantinople, 7; in Soldaia, 7; in Bolgara, 9; in Bokhara, 14–15; with Mongols, 27–30; messenger for Kublai Khan, 37, 40, 69; return to Venice, 39–40, 67–68; remarriage of, 69, 211–12; in Acre, 74–75, 78–80; bound for East, 80; in Anatolia, 83; in Hormuz, 93–96, 155; in Kan Chou, 106–108; received by Kublai Khan, 113; return planned by, 143–45; in India, 150–52; in Tabriz, 160–61, 165; home to Venice, 166–69; identity questioned, 171–72; banquet of, 174–77, 253ff.; natural sons of, 185 & n., 212; death of, 212n., 214–16; tomb of, 215, 244, 246

Porcupines: 98 & n.
Prescriptions: 229
"Prester John": 107 & n., 109
Printing: 35 & n., 124
Procopius of Caesarea: 34n.

Ramusio, Giovanni Battista: 43, 80n., 98f., 111, 120, 122, 135, 144, 161, 171, 173f., 177, 187f., 194f., 200, 202f., 206, 210f., 213, 215, 244, 246n., 251 & n., 256; birth and early life of, 265–66; death of, 267–68; writings of, 267–69 & n.; portrait of, 268

Rhubarb: 64, 118, 157; in medicine, 106 & n.
Rialto, the (in Venice): 4ff., 50f., 63, 173, 183ff., 217ff., 219ff.
Ricci, Father: 336n.
Riva degli Schiavoni (in Venice): 5, 71
Rome: 24n., 32f., 40ff., 49n., 179, 182, 191ff., 265ff.
Roosevelt, Theodore: quoted, 17
Rudders: 5n., 146n.
Ruskin, John: 55n.
Russia: 10n., 21, 24, 237ff., 257ff.
Rustichello of Pisa: 195 & n., 237ff.; collaborator of Marco Polo, 200–201, 203–206, 208; freed from prison, 209

Saba, Persia: 90 & n.
St. Mark: 57ff.; legends of, 44–47
St. Mark's Church: 5ff., 41ff., 48n., 49n., 51n., 54, 63ff., 65ff., 167, 177f., 197ff.; festivals, pageants of, 44; mosaics of, 44, 48, 178; columns of, 47–48 & n., 49; horses of, 49 & n.; gaming in, 49–50
St. Sofia Church (in Venice): 7ff.
St. Theodore (patron saint of Venice): statue of, 49, 70
Salt: 39, 55, 71ff., 98n., 132n.
Samarkand: 20, 101, 102n.
San Giacomo di Rialto (church): 50 & n.
Sanudo, Marino: 77
Sapurgan (Shiburgan, city on Polos' route): 97 & n.
Sea-swine (mythical animal): 73
Sericulture: 34n.
Seven arts, the: 38
Shakespeare, William: quoted, 68
Shamanism: 28 & n.
Shang Tu (palace of Kublai Khan): 37, 82ff.; description of, 110–12
Ships, Chinese: 145–46, 157
Ships, Persian: 94–95 & n., 157
Ships, Venetian: 63, 64n., 65, 206ff., 208f., 213ff., 216; description of, 4–6; see also Venice
Sheep: fat-tailed, 92; in Pamirs, 100
"Silent bargaining": 89 & n.
Silesia: 24n.
Silk: 14, 54ff., 63f., 85ff., 89, 123ff., 157, 217; in Rome, 33–34 & n.

Sinkiang, China: 100, 102n.
Slaves and slavery: 10ff. & n., 11ff. & n., 29, 92, 97, 108n., 158ff., 236ff.
Slaves and slavery in Venice: 65, 191ff.; female slaves, 60, 65n.; *see also* Venice
Soldaia (Sudan): 9, 12
Spain: 10, 25n., 34, 35n., 190ff., 257ff., 260ff., 263f., 266ff.
Sposalizio (marriage): *see* Ascension Day
Steel: 62ff., 92
Sudan: *see* Soldaia
Sudarium (holy handkerchief): 106
Suleyman (merchant): 35n.
Sumatra: 147, 149
Sung empire: 21f., 118, 133n.; fall of, 36–37

Tabriz, Iran: 88, 160, 163; description of, 89; Polos in, 160–61, 165
Tacitus: quoted, 32, 68
Tafur, Pero (Spanish historian): quoted, 11n., 63
Taican (Persian city): 98 & n.
T'ang Dynasty, the: 36, 86
Tatars (Tartars): 10n., 11ff. & n., 12, 13ff., 14–15, 36, 56, 65n., 96f., 103, 107ff., 112ff., 118, 138ff., 142, 171f., 202ff., 215, 217ff., 231, 255; philosophy of, 83; women, 108; wars of, 155
Tattooing: 129
Templars, Knights: 75, 80 & n.
Temuchin: *see* Genghis Khan
Teobaldo (papal legate): 40, 75, 78–79 & n.; *see also* Pope Gregory X *and* Visconti
Tieopolo, Doge Lorenzo: 56–57
Tramontana (Pole star): 82, 147
Tuli (son of Genghis Khan): 22
Tunocain, Persia: 95–96
Turcomania: *see* Anatolia
Turkestan: *see* Sinkiang
Turquoise: 91, 157

Venice: 3f., 9ff., 10n., 11n., 12, 13ff., 15, 31, 39ff., 42ff., 43, 49n., 67, 82ff., 90ff., 99, 117ff., 127ff., 137ff., 149ff., 156, 160ff. 166f., 170f., 176f., 185n., 188f., 195, 202f., 210ff., 213, 215ff., 217f., 222, 229, 234ff., 239f., 243f., 247 & n., 259ff., 262f., 265f., 268ff.; morals and manners of, 4, 51–52, 108ff.; ships of, 4–6, 63, 64n., 65, 206ff., 208f., 213ff., 216; affluence of, 50, 178, 180; executions in, 50; crimes in, 51–54; festivals and pageants of, 54–58, 263ff.; wed to sea, 55n., 56n., 263ff.; arts and crafts of, 57–58; weddings in, 58–60; slaves and slavery in, 60, 65; funerals in, 61; homes in, 61; dress in, 61–62; streets of, 62; artisans of, 63; commerce in, 63ff., 64–66, 179–80, 183ff., 216; arsenal of, 63 & n.; Jews of, 65; harbor boats in, 66; De Canale quoted on, 71; water front of, 72, 74ff.; earthquake, floods in, 177; coins of, 178–79; treaties of, 179, 183f., 190, 209; skirmishes, war of, 181–86 & n., 189, 206–208; strife in, 219–21; decline of, 263–64
Verrochio (sculptor): 49n.
Vietnam: 147 & n.
Villehardouin, Geoffroi de (chronicler of the Crusades): 266
Visconti: *see* Teobaldo
Volger von Ellenbrechtskirchen (German bishop): 52

Weddings, Venetian: 58, 60; *see also* Venice
William of Rubruck (friar): 15–16, 119

Yaballah I (Moslem traveler): 35n.
Yarkand, China: 102
Yurts (Mongol tents): 11, 27, 29

Ziani, Doge: 55

The text for *Marco Polo: Venetian Adventurer* has been set on the Linotype in 11-point Janson, a recutting of the original type face issued by Anton Janson of Leipzig sometime between 1660 and 1687. The paper on which the book is printed bears the water-mark of the University of Oklahoma Press and has an effective life of at least three hundred years.